Towards the end of the eighteenth century, a major transformation took place in British dramatic culture. At the heart of that transformation was the controversial emergence of an illegitimate theatre, and a cultural struggle between London's patent playhouses (Drury Lane, Covent Garden, and the Haymarket) and the new, so-called minor theatres. This is the first book to explore the institutions, genres, and performance history of illegitimate theatre. Jane Moody's lively and original account considers the prohibition of tragedy and comedy at London's minor theatres and describes the various ingenious ways in which performers circumnavigated the law. Moody brings to light illicit productions of Shakespeare and the minor theatres' fascination with dramatic subjects censored on the legitimate stage.

Illegitimate Theatre represents an important contribution to our understanding of nineteenth-century cultural politics and also offers a powerful critique of theatre's position in the literary history of Romanticism.

JANE MOODY is Lecturer in the Department of English and Related Literature at the University of York.

ILLEGITIMATE THEATRE
IN LONDON, 1770–1840

JANE MOODY

CAMBRIDGE
UNIVERSITY PRESS

PUBLISHED BY THE PRESS SYNDICATE OF THE UNIVERSITY OF CAMBRIDGE
The Pitt Building, Trumpington Street, Cambridge, United Kingdom

CAMBRIDGE UNIVERSITY PRESS
The Edinburgh Building, Cambridge CB2 2RU, UK   www.cup.cam.ac.uk
40 West 20th Street, New York, NY 10011–4211, USA   www.cup.org
10 Stamford Road, Oakleigh, Melbourne 3166, Australia
Ruiz de Alarcón 13, 28014 Madrid, Spain

First published 2000

Printed in the United Kingdom at the University Press, Cambridge

Typeface Monotype Baskerville 11/12.5 pt   *System* QuarkXPress™   [SE]

A catalogue record for this book is available from the British Library

Library of Congress Cataloguing in Publication data
Moody, Jane.
Illegitimate theatre in London, 1770–1840/Jane Moody.
p. cm.
Includes bibliographical references and index.
ISBN 0 521 56376 3
1. Theater – England – London – History – 19th century.
2. Theater – England – London – History – 18th century.   1. Title.
PN2596.L6M59 2000 792′.09421′09034–dc21

ISBN 0 521 56376 3 hardback

For my parents, who introduced me to the pleasures of books, libraries and playgoing

Our associations of admiration and delight with theatrical performers, are among our earliest recollections – among our last
regrets. They are links that connect the beginning and the end of
life together; their bright and giddy career of popularity measures
the arch that spans our brief existence.

(William Hazlitt, writing in *The Times*, 25 June 1817)

Contents

Illustrations

Acknowledgements

This book began life as a doctoral thesis at Oxford University, and I am very grateful to the British Academy, and St Edmund Hall, Oxford, for financial support, and to my supervisors, Roy Park and David Mayer, for their help and encouragement. A Research Fellowship at Girton College, Cambridge, gave me the time to develop my ideas and read more widely; I also greatly appreciated the warmth, good humour and intellectual generosity of my colleagues there, especially Chris Cannon, Juliet Dusinberre, Anne Fernihough, Stephanie Palmer, and James Simpson. At York, new colleagues have enriched my ideas in innumerable ways, and provided cheer at crucial moments: special thanks go to Greg Dart, Hugh Haughton, Felicity Riddy and Hugh Stevens. The Department of English and Related Literature kindly provided funds for the illustrations which appear in this book.

Research for this book took me to a variety of libraries in Britain and the US and I am grateful to all the librarians who helped me to locate plays, periodicals and illustrations: special thanks are due to the staff at the Harvard Theatre Collection, and to those at Christ Church Library in Oxford. As the recipient of Fellowships from the Huntington Library in San Marino, California, and the Folger Shakespeare Library in Washington, D.C., I was able to spend many pleasurable hours amidst those wonderful research collections; I should like to thank those institutions, and the Society for Theatre Research, for making these research trips possible.

I am indebted to many colleagues, on both sides of the Atlantic, for inviting me to speak at seminars and conferences, and also for taking the time to discuss my ideas and offer advice. I should particularly like to thank Jonathan Bate, Jacky Bratton, Marilyn Butler, Catherine Burroughs, Gillian Beer, Julie Carlson, Jeff Cox, Tracy Davis, Michael Hays, Peter Holland, Robert Hume, Louis James, Jon Klancher, Marius Kwint, Nigel Leask, Lucy Newlyn, Anne Mellor, Peter Raby and Stanley

Wells. David Mayer continued to read my work, and to share his own research, long after his duties as my thesis supervisor were over: I acknowledge with pleasure his charisma, immense patience, and gentle inspiration. At Cambridge University Press, I have benefited enormously from the calm expertise of Sarah Stanton and Victoria Cooper, as well as from the shrewd and thoughtful comments provided by the Press's anonymous referees. Christine Lyall Grant copy-edited this book with great patience and good sense. On a more personal note, I should like to record my gratitude to my family and to many friends, especially John Allison, John and Peggy Curtiss, Margaret Kirwan, Bill Parry, Jochen Runde, Sinéad Smith and Victoria Tomkinson, for their kindness and encouragement.

Parts of this argument have appeared, in slightly different forms, in *Shakespeare Survey, Texas Studies in Literature and Language,* and *Nineteenth Century Theatre Research*: I am grateful to the editors for granting permission to reprint material which originally appeared there.

Abbreviations

AND	*Acting National Drama*, ed. Benjamin Webster, 1837–59.
BL	British Library.
CBT	*Cumberland's British Theatre*, 1826–1861.
CMT	*Cumberland's Minor Theatre*, ed. D.G. [George Daniel], 1828–43.
CPPS	*Catalogue of Personal and Political Satires*, ed. F.G. Stephens and M.D. George, 11 vols, London: British Museum, 1874–1954.
Devonshire	Duke of Devonshire's collections, Chatsworth House.
Dicks	*Dicks' Standard Plays.*
DBT	*Duncombe's British Theatre*, 1828–52.
Guildhall	Noble collection, Dept. of Prints and Drawings, Guildhall Library, London.
Hazlitt	*The Complete Works of William Hazlitt*, ed. P.P. Howe. 21 vols (London: Dent, 1930–34).
HO	Home Office Papers, Public Record Office.
HTC	Harvard Theatre Collection.
Lacy	*Lacy's Acting Edition, c.* 1849–55.
Lamb	*The Works of Charles and Mary Lamb*, ed. E. V. Lucas, 7 vols. London: Methuen and Co., 1903–5.
Larpent	Larpent collection of MS plays, Henry E. Huntingdon Library, San Marino, California.
LC	Lord Chamberlain's collections of MS plays, British Library.
LH	*Leigh Hunt's Dramatic Criticism 1808–1831*, ed. Carolyn Houtchens and Lawrence Houtchens, New York: Columbia University Press, 1949.
Oxberry	Oxberry, *The New English Drama*, 20 vols., 1818–25.
PRO	Public Record Office.

RMD   *Richardson's New Minor Drama*, ed. W.T. Moncrieff (1828–31).

SC   Report and Minutes of the Select Committee on Dramatic Literature (1832), in Parliamentary Papers, Reports from Committees, 18 vols, 6.

Prologue

This book offers an institutional history of early nineteenth-century theatre in London. That history is populated with hack playwrights and dramatic spies, and explores the pleasures shared by lords, sailors and Whitechapel butchers, as well as recreating the spectacles of blue fire and terrible conflagrations. As we enter this world, we discover playhouses magnificently decorated in gilt and rich velvet, and glimpse a stage displaying oriental palaces and naval victories, urban blackguardism and sensational crimes. My argument will try to capture the wonderful excitement of theatregoing in early nineteenth-century London: the hyperbolic typography of playbills hurriedly posted on walls or jostling for space in shop windows; the sight of the Surrey Theatre, brilliantly lit up on the south bank, to celebrate the one-hundredth performance of *Black-Ey'd Susan*; the expectant crush of carriages, apprentices and placard-waving protestors around the Adelphi at Moncrieff's *Tom and Jerry*. Such details form the imaginative architecture of this book, its sensory and dramatic universe. But while seeking a kind of critical faith to all these pleasures, this book also sets out to define a new framework for interpreting the genres, dramatic institutions and performances in late Georgian London.

Illegitimate theatre is the concept at the centre of my argument. At its simplest, this category refers to the performances staged at those theatres where legitimate drama (tragedy and comedy) was prohibited. As we shall see, the concept of illegitimate theatre makes us think in quite new ways about the politics of institutions in late Georgian London. Moreover, the position of Shakespeare at the heart of this institutional struggle turns on its head that fashionable description of the Romantic period as the historical period during which Shakespeare was transformed into an organic, politically conservative playwright whose work championed the cause of art and nature against the deadening claims of industry and modern capitalism.[1]

---

[1] Cf. John Collick, *Shakespeare, Cinema and Society* (Manchester University Press, 1989), 148; Hugh Grady, *The Modernist Shakespeare: Critical Texts in a Material World* (Oxford: Clarendon, 1991), 36–7.

The concept of illegitimate theatre also encourages us to revise our assumptions about the supposedly apolitical character of late Georgian performance. 'Of the nation's political life almost nothing is traceable in the drama', declared the theatre historian Ernest Bradlee Watson. 'The theatres existed solely by the grace of the king and his chamberlain; therefore nothing but the most slavish deference was tolerated on the stage.'[2] More recently, Michael R. Booth echoes Watson's judgement when he remarks, 'The main reason why the vigorous political life of the century is not reflected in the drama . . . is that the Examiner of Plays would not allow it.'[3] But to what extent did the uncensored plays performed at London's minor theatres challenge these limits of political representation? Here, I shall be considering the significance of illegitimate theatre as a site of political, moral and indeed generic transgression; my argument highlights too the ways in which the production and consumption of these plays defied cherished assumptions about cultural and social hierarchy.

My arguments about illegitimate theatre entail a wide-ranging critique of theatre's position in the literary history of Romanticism. For my starting-point is the conviction that Romantic values and assumptions continue to inhibit the interpretation of early nineteenth-century theatrical practice. In particular, critics implicitly defend the Romantic poet-playwrights for having invented a 'mental theatre' consisting of lyrical, experimental tragedies which brilliantly transcend the irrational and capricious desires of mass audiences and the degraded condition of dramatic institutions such as Drury Lane and Covent Garden. The result of this complicity is that Romantic tragedy has remained the unquestioned cultural apex of late Georgian drama, and the closet the definitive location of authentic Romantic performance.[4] Theatres, by contrast, are briskly dismissed as places of noise, dirt, spectacle and unbridled sexual commerce, where Shakespeare was being mangled into opera, and

[2] E. B. Watson, *Sheridan to Robertson: A Study of the Nineteenth Century London Stage* (Cambridge, Mass.: Harvard University Press, 1926), 5.

[3] M. R. Booth, *Prefaces to English Nineteenth Century Theatre* (Manchester University Press, [1980]), 7.

[4] For Bryon's concept of mental theatre, see *Letters and Journals*, ed. Leslie A. Marchand, 8 vols. (London: John Murray, 1973), VIII:186–7. Before the 1990s, most influential studies defined the drama of the major Romantic playwrights in terms of the plays' disavowal of stage performance. See Alan Richardson's fine study, *A Mental Theater: Poetic Drama and Consciousness in the Romantic Age* (University Park, Penn., Pennsylvania State University, 1988). Cf. Terry Otten, *The Deserted Stage: The Search for Dramatic Form in Nineteenth-Century England* (Athens: Ohio University Press, 1972) and Shou-ren Wang, *The Theatre of the Mind: A Study of Unacted Drama in Nineteenth-Century England* (London: Macmillan, 1990). For a critique of Romantic histories of the stage, see my article, '"Fine word, legitimate!": Towards a Theatrical History of Romanticism', *Texas Studies in Literature and Language* 38, nos. 3 and 4 (1996), 223–44.

ignorant audiences preferred performing dogs to the pleasures of Sheridan and John Gay. Again, Watson's comments sum up a critical position silently assumed by generations of Romantic scholars (and indeed many historians of drama) when he laments that '[a]t the turn of the century the theatres succumbed to the rabble as a weakened constitution might to a virulent disease' (6). The theatre's virtual absence from Romantic scholarship is not hard to understand, for the sights, sounds and smells of a mass cultural public do indeed pose an uncomfortable challenge to that idealist history of Romanticism which has privileged imagination, solitude and critical self-consciousness over the claims of the body, the institution and the market.

In the last decade or so, however, the once impenetrable boundaries between performance and Romantic playwriting have slowly begun to dissolve.[5] Nevertheless, the theatre of Romanticism continues to be described as if it were located beyond theatrical representation. In particular, literary critics still assume, albeit implicitly, that an aesthetic or formal distinction separates a closet drama such as *The Cenci* from popular stage plays such as M. G. Lewis' *Castle Spectre*. Moreover, in what is perhaps the most enduring legacy of Romantic idealism, audiences and playhouses are persistently reinscribed as the sources of aesthetic pollution rather than being acknowledged as the makers, consumers and critics of contemporary theatrical culture.[6] The institutional history presented in this book seeks to question this Romantic historiography of the stage, and to provide a different kind of lens through which to consider theatre's ambivalent position in late Georgian culture.

What was at stake for writers such as Coleridge and Wordsworth in their denunciations of illegitimate theatre? How could dramatic illegitimacy threaten the survival of imagination and indeed the future of the

---

[5] See especially Julie Carlson, *In the Theatre of Romanticism: Coleridge, Nationalism, Women* (Cambridge University Press, 1994). Carlson presents the closeting of Shakespeare by Romantic writers as a form of antitheatricality deeply bound up with fears about public women in the theatre. From a different perspective, Catherine Burroughs' work also questions the notion of a binary opposition between stage representation and a Romantic theatre of the mind and shows the Romantic female closet to be an 'experimental theater' in its own right. Burroughs, *Closet Stages: Joanna Baillie and the Theater Theory of British Romantic Women Writers* (Philadelphia: University of Penn. Press, 1997), 11. See further Michael Evenden, 'Inter-mediate Stages: Reconsidering the Body in "Closet Drama"' in *Reading the Social Body* ed. Catherine B. Burroughs and Jeffrey David Ehrenreich (Iowa: University of Iowa Press, 1993), 244–69; Murray Biggs, 'Staging *The Borderers*: Dragging Romantic Drama Out of the Closet', *Studies in Romanticism* 27 no. 3 (1988), 411–17.

[6] Cf. Manfred Pfister, 'Reading the Body: the Corporeality of Shakespeare's Text' in Hanna Scolnicov and Peter Holland, eds., *Reading Plays: Interpretation and Reception* (Cambridge University Press, 1991), 110–22, 110–11; Brian Vickers, *Returning to Shakespeare* (London: Routledge, 1989), 230.

British political and cultural state? For these Romantic critics, illegitimate theatre connoted vulgarity, lowness, political radicalism and cultural subversion; in the eyes of Hazlitt, Keats and Leigh Hunt, however,
illegitimate performance held out the promise of an anarchic freedom
from dull convention and stultifying precedent. My argument takes an
interdisciplinary form because I seek both to demonstrate the radical
challenge which illegitimate theatre poses to our historiography of the
nineteenth-century stage, and to prove that the politics and iconography
of illegitimacy underpin Romantic playwriting and theatrical criticism.

At a time of extraordinary social and political upheaval, the theatre
represented one of the few kinds of leisure patronised by all social
groups, from kings to kitchenmaids; indeed, spectators, critics and
pamphleteers imagined the playhouses as a miniature parliament of the
nation. As critics such as Thomas Wooler and William Hazlitt recognised, this social inclusiveness also endowed dramatic performance with
a special kind of influence and power. But in the eyes of legislators and
many pamphleteers, this heterogeneity was precisely what made theatre
dangerous and potentially uncontrollable: dramatic performances inev-
itably raised the spectre of social and political disorder. Given such
meanings, arguments about censorship or about which theatres should
be allowed to perform Shakespeare's plays are more than isolated
debates about the eccentricities of dramatic licensing. Rather, they are
concerned with such vexed and controversial questions as the political
control and consumption of culture in a democratic age. Indeed, these
arguments represent one aspect of the stage's importance in the
definition and production of what we might call public Romanticism.[7]

At the heart of my argument is a simple proposition: that the
opposition between legitimate and illegitimate theatre constitutes the
fundamental category of distinction in this period's drama. Such an
opposition, I want to suggest, precedes but in many ways also underpins
that more familiar conflict, as described in literary histories, between the
Romantic closet and the stage. To some extent, this distinction between
the legitimate and the illegitimate follows from the institutional division
between patent and minor playhouses. During the 1660s, by the gift of
Charles II, Thomas Killigrew and William Davenant had acquired
patents for the production of theatre in London. Over the centuries,
these patents had been perceived to confer all but exclusive rights over

---

[7] See especially Jon P. Klancher, *The Making of English Reading Audiences, 1790–1832* (Madison:
University of Wisconsin Press, 1987); Kevin Gilmartin, *Print Politics: The Press and Radical Opposition
in Early Nineteenth-Century England* (Cambridge University Press, 1996) and Paul Magnuson, *Reading
Public Romanticism* (Princeton University Press, 1998).

the staging of tragedy and comedy on two theatres, Drury Lane and Covent Garden. As in Paris, whose theatrical history offers a number of interesting parallels and connections, the other so-called minor theatres like Sadler's Wells and the Royal Circus were licensed only to perform illegitimate forms such as melodrama, pantomime, burletta and spectacle.[8] During the first few decades of the nineteenth century, however, the minor theatres began to challenge their exclusion from legitimate culture.[9] In this struggle, dramatic genres became categories of major ideological dispute,[10] and Shakespeare a major cultural weapon. The evolution of genres on the nineteenth-century stage, the opportunities for dramatic production available to British playwrights, and even the delineation of the closet as a place of imaginary performance: all these are intricately connected to the history of theatrical institutions. The battle for free trade in drama was not only a campaign to overturn a commercial monopoly, but also a deeply political conflict about who should control theatrical culture.

The institutional locations of legitimate and illegitimate theatre might appear to confirm that prevailing opposition between the elite and the popular which has dominated historical interpretations of early nineteenth-century culture.[11] More recently, however, historians such as Roger Chartier have emphasised the way in which the *appropriation* of cultural objects by different social groups complicates and indeed undermines any dichotomy between elite and popular cultures.[12] Chartier's

---

[8] Before the French Revolution the Odéon, Comédie-Française and the Opéra-Comique had a virtual monopoly over dramatic production in Paris. The boulevard theatres remained subject to a set of arcane and wonderfully irrational regulations: characters were permitted to bleed but not to die at one theatre; at others, performances were licensed on the condition that a gauze curtain separated the actors from the audience. In 1790, however, all restrictions on performances at the boulevard houses were abolished. But in 1806 Napoleon concluded that boulevard theatres were having a demoralising influence on public morality. In future, he announced, performances would be permitted at only four boulevard playhouses. On theatrical regulation and political production in Paris, see Marvin Carlson, *The Theatre of the French Revolution* (Ithaca: Cornell, 1966) and especially Michèle Root-Bernstein, *Boulevard Theater and Revolution in Eighteenth-Century Paris* (Michigan: UMI Research Press, 1981).

[9] See further Watson Nicholson, *The Struggle for a Free Stage in London* (London: Constable, 1906) and Dewey Ganzel, 'Patent Wrongs and Patent Theatres: Drama and the Law in the Early Nineteenth Century', *PMLA* 76 (1961), 384–96.

[10] See Joseph Donohue's fine essay, 'Burletta and the Early Nineteenth-Century English Theatre', *Nineteenth Century Theatre Research* 1 (1973), 29–51.

[11] J. Golby and A. Purdue, *The Civilization of the Crowd: Popular Culture in England, 1750–1900* (London: Batsford, 1984); Hugh Cunningham, *Leisure in the Industrial Revolution* (London: Croom Helm, 1980).

[12] See Chartier, 'Culture as Appropriation: Popular Culture Uses in Early Modern France' in Steven L. Kaplan, ed., *Understanding Popular Culture: Europe from the Middle Ages to the Nineteenth Century* (Berlin and New York: Mouton, 1984), 229–53, and Chartier, *Cultural History: Between Practices and Representations*, translated by Lydia G. Cochrane (Cambridge: Polity, 1988).

arguments offer a useful model for thinking about nineteenth-century theatrical culture because, as we shall see, the illegitimate seems to resist both institutional and even generic boundaries. To some extent, certainly, we can define the illegitimate in terms of a set of genres (melodrama, burlesque, extravaganza), a group of London playhouses (including the Surrey, Coburg, Adelphi and Olympic Theatres) and the conventions of gesture and expression associated with those dramatic forms and institutions. In many ways, however, patent and minor cultures also represented overlapping and interconnected domains. The controversy surrounding Edmund Kean's 'electric' performances, for example, takes the form of an impassioned debate – variously conducted through a social discourse of vulgarity and uncouthness, the political language of radicalism as well as through the aesthetic categories of originality and genius – about the intrusion of illegitimate dramaturgy into the performance of Shakespearean tragedy.

In illegitimate culture, plots, playwrights, managers, performers and spectators circulated effortlessly among the Coburg and Covent Garden, Astley's and the Adelphi. The image of Joseph Grimaldi rushing on foot from Sadler's Wells to appear in the afterpiece at Covent Garden aptly sums up the permeable boundaries between the minor and patent theatres. Indeed, one distinctive feature of illegitimate practice was the incorporation of plots and narratives (not to mention images, songs and even a Napoleonic cuirass) borrowed and stolen from a variety of sources, high and low. From Mozart airs and Coleridgean tragedy to Newgate tales and Hogarth engravings, illegitimate theatre delighted in second-hand cultural property. Moreover, these eclectic thefts and adaptations gleefully confound any assumptions we might have about the subjects of high and low cultures and their ostensibly separate audiences. One of the fascinating aspects of illegitimate production is the unexpected variations these dramas often play across narratives and plots not of their own making.

The rise of illegitimate theatre played an important part in the ideological demise of the Theatres Royal. During the first two decades of the nineteenth century, melodrama, romance and other illegitimate forms began to overshadow performances of tragedy and comedy at Drury Lane and Covent Garden: the hallowed boards of Garrick and Siddons abandoned rhetoric for the profits of imperial spectacle. No longer confined to Sadler's Wells and the Royal Circus, illegitimate theatre had taken control of the cultural metropolis. Dozens of articles, pamphlets and reviews began to offer as many explanations for what they perceived as 'the decline of the drama'. 'Who are your successful authors?' demanded 'Philo-Dramaticus' in his open letter to Charles Kemble and Robert Elliston, only to offer his own cutting reply, 'Planché and Arnold, Poole and Kenney; names so ignoble in the world of literature, that they have no circulation beyond the green-room.'[13] Amongst these opportunistic pamphleteers, the stage's degradation would be variously attributed to late dinners, Methodism, the rage for opera and music, monopoly, refinement, tragic dramatists who prized poeticity over action, the economical habits of the middle classes, stage licensing, the malignant criticism of new plays by spectators and reviewers alike, the banishment of politics from the stage, the shameless market for prostitutes in the lobbies and upper boxes at Covent Garden and Drury Lane, and even (ingeniously) the depressive, spectral effects produced by lighting theatres with gas.[14] An old theatrical world seemed to have disintegrated, and its obsolescence foretold the collapse of generic hierarchies and a future of irreversible cultural decline.

The genres and dramaturgy of illegitimate theatre, however, offer a lively riposte to this discourse of dramatic decline. In extravaganza, melodrama and burletta we can find some of the most original and surprising plays of this period; illegitimate plays are also notable for their fascination with the half-comic, half-perplexing experiences of social mobility and technological change. In this period, too, illegitimate theatre became the dramatic newsreel of the modern metropolis. If we are to understand how British imperialism was being transformed into dramatic spectacle at Drury Lane and Covent Garden, or how performance participated in contemporary debates about the abolition of slavery, for example, then it is to illegitimate genres – rather than to the decaying forms of tragedy and comedy – that we must turn.

Hazlitt's theatre criticism provides an elegant thread which runs through the various arguments I present here. One of Britain's greatest dramatic critics, Hazlitt is also perhaps its most eloquent spokesman on

---

13 Philo-Dramaticus (pseud.), *A Letter to C. Kemble and R. W. Elliston on the Present State of the Stage* (London: Marsh 1825), 730.

14 See *inter alia* 'The English Stage', *Theatrical Inquisitor*, November 1813, 3: 201ff.; 'On the Decline of the Stage and the Power of the Licenser', from Drakard's paper, reprinted in *Theatrical Inquisitor*, January 1814, 3: 339–45; 'On Lighting the Theatres with Gas', letter published in *Theatrical Inquisitor*, October 1820, 16: 271–2; 'The State of the Drama', *New Monthly Magazine* (1832), part I, 34: 131–5. See also Edward Bulwer (became Baron Lytton of Knebworth and added Lytton to his surname; he is referred to throughout as Bulwer-Lytton), *England and the English*, 2 vols. (New York, 1833), II: 93; Francis Place, manuscript notes on the decline of the drama, BL MS 27833 fols. 7–34. See in particular *Report and Minutes of the Select Committee on Dramatic Literature* (1832) in Parliamentary Papers, *Reports from Committees*, 18 vols., VII.

the politics of theatrical legitimacy. His willingness to be delighted by the acrobatic grace of Jack Richer (the celebrated slack-rope dancer at Sadler's Wells), as well as by the tragic pathos of Sarah Siddons in the role of Lady Macbeth, represents a polemical form of critical opposition to rigid institutional distinctions between high and low culture. But what is so compelling about Hazlitt's theatrical writing is its honest confusion and conflicting loyalties. For even as he acknowledges these pleasures, Hazlitt also reveals his intense fears about the consequences of an unrestrained cultural democracy in which spectators might make an *auto-da-fé* of their favourite performer, 'as they formerly burnt a witch'.[15]

I am conscious that this is a book about British theatre which nonetheless deals exclusively with professional dramatic performances in London.[16] My interest in the institutional history of metropolitan performance also tends to take precedence in this study over more detailed explorations of particular plays and companies. But fine histories of individual playhouses, notably the Coburg (renamed the Victoria in 1833), Astley's Amphitheatre and the Surrey, are available to theatre historians;[17] similarly, melodrama and pantomime in this period have already been the subjects of distinguished monographs.[18] My aim here

---

[15] *Examiner*, March 1828, *Hazlitt* xviii:375.

[16] Private theatricals did of course play a rich part in London's theatrical life. The controversy over the Pic Nics' performances at Tottenham Street offers an amusing example of opposition to the decadence of the leisured *dilettanti*. See *The Times*, 16 and 18 March, 5 and 8 April 1802; W. Cutspear (pseud.), *Dramatic Rights: or, Private Theatricals, and Pic-Nic Suppers, justified by Fair Argument* (London: T. Burton, 1802) and a variety of graphic satires, notably James Gillray, 'Blowing Up the Pic Nics' (*CPPS* no. 9916) and S.W. Fores, 'A Peep into Tottenham Street or Dillitanti Performers in Training' (Theatre Museum). On London's booth theatres and penny gaffs, see James Grant, *Sketches in London* (London: Orr and Co., 1838), chapter 5, and Paul Sheridan, *Penny Theatres of Victorian London* (London: Dennis Dobson, 1981).

[17] See Dennis Arundell, *The Story of Sadler's Wells 1683–1964* (London, Hamish Hamilton, 1965); John Booth, *A Century of Theatrical History 1816–1916: The Old Vic* (London: Stead's, 1917). See also Marvin Carlson, 'The Old Vic: A Semiotic Analysis' in Carlson, *Places of Performance: The Semiotics of Theatre Architecture* (Ithaca: Cornell University Press, 1989), 56–74. On the history of the Royal Circus/ Surrey, see William Knight, *A Major London 'Minor': the Surrey Theatre 1805–1865* (London: Society for Theatre Research, 1998). Marius Kwint's study of Astley's Amphitheatre is forthcoming from Oxford University Press.

[18] See David Mayer's seminal history of Regency pantomime, *Harlequin in his Element: The English Pantomime, 1806–1836* (Cambridge, Mass., Harvard University Press, 1969). Despite the publication of many fine articles about particular plays and subgenres, the best historical survey remains Michael R. Booth, *English Melodrama* (London: Herbert Jenkins, 1965). See also Martha Vicinus, '"Helpless and Unfriended": Nineteenth-Century Domestic Melodrama', *New Literary History* 13 (1981), 127–43; Gabrielle Hyslop, 'Deviant and Dangerous Behaviour: Women in Melodrama,' *Journal of Popular Culture* 19 (1985), 65–77, and Jacky Bratton, 'The Contending Discourses of Melodrama' in Jacky Bratton, Jim Cook and Christine Gledhill, eds., *Melodrama: Stage, Picture, Screen* (London: British Film Institute, 1994), 38–49. See also Michael Hays and Anastasia Nikolopoulou, eds., *Melodrama: The Cultural Emergence of a Genre* (New York: St Martin's Press, 1996) which includes an impressive range of essays on British, continental and colonial melodrama.

is to bring together the history of theatrical institutions and that of dramatic genres, and to demonstrate the importance of illegitimate theatre for a richer understanding of theatrical and literary history alike. To be sure, the metropolitan theatre of the late Georgian period was dominated by internecine warfare, bankruptcy and institutional corruption. But this was also a place of extraordinary cultural and emotional power. If it is tempting sometimes to remember the most absurd moments of its history – a furious William Glossop, manager of the Coburg, confronting the Drury Lane lessee with a horsewhip over the theft of a play, or George Colman the Younger, then Examiner of Plays, painstakingly explaining to a Parliamentary Committee why he had decided to censor all references to angels in the theatre – then we need to recall too that in this period the performances of John Philip Kemble, Sarah Siddons, John Liston, Joseph Grimaldi, Edmund Kean, Eliza O'Neill and Céline Céleste delighted, shocked and entranced a generation of playgoers and critics. *Illegitimate Theatre* seeks to describe the institutional history which defined the professional lives of these performers and to bring to life the theatrical revolution in which they participated.

CHAPTER ONE

The invention of illegitimate culture

Towards the end of the eighteenth century, a fundamental cultural transformation took place in the nature of London theatre. At the heart of that transformation was the emergence of an illegitimate theatrical culture. We shall trace the varied origins of illegitimacy, in the unlicensed theatrical sphere of eighteenth-century London, amidst contemporary discourses of generic monstrosity and amongst the burlesque productions of Henry Fielding and Samuel Foote at the Haymarket Theatre. We then explore the emergence and institutional position of London's minor playhouses, including the Surrey, Coburg, Adelphi and Olympic Theatres. The fall of the Bastille, and England's war against Napoleon, provided the iconographic catalyst for the rise of an illegitimate drama. This theatre of physical peril, visual spectacle and ideological confrontation challenged both the generic premises and the cultural dominance of legitimate drama. In the theatrical revolution which followed, the minor playhouses and illegitimate genres would become the dramatic pioneers of the modern cultural metropolis.

'MONSTROUS MEDLIES': GENRE AND THEATRICAL REGULATION

The original patents granted by Charles II in 1662 to Thomas Killigrew and William Davenant permitted the performance of 'tragedies, comedies, plays, operas, music, scenes and all other entertainments of the stage'.[1] The King's gift of patents to his loyal courtier playwrights, together with permission to build 'two houses or theatres with all convenient rooms and other necessaries thereunto appertaining'[2] would transform the transient, portable companies of Elizabethan and Jacobean London into permanent London theatrical institutions, later

[1] Killigrew's patent, 25 April 1662, now in the possession of the Theatre Museum, London.
[2] Warrant granted by Charles II to Killigrew and Davenant, 21 August 1660. The warrant is conveniently reprinted in the excellent collection of documents edited by David Thomas in *Restoration and Georgian England, 1660–1788* (Cambridge University Press, 1989), 9–10.

identified with Drury Lane (1663) and Covent Garden (1732). At the same time, Charles II's patents inaugurated a system of dramatic classification based (somewhat haphazardly) on theatrical genres. That system equivocated between literary specificity (tragedies and comedies), and generic inclusiveness (other, by implication, non-literary entertainments of the stage). Having successfully circumvented the ban on playing during the Commonwealth by categorising his plays as 'operas' Davenant may have influenced this portmanteau definition of theatrical kinds, for this classification both assumed and simultaneously dissolved the hierarchy of theatrical genres.

The patents bestowed by Charles II were a masterpiece of sophistry and ideological obfuscation. They introduced a system of monarchical patronage and cultural monopoly – as well as providing for the transfer of female roles from actors to actresses – as an institutional antidote to the theatre's profanity, obscenity and scurrility. As if by alchemy, the theatre's moral pollution ('diverse companies of players' acting without authority, representing plays which 'do contain much matter of profanation and scurrility', and thus tending 'to the debauching' of their audiences' morality) was to be transformed, through the agency of the patentees, into 'innocent and harmless divertissement' featuring 'useful and instructive representations of human life'.[3] Yet, having been granted a commercial monopoly in perpetuity, the heirs and assigns of Killigrew and Davenant would inherit a weighty burden of moral and cultural stewardship which would remain inextricably associated with the monarchy's restoration.

Profanation and scurrility, glimpsed in the moral volatility of theatre which the bestowal of patents claimed to exorcise, are of course rarely far from view in theatrical history. In any case, by the end of the eighteenth century pamphleteers and radical journalists had vigorously challenged any remaining sanguinity about the beneficial, let alone the purgative, role of the patent theatres. Indeed, according to many commentators, the spectacular drama being promoted at the patent theatres simply promoted vulgarity, coarseness and cultural defilement.

Despite the theatrical monopoly, various dramatic competitors (first stubborn George Jolly, then the rebellious Thomas Betterton, who acquired a licence from the Lord Chamberlain in 1694/5)[4] continued to vex the patentees. Several unlicensed theatres also opened their doors.

---

[3] Quotations are from the 1660 warrant cited in note 2, with the exception of the last, which is from Killigrew's patent of 1662.

[4] See Allardyce Nicoll, *A History of English Drama 1660–1900*, 6 vols. (Cambridge University Press, 1952–9), I: 308–16; 331–6.

Some, like Goodman's Fields (1729) in Ayliffe Street, appeared on the cultural and geographic fringes of London; others, such as Thomas Potter's Little Theatre in the Haymarket (1720), were located in the city's cultural centre. And although historians have often interpreted the production of Fielding's political satires at the Haymarket as the theatrical catalyst for Walpole's introduction of the controversial Licensing Act, that legislation is in fact inextricable from a concerted campaign to suppress the unlicensed theatres.

Meanwhile, the introduction at Drury Lane and Covent Garden of immigrant cultural forms such as pantomime and Italian opera had produced a flood of visual, textual and theatrical critiques.[5] In particular, critics mocked the miscellaneous interweaving of music and visual spectacle with elaborate stage machinery, virtuosic dance and, in the case of pantomime, the silent, gestural language of mime. To some extent, this pervasive antipathy about opera and pantomime is a cultural sign of Britain's resurgent national self-consciousness: 'Rule Britannia', for example, was first performed in 1740. But what concerns me here is the decisive emergence of an absolute opposition between authentic and spurious theatrical forms, an opposition which soon begins to be imagined as a nightmarish confrontation between quasi-ethereal textuality and grotesque corporeality.

In periodicals such as the *Tatler* and the *Prompter*, or amidst the apocalyptic Dulness of Pope's *Dunciad*, writers and graphic satirists identified 'monstrous' theatrical kinds – namely pantomime, opera, puppet shows and farce – as the definitive sources of cultural pollution in the English theatre. In the *Dunciad*, for example, John Rich, the celebrated Harlequin and manager of Covent Garden, sits calmly 'mid snows of paper, and fierce hail of pease'. Drama at the patent theatres has been abandoned in favour of the spectacular attractions of sable sorcerers and ten-horned fiends, storms, whirlwinds and conflagrations. Writers and graphic satirists blamed these monstrous productions for what they perceived as a process of generic miscegenation (farce and epic 'get a jumbled race'; the arrival of *castrati* on the English stage becomes in these critiques a physical symbol of opera's effeminacy and sexual transgression) and for the disintegration of generic and social hierarchies

---

[5] See *inter alia* 'Punch Kicking Apollo', (*CPPS* no. 1832), published 1729; Hogarth, 'A Just View of the English Stage, or Three Heads are Better than None' (*CPPS* no. 1761), published 1725; [James Miller], *Harlequin-Horace: or the art of modern poetry* (*CPPS* no. 1835), published 1729; John Gay, *The Beggar's Opera* (Lincoln's Inn Fields, January 1728) and Henry Fielding's theatrical satires, *Tumble-Down Dick; or, Phaeton in the Suds* (Haymarket, April 1836) and *Eurydice Hiss'd* (Drury Lane, February 1737).

(farce, 'once the taste of Mobs, but now of Lords').[6] Careless of the generic licence which the terms of patent monopoly seem to have permitted, this critique of monstrosity now demanded an absolute and inviolable distinction between a text-based canon of English drama (defined by Richard Steele as 'Shakespear's Heroes, and Jonson's Humourists') and a miscellaneous realm of non-textual, physical entertainment allegedly imported from Bartholomew Fair ('Ladder-dancers, Rope-dancers, Juglers, and Mountebanks').[7]

Such theatrical critiques shared a recurring, often scatological nightmare of institutional miscegenation whereby kings, authors and dramatic language would be suddenly cast aside in favour of a physical theatre defined in terms of frenetic movement, the tyranny of spectacular objects and the wizardry of quacks, freaks and charlatans.[8] In the metatheatrical frontispiece to *Harlequin Horace*, for example, Harlequin raises his wooden sword to beat a distressed yet effulgent Apollo while Punch adds a vigorous kick of his own; on the stage floor lie the discarded works of Shakespeare, Jonson and Rowe. Indeed, this image of Britain's leading dramatists being thrown away like so much cultural rubble soon becomes a favourite visual trope in Georgian graphic satire. A few decades later, the actor-manager David Garrick dramatised Harlequin's attack on British drama – a national *œuvre* characteristically represented by Shakespeare – as a full-scale invasion in flat-bottomed boats. But at the end of *Harlequin's Invasion* (Drury Lane, 1759), in a striking dramatic image of the stage's capacity to reform itself, that usurpation was defeated in a spectacular *coup d'état*: Harlequin sank through the trap door, and Shakespeare rose up in triumph.[9]

The prominence of beleaguered texts and authors in these satirical images and narratives figured contemporary anxieties about the disintegration of the nation's dramatic corpus into nonsense and corporeal buffoonery. In the *Prompter*, Aaron Hill offered his readers a disturbing and evocative prophecy of cultural decadence. Should these monstrous theatrical forms triumph, he argued, actors would be transformed into

---

[6] *Dunciad* Bk 3, lines 257–8; Bk 1, line 68; *Imitations of Horace*, Epistle II.i line 311 in *The Poems of Alexander Pope* ed. John Butt (London: Methuen, 1965).

[7] *The Tatler*, ed. Donald F. Bond, 3 vols. (Oxford: Clarendon 1987), 7 May 1709, I: 107.

[8] The catalogue of Queen Ignorance's hostages, as introduced by Harlequin, in Fielding's *Pasquin* is a good example. This arbitrary collection of dramatic personages – 'a tall man, and a tall woman, hired at a vast price', 'two human cats' and a 'set of rope-dancers and tumblers from Sadler's-wells' – is designed to highlight the disintegration of knowledge and dramatic culture at the patent houses. See *Works of Henry Fielding*, 14 vols (London: J. Johnson, 1808) V: v.i.341.

[9] Given Garrick's dependence on the profits of pantomime during his management of Drury Lane, Shakespeare's triumph in *Harlequin's Invasion* is a little disingenuous.

'tame vocal puppets'.[10] As puppets, performers would become no more than lifeless signifiers of human beings, devoid of individual identity, and capable of language only through the intermediary presence of their puppeteer. Hill's image is worth remembering when we come to consider *The Handsome Housemaid* (Haymarket, 1773), Samuel Foote's lively, satirical puppet play. This is because Foote's dramatic satire unwittingly inverts Hill's ideological terms, presenting the Haymarket puppets as the desiccated, wooden embodiment of patent theatrical culture. From the controversial vantage-point of mid-eighteenth-century pantomime, we can also look forward to Joseph Grimaldi's transformation of the Clown into the whimsical, practical satirist of the Regency city. For writers such as Hazlitt and Leigh Hunt, Grimaldi's sensuous, ingenious, parti-coloured Clown became a precious symbol of social licence; Harlequin's episodic violence, meanwhile, suggested the pleasures of a delicious political retribution.

LICENSING THE UNLICENSED

Opposition to the Goodman's Fields theatre, which had opened in 1720 with neither patent nor licence, was conducted in a familiar discourse alleging the dangers of economic and moral pollution. Erecting the theatre, warned a Justices' order, 'will draw away Tradesmens Servants and others from their lawful Callings, and corrupt their Manners, and also occasion great Numbers of loose, idle, and disorderly Persons'.[11] Commentators in this period invariably recognised the neighbourhoods surrounding Drury Lane and Covent Garden as part of a regrettable but licensed topography of pleasure. By contrast, opposition to unlicensed theatres beyond Westminster persistently cited the supposed danger to the economic health of manufacturing neighbourhoods (in the case of Goodman's Fields, the manufacture of silk and wool)[12] and especially to their lower-class inhabitants.

After several inconclusive attempts to silence performances at Goodman's Fields, as well as the threat of a new unlicensed theatre in St Martin's le Grand, Sir John Barnard proposed a Bill 'to restrain the Number and scandalous Abuses of the Play-Houses'. Notwithstanding

---

[10] Aaron Hill and William Popple, *The Prompter: A Theatrical Paper*, selected and edited by William W. Appleton and Kalman A. Burnim (New York: Benjamin Blom, 1966), 30 January 1735, 150.

[11] Arthur Bedford, *The Evil and Mischief of Stage-Playing . . . occasioned by the erecting of a Play-house in the Neighbourhood*, 2nd edition (London, J. Wilford, 1735), 40.

[12] See the petition submitted by the Lord Mayor and city aldermen, 1729–30, PRO LC 7/3, fol. 28.

the terms of the patent, he argued, 'diverse ill-disposed and disorderly Persons, have of late taken upon themselves, without any legal authority, to act and represent Tragedies, Comedies, Plays, Operas, and other Entertainments of the Stage'. The Bill's aim was the suppression of unlicensed theatres in London by means of a revival of vagrancy legislation: those performing without authority would be classified and punished as 'rogues, vagabonds and sturdy beggars'. But Barnard's legislation failed when Walpole met stern opposition over his attempt to graft on to the suppression of unlicensed theatres measures which would have expanded the Lord Chamberlain's powers to control the licensing of plays.[13]

Apart from a petition submitted by 'several eminent Merchants, Shopkeepers, Silk-Men, Weavers, Packers, Dyers, Factors, and other Tradesmen and Inhabitants of the City of London', little support had been forthcoming for Goodman's Fields. In the *Prompter*, however, Hill questioned the expediency of closing unlicensed theatres, and ironically recommended the reversal of existing institutional hierarchies. The unlicensed theatres should be permitted to perform tragedy and comedy alone, he suggested, while the patent and licensed establishments would be restricted to the profitable theatrical kinds ('farce, Harlequinery, buffoonery, . . . dancing, singing, dumb or deserving-to-be dumb entertainment').[14] Hill's ironic solution to the problem of reconciling dramatic legitimacy and patent profit rehearses questions of genre and cultural stewardship which would preoccupy critics, managers and pamphleteers for many years to come.

During the 1730s, political and partisan dramas of various kinds were being performed at London theatres. So, as Robert Hume has pointed out, the argument that Henry Fielding's vituperative anti-Walpole satires were solely responsible for the hurried passing of the Licensing Act cannot be sustained. But what Hume's thesis perhaps underplays is the pivotal position of the Haymarket as an unlicensed institution. For the Haymarket's repertoire, featuring lively burlesques and topical satires, already represented a powerful form of *cultural* opposition to Rich's Covent Garden and Fleetwood's Drury Lane. In particular, *The Historical Register for the Year 1736* and *Eurydice Hiss'd*, both performed at the Haymarket in 1737, audaciously dramatise the systemic relationships between political corruption and patent theatrical practice.

[13] See Vincent J. Liesenfeld, *The Licensing Act of 1737* (Madison, University of Wisconsin, 1984) 52–9; Robert D. Hume, *Henry Fielding and the London Theatre: 1728–1737* (Oxford: Clarendon, 1988), 197–9.   [14] *Prompter*, 63.

In these plays, Fielding represents what the character of Medley calls a 'strict resemblance between the states political and theatrical' (*Historical Register*, II. ii. 38). Here, theatrical managers resemble lawless prime ministers, prime ministers resemble Harlequins, and both actors and politicians are bought at exorbitant prices. The unlicensed status of the Haymarket Theatre enables Fielding to create an unprecedented indictment of the institutional collusion which characterised government, state institutions and patent theatrical management at Drury Lane and Covent Garden.[15] In the final scene of *Tumble-Down Dick*, a cartload of performers from an unlicensed theatre are about to be committed to prison under the vagrancy legislation of 1713. But when the Justice is offered a financial inducement to waive this punishment, he suddenly decides to become a performer himself, and is promptly transformed into Harlequin.[16] In this way, Fielding's self-reflexive satire on legal corruption reminds his audience of the Haymarket's precarious position beyond the law. That position, as Fielding no doubt realised, was too precarious to last.

Like Sir John Barnard's Bill, the Licensing Act (10 Geo. II, c. 28) revived the classification of actors as vagrants (see 12 Anne II, c. 23); not until 1843 did performers begin to be distinguished in law from vagrants. Any individual performing an 'Interlude, Tragedy, Comedy, Opera, Play, farce or other entertainment of the Stage' not previously sanctioned by letters patent or licensed by the Lord Chamberlain 'for hire, gain or reward' would now be liable to punishment as a rogue and a vagabond.[17] Unlike the earlier Bill, however, the Licensing Act also succeeded in imposing a system of textual censorship by which the play texts for Drury Lane and Covent Garden – and later, as we shall see, other minor theatres within Westminster such as the Adelphi and the Olympic – had to be scrutinised before performance by the Lord Chamberlain.[18] But by restricting the king's power to grant letters patent for the erection of theatres in London to Westminster and its liberties, the Licensing Act indirectly contributed to the emergence of an uncensored theatrical terrain beyond the control of the Lord Chamberlain. The Haymarket's unique institutional position, on the border between the patent theatres and the unlicensed playhouses, is one interesting

---

[15] *Works of Fielding*, v. [16] *Ibid.*, 118.

[17] See Thomas, *Restoration and Georgian England*, 207–10. My account is indebted to the detailed studies by Liesenfeld, *Licensing Act of 1737*, and Hume, *Henry Fielding*.

[18] On theatre censorship in this period, see Leonard Conolly, *The Censorship of English Drama 1737–1824* (San Marino, CA: The Huntington Library, 1976).

consequence of this legislation. But my discussion here concentrates on the unwitting creation of an illegitimate domain within metropolitan theatre – a domain which would evoke the spectre of political radicalism, the promotion of plebeian immorality and the uncontrollable reproduction of urban criminality.

The Act initially achieved its aim of suppressing the unlicensed theatres as well as ending altogether Fielding's career as playwright and theatrical manager. In 1740, however, Henry Giffard reopened Goodman's Fields, cleverly avoiding the provisions of the Licensing Act (notably the clause about performing 'for hire, gain or reward') by charging spectators to listen to music, and then offering *gratis* comedies such as George Farquhar's *The Beaux' Stratagem*. But the much-publicised engagement of the celebrated actor David Garrick, who performed *Richard III* in 1741, incurred the wrath of the patentees and Giffard was forced to close the theatre. Cibber's production of *Romeo and Juliet* at the Haymarket similarly provoked a sharp rebuke from the Lord Chamberlain.[19] Despite these threats and prosecutions, however, the minor theatres would continue to defy the patentees throughout this period by staging performances of Shakespeare (see chapter 4).

After Goodman's Fields, the Little Theatre in the Haymarket and Lincoln's Inn Fields had been silenced, complaints soon began to recur about disorderliness at establishments such as Sadler's Wells (which had been staging rope-dancing, acrobatics, music and singing since 1740), and a theatre in Well's yard. In order to oversee more closely such 'public entertainments', Parliament introduced an Act in 1752 'for the better preventing thefts and robberies, and for regulating places of public entertainment, and punishing persons keeping disorderly houses'.[20] This legislation represented unlicensed playhouses as places of plebeian immorality (where 'the lower sort of People' were spending money in 'riotous Pleasures') as well as a serious threat to property and social order. The Act therefore established a system of annual licences for 'music, dancing, and other entertainments of the like kind' which would be administered by local magistrates. By contrast with Barnard's Bill and the Licensing Act, both of which implicitly defined theatres as special and potentially subversive cultural institutions, these later Acts simply regulated unlicensed playhouses as part of an undifferentiated realm of 'public entertainment'.

This legislation unwittingly established an enduring division in the

[19] PRO LC 5/161, 192.   [20] 25 Geo. II, c. xxxvi; see also 28 Geo. II, c. xix.

regulation of London theatre. The Act of 1752 was based on the assumption that the public entertainments offered at Sadler's Wells and other unlicensed theatres within a 15-mile radius of Westminster represented a non-dramatic sphere of bodily performance utterly distinct from the drama staged at Drury Lane and Covent Garden. No provision was made for the textual scrutiny of these entertainments, for what preoccupied legislators was not the threat of political subversion but rather the moral and social pollution spilling out from plebeian pleasure. In any case, how could a system of censorship be imposed on performances for which no texts existed? But from within this portmanteau category of public entertainments, illegitimate theatre would begin to evolve.

As if Fielding's burlesques had permeated the building's very fabric, the 1760s and 1770s revealed the irrepressible character of the Haymarket. In the last decades of the century, the playhouse seemed to relish its own status as an historical place of political and cultural opposition. After a riding accident witnessed by the Duke of York, in which Samuel Foote had lost a leg, the actor and dramatist succeeded in acquiring – by way of theatrical compensation – a summer patent for the representation of 'tragedies, plays, operas and other performances on the stage' at the Haymarket. In one of those tricks of patronage which so often shape stage history, the unlicensed Haymarket now became the playhouse on the institutional border between the monopolists (Drury Lane and Covent Garden) and the minor establishments, a position the theatre would exploit in a variety of ways for the next fifty years.

Samuel Foote (the English Aristophanes, as he was often described) and his successor, George Colman the Elder, inherited an institution whose cultural position and generic traditions had been defined and shaped by Henry Fielding. In his burlesque prelude *The Election of the Managers* (1784), for example, Colman followed Fielding's lead in his daring fusion of a political election and a rehearsal play.[21] In this occasional piece, written for the opening of the Haymarket season, and full of allusions to Britain's war against America, Colman transformed into theatre managers the parliamentary candidates who had taken part in the controversial recent election for the City of Westminster. Indeed, the election hustings had taken place only a stone's throw from the Haymarket, under the portico of St Paul's in Covent Garden. In *The Election* the government candidates, Lord Hood and Sir Cecil Gray, become Laurel and Ivy, the colluding and corrupt managers of Covent

[21] Larpent MS 659.

Garden and Drury Lane, fighting under the slogans 'Prerogatives of Tragedy' and 'Privileges of Comedy'. Charles James Fox, leader of the Rockingham Whigs, appears as Bayes, the patriotic proprietor of 'old English humour' at the Haymarket who vociferously opposes the 'Puppet Shew Managers' at the patent houses. Georgiana, the Duchess of Devonshire, also features in Colman's prelude as Mrs Buckram, the tailor's irrepressible wife, who insists that women are 'the most active and able Canvassers' at an election and expresses her staunch conviction that women should be allowed to become Members of Parliament.[22]

The Examiner of Plays made sporadic deletions to the licensing manuscript of *The Election*. John Larpent erased references to Laurel and Ivy which portrayed these 'two Consuls' presiding over the 'literary Republick'. But elsewhere in the play Larpent ignored a series of references to Laurel's and Ivy's imperialist ambitions (see Blarney's speech to the electors describing them as 'Managers of Great Britain and Ireland') and repeated allusions to various kinds of political and theatrical corruption (according to Type, a reviewer, 'The State & the Theatre are equally at our devotion. Managers and Ministers, all know that no piece & no measure can possibly go down without our assistance'). Notwithstanding its patriotic claptraps and hackneyed appeals, Colman's prelude presented the Haymarket as a place of heroic, patriotic opposition to the insidious, corrupt alliance of the patent theatres.[23] In this sense, *The Election of the Managers* laughingly anticipates that later, radical critique of the collusive relationships between the political and the theatrical states mounted by critics such as John Thelwall and William Hazlitt.

The Haymarket manager was required to await the closure of Drury Lane and Covent Garden Theatres before opening for his own summer season. In the winter of 1772–3, infuriated by Garrick's nonchalant, tactical extension of his season at Drury Lane (this strategy of encroachment became a favoured, though unsuccessful, tactic by which to erode the Haymarket's receipts), Samuel Foote decided to evade the terms of his patent. To perform tragedy or comedy, as Foote well knew, would certainly have incurred the threat of prosecution. Instead, Foote created an illegitimate dramatic entertainment – *The Handsome Housemaid; or, Piety in Pattens* – whose avoidance of dramatic dialogue and eschewal of human performers was calculated to escape legal definition as drama.

---

[22] For the Duchess of Devonshire's participation and the role of gender in this election, see Linda Colley, *Britons: Forging the Nation, 1707–1837* (Yale University Press, 1992), 242ff.

[23] These tactics were somewhat disingenuous for, as the play comically acknowledged, Colman's own managerial career had been closely connected with Covent Garden.

Thus far, Foote's production might be seen as an extension of those unlicensed ruses which had included his own 'Dish of Tea' performances in which drama had been performed *gratis*, with a charge made for the spectators' refreshment. But the 'Primitive Puppet Show' exceeded mere formal subterfuge. Once a sign of cultural vulgarity, the puppets exhibited by Charlotte Charke and others had recently become a modish form of metropolitan entertainment, patronised by leading writers and public figures such as Samuel Johnson.[24] The semiotic medium of a puppet show, filtered through a parody of Richardson's *Pamela*, offered Foote not only a kind of legal equivocation, but also a form of mimicry which literally embodied its own critique.[25]

In the show, the handsome housemaid Polly Pattens heroically rejects the seductive overtures of both the Squire (who promises to take her off to London where she will have 'a round of delights') and the Butler. But this narrative of triumphant virtue, in which Polly proves 'how truly delicate a House Maid can be' is no more than a flimsy pretext. What the puppet show effectively provides is a cultural form through which to mock the 'woodenness' of performance and sentiment at the patent theatres. For his spectators, of course, jokes about wood and woodenness (the Squire refers to the Butler as 'a wooden headed rascal' to which Polly indignantly replies that he is 'made of the same Flesh & Blood as myself') had an immediate and comic visual corollary in Foote's own wooden leg. Foote's cleverness, however, was to present woodenness as a form of satirical iconography. In *The Handsome Housemaid*, therefore, the wooden body, awkward movement and ventriloquised speech of the puppets provide a visual and physical analogy for the hollowness of language, gesture and emotion which characterise theatrical productions at Drury Lane and Covent Garden. In particular, as the *St James's Chronicle* recognised, the Primitive Puppet Show burlesqued 'those hackneyed and disjointed Sentiments which are become so fashionable of late' in English patent drama.[26]

Foote's puppets embodied, literally and metaphorically, the insipidity of contemporary theatrical culture (a theme which would also preoccupy Hazlitt) as well as its slavish dependence on foreign performers and

---

[24] See Scott Cutler Shershow, *Puppets and 'Popular Culture'* (Ithaca: Cornell University Press, 1995).
[25] A manuscript of *Piety in Pattens* can be found in the Larpent collection, MS 467. A valuable modern edition now exists which includes an excellent essay on Foote and the revolt against sentimental drama as well as a useful commentary on the show's production and reception. See '*Samuel Foote's Primitive Puppet-Shew* featuring *Piety in Pattens: A Critical Edition*', ed. Samuel N. Bogorad and Robert Gale Noyes, *Theatre Survey* 14 no. 1a (Fall 1973).
[26] 13–16 February 1773.

plays. At Drury Lane and Covent Garden, Foote's prologue explains, 'we have frigid actors hewn out of petrified blocks; and a theatrical manager upon stilts made out of the mulberry tree'. This theatrical punning on the disembodied character of the puppets is brilliantly underlined by Foote's ironic framing of the Primitive Puppet Show in terms of a collapse of legal classifications. In an extension of the legal farce dramatised in his *Trial of Samuel Foote*, *The Handsome Housemaid* ends with the metatheatrical arrest of Foote and his puppets for vagrancy. Finally, however, all the performers are released, for the learned court is unable to decide whether Foote should be classified as man or puppet. (If he is committed as a man, the puppet part of him should have a right to action for damages, argues Quibble; if committed as a puppet, then the body might sue for false imprisonment.)[27] The Primitive Puppet Show's dissolution into legal quibbling thus highlights the performance's semiotic status as a dramatic equivocation. The puppets' woodenness is suddenly revealed to be doubly deceitful, the puppets themselves a delightful legal sham.

Sophisticated puffing and tantalising advance publicity had ensured that the Haymarket Theatre was packed to the rafters for the opening night of *Piety in Pattens*; according to the *General Evening Post* (16 February), MPs even deserted their debate in the House of Commons to come and watch Foote's puppets. But some of the Haymarket spectators were not impressed by Foote's satirical puppetry. In particular, spectators in the gallery objected vociferously to the absence of any physical combat in Foote's puppet show, and proceeded to express their frustration about this unwise omission by taking limited revenge on the fabric of the auditorium and breaking down the orchestra. The spectators' disruption thus offers an ironic postscript to the relationships between critique and convention in *The Handsome Housemaid*. In a revised and lengthened version, however, Foote's puppet play was regularly performed at the Haymarket until the mid-1790s.

Foote's appropriation of puppetry as a cultural practice which cannot be classified as *drama* marks a turning-point in the delineation of an illegitimate theatre. Before exploring the evolution of illegitimate genres, however, we need to take note of the first direct challenge to the Licensing Act. In some ways, the controversy over the Royalty Theatre in Wellclose Square rehearsed now familiar themes. A petition submitted by 'many of the most respectable and opulent Merchants,

---

[27] See the *Morning Chronicle* review, 16 February 1773.

Shipbuilders, Ropemakers, and other Gentlemen resident in the vicinity of the Tower'[28] alleged for example that the theatre would increase dissipation, economic indiscipline and criminal activity in the neighbourhood. The patentees responded with litigious alacrity to the unlicensed performance of a Shakespeare play (*As You Like It*). And the Royalty's manager – the comic actor known as 'Plausible Jack' Palmer – discovered another strategy by which to negotiate the ban on playing 'for hire, gain or reward'.

So what distinguished the Royalty from earlier unlicensed ventures such as Goodman's Fields? For the first time since the Licensing Act, the manager of an unlicensed playhouse had announced his intention openly to defy the monopoly by representing legitimate drama. In defence of his illicit performances, Palmer invoked various legal justifications, notably the semi-autonomous legal status of the neighbourhood around the Tower of London in which the Royalty was situated.[29] But what made this defiance all the more galling to the patentees was Palmer's audacious proposal to stage Shakespeare, the quintessential dramatist of theatrical legitimacy, on the Royalty's opening night, to be followed by another play from the stock repertoire, Garrick's *Miss in her Teens*. When they discovered this plan, the patentees began their sabre-rattling. By publishing extracts from the Vagrant and Vagabond Acts, they signalled their intention to use the process of law to transform the players of Shakespeare into rogues and vagabonds.[30] Only mildly alarmed by these threats, the indefatigable Palmer decided to perform *As You Like It* for the benefit of the London Hospital.

Whereas the Goodman's Fields Theatre had sparked almost implacable opposition, opinion was now much more divided about the moral and cultural status of a popular theatre. When local magistrates declined to given Palmer a licence for the Royalty, they cited the recent royal proclamation about 'disorderly practices' as well as making the familiar argument that stage performances would be 'a nuisance peculiarly mischievous in that part of the metropolis'.[31] This refusal, which may

---

[28] Memorial, passed from the Home Office to magistrates in Whitechapel, Shoreditch and Shadwell, opposing the renewal of the Royalty licence in 1798, HO 65/1, 22 January 1798, PRO.

[29] See letter from 'Boni Hominis Age' entitled 'Powerful Reasons against the Playhouse in Goodman's Fields' (1786), undated cutting, Tower Hamlets Public Library.

[30] Sheridan and Harris claimed (implausibly) to have spent £7,200 prosecuting their case against the theatre. See their MS letter, 14 February 1816, to the Secretary of State for the Home Department, LC 7/4.

[31] Unidentified cuttings, Theatre Museum. On the proclamation and moral reform, see M. J. Roberts, 'The Society for the Suppression of Vice and its Early Critics', *Historical Journal* 26 (1983), 159–76.

have been influenced by pressure from the Lord Chamberlain,[32] was followed by a series of decisions which seem to reveal the magistrates' conflicting loyalties. Having granted a licence in 1788, they declined to renew it in 1802, only to license the Royalty again in 1803. The pamphlet war surrounding the Royalty was similarly divided, accusatory and acrimonious. Several writers argued that a theatre would help to promote the circulation of money, as well as providing employment for hackney coachmen, porters and labourers; another claimed that drama helped to promote female virtue by depicting the evils perpetrated by the 'despoilers of private tranquillity', while another made the argument that the Royalty might counterbalance the insidious influence of those associations 'inimical to government', said to flourish in Spitalfields, Ratcliffe Highway and around Tower Hamlets. But the Royalty's opponents maintained that the beneficial effects of the nearby National and Sunday Schools would be utterly nullified if the theatre were to be granted a licence, and held out the prospect of 'our industrious mechanics' and 'sober apprentices' deserting their gunmaking orders to visit the Royalty. And it was but one short imaginative step from men abandoning their workshops to losing the war with France. At a time when 'a formidable enemy is at our gates, and threatens to howl destruction on our devoted country', the licensing of the Royalty was portrayed as an issue of national and patriotic concern.[33]

Carriages and coaches swept up for the Royalty's first performance. But Plausible Jack's foray into unlicensed Shakespeare lasted only one night, because the patentees immediately commenced legal proceedings against both Palmer and the members of his company. Indeed, several Royalty performers were subsequently imprisoned by Justice Staples, only to be bailed by the magistrates of Tower Hamlets, whose ruling was then overturned on appeal to the King's Bench.[34] So when the Royalty

---

[32] See Peter Pindar (pseudonym of George Daniel), *The Plotting Managers, a Poetical Satyrical Interlude* (London: J. James, 1787).

[33] *A Letter . . . on the Statutes for the Regulation of Theatres, the Conduct of Mr. Palmer, of Mr. Justice Staples, and the Other Justices* [1787]; *A Review of the Present Contest . . .* (London: Charles Stalker, 1787); [George Colman], *A Very Plain State of the Case . . .* (London: J. Murray, 1787); [Isaac Jackman], *Royal and Royalty Theatres . . .* (London: J. Murray, 1787); Augustus Polydore (pseud.), *The Trial of Mr. John Palmer, Comedian . . . Tried in the Olympian Shades before the Right honourable Lord Chief-Justice Shakspear . . . John Milton, Joseph Addison, Thomas Otway . . .* (London: J. Ridgeway, 1787); *Case of the Renters of the Royalty Theatre* (n.d.); [John Palmer], *Case of the Theatre in Well Street* (1790); [An inhabitant of the Tower], *The Tendency of Dramatic Exhibitions* (?1794); Revd Thomas Thirlwall, *A Solemn Protest against the Revival of Scenic Exhibitions and Interludes at the Royalty Theatre . . .* (London: T. Plummer, 1803).

[34] See *Gentleman's Magazine*, March 1788, 50: 267; James Lawrence, *Dramatic Emancipation; or Strictures on the State of the Theatre . . .* in the *Pamphleteer*, 1813, 2: 382; unidentified cuttings, Tower Hamlets Library.

reopened two weeks later, the repertoire carefully avoided the litigious genres of tragedy and comedy.[35] Moreover, in the wake of Palmer's transgression, the patentees tried to impose a new and unprecedented definition of their own privileges. Sheridan and Harris now declared that their monopoly of dramatic forms also extended to a monopoly over the spoken word. They therefore threatened to prosecute Palmer if any of his performers should speak, even in a pantomimic performance. Indeed, the famous clown Carlos Delpini was actually prosecuted for having spoken the words 'roast beef' unaccompanied by music.[36] Whether or not these were the only words spoken by Delpini on stage, it seems a little ironic that roast beef, traditional food of John Bull, and by then inextricable from the defence of robust British political culture, should suddenly become associated with theatrical transgression. The corporeal semiotics of pantomime – all bodily excrescences and uncontrollable consumption – seemed to have passed with their own irrepressible energy into the newly monopolised world of dramatic speech.

Infuriated by Palmer's jaunty escapade at the Royalty, the patentees pursued the actor to his engagement at the Royal Circus in 1789. Here in St George's Fields, Charles Dibdin the Elder had attempted to realise his dream that horsemanship, if divested of blackguardism and 'made an object of public consequence', might form the basis for an entertainment which profitably combined the traditions of stage and circus. From the beginning, the Royal Circus managers had also announced their resolution to perform dramatic entertainments including 'speaking pantomime, opera, medleys, drolls and interludes'.[37] In the early years, however, the Circus' history had been stormy ineed: a catalogue of licences refused, pecuniary embarrassments and acrimonious disputes involving Charles Hughes, the dastardly manager of the horses. The engagement of Palmer, then conveniently living 'within the rules' of the King's Bench prison (i.e., as a debtor) therefore represented a determined attempt to prove the theatrical distinction of the Circus.

[35] The fate of the Royalty prompted Sadler's Wells, Astley's and the Royal Circus to seek Parliamentary protection for their entertainments. But by shrewdly invoking the spectre of popular vice and the need to protect patent property, Sheridan neatly filibustered the proposed Interlude Bill. See *Journal of the House of Commons*, 43: 299, 7 March 1788; *Gentleman's Magazine*, supplement for 1788, 1146.

[36] Lawrence, *Dramatic Emancipation*, 382; Edward Brayley, *Historical and Descriptive Accounts of the Theatres of London* (London: J. Taylor, 1826), 80. See also *The Memoirs of J. Decastro, Comedian*, ed. R. Humphreys (London: Sherwood, 1824), 123ff.

[37] LC 10–12 October 1782, cited in Robert Fahrner, *The Theatre Career of Charles Dibdin the Elder (1745–1814)* (New York, New York: Peter Lang, 1989), 96.

The Bastille's extraordinary run of more than seventy nights aroused 'the envy, dread, and opposition of the Theatres Royal'.[38] Whilst playing the hero, Henry du Bois, in John Dent's play, Palmer was prosecuted by the notorious Justice Hyde for 'speaking Prose on the Stage' and sent to the Surrey gaol as a rogue and vagrant.[39] Throughout this period, the patentees almost invariably selected for prosecution those minor productions which featured a well-known performer. They no doubt found sweet revenge, too, in having the dramatic hero of French liberation imprisoned in an English prison. But despite all these attempts at intimidation, the representation of revolution and of war had become a spectacular catalyst. The minor theatres now began to abandon the pretence of dramatic silence for the litigious controversies of dramatic speech.

John Dent's *Bastille* (Royal Circus, October 1789) is a sentimental comedy in illegitimate disguise.[40] In its semiotic conventions, the play appears to conform to the regulations governing the minor theatres: the text of *The Bastille* consists entirely of recitative, interspersed with songs; the play also incorporates topical descriptions of 'the dreadful sufferings' endured by the Bastille prisoners and the 'uncontrollable effervescence of popular heroism which led to the destruction of that horrid fortress'.[41] In many ways, however, Dent's play closely follows the conventions of sentimental comedy: Henry, whose love for Matilda is opposed by her father, overcomes that characteristic barrier to romantic happiness by rescuing him from the Bastille. Love and revolution are then interwoven in a patriotic, allegorical transformation. At the end of the play, accompanied by 'low music', Britannia descends, seated in her triumphal car, bearing two transparent portraits of King George III and Queen Charlotte. According to Brittania, the fall of the Bastille represents the happy translation of British liberty across the Channel: 'From Britannia you caught the Patriot flame, / On Britain's plan then build your future fame / Let liberty and reason rule each part / And form the Magna Charta of the heart' (23). After Britannia's song, the statue of liberty joyfully tramples

---

[38] Address, John Dent, *The Bastille* (London: W. More, 1789); *Memoirs of Decastro*, ed. Humphreys, 124.

[39] *Memoirs of Decastro*, 125; Brayley, *Historical and Descriptive Accounts*, 71–2. According to Brayley, Palmer was released after Hyde extracted an assurance that the Circus season would be limited in future to the period between Easter and Michaelmas. Having settled his financial affairs, Palmer returned to Drury Lane and played Joseph Surface (a role Sheridan claimed to have designed especially for him) in *The School for Scandal*.   [40] Dent, *The Bastille*.

[41] Brayley, *Historical and Descriptive Accounts*, 71.

An Amphitheatrical Attack of the Bastile.

1. The illegitimate revolution begins. *An Amphitheatrical Attack of the Bastile.*

on the figure of despotism and then ascends to the sounds of a patriotic chorus. What is notable about *The Bastille* is John Dent's skilful marriage of illegitimate dramaturgy and the legitimate conventions of benevolence and sentimental reconciliation.

Collings' engraving, 'An Amphitheatrical Attack of the Bastile' (plate 1) is a metatheatrical satire on this illegitimate innovation. The image features a number of humorous scrolls (the hapless Bastille governor holds one which reads 'D--N YOU WHAT DO YOU WANT') and even the (paper-thin) drawbridge is ironically labelled as such. What is more, the supposed revolutionaries are a motley, hollow-eyed crew who look utterly incapable of even holding up their Standard of Liberty, let alone of storming the Bastille. On the stage floor, next to the exploding cannon, we can also see a scrap of paper whose text satirically punctures the proud verisimilitude of the Royal Circus's production. Indeed, the miniature announcement written here is almost like another scroll, left behind by accident. It reads: 'Mr. Centaur can assure the publick since his return from ~~Dublin~~ Paris that this here Bastile is the most exactest of any of the Bastiles existin.' But despite the mocking laughter engendered by this image, *The Bastille* had transformed for ever what could be represented on a minor stage.

The fall of the Bastille, and Britain's war against Napoleon, provided the minor theatres with a collection of topical, spectacular narratives perfectly suited to illegitimate representation. Beyond the control of the Examiner of Plays (who had banned Covent Garden's Bastille play),[42] and forbidden to represent legitimate drama, Astley's, the Royal Circus and Sadler's Wells Theatre began to pioneer their own physical dramaturgy of war. In these shows military knowledge, technical innovation and topographical illusion went hand in hand: managers like the gruff, blunt Philip Astley (who had received four horses in gratitude for his gallantry at the siege of Valenciennes) shrewdly exploited his first-hand knowledge of military strategy and organisation. At the Amphitheatre, Astley created a series of elaborate equestrian spectacles such as *Paris in an Uproar* (August 1789), *The Champ de Mars* (July 1790) and *Bagshot-Heath Camp* (August 1792).[43] Meanwhile, the managers of Sadler's Wells

---

[42] See Conolly, *Censorship*, 91–2.
[43] Astley's playbills often included detailed explanations of weaponry and battle formations. See for example the bill advertising *The Surrender of Condé* (Astley's, August 1793 in HTC) which promised its audience 'cannon of different calibres' and ammunition wagons, and even offered an explanation of a blockade including glacis, counterscape and ditch.

exploited the theatre's proximity to the New river in their production of an aquatic theatre of war featuring the ingenious reconstruction of sea battles including Charles Dibdin's *The Siege of Gibraltar* (1804).

Revolution and war now provided the script for an illegitimate theatre of peril, danger, and spectacular illusion. The physical materials as well as the iconography of these martial spectacles originated from contemporary warfare. Craftsmen from the Woolwich dockyard, for example, were making the model ships for the naval battles staged at Sadler's Wells; 'Redfire', a new substance manufactured for use as a military explosive from strontia, shellac and chlorate of potash, produced the spectacular flame effects to be seen at Sadler's Wells.[44] The dramaturgy of these topical plays also represents a noticeable departure from the conventions of legitimate drama, and especially from the traditions of benevolence and reconciliation at the heart of sentimental comedy. Here, by contrast, good and evil are irreconcilable opposites, and the confrontation between them is characteristically imagined in physical terms. A recurring topos in these plays, for instance, is the 'blow-up', a spectacular explosion which destroys the tyrant's or usurper's castle. In many ways, the blow-up might seem to exemplify that theatre of meretricious spectacle so lamented by the defenders of 'The Drama'. But from a different perspective the blow-up actually marks a radical departure in the dramatisation of nation and empire. It makes representable in an entirely new way that irreducible confrontation between freedom and despotism, good and evil. In so doing, the dramaturgy of illegitimate theatre implicitly reveals the failure of rationality, the inadequacy of rhetoric and the impossibility of benevolence. What the blow-up silently confirms, in other words, is the collapse of legitimate genres such as sentimental comedy as ideological models for the dramatisation of a modern nation.

The dramaturgy of war at the minor theatres evolved in the face of legal contingency, namely an unwritten ban on spoken dialogue. But did this mean that performers must be mute? On the contrary, rhyming couplets and dramatic recitative, accompanied by music, provided two important kinds of illegitimate speech at the minor theatres. Then, from the 1790s onwards, playhouses began to circumvent the ban on spoken dialogue by the use of linen scrolls, also known as flags or banners. The scrolls were inscribed with small portions of dramatic speech (idiosyncratic spellings often provided a source of amusement for some educated

---

[44] Arundell, *The Story of Sadler's Wells*, 60 ff.

spectators) and held aloft on stage by the performers for the audience to read.[45] John Cross' *Circusiana* plays provide a useful example of these techniques in practice.

The *Circusiana* exist in a theatrical hinterland between circus and theatre, between physical spectacle and dramatic forms based on the primacy of rhetoric.[46] Cross's plays include *Sir Francis Drake and Iron Arm* (Royal Circus, August 1800) 'in which the cool courage, and exemplary humanity of the English admiral, is forcibly contrasted by the cruelty, meanness, and perfidy of a savage outlaw',[47] *The Fire King; Or, Albert and Rosalie* (Royal Circus, June 1801) and a collection of overtly patriotic pieces such as *Our Native Land, and Gallant Protectors* (Royal Circus, July 1803). Variously defined as *ballets d'action*, spectacles and melodramas, the plots of Cross' musical plays, several of which were staged at the patent theatres, included mythological narratives and a Kotzebue drama as well as popular tales of Gothic skulduggery. Sometimes implicitly, more often overtly, the *Circusiana* exploited audiences' enthusiasm about seeing Napoleonic bogeymen and sturdy British heroes portrayed on stage. Melodramas such as *The Great Devil; or, The Robber of Genoa* (1801) and *Jack the Giant Killer* (1803) at Sadler's Wells, many written with starring parts for Grimaldi, and music by Russell and Reeve, shared similar themes of menace, devilish treachery and triumphant patriotic virtue.[48]

These plays abound with Gothic horrors in the form of skeletons and apparitions. Most are set in wild and picturesque scenery, whether in the Appenine mountains (*Rinaldo Rinaldini*), in a distant sea view after a tempest (*The False Friend*) or on the edge of a precipice in the West Indies (*Blackbeard; or, The Captive Princess*). Airs, ballads and choruses punctuate the dumbshow action, as well as dances and 'warlike', 'slow' or 'soft' musical accompaniments. Cross' texts carefully notate the bodily expression of emotion: characters shudder, tremble and form a group 'expressive of the utmost terror' and at the sight of a figure in transparent armour, Sitric the villainous Dane appears 'with all the horror of guilt marked on his countenance and trembling limbs'.[49]

---

[45] See report in *Morning Chronicle*, 21 January 1812. On the fashion for transparent inscriptions, and a theatrical accident arising from the last-minute preparation of scrolls, see Charles Dibdin, *Memoirs of Charles Dibdin the Younger*, ed. George Speaight (London: Society for Theatre Research, 1956), 100.

[46] *Circusiana; or A Collection of the most favourite Ballets, Spectacles, Melo-dramas, &c. performed at the Royal Circus, St. George's Fields*, 2 vols. (London: T. Burton, 1809). Reprinted as *The Dramatic Works of J.C. Cross* (London: printed for the author, 1809). [47] *Monthly Mirror*, August 1800, 111.

[48] Charles Dibdin, *The Great Devil; or, The Robber of Genoa, CMT* xiv.

[49] *The Round Tower; or, The Chieftains of Ireland* (Covent Garden 1797), in *Circusiana* 1: 17.

At the heart of the *Circusiana* is that archetypal narrative of the villain-ous usurper finally defeated. What interests me here, however, is the way in which the scrolls served to make virtue visible to spectators in textual form. At the Dargle by midnight, through a fragment of the rock, the audience watching *The Round Tower* read the transparent letters 'mur-derer despair and die' (scene viii, p. 8); in *Julia of Louvain*, a series of scrolls ('Remember your Vow'; 'Death or St Pierre') mirror the heroine's stark, moral choice between resistance and forced acquiescence to St Pierre. By solemnly kissing the word death on the scroll, Julia silently transforms unspoken language into a solemn oath.[50] The *Circusiana* scrolls, including the blood-red letters in the Book of Blood (*Rinaldo*) or the patriotic declaration in *Blackbeard* ('THE ENEMY IS BRITISH AND WILL DIE OR CONQUER')[51] present language as a physical, embodied object, tangible, prophetic and incontrovertible.

Cross' plays also marked a watershed in the publication of illegitimate theatre. Many of the Royal Circus pieces were printed soon after their first performance; encouraged by the Earl of Craven, Cross also had his collected dramas published by subscription. By the late 1820s, of course, publishers like Richard Cumberland were beginning to exploit the market for minor plays by introducing their own collections. But the appearance of the *Circusiana* – in his Preface, Cross self-consciously described his plays as 'Minor Dramas' – indicates the emergence of the minor play as a text to be read and imagined in the closet, not simply enjoyed as theatrical spectacle.

Quadruped theatre, aquadrama and circusiana represent the innova-tive and technically sophisticated forms of war and revolution pioneered at the minor theatres. These plays not only enhanced the dramatic rep-utations of Sadler's Wells, the Royal Circus and Astley's, but also made topical spectacles an object of commercial envy at the patent houses. But to stage such plays at Drury Lane and Covent Garden was to invite accu-sations about the monopolists' treacherous betrayal of legitimate culture. As a skirmishing corps of 'hostile sharp-shooters' are reported to have shouted from the Covent Garden gallery in response to one of Tom Dibdin's songs, 'It vont do! it vont do, I tell you! take it away! take it to Sadler's Wells!'[52]

[50] *Julia*, scene vii, 109.
[51] *Rinaldo* (Royal Circus, 1801), scene iii, 147, in *Circusiana* II; *Blackbeard* (Royal Circus, 1798), scene x, 43 in *Circusiana* I.
[52] Thomas J. Dibdin, *The Reminiscences of Thomas Dibdin*, 2 vols. (London: Henry Colburn, 1827), I: 337–48: 341. The apparently predetermined uproar arose in response to Dibdin's song about the beauty of Jewish ladies in his opera *Family Quarrels* (Covent Garden, 1802).

The success of the early minor theatres also encouraged dramatic entrepreneurs to open playhouses within Westminster. In 1806, the colour merchant John Scott established the Sans Pareil as a small theatre to display the talents of his daughter Jane Scott, and persuaded the Earl of Dartmouth (then Lord Chamberlain, and, indeed, no friend to Drury Lane and Covent Garden) to license his playhouse for winter performances between Michaelmas and Passion Week.[53] Meanwhile, Astley's profits at his Amphitheatre on the south bank convinced him that the time was now ripe to take circus into Westminster itself. The flamboyant, tent-like Olympic theatre, a structure quickly improvised from the remains of a French warship, with a tin roof to keep out the rain, soon appeared on Wych Street, an insalubrious location just off the Strand (see plate 2). Although the Olympic did not thrive under Astley's management, Scott and Astley nonetheless had laid the foundations for theatrical competition to take place on the patentees' own geographical territory of Westminster.

As the proprietors of Drury Lane soon complained, theatre was now being licensed 'almost under the Porches of the two Patent Theatres'.[54] They objected in particular to the way the new theatres were beginning to stage drama under the guise of burletta. Defined as 'strict musical pieces without dialogue', usually in three acts and containing about six songs, burletta's musical form perfectly served legal contingency and the expressive, gestural traditions of illegitimate theatre. In other words, burletta did indeed provide a convenient generic disguise for the introduction of dramatic dialogue at the minor theatres.[55] Jane Scott's Gothic burlettas including *Asgard, the Demon Hunter* (Sans Pareil, 1812) and *The Old Oak Chest* (Sans Pareil, 1816), represent two early examples of these illegitimate transgressions within Westminster.[56] But by 1818 the patentees were besieging the Home Office with complaints about the perversion of burletta at the Sans Pareil and the Olympic. Evidence for their claims was provided in the form of statements made by the theatres' employees, who were being sent to spy on performances at the offending playhouses. Thomas Wakerly's deposition, for example, alleged that *The*

[53] Brayley, *Historical and Descriptive Accounts*, 85–6.

[54] Letter from the proprietors of Drury Lane to the Secretary of State for the Home Department, 14 February 1816, in LC 7/4.

[55] Philip Astley had applied to perform burletta at the Amphitheatre in 1787. For Scott's petition to perform burletta, and a letter from the Deputy Chamberlain to Lord Dartmouth, see Historical Mss. Commission Report XIII (v), 1892; Report XVI, Appendix I (Dartmouth II), 1896, 505

[56] See J. S. Bratton's chapter, 'Jane Scott the writer-manager' in Tracy C. Davis and Ellen Donkin, eds., *Women and Playwriting in Nineteenth-Century Britain* (Cambridge University Press, 1999), 77–98.

2. Circus migrates to Westminster. Astley's Olympic Theatre in Wych Street.

Old Oak Chest was now performed in regular dialogue without accompaniment except for the songs; at the Olympic, '*Dialogue* is substituted for Recitative in Rhyme, and carried on without accompaniment by the Orchestra.'[57] Without trespassing on the legitimate genres of tragedy and comedy, however, the Adelphi and the Olympic had already succeeded in forging their own distinctive repertoire. Moreover, with the apparent connivance of a liberal Lord Chamberlain, the Westminster playhouses had already begun to abandon recitative, scrolls and the other signs of theatrical illegitimacy.

THE RISE OF THE MINOR THEATRES

By 1831, Leigh Hunt would applaud Davidge's allusion to the Coburg's distinguished position, on 'the side on which the olden Theatres once stood, where Shakspeare, Massinger and Ben Jonson wrote and acted'. In future, predicted Hunt, 'the trade of a theatrical critic' would take place on the south bank of the river rather than in 'the once witty neighbourhood of Covent-Garden.'[58] Hunt's polemical comments were intended to alert his readers to the disintegration of old hierarchies and the emergence of new forms and places of dramatic performance.

In an earlier article, Hunt had castigated the complacency of the Theatres Royal whilst praising the freshness and originality of certain minor plays. The dramas at Drury Lane and Covent Garden, complained Hunt, 'consist of spectacle and show with dogs and horses, and nautical afterpieces in the Adelphi style dramas'; even the very best pieces produced here, he continued, 'are such as those which the Olympic, the Adelphi, Mr. Arnold's theatre, and Mr Morris's have been producing every day' while the patent pantomimes 'are in the universal opinion of the town inferior to the pantomime at the Adelphi':

The Adelphi is constantly producing new pieces that do it great credit; the Olympic, in its light way, promises to do as much . . . and from what we hear of the Coburg and the Surrey, and have seen of a variety of printed dramas which have been sent us, performed at those theatres, and written by Mr. Jerrold, they have been making the most praiseworthy exertions for informing as well as

---

[57] See Joint Memorial from Harris and Ward against the infringements of the minors, 2 November 1815 in PRO 7/4.

[58] Playbill advertising the engagement of Edmund Kean, 1 July 1831. Cf. Coburg's 'Address to the Public' (25 October 1833) which pointed out the neighbourhood's associations with Shakespeare, Jonson, Beaumont and Fletcher. Leigh Hunt's comments are taken from the *Tatler*, 7 July 1831, 3: 24: 'The best thing said by a manager in his playbills . . . is what Mr. Davidge of the Coburg has said, relative to the classical ground of Southwark.'

amusing the important multitudes that visit them; a circumstance, we may venture to say, which is not unworthy the serious consideration of the Lord Chancellor, as serving to shew him the importance of exciting intellectual emulation among a variety of play-houses.[59]

Hunt's *Tatler* essay is a miniature manifesto for dramatic free trade. In his lightning tour of the cultural metropolis, the patent theatres are portrayed as jaded, obsolete institutions no longer capable of dramatic innovation. With this transformation in mind, we now need to explore the geography of this emerging theatrical metropolis.

On the south bank of the Thames, at the intersection of the seedy New Cut which connected the Blackfriars and Westminster Roads, was the Coburg, still standing today as the Old Vic (see plate 3). Designed by Rudolph Cabanel in the style of the French minor theatres, and featuring a grand proscenium extravagantly embellished with images of comedy and tragedy, this vast playhouse could hold well over three thousand spectators. As at the Surrey, two large galleries provided a large proportion of the seats. Indeed, the galleries at the Coburg extended all the way around the house. This unusual design (or 'blemish' according to the *British Stage*) brought 'into a most conspicuous point of view a number of gentry, who, though they contribute largely to the treasury of a theatre, by no means add to the elegance of its appearance.'[60]

Sometimes known as the 'Blood Tub' in deference to its penchant for staging violent, sensational melodrama, the Coburg courted notoriety and respectability by contradictory turns. On the one hand, spectacular panoramic scenery, painted by leading artists such as Clarkson Stanfield, helped to establish the Coburg's reputation as a spectacular place of visual pleasure. On the other, the Coburg's historical melodramas including McFarren's sanguinary drama, *Guy Faux; or, The Gunpowder Conspiracy* (August 1822) and Milner's *Lucius Catiline, the Roman Traitor* (June 1827), which promised 'a faithful picture of the Manners, Warfare, Religious and Civil Ceremonies, &c. of the Ancient Romans'[61] were clearly intended to draw the seekers of immoral thrills as well as educated middle-class spectators. Above all, the Coburg attracted controversy. Whether in the risky 'melodramatisation' of *Richard III* in 1819 or in the jaunty adaptation of Fielding's *Tom Thumb*, staged amid the Reform crisis of 1832, the Coburg seemed to relish theatrical, moral and political brinkmanship.

[59] *Tatler*, 27 January 1831, 2: 497–8, 498.
[60] *British Stage, and Literary Cabinet*, ed. Thomas Kendrick, June 1818, 2: 136.
[61] Playbill, 11 June 1827.

3. Circus and stage in St George's Fields. The Royal Circus Theatre in 1809.

After a period of dark uncertainty, and its destruction by fire in 1805, the Royal Circus had been rebuilt from a design by Rudolph Cabanel. Ackermann described the new building as 'a very handsome theatre' with 'various and beautiful scenery' and an auditorium offering 'a very pleasing *coup d'œil* of taste and elegance'.[62] Plate 4 shows Rowlandson's and Pugin's watercolour of a full house at the Surrey enjoying a pantomime; the image emphasises the theatre's size and grandeur, especially the elaborate patterns and mythological decoration on the ceiling. At this period, performances still took place both on stage and down in the circus ring (here opened to spectators).

Renamed the Surrey by its new lessee, Robert Elliston (a change of name which shrewdly capitalised on neighbourhood pride as well as discreetly erasing the playhouse's association with the circus),[63] the Surrey soon acquired a reputation as the most respectable of the minor theatres. 'Of all the old established Minor Theatres', remarked a correspondent in the *Theatrical Inquisitor*, 'the *Surrey* is the only one which lays claim

[62] R[udolph] Ackermann, *The Microcosm of London; or London in Miniature*, 3 vols. (London: R. Ackermann, 1808–10), III: 17.   [63] Brayley, *Historical and Descriptive Accounts*, 73.

4. Royal Coburg Theatre, 1818.

to rational approbation.'[64] At the outset, Elliston had petitioned to stage entertainments 'accompanied with *Dialogue*, in the ordinary mode of dramatic representation', but his request was peremptorily refused.[65] Nevertheless, his successful and profitable management (1809–19), featured a well-judged mixture of melodrama and burletta, interspersed with illegitimate versions of *Macbeth, The Beaux' Stratagem* and *The Beggar's Opera*, each methodically transformed into burletta, complete with rhyming dialogue, musical accompaniment and scrolls.

Under the management of Thomas Dibdin, the Surrey again became a fashionable transpontine theatre. Dibdin continued Elliston's policy of melodramatising legitimate dramas: in his *Reminiscences*, he records gleefully how the tragedy of *Douglas*, 'without omitting a single line of the author, made a very splendid melo-drama, with the additions of Lord Randolph's magnificent banquet, a martial Scotch dance, and a glee . . . exquisitely set by Sanderson'.[66] Dibdin's adaptations of Scott's novels, including *The Bride of Lammermoor; or, The Spectre at the Fountain* (1819) – carefully omitting Lucy Ashton's assassination of her husband – and

[64] Letter from 'Peeping Tom', *Theatrical Inquisitor*, January 1819, 14: 21.
[65] George Raymond, *Memoirs of Robert William Elliston*, 2 vols. (London: John Mortimer, 1844), I: 432–4.   [66] Thomas Dibdin, *Reminiscences*, II:270.

Ivanhoe: or, The Jew's Daughter (1820) also attracted thousands of spectators to the Surrey; West End carriages swept across Waterloo Bridge to St George's Fields to see realised on stage the works of the nation's most celebrated novelist. Walter Scott, declared the playwright Edward Fitzball, represented a 'mighty luminary which reflected its lustre upon the so-called illegitimate drama'.[67] Certainly, dramatic adaptations of Scott created a great deal of favourable publicity for the minor theatres.

Travelling out of Westminster towards the neighbourhood of the old Goodman's Fields theatres, we might wonder what had happened to the Royalty. Later renamed the East London (a change of title which, like the Surrey, suggests the perceived commercial advantage of a local identity), the theatre had survived until it was destroyed by fire in 1826. Two years later, an elegant and commodious new playhouse, named the Royal Brunswick, was built by subscription on the site.[68] Designed as 'an appropriate Ornament to the wealthy and extensive District of Eastern London' (with a façade said to resemble that of San Carlos at Naples),[69] the Royal Brunswick had been open only a few days in 1828 when fire swept through the building, killing several carpenters and passers-by.[70] The episode provided a tragic reminder of how precarious an activity theatrical speculation can be. As he struggled amongst the ruins to rescue the injured, a local minister could not help but reflect that 'so extraordinary had been the haste to put up this Theatre, that even the holy day of God . . . had been violated'. Nor was Smith able to resist giving a miniature sermon about theatre's profanity. He even told one terrified woman whom he had just rescued that she would have to thank God for the rest of her life, for 'you would not die in a Theatre, of all other places'.[71]

Not long after the Brunswick fire, the Pavilion Theatre began to emerge from the shell of an old clothes factory on Baker's Row in Whitechapel. From 1828 until the opening of the Britannia at Hoxton in 1841, the Pavilion would remain the leading East End playhouse. In this seafaring neighbourhood, nautical melodrama dominated the repertoire, together with sensational melodramas such as *Romanoff the*

---

[67] Edward Fitzball, *Thirty-Five Years of a Dramatic Author's Life*, 2 vols. (London: T. C. Newby, 1859), I: 270.

[68] A report in *The Times*, 1 March 1828, alluded to numerous free invitations having been issued to 'respectable inhabitants' in the neighbourhood to persuade them to support the theatre's opening. [69] John Timbs, *Curiosities of London* (London: John Camden Hotten, 1855), II: 47.

[70] Moncrieff, *Remarks* to James Thomson, *An Uncle Too Many, RMD* I.

[71] Rev. George Smith, *Dreadful Catastrophe. Destruction of the Brunswick Theatre, Wellclose Square*, 3rd edition (London: W. K. Wakefield, [1828]).

Regicide (decorously billed as a 'Terrific Legendary Recreation').[72] At the Pavilion, Frederick Tomlins claimed, 'the Newgate calendar and tales of terror stand in the same place as Homer did to the ancient dramatists'; the Pavilion ruthlessly traded on 'the deepest atrocities, the most squalid miseries'.[73] But Tomlins perhaps overstated his case for rhetorical effect, for the Pavilion also staged a range of original dramas (including, for example, *Esther, The Royal Jewess*, Elizabeth Polack's tragedy of ethnicity and ambition), and also presented more of Shakespeare's plays than any other minor theatre.

Few members of the House of Lords, we can safely assume, had patronised any of the East End theatres. But Garrick's Subscription Theatre, which opened close to the Pavilion in 1831, momentarily acquired a special kind of notoriety during the Lords' debates on the Dramatic Performances Bill. According to the Bishop of London, a deputation of 'respectable inhabitants' had complained to him of the 'great evils' produced by the Garrick Theatre on 'the moral character of the neighbourhood', and especially on the morality of women and apprentices; as we have seen, many commentators portrayed the East End theatres as a threat to social order and economic discipline.[74] Like the Pavilion, the Garrick specialised in nautical plays and dramas of criminal sensation, including Dibdin Pitt's dark dramas, *Ada the Betrayed* and *Richard the Ruthless; or, The Felon Father*.[75] And in vengeful plays such as Fitzball's *The Negro of Wapping; or, The Boat-Builder's Hovel* (April 1838), starring a cynical negro sweep 'dragged on board a ship, and doomed to labour . . . then left to beg, or rob, or die of famine in a stranger land', the Pavilion also staged disconcerting images of ethnicity in the modern city.[76]

The production of *Rochester* (Olympic 1818), Moncrieff's saucy costume burletta of aristocratic rakery, with Elliston in the title role, marked the beginning of a new kind of competition for the patronage of fashionable audiences. Moncrieff himself would confidently proclaim *Rochester* to be 'the first original piece produced on the Minor Stage, claiming any pretensions to the rank of a regular drama'. Though that description may be questionable, Moncrieff could certainly take credit for attracting the *beau monde* to the Olympic, a theatre previously considered 'low'.[77] Until the arrival of Eliza Vestris as lessee in 1830, however,

---

[72] Playbill, 14 April 1828, Tower Hamlets Library.   [73] Tomlins, *Brief View*, 65.
[74] See *Morning Chronicle*, 5 August 1832.
[75] Many of Dibdin Pitt's plays concern the vicissitudes of women. Cf. *Susan Hopley; or, The Vicissitudes of a Servant Girl* (Victoria, 1841); *Charlotte Hayden; or, The Victim of Circumstances* (Britannia, 1844).   [76] *DBT* XXIX, II.iii.21.   [77] Moncrieff's preface, *RMD* I.

the Olympic's fortunes remained uncertain: between 1819 and 1825, the theatre bankrupted several managers. By contrast, the nearby Adelphi rapidly acquired a settled place in the metropolitan economy of pleasure, particularly amongst Regency bucks who arrived at half-price to enjoy the afterpiece as part of a night on the town. Moreover, under the management of Jones and Rodwell the Adelphi also declared its policy of approaching 'as near the regular drama as the exclusive privileges of the great theatres will permit'.[78] Two years later, seats at the Adelphi were being taken weeks in advance; peers and apprentices, dukes and dustmen mobbed the theatre to obtain admission,[79] whilst Methodists could be found angrily placarding the Adelphi's performances. The play, of course, was *Tom and Jerry* (1821), adapted by William Moncrieff from Pierce Egan. This drama, which featured a rich collection of popular songs as well as brilliantly realising Cruikshank's illustrations, transformed the Adelphi almost overnight into London's most popular theatre. Thomas Dibdin, who claimed to have turned down *Tom and Jerry* in the belief that its production would deprive him of the local magistrates' good opinion, and indeed that of his Surrey public, must have been seething quietly.[80]

In the wake of *Tom and Jerry*, which rapidly spawned many burlesques and imitations,[81] the Adelphi marketed itself as a theatre of metropolitan flash, vulgarity and low life. The theatre's audiences, too, sometimes contributed to this atmosphere of general vulgarity: in 1835, the *New Monthly Magazine* alleged that scenes 'similar to those which may be witnessed among the most dissolute class frequenting the booths that disgrace a race-course' had been reported at the back of the theatre.[82] Moreover, the Adelphi's stars included a number of London's most celebrated 'low' comedians such as John Buckstone, John Reeve and Frederick Yates. In many ways, the theatre's repertoire does confirm this disreputable reputation, for the Adelphi delighted in the production of diabolical melodramas such as Fitzball's *Vanderdecken*, grotesque burlesques including *The Elbow Shakers* (set in the Blue Moon public house at Wapping) and unfashionable farce (see chapter 6). During the same period, nevertheless, the Adelphi also pioneered picturesque, romantic

---

[78] Adelphi theatre scrapbook, cutting for 10 October 1819.
[79] Moncrieff's Preface to *Tom and Jerry*, *RMD* I.   [80] Thomas Dibdin, *Reminiscences*, II: 214.
[81] These included Charles Dibdin the Younger, *Life in London; or, The Day and Night Adventures of Logic, Tom and Jerry* (Olympic, November 1821) and *The Death of Don Giovanni; or, The Shades of Logic, Tom and Jerry* (Olympic, December 1823), as well as *Green in France; or, Tom and Jerry's Tour* (Adelphi, January 1823). In the last, the Examiner deleted references to the Queen Caroline affair and a scene in which the tourists drank the health of French and English ladies. See Larpent MS 2330.
[82] 45: 521. On the Adelphi's lowness, see Charles Mathews, SC 3088.

dramas such as *The Wreck Ashore* (1830), *Victorine; or, I'll Sleep On It* (1831) –
a minor play widely praised for its 'legitimacy' at the Parliamentary
Select Committee[83] – *Isabelle, or, Woman's Life* and *Henriette the Forsaken*.
Like Buckstone's subsequent hit plays, *The Flowers of the Forest* (1847) and
The Green Bushes (1845), what distinguished many of these Adelphi
dramas was their fascination with the conflicting emotions of forsaken
women.

In the vicinity of Exeter Change, Samuel Arnold's English Opera
House, also known as the Lyceum, had succeeded in acquiring a licence
to stage musical farces and ballad operas during the summer months.[84]
Arnold's patriotic revivals of English opera irked the patentees; so did
the Lyceum's genius for identifying hit plays such as Planché's diabolical
drama, *The Vampyre; or, The Bride of the Isles* (1820) and Richard Brinsley
Peake's celebrated adaptation of *Frankenstein* (1823), in which the sailor
hero T. P. Cooke starred as the monster. One of the earliest theatres to
install gas lighting (an innovation much trumpeted in playbills), the
Lyceum also followed the Haymarket in mocking, defying and burlesquing patent monopoly. Arnold's preludes and opening addresses comically highlighted the constraints on the Lyceum's performances: 'So
Shakespeare says – and adds, pray Criticks note him, / We must not *act*
him here, but we may quote him.'[85] The ironic, Malthusian prelude,
Patent Seasons, whimsically imagines the utter oblivion of the patent theatres (whose roofs will be dug up one day by farmers reaping their corn),
whilst the distressed Lyceum manager plangently complains to
David Garrick that the large houses have 'devoured up our discourse'.[86]

---

[83] See J. Payne Collier, SC 304 where *Victorine* is described as 'a well-conducted piece' with 'a most
unexceptionable moral' and 'of the most ingenious and fanciful construction'. Cf. SC 746, 2453,
2999–3003.

[84] For Drury Lane's complaints that Arnold was staging stock plays, see letter of 14 February 1816
in LC 7/4.

[85] Arnold's address, 15 June 1816. See also Arnold's unlicensed *Soirées Amusantes*, staged during
the winter of 1820–1. Outside the terms of his summer licence, Arnold was forbidden to offer
dramatic entertainments. The Lyceum therefore advertised the *Soirées* as a glorious 'mis-
representation' or 'burlesque Olio' which, like Foote's Primitive Puppet Show, defied any definitions of drama. The *Soirées* featured various entertainments including a show modelled on the
Ombres Chinoises (in which gauze separated the performers from the audience), a Lecture on
Living Heads, and a puppet show.

[86] [Arnold and Peake], *Patent Seasons*, Larpent MS 2166. Arnold staged the play to draw attention
to Elliston's tactic of extending his Drury Lane season in order to erode the Lyceum's receipts.
While admiring these comic hits at Arnold's 'overbearing rival', Hazlitt suggested that the
Lyceum's confession of 'weakness' and 'poverty' might damage the theatre's success. 'Every one
is inclined to run away from a falling house; and of all appeals, that to humanity should be the
last . . . Talk of 170 distressed families dependent on a distressed manager . . . and the sound
hangs like a mill-stone on the imagination, "or load to sink a navy."' See *London Magazine*,
September 1820, *Hazlitt* xviii:366.

A consummate publicist and modern entrepreneur, Samuel Arnold ensured that the Lyceum's satirical vitality and dramatic celebrity would continue to trouble the dreams of the patentees.[87]

OVERTURNING MONOPOLY

Beleaguered and threatened by turns, Drury Lane and Covent Garden attempted to suppress their minor rivals by law. The perceived hypocrisy of these tactics increased when Elliston became the new lessee of Drury Lane. There, to the consternation of critics such as Hazlitt and Hunt, the former Surrey manager staged a spectacular version of George IV's coronation (complete with 'the Vauxhall style of refreshments and music' and 'the Royal Circus exhibition of the Man in Armour'), and a production of *Coriolanus* which included processions 'some of which were lengthened out as if they would reach all the way to the Circus'.[88] Elliston's management had sounded the death knell for legitimate drama: now the illegitimacy of the patent establishment finally began to seem irreversible.

Not content with illegitimising Shakespeare at Drury Lane, Elliston was also determined to crush his former transpontine rivals. He therefore decided to prosecute Glossop for the Coburg's unlicensed production of Shakespeare's *Richard III*. But although Elliston won the case, and Glossop was fined £100, the prosecution only increased public sympathy for the cause of the minor theatres. Periodical critics mocked Elliston's litigious pursuit of his old rival, and in the *Examiner* Leigh Hunt demanded the end of monopoly: 'The justice of the case, we think, is all on Mr. GLOSSOP's side.'[89] Moreover, in a series of bold articles entitled 'Attempt to Suppress the Minor Drama' Glossop protested against this campaign to 'deprive the public of a very gratifying portion of their amusements, by reducing the present performances of the Coburg and similar Theatres, "to inexplicable dumb shew"'. To compel the minor theatres' return to 'ribaldry, nonsense, scrolls, and orchestra tinklings',

---

[87] Compare the fracas in 1830 when, after the Lyceum's destruction by fire, Arnold applied to perform throughout the year in order to recoup his losses. See *Morning Chronicle* 25 and 26 January, 1 and 26 February 1831. Amid concerted opposition from the patentees, who accused Arnold of performing 'bastard comedies' and travesties of all kinds, Leigh Hunt bombarded his *Tatler* readers with a series of articles defending Arnold's position. See 'Twenty-Three Reasons Why the Managers of the Great Theatres Ought Not to Prevail against Mr. Arnold', *Tatler*, 25 January 1831, 2: 489–90 and following issues. The Lord Chancellor eventually advised that the Lyceum season should be limited to the period between May and October.

[88] Hunt, 'Kings and Coronations', *Examiner*, 22 July 1831, 449–50; *London Magazine*, February 1820, *Hazlitt* XVIII:291. [89] *Examiner*, 9 January 1820, 25.

declared Glossop, would represent 'an outrage on the intellectual character of the nation' and 'an injury to public order and christian morality'.[90] This was the most persuasive argument yet published about the morality and respectability of minor culture.

Undeterred by public sympathy for the Coburg, the patentees quickly gave notice of their intention rigorously to enforce the existing theatrical laws.[91] By 1828, Davidge had been convicted at the Surrey assizes for the Coburg's unlicensed performances of *Douglas* and *Richard III*; the patentees had also threatened the Surrey for its illegal performances of legitimate plays.[92] The minor theatres therefore added to their licences nebulous portmanteau phrases ('and other like entertainments') in the vain hope of protecting themselves from the patentees' litigious ambitions.[93] At the same time, the defiant Coburg Theatre established a fighting fund to defray the costs of further prosecutions.[94] What provided the catalyst for theatrical reform, however, was the decision by Chapman and Melrose, managers of the Tottenham Street Theatre, to stage a short season of legitimate plays starring the celebrated actress Eliza Vestris.

In 1830, Charles Kemble had written to the Drury Lane Committee, stating that his solicitors were now examining the Drury Lane patent 'with reference to proceedings against the Minor Theatres, in which, the Proprietors of this establishment hope to be joined by you'.[95] Under Kemble's leadership, the patentees then established a network of spies, recruited from employees of Covent Garden and Drury Lane, to inform upon illegal performances at minor theatres such as the Panharmonion in St Pancras, the Surrey and the unlicensed New Strand, as well as the

[90] *Theatrical Inquisitor*, February 1820, 16: 99–102.
[91] See MS letter, dated 3 April 1820, from Ward and Harris to Beverley, manager of the West London theatre, bound in a volume entitled 'Charles Kemble and the Minor Theatres' (hereafter HChK) in the Harvard Theatre Collection. An injunction also seems to have been obtained against Glossop for acting *Thérèse*, but this was subsequently dismissed on a technicality. See *Drury Lane Journal: Selections from James Winston's Diaries 1819–1827* ed. Alfred L. Nelson and Gilbert B. Cross (London: Society for Theatre Research, 1974), 26.
[92] See SC 1218 where Davidge hinted that public support for the Coburg had inhibited Drury Lane from bringing further prosecutions: *Stage* no. 4 (November 1828), 135. Forbes, SC 1863–5 claimed that he had prosecuted the Adelphi but never obtained damages because the defendants were bankrupt. He also suggested that the magistrates had declined to convict the defendant without the involvement of the Lord Chamberlain.
[93] See Surrey Quarter Sessions report, *Morning Chronicle*, 16 October 1828; *Dramatic Gazette*, 30 October 1830, 1: 49–50.
[94] *The Times*, 9 March 1829. See also *Dramatic Magazine*, April 1829, 1: 55.
[95] Covent Garden Theatre, *Letter Book of H. Robertson 1823–1849*, BL Add. MS 29643. *The Times*, 18 June 1830, also reported the decision of Covent Garden and Drury Lane Theatres to oppose the renewal of the minors' licences on the grounds of their recent infringements.

Clarence, Garrick and New City Theatres.[96] The Tottenham Street playhouse was the first to be prosecuted under this new system of dramatic espionage.

'Does this theatrical *charlatan* suppose that the public are blind to his quackeries, and persecution of his more able competitors, the Minor Theatres?' demanded the *Age* (28 November 1830). 'Unflinching resistance to the oppressive Statute', promised the Tottenham Street playbills and broadsides, threatening darkly that the audience would inflict its own 'summary punishment on Kemble's theatrical spies'.[97] At the packed and disorderly court hearing (attended by dozens of performers and playwrights including Davidge, Grimaldi and Barrymore), the Tottenham Street defence spectacularly turned the theatrical tables, alleging that the patent houses had transformed the 'boards trodden by Garrick and Siddons' into an arena for the exhibition of beasts, and men in the shape of beasts. Cowed by these indictments, and by the raucous insults of 'a numerous assembly of groundlings', the patent informers suddenly declined to give evidence, and Thomas Halls and Sir Richard Birnie – the unashamedly partisan magistrates – promptly dismissed the case.[98] But the subsequent conviction of the Tottenham Street managers at the King's Bench, not to mention a fine of £350, convinced managers, performers and spectators alike of the urgent need to seek parliamentary authority for a change in the dramatic laws.[99]

Emboldened by enthusiastic public support and confident, perhaps, of eventual victory, the minor theatres enjoyed drawing the public's attention to the absurdities and injustices of their institutional position. Coburg playbills laughed at the way in which the patent theatres, these 'Lords of Histrionic Legitimacy, Legality and Regularity', simultaneously represented themselves as the 'Monopolists of Melo-Drama' and 'Proprietors of Pantomime'.[100] Performance, too, provided innumerable opportunities for satirical jibes and mocking laughter. When Covent Garden pilfered *The Pilot*, Fitzball's highly successful nautical melodrama based on James Fenimore Cooper's story, the Adelphi responded

---

[96] The informers' correspondence can be found in HChK.

[97] 'Charles Kemble's Mercies or the 999 Increasing', broadside in HChK; see also Tottenham Street bills for 22, 25 June, 2 July 1830. A variety of periodicals expressed support for Tottenham Street: see the *Theatrical Rod* no. 1 [?1831], 2, and the cuttings in the Tottenham Street file, Theatre Museum. On the 'bombast' and 'coarseness' of Tottenham Street's tactics, see *Dramatic Gazette*, 18 December 1830, 1:182–3; *Athenaeum*, 27 November 1830, 749.

[98] See *Morning Chronicle*, 7 December 1831; *New Monthly Magazine*, August 1830, 30: 332–4.

[99] The patent houses publicised the success of this prosecution in order to intimidate other theatres. See the report in the *Age*, 25 December 1831, 44.   [100] Playbill, 22 February 1830.

with a retributive burlesque by Buckstone entitled *The Pilot; or, A Tale of the Thames* (November, 1830). Here, the war between England and America was comically translated to London, and military conflict reconfigured as a succession of rescues, resurrections and hair-raising escapes. The prelude, spoken by Frederick Yates – and tactically omitted from the licensing text submitted to the Examiner of Plays – mocked Covent Garden's dramatic theft of *The Pilot*. One reviewer welcomed 'some hard hits at the major receivers of stolen goods' and declared that the minor theatres 'should never let an opportunity pass for planting a heavy blow upon the Patent Monopolists'.[101] In *The Witch of the Volcano; or, Harlequin and the King of the Coral Isle* (Pavilion, 1831), the manager John Farrell seems to have interpolated additional scenes prophesying the collapse of monopoly. As one reviewer commented, 'The introduction of an *outré* figure, ten feet high, as *Major Monopoly*, called forth some strong indications of the odour in which the recent attempt of the patent managers to crush their humble competitors is likely to be viewed, and afforded an excellent opportunity . . . to indulge in a rich strain of equivoque at the expense of the major theatres.' The destruction of this figure by Captain Minimus, he continued, took place 'to the great delight of the audience, who testified their approbation and their feelings on the subject by three distinct rounds of applause'.[102]

The indefatigable excitement surrounding the cause of parliamentary reform, the popularity of laissez-faire principles in economics, and even the topical issue of religious toleration all provided powerful momentum for the minor theatres' campaign against dramatic monopoly. As political economists, argued a Clerkenwell spectator, it was in the interests of the public to support the minor theatres in order to obtain reasonably priced entertainment.[103] For the barrister Charles Wilkins, the defence

---

[101] See LC MS 42905 fols. 123–46; *Age*, 5 December 1830, 390 and cf. *Dramatic Magazine*, December 1830, 2: 380.

[102] Unidentified review, 30 December 1831, in Pavilion file, Theatre Museum. Between 1832 and 1833, two unlicensed theatres staged burlesque dramas mocking theatrical monopoly. *Professionals Puzzl'd; or, Struggles at Starting* (Strand, January 1832) and *The Dramatic Committee; or, Majors and Minors* (Clarence August 1833) were both written by William Rede. A review of *Professional Puzzl'd* reported that the piece 'may be considered more as the statement of a case drawn up on behalf of "the Minors against the Majors"' (*Morning Chronicle*, 28 January 1832). The Clarence playbill advertising *The Dramatic Committee* announced that Rede's 'Hyperbolical, Diabolical, and Inquisitorial Drama' would conclude with a 'Picture-esque Representation of THE GRAND PANACEA FOR THE WRONGS OF THE DRAMA, AND THE RIGHTS OF THE PEOPLE!!!' (playbill, 26 August 1833).

[103] See report in *Morning Chronicle*, 2 March 1832 and cf. *Westminster Review*, January 1833, 36: 43. Here the writer voices approval for the idea of extending the principles of political economy to the arts of amusement.

of monopoly resembled that 'used by the slavemaster with the whip in his hand . . . enforced in the House of Commons . . . against the transfer of the representation of the pigsties and rubbish of Gatton and Old Sarum to more populous districts'.[104] The 'spirit of Reform is abroad', the *Age* had announced smugly to the patentees, and it will extend to the abolition of your patent rights; 'I am a Reformer – a *Dramatic* Reformer! I would have *Shakspeare* and the *People* duly represented!' quixotically declared 'Philo-Dramaticus'.[105] In a variety of ways, the cause of the minor theatres dovetailed with fervent enthusiasm for political reform and a pervasive antipathy to commercial monopolies.

Reviewers had once dismissed the patrons at the minor theatres as 'dead to the workings of fancy in its fairest shapes' and in need of 'powerful provocatives to awaken their glutted appetites'.[106] Now, well-known playwrights such as Douglas Jerrold and Thomas Shee, and famous performers such as John Reeve and John Buckstone, as well as loyal spectators from a variety of neighbourhoods, supported the campaign, as did leading journalists, members of the aristocracy (the Duke of Somerset, and the Marquis of Clanricarde), Westminster radicals (Francis Burdett, Francis Place and Sir John Hobhouse) as well as other Whig and radical MPs (Colonel Evans and Colonel Mahon).[107] This eclectic consensus, a haphazard configuration of financial interests, cultural loyalties and political opportunism, is aptly summed up by the idiosyncratic collection of shops, institutions and meeting-places at which the petition in support of the minor theatres could be signed. These included Walker's Glove Manufactory in Lincoln's Inn Fields, a grocer's in the London Road, an auctioneer in Cannon-street; the City of London Coffee House, a paper-hanger in Fleet Street and a stationer's in Holborn Hill.

The minor theatres' campaign, culminating in a petition presented to the House of Commons, led to the setting up of a Select Committee to enquire into the state of dramatic literature and the regulations governing theatre. Under the leadership of Edward Bulwer-Lytton, the

---

[104] Report in *Morning Chronicle*, 23 March 1832.
[105] *Age*, 19 December 1830; letter cited in *Remarks* to George Almar's play, *The Rover's Bride; or, the Bittern's Swamp*, *CMT* VI.
[106] See the Living Dramatist series on William Moncrieff, *Theatrical Inquisitor*, August 1820, 16: 11.
[107] Many playwrights also took the opportunity to publicise the issue of copyright for dramatic authors. See report of 24 February meeting in the *Edinburgh Spectator*, 3 March 1832 and John Stephens, *The Profession of the Playwright: British Theatre 1800–1900* (Cambridge University Press, 1992), chapter 4. For the minor theatre supporters, see *Age*, 11 December 1831, 398; unidentified notice at the Garrick Club entitled 'Cause of the Drama'; *Morning Chronicle* reports, 25 February 1832, 23 March 1832 and unidentified cuttings, Theatre Museum. On Francis Place's involvement, see BL Add. MS 27833 fols. 21ff & 35149 fols. 273–4.

Committee questioned a variety of witnesses including the Examiner of Plays, patent and minor managers, performers and dramatic authors. The collected evidence offers an intriguing, bizarre and often farcical snapshot of early nineteenth-century theatre: *Othello* performed as a burletta, with a low accompaniment from the piano every five minutes; playwrights miserably unpaid; George Colman's obsessive determination to delete all references to angels in the scripts submitted to him as Examiner of Plays; absurdly contradictory definitions of legitimate drama and burletta, and all but incomprehensible histories of the Drury Lane and Covent Garden patents. The true construction of the current law, remarked the *Athenaeum* critic, with a mixture of wry amusement and despair, remained 'as unattained a point to the Committee, the public, and themselves, as the North Pole is at present to any other government explorer'.[108]

Should the Lord Chamberlain's authority be extended to all London theatres? Could public taste, backed by the 'vigilant admonition of the public Press', be trusted 'for the preservation of theatrical decorum'? The fear that the minor theatres encouraged popular immorality, social disorder and even sedition still haunted legislators.[109] But the balance of evidence suggested that a theatrical culture once perceived as monstrous, plebeian and immoral had proved itself to be rational, respectable and even original. The Select Committee therefore proceeded to recommend the abolition of the patentees' monopoly over legitimate drama.[110] Opposition in the House of Lords, however, narrowly prevented the passage of the Bill into law – Francis Place sarcastically attributed this defeat to patrician apathy about popular amusements[111] – and it was not until the Theatre Regulation Act of 1843 (6 & 7 Vict c. lxviii) that the minor theatres would finally gain the right to stage legitimate drama. Nevertheless, in 1833 theatrical monopoly had been abolished in all but name. Having given up the defence of their own cultural prop-

---

[108] *Athenaeum*, 3 November 1832, 713–14.

[109] On the contradictory views of witnesses about political censorship, see *Hansard's Parliamentary Debates*, House of Commons, 31 May 1832, 13: 244–5. For Place's controversial remarks that theatres 'ought to be made the means of political excitement', cf. *Morning Chronicle*, 16 July 1832. Payne Collier, SC 426 evokes the lawlessness of the minor theatres; cf. William Moore, SC 4041. On the respectability of the minor theatres, see the Marquis of Clanricarde's comments in the House of Lords, reported in *Morning Chronicle*, 5 August 1833. Reporters frequently emphasised the respectability of those attending the public meetings in support of the minors. See *The Times*, 4 January 1832; *Morning Chronicle*, 2 August 1833.

[110] See Watson Nicholson, *Struggle for a Free Stage*, chapter 13.

[111] Francis Place, 'A Brief Examination of the Dramatic Patents' in *Monthly Magazine*, March 1834, 12. See *Mirror of Parliament*, ed. J.H. Barrow, 1st series, 11th Parliament, 1: 3490–4.

erty, the Theatres Royal now proceeded to turn a a blind eye to the still illicit performances of their rivals. The illegitimacy of the illegitimate was beginning to disappear.

As Davidge observed, the right to perform legitimate drama, 'is a matter more cavilled at than is warranted by any real advantage that might be derived from it'.[112] The end of monopoly did not witness a sudden increase in performances of Shakespeare or Sheridan, Otway or Massinger at the minor theatres. Within a decade, however, both Charles Kean (at the Princess Theatre) and Samuel Phelps (at Sadler's Wells) had attracted large audiences to their productions of Shakespeare. To a large extent, however, the victory of the minor theatres was a symbolic rather than a practical one. After the Theatre Regulation Act, speculators may have abandoned former reservations about the safety of their capital at a minor theatre; performers now knew that they could not be prosecuted while engaged at the Surrey or the Coburg.[113] Of such intangible risks, however, few traces remain; the economic and artistic consequences of monopoly's abolition are in any case beyond the scope of this book. Rather, what my story has sought to establish is that for more than four decades theatrical monopoly had irrevocably shaped the nature of dramatic writing, performance, management and spectatorship.

---

[112] SC 1290.

[113] On actors' fears about being prosecuted for performing at the minor theatres, see Payne Collier, SC 279 and Thomas Serle, SC 2098.

CHAPTER TWO

The disintegration of legitimate theatre

REVOLUTION

The French Revolution and its aftermath helped to unleash a whirlwind of anxiety about the morality of public entertainments in general and the seditious potential of theatrical performance in particular. By late 1795, after repeated, violent outbursts of democratic sentiment, the Drury Lane managers withdrew Thomas Otway's tragedy, *Venice Preserv'd* from the repertoire: the speeches of Pierre and the conspirators were now alleged to 'feed the flame of lurking sedition'.[1] So edgy was John Larpent, the Examiner of Plays, about displays of political feeling at the patent theatres that he even censored anti-revolutionary plays such as Edmund Eyre's drama, *The Maid of Normandy; or, the Death of the Queen of France* (1794).[2] Meanwhile, in the rearguard cultural action mounted to defend Britain against the dangers of radicalism and revolution, the 'flood', 'disease' or 'plague' of sentimental and humanitarian dramas, then appearing in print and also on the stage, came to represent all that was morally and politically subversive about contemporary drama. In particular, the 'noxious', 'poisonous' qualities of German drama, its 'levelling morality' and 'shining cant', seemed to endanger the moral and political security of the British nation. Kotzebue's plays, declared the *Anti-Jacobin*, hold up 'to esteem and respect, women who have deviated from the paths of virtue', render 'the characters of rank vicious' and confine goodness 'to low factions'. When plays such as

---

[1] *The Times*, 27 October 1795. For political excitement over *Venice Preserv'd*, see reviews in the *Morning Chronicle* 22 and 27 October 1795. One of the most controversial moments in the play was Pierre's speech, 'We've neither safety, unity, nor peace; / The foundation's lost of common good', in which laws are portrayed as serving 'but for the instruments of some new tyranny'. John Thelwall's applause for these sentiments (rapidly joined by his friends, and then by the audience, producing general uproar in the theatre), had been one of the counts against him in the treason trial of 1793–4. See *The Life of John Thelwall*. By His Widow (London: John Macrome, 1837), 285–7.

[2] On anti-revolutionary plays, see also Jeffrey N. Cox, 'Ideology and Genre in the British Antirevolutionary Drama of the 1790s', *English Literary History* 58 (1991), 579–610.

Pizarro are exhibited, argued a correspondent in the *Anti-Jacobin*, 'it indeed becomes a serious question how far a good Government should interfere.'[3]

The 'loud trampling of the German Pegasus on the English stage', Hazlitt later recalled, strikes the hearer 'by overturning all the established maxims of society'. Extravagant action, improbable fables and moral controversy captivated spectators, Hazlitt believed, by embodying 'the extreme opinions which are floating in our time'.[4] Yet the capacity of German drama to hit 'the temper of men's minds' – the sheer, compulsive fascination generated by plays such as *The Stranger* and *Pizarro* – was precisely what troubled contemporary reviewers and many pamphleteers. German drama seemed to offer a seditious blueprint for the disintegration of an aristocratic, Christian political state.

In this atmosphere of fearfulness bordering on cultural paranoia, reviewers watchfully scrutinised the political loyalties of plays by known Jacobin sympathisers such as Elizabeth Inchbald and Thomas Holcroft. A recurring feature of these reviews is a telling form of ideological shorthand: critics dispute the probability of a drama as a means by which to question its political loyalty and moral integrity. The reception of Elizabeth Inchbald's play, *Every One Has His Fault* (Covent Garden, January 1793), offers a useful example. 'We are at a loss what to term this new species of composition', declared the *True Briton*, ''tis neither Comedy, nor Tragi-Comedy, but something anomalous in which the two are jumbled together'. The play's generic deviance (the 'pathetic' and the 'ludicrous' are 'most unaccountably blended', alleges the writer) provides an ostensibly *aesthetic* framework for the reviewer's political critique of *Every One*. Allusions are made, the *True Briton* reveals, 'to the dearness of provisions in this Metropolis' (expunged from future performances: famine would remain a dangerous subject on stage for several decades), 'and in several sentences the *Democrat* displays a cloven foot'. In particular, Inchbald's poignant dramatisation of necessity seems to have infuriated the *True Briton*'s critic. Can it be conceived, demands the reviewer, that a military officer, even while distracted by misfortune, would commit a robbery in a public street? By dismissing Captain Irwin's theft of a pocket-book as *improbable*, the *True Briton*'s critic subtly transposes an

---

[3] *Anti-Jacobin*, August 1799, 3: 439; September 1800, 7: 61–21; December 1800, 7: 515–18. On German drama as political and moral contamination, see *inter alia* [John Britton], *Sheridan and Kotzebue* (London: J. Fairburn, 1799), 130; Hannah More, *Strictures on the Modern System of Female Education*, first published 1799, 2 vols. (London: Cadell, 1826), 1: 39–45.
[4] [On the German Drama], *Lectures on the Dramatic Literature of the Age of Elizabeth*, Lecture 7, *Hazlitt* VI: 345–64.

ideological objection (that a military man should be capable of a criminal action) into the apparently neutral discourse of aesthetic probability.[5]

The 'anomalous' character of *Every One Has His Fault* is proved here by means of a political critique pointedly framed in generic terms. The *True Briton*'s preoccupation with definitions of genre and probability is characteristic. Reviewers repeatedly castigated the failure of new plays to conform to the established genres of tragedy and comedy; the improbability of these plots, they implied, offered disturbing evidence of more intangible forms of dubious innovation. The reception of *The Castle Spectre*, M. G. Lewis' Gothic play, provides a good example of the confusion – and subliminal political anxiety – surrounding mixed genres. According to the *Morning Herald* (16 December 1797), *The Castle Spectre* should be termed a '*Speaking Pantomime*'. With evident suspicion, the *True Briton* (16 December 1797) declared the play to be 'a Drama of strong interest, but of a very improbable kind' while the *St James's Chronicle* (16–19 December 1797) noted that Lewis' *The Castle Spectre* was 'a drama of a mingled nature, Operatic, Comical and Tragical'. There was also a wary, satirical subtext in the *Morning Chronicle*'s description (21 January 1797) of George Colman the Younger's *Feudal Times*: 'an exhibition of music and dialogue, pantomime and dancing, dresses and armour, thunder and lightning, fire and water.' Similarly, the *True Briton*'s review of *The Iron Chest* (Colman's adaptation of Godwin's *Caleb Williams*) called the play a 'Serio-Comic Drama interspersed with Songs' and lamented that it contained 'nothing that would rationally gratify'.[6] In January 1798, this persistent anxiety about dramatic genres even found expression in the auditorium: spectators threw handbills 'of a most inflammatory nature' into the Drury Lane pit in protest at the production of *Blue-Beard*, a play which *The Times*' critic also dismissed as 'a mere prating Pantomime'.[7] The *Morning Chronicle*'s bemused reaction to *A Tale of Mystery* (Covent Garden, 1802) neatly encapsulates this powerful conviction of unprecedented dramatic change and perplexing generic fragmentation. *A Tale*, declared the reviewer, seemed 'quite unlike any thing that has thereto been brought out upon the English stage'.[8]

---

[5] *True Briton*, 30 January 1793. For more placatory comments about Inchbald's play, see *ibid.*, 1 February 1793.   [6] 14 March 1796.

[7] See *The Times*, 17 January 1798. The bills 'contained a severe invective against Pantomime in general' and called on the audience to banish *Blue-Beard* from the theatre. The reviewer continued, 'This illiberal and unjustifiable attack on an Exhibition which, properly speaking, cannot be called a Pantomime, or if viewed in that light, must be pronounced the least objectionable of any which have hitherto appeared, was received, as such envious and malignant attempts must ever be an impartial Public, with the utmost contempt.'   [8] 15 November 1802.

According to certain Anti-Jacobin critics, that contagious disease called *Kotzebue-mania* (the symptoms of which allegedly included the suspension of common sense, a strange admiration for ghosts, as well as 'mouldering castles, sulphurous flames, bloody daggers, and other terrific images of a distempered imagination') was primarily responsible for the apparent glut of supernatural wonders and dramatic irrationality in contemporary British theatre.[9] My concern here is not with that exciting collision of traditions (sentimental, Gothic, humanitarian) at the heart of dramatic innovation during the late 1790s,[10] but rather with the perceived relationships between improbability, genre and political subversion. For what this discourse of improbability reveals is the pervasive fear that modern drama might disavow the established, monarchical genres of tragedy and comedy in favour of an anarchic miscellany of dramatic forms; in other words, that generic innovation might somehow be proleptic of social and political revolution.

The emergence of the term 'legitimate' as a category of dramatic classification during the late 1790s reflects this feverish desire to distinguish between authentic and spurious dramas and between loyal and seditious performances. Legitimate drama, like 'regular drama', and 'national drama',[11] with which it is essentially interchangeable in this period, usually referred to the established genres of tragedy and comedy. More broadly, the legitimate came to connote the stock dramatic repertoire, thus encompassing dramatists such as Shakespeare, Otway and Massinger as well as those contemporary playwrights (notably Sheridan and George Colman the Younger) whose work was perceived to conform to dramatic tradition.[12] But was the legitimate a fixed or historically relative category? Would it be possible to describe a modern classic such as *Victorine*, Buckstone's three-act comedy, as a legitimate drama? Such questions continued to perplex reviewers, legislators and pamphleteers

---

[9] *Oracle*, 1802, cited Cecil Price, *The Dramatic Works of Richard Brinsley Sheridan*, 2 vols. (Oxford: Clarendon 1973), II: 637.

[10] Bertrand Evans' study, *Gothic Drama from Walpole to Shelley* (Berkeley: University of California Press, 1947) is still the most authoritative guide; see also Paul Ranger, '*Terror and Pity Reign in Every Breast*': *Gothic Drama in the London Patent Theatres, 1750–1820* (London: Society for Theatre Research, 1991).

[11] See especially *The National Drama; or the Histrionic War of the Majors and Minors* (London: E. Muers, 1833).

[12] Although the Licensing Act of 1737 provides the legislative framework for definitions of legitimacy, the term did not become widely used until the 1790s. See, for example, the *Morning Chronicle*'s review of Holcroft's play, *The Deserted Daughter*, 4 May 1795, in which the critic classifies the piece as a 'legitimate' drama. In his translation of Johannes Brandes' play, *The German Hotel* (Covent Garden, 1790), Holcroft apparently burlesques the discourse of legitimacy when McCarnock jokes about drama being the 'legeetimate' child of the Muses. See *The German Hotel* (London: G.C,J. and J. Robinson, 1790), ix.

throughout this period. I now want to suggest that the controversial status of the legitimate as a theatrical term in the early nineteenth century can be traced to Edmund Burke's influential definitions of political culture.[13]

At the heart of Burke's *Reflections on the Revolution in France* (1790) is an opposition between legitimate and illegitimate government. In *Reflections* Burke sets out to counter the revolutionary proposition, advanced in Richard Price's famous lecture, that a system of representation based on the sovereignty of the people constitutes the basis of all 'legitimate' government.[14] In the absence of representation, according to the Revolution Society, a government is illegitimate or 'bastardized' (120–1). Burke's defence of the unwritten English constitution, of course, dramatically reverses these terms: the 'natural' symmetry of the English state and its system of *virtual* representation are what constitute its political legitimacy. What legitimacy connotes, then, is an extensive set of institutions and associated moral values based on aristocracy, property, heredity, monarchy and the Established Church. 'We fear God,' declares Burke, 'we look up with awe to kings; with affection to parliaments; with duty to magistrates; with reverence to priests; and with respect to nobility' (182). Whereas legitimacy arises naturally from the values of chivalry and civility, the illegitimacy of revolutionary philosophy can be aptly summed up by its perversion of moral as well as political values. In an illegitimate state, then, a king is no more than a chief of bumbailiffs, jailors and hangmen (317); his subjects inhabit a country whose values are those of plunder, barbarity, bastardy, perversion and 'promiscuous slaughter' (164).[15] In other words, monarchy and social hierarchy actually guarantee moral order; their overthrow produces an anarchic miscegenation which permeates every aspect of public and private life.

Dramatic genres play an important role in Burke's exposure of revolution's illegitimacy. At the spectacular centre of *Reflections*, the murder of monarchy is imagined as an act of generic miscegenation – that 'monstrous tragi-comic scene'. Like the comedians of a fair, Burke declares, the French 'have inverted order in all things' so that 'the gallery

---

[13] The problem of defining the legitimate is a recurring theme in the Select Committee evidence. See especially *SC* 329, 2983–4. Cf. 'What is the Legitimate Drama', a letter from 'Free and Easy' in *Theatrical Inquisitor*, May 1819, 14: 351 which mocks the proliferation of terms such as 'legitimate', 'classical' and 'genuine' drama; Alfred Bunn, *The Stage: Both Before and Behind the Curtain*, 3 vols. (London: Richard Bentley, 1840), 1: xix.

[14] Edmund Burke, *Reflections on the Revolution in France*, first published 1790 (London: Penguin, 1968), 145–7. Subsequent page references are cited within the text.

[15] Compare Burke's portrayal of Rousseau as a symbol of revolutionary sexual deviance. See further Seamus Deane, *The French Revolution and Enlightenment in England, 1789–1832* (Cambridge, Mass.: Harvard University Press, 1988), chapter 1.

is in the place of the house' (161). In Burke's argument, revolution is imagined as the collapse of monarchical genres: the National Assembly, antithesis of legitimate government, has exchanged the sanctity of political hierarchy for the anarchy of 'profane burlesque' (161).

Burke's depiction of burlesque and tragi-comedy as disorderly, plebeian forms, the degraded antitypes of a legitimate political culture, haunts the interpretation of contemporary drama. Just as Burke had sought to distinguish an aristocratic political culture from the anarchic, revolutionary state, so Anti-Jacobin commentators attempted to delineate a hereditary, hierarchical, loyalist drama – the repository of political and moral tradition – from a deluge of dangerous, deviant theatrical change. Throughout the 1790s, the language of cultural nationalism began to be appropriated in the cause of a theatrical war between two apparently irreconcilable kinds of dramaturgy. As we can see from *The Rovers; or, The Double Arrangement* (1798), a burlesque German drama written by George Canning and John Frere, and published in the *Anti-Jacobin*, dramatic satire played an important role in demonising theatrical innovation.[16]

The Rovers is a delightfully improbable play featuring Matilda (in love with Rogero and mother to children fathered by Casimere, a Polish officer, who is also married to Cecilia) and the hapless Rogero, immured for eleven years in a subterranean vault of the Abbey at Quedlinburgh. At the play's climax, a band of troubadours storm the Abbey, beheading the Count of Weimar and imprisoning the corpulent Prior in the dungeon, before setting off to rescue Rogero. According to Mr Higgins, the play's Godwinian author, the staging of *The Rovers* will 'do much to unhinge the present notions of men with regard to the obligations of civil society' substituting for 'sober contentment' and a 'regular discharge' of those duties incident to a man's peculiar situation 'a wild desire of undefinable latitude and extravagance' (326).

The absurd parody of Schiller's *The Robbers* and Goethe's *Stella* which takes place in *The Rovers* mimics the anarchic decomposition of society which German drama is alleged to rehearse. As in other Anti-Jacobin attacks, a critique of improbability – notably the 'double arrangement' in *Stella* by which a man is endowed with two wives – comically highlights the plays' immorality. But, though perhaps the most important, German drama is only one of Canning and Frere's satirical targets here.

---

[16] The play is printed in Simon Trussler's collection, *Burlesque Plays of the Eighteenth Century* (Oxford University Press, 1969): references are cited within the text. In 1811, George Colman the Younger adapted Canning and Frere's drama for his satire on Covent Garden's production of quadruped plays. See *The Quadrupeds of Quedlinburgh; or, The Rovers of Weimar* (Haymarket, 1811), Larpent MS fiche 254/502.

Rogero's imprisonment, for example, amid coffins, scutcheons and a death's head, brilliantly parodies the captivity of Reginald in 'Monk' Lewis' drama of supernatural horror, *The Castle Spectre* (Drury Lane, 1797). And in many ways *The Rovers* represents as commensurable the immorality of German drama and the cultural degradation represented by Lewis' Gothic theatre. The extravagant gestures which punctuate *The Rovers*' satirical dramaturgy, for instance, confirm this shared legacy. Rogero 'dashes his head repeatedly against the walls of his Prison' (336), Cassimir speaks 'in a paroxysm of agitation' (337), and Beefington 'falls into an agony' (341). Such hyperbolic iconography, of course, provides a humorous corollary for the play's self-consciously improbable plot. But Canning and Frere's drama also unwittingly reveals how the production of German drama and Gothic plays was transforming the representation of feeling on stage.

In the first two decades of the nineteenth century, a miscellaneous collection of illegitimate genres – melodrama, romance and pantomime, amongst others – succeeded German drama as the monstrous antitypes of legitimate dramatic culture. The plays of Sheridan, Goldsmith and Shakespeare, insisted reviewers, were now threatened by 'vilest buffooneries' and 'vamped-up' pieces of 'barbarism', 'founded in absurdity' and 'supported by improbability'.[17] Illegitimate drama, whether in the 'contemptible' conversion of *Macbeth* into a ballet of action, the lurid dramatisation of murder and criminal sensation, or the exhibition of horses and elephants on the patent stages, seemed to display a lawless disregard for morality, decorum and dramatic tradition.[18]

Above all, melodrama came to represent the source and origin of theatrical decadence. According to many detractors, melodrama had transformed acting into mere rant, dramatic authorship into cheap theatrical commerce, and plots into a motley collection of spectacular effects.[19] The *Theatrical Inquisitor* gave comic voice to these complaints by

---

[17] See, for example, *Theatrical Inquisitor*, October 1814, 5: 117–18 and 264–5, and 'On the Decline of the English Drama', a letter to the editor, signed 'E. R.' in the issue for February 1818, 12: 73–6, especially 74.

[18] For these critiques see, *inter alia* [F. G. Tomlins], One of the Public (*pseud.*), *Major and Minor Theatres, A Concise View of the Question*, 16, and Tomlins, *The Nature and State of the English Drama* (London: Mitchell, 1841), 19–20. On the usurpation of legitimate drama by 'bombastic show' and 'pantomimic absurdity', see John Denman, *The Drama Vindicated* (Cambridge: W.H. Smith, 1835).

[19] On the vehemence of melodramatic acting, see the *Theatrical Observer*, 5 March 1825, 74–5. Compare the *Remarks* to Fitzball's *The Inchcape Bell*, *CMT* 1, where George Daniel declares that he has no objection to melodrama in its 'proper region' (i.e. a minor theatre). Our 'sharpest tirades', he continues, 'have been directed, not at its existence, but its introduction into temples professedly devoted to the dramatic muse'.

ironically advertising the 'complete ingredients for a Melo-Drama, formerly the property of Drury Lane' consisting of 'some brown paper for snow, two ounces of gunpowder, a dozen of old songs newly set to old tunes, four escape ladders . . . a barrel of tar . . . the necessary ingredients for a storm.'[20] In this satirical publicity, authorship and textuality are mockingly depicted as no more than a formulaic, commercial recipe of physical properties.

The prominence of food, eating and appetite in these critiques derisively signalled the perceived collapse of theatrical taste into the dangerous irrationality of mass, sensuous gratification. In 'The Monster Melodrama', for example (see plate 5), contemporary writers including Thomas Holcroft, Lumley Skeffington, 'Monk' Lewis and Frederic Reynolds are depicted feeding from the teats of a many-headed, half-canine monster. The monster's heads would have been easily recognisable to viewers of the cartoon as those of R. B. Sheridan, John Philip Kemble and Joseph Grimaldi, while the monster's tail is tellingly inscribed with the title of Holcroft's famous melodrama, *A Tale of Mystery*. Legitimate dramatists, including Congreve, Fletcher and George Colman, lie under the monster's front paws, and Shakespeare's works can be glimpsed under one of its back legs. The cartoon offers a visual image of monstrous generic hybridity in which the body of melodrama is indeed unrecognisable by the laws of nature. The grotesque maternity depicted here implicitly represents melodramatic authorship as a form of quasi-incestuous sexual deviance. Moreover, the cartoon cleverly blurs distinctions between writing and production, between melodramatic authorship and performance: the textual and the corporeal seem to have become indistinguishable.

The denunciation of illegitimate theatre also became a Romantic project. Both the Bartholomew Fair passage in Wordsworth's *Prelude*, Book 7, and Coleridge's various attacks on contemporary theatre invoke a Burkean discourse of legitimacy. The poems which make up *Lyrical Ballads*, of course, had purported to offer a cultural remedy for that 'craving for extraordinary incident' (the image of degraded pleasures as sensuous consumption is, as we have seen, characteristic) discernible in the popularity of 'silly German tragedies'.[21] But what lies behind Wordsworth's anxiety about Bartholomew Fair and Coleridge's

[20] See Lot 15 of the mock sale, *Theatrical Inquisitor*, August 1814, 5: 86–90, 88.
[21] *Preface to Lyrical Ballads* (1802) in *William Wordsworth*, ed. Stephen Gill (Oxford University Press, 1984), 599.

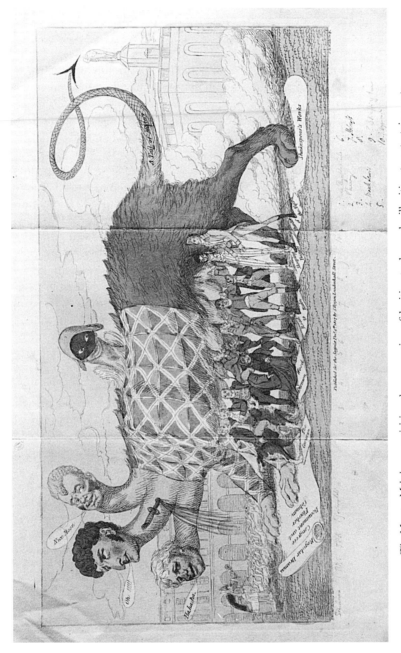

5. *The Monster Melodrama*, satirising the usurpation of legitimate drama by illegitimate entertainments.

mockery of sentimental drama is that Burkean nightmare about the licentious performances sponsored by a 'parliament of monsters'.[22]

Wordsworth's description of Bartholomew Fair – a world of 'anarchy' that is 'barbarian', 'infernal' and 'perverted' – conspicuously highlights political and religious categories; the fair seems to dramatise an illegitimate state in which social hierarchies and monarchical order have been destroyed. In this context, Wordsworth's allusion to Madame Tussaud's waxworks (line 686) is especially poignant, for at that exhibition, new in the year of Wordsworth's visit, visitors to Bartholomew Fair would have seen various models of the French Revolution's leaders and victims. The fair's 'parliament of monsters' also recalls the 'monstrous tragi-comic scene' described in *Reflections* (compare, too, Burke's reference to the members of the French Assembly behaving 'like the comedians of a fair before a riotous audience', 161). Indeed, Wordsworth's revisions to *The Prelude* for the 1850 text point up this Burkean interpretation: in an interpolated passage, written in 1832, Wordsworth appeals directly to Burke, asking him to forgive 'the pen seduced / By specious wonders' (1850 text, 7: 512–43). This self-conscious invocation seems to establish a parallel between performance and revolution as similarly delusive spectacles: 'bewildered men / Beginning to mistrust their boastful guides' (1850 text, 7: 514–15). Amidst the spectacular pleasures described in Book 7 (Sadler's Wells, the experience of watching Shakespearean tragedy and the memory of a 'bright cavern of romance' glimpsed in childhood, through a fractured wall at a country playhouse, 455), Bartholomew Fair symbolises the anarchic threat posed to political and social order by the cacophonous disorder permitted in the name of plebeian entertainment.

Coleridge, however, is the Romantic critic who canonised an absolute distinction between legitimate and illegitimate drama.[23] In the Satyrane letters, presented as a dialogue between a Coleridgean Plaintiff and a Defendant of modern sentimental drama, Coleridge notoriously denounces the 'system' of contemporary drama as 'a moral and intellectual Jacobinism of the most dangerous kind' (*Biographia*, 440). Amidst

---

[22] William Wordsworth, *The Prelude* 1799, 1805, 1850, ed. Jonathan Wordsworth, M.H. Abrams and Stephen Gill (New York: W. W. Norton, 1979), Book 7: 692. Subsequent references are cited within the text.

[23] Amongst Coleridge's varied writings on theatre, see especially the Satyrane letters, originally published in *The Friend*, 7 December 1809, later reprinted in *Biographia Literaria*, chapter 22 (hereafter cited as *Biographia*) and the letters on drama (*Courier*, 29 August, 7, 9, 11, 19 September 1816, reprinted in *Essays on his Times* 2: 435–40), many parts of which were later included in *Biographia*, chapter 23. References are given, unless otherwise indicated, from *Biographia*.

the dialogue's light-hearted Anti-Jacobin irony (see the Plaintiff's mockery of the 'valiant tars', 'philanthropic Jews' and 'tender-hearted braziers' alleged to populate modern English plays, 439), Coleridge sets out to define 'sentimental drama' (a category whose capaciousness in this argument seems very deliberate) as the dangerous antithesis of that legitimate culture represented by Shakespeare, Ariosto, Milton and Molière. The juridical structure of Coleridge's dialogue enhances the idea of an absolute opposition between comedy and legitimate tragedy (which wise men of old, Coleridge recalls, perceived to be the highest effort of human genius), and the moral, political and aesthetic deviancy of the sentimental muse. Tragedy is a writerly drama, Coleridge argues, whose heroes are aristocratic, whose subject is human nature, and whose pleasures arise from poetic language and the dynamic action and reaction of human passion. In sentimental drama, by contrast, 'the opulent and high-born themselves confess, that virtue is the only true nobility' (440). Here, the 'poor, pettifogging nature' of lowly human beings has become the sole theatrical subject. Moreover, the anti-aesthetic of sentimental drama merely privileges the slavish, sensational replication of ordinary life, as comically proved by the Defendant's otherwise incomprehensible admiration for the 'astonishing naturalness' of a 'deafening explosion' on stage.

Coleridge's argument is predicated on a stark opposition between the classical legacy of European culture and an undifferentiated morass of contemporary dramatic 'garbage', gobbled from a 'common trough' (*Biographia*, 437). Elsewhere, this opposition reappears as a distinction between the legitimate, aristocratic drama of Shakespeare, and Kotzebue's deviant, immoral theatre.[24] Above all, in his interpretation of *Bertram*, first published anonymously in 1816, Coleridge portrays Maturin's controversial Gothic play as the demonic symbol of an illegitimate culture which trades in moral and political subversion.

Bertram is a Byronic drama about a disgraced lord, now leader of a band of robbers. After his rescue from a shipwreck, Bertram finds himself at the castle of St Aldobrand, where he discovers that Imogine, his former lover, has married Lord Aldobrand in order to save her own father from

---

[24] Lecture 1 of *Lectures on Shakespeare and Education*, delivered at Bristol in 1813, published in *Lectures 1808–1819 on Literature, The Collected Works of Samuel Taylor Coleridge*, gen. ed. Kathleen Coburn, 16 vols. (Princeton University Press, 1971–), vol. v part 1, 520. Here, Coleridge praises Shakespeare for '*keeping at all times the high road of life*; with him there were no innocent adulteries, he never rendered that amiable which religion and reason taught us to detest; he never clothed vice in the garb of virtue, like *Beaumont* and *Fletcher*, the *Kotzebues* of this day'. See also the lectures of 1808, lecture 15: 117.

poverty. In Aldobrand's absence, Bertram seduces Imogine, whose remorse later drives her insane. After Imogine's death, the guilt-stricken hero finally takes a knife from his prison guard and kills himself, exulting that by this act he dies as a warrior and not as a felon. According to Coleridge, *Bertram*'s success at Drury Lane offers 'a melancholy proof of the depravation of the public mind' (469). He mocks the play's manifold improbabilities, 'solecisms' and 'corrupt diction' as well as deriding the inclusion of 'a number of mute dramatis personae' who 'afford something to be *seen*, by that very large part of a Drury Lane audience who have small chance of *hearing* a word' (471). As reprinted in *Biographia*, Coleridge's account forms the symbolic climax to his denunciation of sentimental drama. In this description, we are transported into Drury Lane Theatre, as if to hear for ourselves the 'thunder of applause' which greeted the actor Edmund Kean at the opening of Act IV, when Bertram appeared after his seduction of Imogine 'reeking from the consummation of this complex foulness and baseness' (469). Here, the sound of clapping – 'plaudits, which, but for the rivalry of the carts and hackney coaches, might have disturbed the evening prayers of the scanty weekday congregation at St Paul's cathedral' (471) – powerfully evokes the moral cacophony of illegitimate culture. In particular, the audience's injudicious applause subtly confirms for Coleridge's purposes the dangerous consequences of allowing 'the right of cultural suffrage' to become 'too widely diffused'.[25]

Coleridge, together with the 'plain, elderly man' sitting next to him who is so dumbfounded by Bertram's adultery, become the sole questioners of *Bertram*'s triumph, the solitary, heroic rebels against theatrical illegitimacy. Yet, as critics from Hazlitt onwards have pointed out, Coleridge had powerful reasons for denouncing Maturin's play.[26] The poet's most immediate interest was his own questionably Jacobin tragedy, *Remorse*; Drury Lane's recent rejection of *Zapolya* had only added insult to injury. So is it not possible, declared Hazlitt slyly, that 'the charge of sophistry and paradox, and dangerous morality, to startle the audience, in lieu of more legitimate methods of exciting their sympathy, which he brings against the author of Bertram, may not be retorted on

[25] Letter to the editor of the *Courier*, 29 August 1816, in *Essays on his Times*, part 2, 436, not included in *Biographia*.

[26] See Alethea Hayter, 'Coleridge, Maturin's *Bertram*, and Drury Lane' in Donald Sultana, ed., *New Approaches to Coleridge: Biographical and Critical Essays* (London: Vision Press, 1981), 17–37; John David Moore, 'Coleridge and the "Modern Jacobinical drama": *Osorio, Remorse* and the development of Coleridge's critique of the stage, 1779–1816', *Bulletin of Research in the Humanities* 85 (1982), 443–64.

his own head?'[27] Even when he returned to the subject some years later, Hazlitt could not resist another jibe at what he regarded as Coleridge's hypocrisy on the subject. In his apparently uncontentious description of *Remorse*, *Bertram* and Milman's *Fazio* as examples of 'the more legitimate and higher productions of the modern drama', Hazlitt is in fact rubbing yet more salt into Coleridge's wounds by disputing again *Bertram*'s supposed illegitimacy.[28]

Modern critics have certainly acknowledged Coleridge's political partisanship; many have also recognised the contradictions between his theory and his dramatic practice (*Remorse*, for example, borrows much of its dramaturgy from the same Gothic tradition as *Bertram*). But many scholars nonetheless accept without question Coleridge's absolute distinction between an elite, poetic drama and a vulgar, illegitimate theatre.[29] True, Coleridge was by no means alone in his vituperative reaction to Maturin's Gothic tragedy. *Bertram*'s adulterous love for Imogine, not to mention a controversial and questionably blasphemous scene depicting a high altar prepared for the sacrament, attracted furious condemnation from a number of reviewers. 'The strongest objections to be urged' against Maturin's plays, argued the *Theatrical Inquisitor* (October 1817, 945) 'consist in a direct proof of their illegitimate order, drawn from the certitude of their foundation upon a dramatic practice abhorrent to the sense and simplicity of our ancestors.' The conservative *British Review* similarly denounced *Bertram*'s '[r]otten principles' and 'bastard' sentiments which, the writer declared, had been 'imported into this country from German moralists and poets'.[30] Yet the very same reviewer also acknowledged the 'deep distress in the story of this tragedy' and its 'very considerable force in the expression of feeling and passion'. In this context, it is striking (and, in terms of my argument,

---

[27] *London Magazine*, April 1820, *Hazlitt* xviii:309. Cf. Hazlitt's earlier critique in the *Yellow Dwarf* (1818), *Hazlitt* xix: 206–10, in which Hazlitt mocks Coleridge's vain attempt to prove *Bertram* 'quite different in its philosophical tendency from his own sweet injured *Zapolya*'. Hazlitt cruelly compounds his laughter at Coleridge's expense by reminding his readers that an unauthorised version of *Zapolya* may now be seen 'represented to the life' at the Royal Circus, 'accompanied with music, and compressed into three acts, to make it "tedious and brief."' For Coleridge's fury over Drury Lane's rejection of *Zapolya*, see *Collected Letters of Samuel Taylor Coleridge*, ed. E. L. Griggs, 6 vols. (Oxford: Clarendon 1956–71), 15 April 1817, iv:720.

[28] *London Magazine*, April 1820, *Hazlitt* xviii: 304.

[29] See Alethea Hayter, 'Coleridge', who argues that the critique proves the inattention of contemporary audiences: '[n]o drama of ideas, no sustained philosophical theme, no subtle imagery, could possibly be put across to an audience in such conditions' (21). Cf. John Moore's claim in 'Coleridge and the "Modern Jacobinical drama"' that *Remorse* is a play designed 'to stem the rising tide of a lower-class drama addicted to sensational entertainment' (464).

[30] August 1816, 8: 64–81. See also *Monthly Review*, June 1816, 80: 179–80.

ironic) to note that the other text discussed in this review is Coleridge's new poem *Christabel*. And the critic of the *British Review* has no doubts about the relative merits of these two ambitious explorations of innocence and evil. Whilst *Bertram* represents 'a production of undoubted genius', the writer dismisses *Christabel* as nothing more than 'a weak and singularly nonsensical and affected performance' (80). Whether or not we regard as plausible these relative claims about critical value, there is no doubt that many Romantic critics have been slow to challenge Coleridge's arguments about *Bertram*.

Yet for Lord Byron, Walter Scott, and other reviewers, *Bertram* represented one of the most innovative and compelling dramas on the contemporary stage.[31] *The Times'* critic praised the play's 'matchless force', 'elegance of expression', 'profuse imagination' and 'pathos the most exquisite and profound'; the *Morning Chronicle* declared that *Bertram* contained passages 'of such burning and electrical effect, as to make it impossible to remain untouched by their force'.[32] What we see in this violent clash of opinions over *Bertram* is a set of contradictory responses to the breakdown of an old theatrical order. The fragmentation and mutation of dramatic genres, the unprecedented changes taking place in theatrical patronage, and the disintegration of Drury Lane and Covent Garden as national cultural institutions: these are the fears and forms of knowledge lurking in the shadows of Coleridge's critique. Above all, *Bertram* seemed to evoke that Burkean description of an 'unnatural' state where the stage boxes will be half-empty and culture tyrannically ruled by 'promiscuous' plebeian desires.

Coleridge's distinction between an elite, moral, legitimate dramatic culture and its illicit, plebeian, opposite becomes the consummate Romantic disavowal of illegitimate theatre. That disavowal, however, jars uneasily against Coleridge's own dramatic practice, not to mention his desire to produce a number of illegitimate plays, including 'Laugh till you lose him' (a dramatic romance), an oriental entertainment, a speaking ballet, and a pantomime based on the Tartarian tales.[33] So Coleridge's critique should encourage us to be cautious about making rigid distinctions between the legitimate and the illegitimate: as Hazlitt gleefully realised in the debate over *Bertram*, neither category is pure or absolute. If we turn now to the Old Price riots at Covent Garden, we can examine how growing opposition to the policies and repertoire of

---

[31] For Scott's and Byron's enthusiasm about *Bertram*, see Robert E. Lougy, *Charles Robert Maturin* (Lewisburg: Bucknell University Press, 1975), 41–8.
[32] *The Times*, 10 May 1816; *Morning Chronicle*, 10 May 1816.   [33] Coleridge, *Letters* IV: 606.

the patent theatres was shaping perceptions about the institutional legitimacy of Covent Garden and Drury Lane.

THE OLD PRICE RIOTS

During the autumn of 1809, performances at Covent Garden became a near-inaudible dramatic sideshow for almost three months. The main show had moved to the auditorium where protestors, armed with banners and slogans ('Old Prices'; 'John Bull against John Kemble'; 'No Italian Private Boxes'), climbed onto the pit benches, harangued the manager, John Philip Kemble, and created their own noisy, carnivalesque performances in the form of Old Price songs and dances (accompanied by marrow-bones, cleavers and a dustman's bell), pugilistic combats and sword-play. The banging of sticks against pit seats, the screeching sounds of whistles, and the menacing crackle of Old Price rattles: these sounds of ritual disorder might seem only to confirm the triumph of mob rule in the early nineteenth-century theatre. But in many ways the Old Price riots represent a rational response to what the protestors identified as Covent Garden's capitulation to decadent luxury and social exclusivity.

As Marc Baer and Gillian Russell have shown, the riotous festivities at Covent Garden raise important questions about the relationship between spectatorship, class and concepts of national identity. In particular, Baer's monograph offers a persuasive account of the relationship between the Old Price disturbances and Westminster radicalism.[34] First, I want to suggest that the riots helped to extend and develop the idea of a 'national' or 'legitimate' drama. Secondly, the dispute between the audience and the Covent Garden manager brought to light a symbiotic relationship between theatrical and political power. The events at Covent Garden drew popular attention, in other words, to the hidden relationship between the patent institution and the state.

John Thelwall's lectures on the politics of the patent establishment provide an important precedent for the arguments put forward by the Old Price rioters. In the mid-1790s, the radical journalist and lecturer had delivered two lectures entitled 'On the Political Prostitution of our Public Theatres'.[35] According to Thelwall, the mystification of politics

---

[34] Marc Baer, *Theatre and Disorder in Georgian London* (Oxford: Clarendon, 1992); Gillian Russell, 'Playing at Revolution: The Politics of the O.P. Riots of 1809', *Theatre Notebook* 44 (1990), 16–26.

[35] These lectures, given in April 1795, were later published in the *Tribune* (London: printed for the author, 1796), 279–318. Together with Hardy and Horne Tooke, Thelwall was acquitted in the treason trials of 1793–4. Pitt and Greville's so-called Gagging Acts were introduced partly in order to prevent Thelwall's exploitation of the lecture as a political platform.

as an elite science 'with which the mass of the people have no sort of business or connection', had long served to disguise the manipulation and corruption of public amusements for political ends (280). Having illustrated his thesis with examples from a variety of historical epochs, Thelwall turned to the contemporary 'prostitution' of the patent theatres to the political establishment. Now, by 'the prudent device of a monopoly, and the sapient intervention of a Lord Chamberlain', England had produced an ideological replica of theatre's political prostitution in Roman society. Not only did the institution of monopoly infect 'the morality and justice of the whole country', but it also dictated 'the particular sentiments to be uttered, the opinions that are to be propagated, and the factions, however despicable, to which all talents are to be prostituted' (282). What is interesting about Thelwall's argument is the way in which he conceives of theatrical performance as a valuable yet fragile form of political culture which is always dangerously vulnerable to state intervention and control. Theatrical prostitution, he maintains, violates 'the imprescriptible rights of man'.

Thelwall's polemic is occasionally intemperate and sometimes wrong-headed. The claim that even Shakespeare 'too often wielded the pen of political prostitution', for instance, would seem to beg several questions which remain unanswered here. But the importance of 'On the Political Prostitution of our Public Theatres' lies rather in Thelwall's interpretation of monopoly and censorship as political structures. For, as Thelwall recognises, the institution of monopoly actually defines what may be represented on the stage. The discourse of the Old Price riots shares many of Thelwall's preoccupations, and exposes in particular that insidious collusion between the political and cultural states at the heart of which lay patent monopoly.

After the disastrous fire at Covent Garden in 1808, Sheridan and John Philip Kemble had raised vast sums of money in order to construct one of the finest examples of neoclassical architecture in late Hanoverian London. The new Covent Garden Theatre cost an extraordinary £150,000. Robert Smirke had copied the portico from the Temple of Minerva in the Acropolis; inside, figures of Aeschylus, Aristophanes and Menander adorned the panels, whilst Rossi's statue of Shakespeare in yellow marble stood in the anteroom. Sheridan and Kemble also continued their controversial policy of converting Covent Garden into a theatre of social exclusivity. Not only did the new Theatre include three whole tiers of boxes, but one of those tiers was reserved exclusively for private use. What is more, in order to make space for these wealthy spectators (and, more to the point, according to the rioters, for the prostitutes who accompanied many of them), the gallery audience was now accommodated still further away from the stage in an area soon known as the 'pigeonholes'.

Sheridan's conception of the new Covent Garden can be surmised from the pseudonymous puff he sent to the *Morning Post* advertising the opening of a 'New Grand Imperial incombustable [*sic*] Theatre'.[36] Reviewers and pamphleteers agreed, hailing the new Covent Garden Theatre as the 'pre-eminent monument of British taste'.[37] During the Old Price riots, however, this language of imperial self-congratulation clashed violently against a traditional rhetoric of theatrical chauvinism redolent with suspicions about foreign performers (notably Angelica Catalani, an Italian opera singer recently employed by Kemble at an extortionate salary), foreign theatrical forms (opera, melodrama), and questionably foreign, immoral practices (the provision of private boxes in a public theatre).

Increased prices, a reduced one-shilling gallery, enlarged private boxes, the employment of Catalani: the immediate causes of the Old Price riots were multifarious. During the autumn of 1809, the disruption at Covent Garden provided a theatrical bandwagon for numerous causes and complaints, including angry fulminations about the visibility of prostitutes at Covent Garden and chauvinistic opposition to Italian opera ('extremely injurious to the genuine principles of religion and morality' remarked 'A True Briton'; another protester argued that 'The Italian Frenchified operas have ruined the British drama, and will ultimately ruin the British constitution').[38] As in earlier theatre protests, the Old Price rioters claimed that the new theatre deliberately promoted class division and exclusivity, as the private boxes, with their separate entrances and stairs, permitted the aristocracy to 'purchase their exemption from mingling with the body of the people'.[39] In the *Examiner*, Leigh Hunt described the private boxes as a 'foreign piece of indulgence'

---

[36] The puff, signed 'Gregory Gull', was published 20 October 1809. See *The Letters of Richard Brinsley Sheridan* ed. Cecil Price, 3 vols. (Oxford: Clarendon, 1966), III: 71. Sheridan had been compelled to resign from the management of Covent Garden in 1809 because of his now-perilous financial position.

[37] Anon, *The Life of John Philip Kemble* (London: J. Johnston, 1809), 39.

[38] A True Briton, *Strictures on the Engagement of Madame Catalani . . . and on the Italian Opera* (London: Cox & Baylis, 1809), 3; *Political Review*, 28 October 1809.

[39] *Dramatic Censor*, April 1811, 226; see also letter to the Earl of Dartmouth in *The Times*, 7 November 1809. Although the Old Price protesters doggedly portrayed this innovation as a symbol of aristocratic exclusivity, fashionable society in general (that social group often referred to as the *beau monde*) also patronised the private boxes. See OP. *The Interesting Trial at Large of Henry Clifford, Esq . . .* (London, 1809), 9. In the *Political Review* of 4 November 1809, Henry Yorke caustically refers to these people of fashion as 'that hermaphrodite race of feeble creatures'.

declaring, 'a whole circle of the Theatre taken from them to make privacies for the luxurious great is a novelty so offensive to the national habits, both on account of its contemptuous exclusions, and the ideas of accommodation it so naturally excites, that the Managers deserve to suffer still more for their mercenary and obsequious encouragement of pride and profligacy'.[40]

The emergence of 'national drama' as a popular rallying-cry during the riots ('National Theatre: Fair Prices: English Drama: *No Catalani*')[41] was accompanied by the chauvinistic repudiation of new and especially 'foreign' theatrical forms. According to one pamphleteer, the Covent Garden managers preferred to gratify spectators' curiosity (and to fill their own coffers) 'with singing and dancing, with monsters, eunuchs, or any other exotic rarity' rather than to furnish 'the food of the mind' with legitimate drama; Henry Yorke dismissed Covent Garden's repertoire of opera and melodrama, 'execrable fooleries and sing-song lullabies' as 'detestable trash'.[42] Like the anti-Jacobin reviewers, the Old Price rioters castigated Covent Garden's promotion of miscellaneous, bastardly theatrical forms: the 'promiscuous' jumbling of comedy and tragedy together with a 'new species of mummery, called melo-dramatic writing'.[43]

In their sturdy demands for 'the national drama', the Old Price rioters coined a phrase which succinctly conflated the nostalgic claims of cultural patriotism and also the topical rhetoric of popular constitutionalism. Through this clarion call, the rioters attempted to mythologise as pure and unadulterated a British theatrical tradition in truth continuously shaped by the influences of continental forms, performers and playwrights. In particular, the rioters perceived the innovative mixing and mutation of genres in contemporary theatre as yet another example of cultural and moral decay. As we have seen, the national drama was essentially a cultural symbol rather than a recognisable collection of British plays. But in an era marked by extraordinary changes in theatrical genres (not to mention those taking place in political culture), this category provided the rioters with a useful weapon of aesthetic distinction, a means by which to defend a reactionary set of cultural values. A few

[40] *Examiner*, 24 September 1809, *LH* 33.
[41] *The Rebellion: or All in the Wrong* (London: Vernon, Hood & Sharpe, 1809), 23.
[42] Henry Yorke, *Considerations on the Past and Present State of the Stage* (London: C. Chapple, 1809), 39; *Political Review*, 16 September 1809. For similar references, see also entries for 16 January 1808, 23 September 1809 and 6 January 1810.
[43] See Yorke in J. J. Stockdale, ed., *Covent Garden Journal*, 2 vols. (London: J. J. Stockdale, 1810), 2: 416, 417 and see also II: 391; hereafter *CGJ*.

6. The forces of law employed to crush public opposition. *Acting Magistrates commiting themselves being their first appearance on this stage as performed at the National Theatre, Covent Garden.*

decades later, too, the minor theatres would also seize on the rhetoric of 'national drama', this time as a patriotic defence of their own unlicensed performances. In 1832, for example, a Surrey playbill described the proprietor having been 'waited on by a Deputation of Gentlemen, and others from the neighbourhood' requesting the performance of 'some part of the NATIONAL DRAMA'. Osbaldiston was quick to comply, and the Surrey proceeded to stage *The Venetian Moor*, a burletta 'interspersed with Melo-dramatic Music, founded on Shakspeare's Othello'.[44] The Old Price riots had given ideological currency to a slogan which could now be evocatively mobilised to promote illegal productions of legitimate plays.

Like earlier critics and protestors, the Old Price rioters defined theatrical monopoly as a contract held from government under a 'tacit tenure, for the benefit, amusement, and instruction of the people'.[45] But what distinguished the Old Price riots was a pervasive conviction that Covent Garden's degraded repertoire proved this contract's collapse. Unlike Anti-Jacobin reviewers, however, the rioters' critique of miscellany and monstrosity went hand in hand with an unprecedented attack on Covent Garden as a monopolistic institution. Once perceived as a cultural parliament of the nation, the new Covent Garden Theatre seemed to have broken its unwritten constitutional pledges. 'The legitimate British theatre,' argued one pamphleteer, 'resembles our invaluable constitution. It has, from time immemorial, been fairly open to all classes of the public, in their several ranks and degrees.'[46] The appearance of magistrates on the Covent Garden stage to read the riot act (see plate 6), and the systematic arrest of Old Price protestors (including Henry Clifford, the well-known barrister), seemed to confirm the management's determination forcibly to crush the Old Price opposition. In the Cruikshanks' engraving, the theatre is packed with placard-waving protestors ('No Italian Private Boxes'; 'John Bull against John Kemble'); almost all the spectators appear to be on their feet whilst the unfortunate magistrates look utterly bewildered and not a little alarmed at their cacophonous dramatic reception. (The cartoon's title, 'Acting Magistrates committing themselves being their first appearance on this stage as performed at the National Theatre, Covent Garden', not to mention the laughable figure of Kemble solemnly applauding them at the back of the stage, also draws satirical attention to Covent Garden's theatrical *production* of the state's legal authority in an attempt to quell the disruption.)

---

[44] Playbills for 16 and 30 January 1832. [45] *Covent Garden Theatre!! Remarks*, 4.
[46] *Considerations on the Past and Present State of the Stage*, 32–3.

Throughout the riots, songs, broadsides, caricatures and slogans mockingly portrayed Kemble as 'the Great Dramatic Tory'; resistance to the Theatre's imposition of new prices soon became synonymous with popular resistance to unfair taxation.[47] Moreover, a range of more illicit tactics, including Kemble's alleged applications to the Bank and the Treasury (in the hope of preventing their employees from attending the Theatre) and his decision to employ pugilists to control the rioters within the playhouse, led to the charge that Covent Garden represented an insidious extension of the political establishment. Such attacks on the '*personal liberty*' of the audience, William Cobbett declared, transformed the riots into a political issue.[48] As a correspondent in the *Theatrical Inquisitor* would later remark, 'It is thus that in monarchies purely despotic, the unjust sovereigns are murdered by the people, by the army, or by the ministers, when they oppress them too far.'[49]

After three months of excited tumult and raucous festivity, the Old Price riots ended with the capitulation of Kemble and the Covent Garden proprietors, the removal of private boxes, the restoration of Old Prices in the pit, and the dismissal of Angelica Catalani. Two decades later, F. G. Tomlins would remember the Old Price rioters as the heroic opponents of monopoly, 'justly indignant at the insolence of an obstinate man'.[50] Francis Place also recognised the events of 1809 as a decisive turning-point in the public's attitude towards Covent Garden. 'The public took the advice so absurdly and arrogantly given', he declared, 'they staid away; and we now see the consequences'.[51] Far from closing a chapter in theatrical history, as Baer's argument suggests, the Old Price riots marked a watershed in the financial and ideological collapse of the patent theatres. In their wake, the nature of monopoly now began to be scrutinised far more closely; meanwhile, the minor theatres started to exploit demands for a national drama by staging legitimate plays in defiance of the monopolists. In a variety of ways, Walter Scott's later description of the new Covent Garden theatre as based on 'a plan too ample for its legitimate purpose'[52] quietly sums up a widespread conviction that the new Covent Garden building – not to mention the assump-

---

[47] *What-Do-You-Want? explained in a Poetical Epistle from O.P. to all the Aitches* (London, n.d.), 20–1.

[48] *Cobbett's Political Register* [ed. William Cobbett], 9 December 1809, XVI: 891. On Kemble's attempts to influence the Bank and Treasury, see *CGJ* I: 108.

[49] Letter from 'A Lover of Justice and the Drama' in *Theatrical Inquisitor*, March 1814, 4: 161–2, 161; cf. *CGJ* I: 23.   [50] [F. G. Tomlins], *Major and Minor Theatres. A Concise View of the Question*, 12–13.

[51] [Place], *A Brief Examination of the Dramatic Patents*, in *Monthly Magazine*, March 1834, 11.

[52] [Walter Scott], [Review of] *Memoirs of the Life of John Philip Kemble*, *Quarterly Review* 34 (1826), 196–248, 235.

tions about spectatorship implicit in that building's design – had breached a symbolic contract between patent managers and the theatrical public, a contract whose widening cracks would now become irreparable.

BLUE-BEARD, *TIMOUR*, AND QUADRUPED DRAMA

Faced with fast-increasing bills and diminishing audiences, the treasuries at Covent Garden and Drury Lane edged ever closer towards insolvency. After a revival of the Old Price riots at the beginning of the 1810–11 season, Kemble had been compelled to remove another eight private boxes in order to secure peace: the enforced loss of twenty-six private boxes stripped more than £10,000 per annum from the Theatre's revenues.[53] Covent Garden's response to this financial crisis would later go down in theatrical history as the apotheosis of patent illegitimacy.

Kemble and Henry Harris must have heard with dismay of the enthusiastic crowds gathering at the Royal Circus where, for the last two seasons, Robert Elliston had been staging legitimate plays such as *Macbeth* and *The Beggar's Opera* under the guise of burletta. Nearby, on Westminster Bridge, Astley's Amphitheatre had performed to great acclaim an equestrian spectacle entitled *The Blood Red Knight*. Presented in dumbshow, and interspersed with grand chivalric processions, the show featured Alphonso's rescue of his wife Isabella from her imprisonment and forced marriage to the evil knight Sir Rowland, and concluded with the spectacular, fiery destruction of the castle and Sir Rowland's death. In an extraordinary run of 175 performances, *The Blood Red Knight* had brought in £18,000.[54] Quaduped drama had certainly captured the public imagination.

Bitter arguments ensued between Kemble and Harris over how to reduce Covent Garden's deficits.[55] Perhaps Kemble anticipated the storm of protest which would erupt after the decision to hire Astley's stud of horses (an innovation which required the rapid reinforcement of the Covent Garden stage as well as the provision of stable quarters) for an equestrian revival of Colman's controversial melodramatic romance, *Blue-Beard*. Certainly, the coupling of *Blue-Beard* with Shakespeare's *The Comedy of Errors* suggests a calculated attempt to deflect damaging

---

[53] Henry Saxe Wyndham, *Annals of Covent Garden Theatre from 1732 to 1897*, 2 vols. (London: Chatto and Windus, 1906), I: 348.   [54] Decastro, *Memoirs*, 101.

[55] See *Morning Chronicle* 3 May 1811; James Boaden, *Memoirs of the Life of John Philip Kemble*, 2 vols. (London: Longman, 1825), II: 542.

accusations about the burgeoning illegitimacy of Covent Garden's repertoire.

Blue-Beard is an oriental drama about forbidden desire. At its climax,
Fatima discovers the fearful blue chamber, full of supernatural figures,
and a huge skeleton who sits beneath a chilling inscription written in
characters of blood: 'The Punishment of Curiosity'. The decorative
magnificence of Colman's play was never in dispute. Audiences were
entranced by a succession of memorable scenes, including the Satrap's
picturesque procession through the hills, and the wonders of an articulated skeleton, not to mention the final storming of the Bashaw's castle,
during which 'the whole depth of the scene was filled with combatants,
foot and horse' (*The Times*, 19 February 1811). In financial terms, too, the
equestrian *Blue-Beard* exceeded the managers' most optimistic expectations, taking £21,000 in its first forty-one nights.[56] But critical reaction
ranged from half-condescending rebukes about the play's alleged lack of
oriental verisimilitude to downright fury. At the Theatre, placard-
holders opposed to the introduction of horses (not to mention elephants
and camels) protested loudly during the performance on the opening
night. Reviewers also objected to the display of a room containing portraits, in defiance of Muslim precept, and criticised the careless incoher-
ence of Fatima's oriental costume ('neither Turkish, Persian nor
Christian . . . an awkward compilation of shawls and silks, without propriety or elegance').[57] Amongst the loudest detractors was the *Morning
Chronicle*, whose reviewer deplored this extravagant prostitution of
Covent Garden to 'buffoonery and shew', and peremptorily demanded
that *Blue-Beard* should 'be transferred to its proper sphere, which is
Astley's Amphitheatre'.[58]

Meanwhile, prominent reviewers and dramatic editors joined the fray.
John Williams, editor of the recently established *Dramatic Censor* – a periodical which had dedicated itself to supporting the 'morality' and
'dignity' of the drama[59] – soon began to take up rhetorical cudgels
against the patentees. According to Williams, *Blue-Beard* represented the
theatrical climax of that contempt and patrician arrogance displayed by
Kemble during the Old Price riots. Leigh Hunt agreed, denouncing
Blue-Beard as 'one of those wretched compounds of pun and parade'
which form 'the nightly boast of this "*classical*" theatre.' Such exhibitions, he argued

---

[56] Frederic Reynolds, *The Life and Times of Frederic Reynolds*, 2 vols. (London: Henry Colbourn, 1826),
II: 404.
[57] See Leigh Hunt's comments in the *Examiner*, 24 March 1811, *LH* 45, and a report in *The Times*,
19 February 1811.   [58] 19 February 1811.   [59] See subtitle to the first issue, January 1811.

are too powerful a stimulus to the senses of the common order of spectators, and take away from their eyes and ears all relish for more delicate entertainment. The managers and the public thus corrupt each other; but it is the former who begin the infection by building these enormous theatres in which a great part of the spectators must have noise and shew before they can hear or see what is going forwards.[60]

Kemble and Harris, however, airily dismissed these expressions of discontent, and promptly commissioned another quadruped play, this time from the novelist, playwright and Regency dandy, Matthew ('Monk') Lewis, author of *Adelmorn* and *The Castle Spectre*. Like Colman, Lewis based his play on a well-known oriental narrative, already familiar to audiences and play-readers from Marlowe's play, and especially from *Tamerlane* (1701), Nicholas Rowe's militaristic stock drama. First performed on 29 April 1811, *Timour the Tartar* would run for more than forty nights, and be revived all over Britain for many years afterwards.

'Monk' Lewis's *Timour*, which I discuss more fully in chapter 3, dramatises the spectacular overthrow of an oriental tyrant by the legitimate heir to the Georgian throne. The opening night of the play, however, immediately revived the controversy stirred up by Covent Garden's equestrian *Bluebeard*. From the upper boxes and the pit, spectators intent on voicing their opposition to quadruped drama launched handbills, which were promptly torn to shreds, amidst loud hissing by rival groups.[61] 'Some displeasure,' reported *The Times*' reviewer (30 April 1811), 'appears to have been predetermined on by the critics in the pit'; the paper's critic nonetheless declared, with characteristic loyalty, that the dénouement of *Timour* had been greeted with 'a roar of approbation'. The *Morning Chronicle* demurred, referring to the production as 'contemptible mummery', while the *Dramatic Censor* similarly condemned *Timour* as 'another vandal experiment on the public taste for scenery, horsemanship, and mummery'.[62] Covent Garden's 'prostitution' of the stage, alleged one newspaper correspondent, resembled the decadence of imperial Rome; the *Morning Chronicle* even published a satirical poem entitled 'On the New Hippodrome at Covent Garden'.[63] At the minor theatres and the Haymarket, mock equestrian dramas soon became all the rage. Leigh Hunt remarked with obvious satisfaction that the final chaotic battle scene of *Quadrupeds; or, The Manager's Last Kick* (July

---

[60] *Examiner*, 24 March, 1811, *LH* 47–8.
[61] *European Magazine*, May 1811, 59: 377; *Morning Chronicle*, 30 April 1811. For a later confrontation, see *The Times*, 1 April 1812. [62] May 1811, 241.
[63] Letter from Oliver 'Old Times', *Morning Chronicle*, 2 May 1811; *Morning Chronicle*, 22 April 1811. For a classical riposte to these allegations, compare Whibread's arguments at the second reading of the London Theatre Bill, reported in the *Morning Chronicle*, 21 March 1812.

1811) 'affords a good and palpable ridicule of the Kemble horses', and 'looks like Hogarth's picture of the battle of *Hudibras*, brought into life'.[64] In Parliament, meanwhile, the petitioners for a third theatre in London explicitly charged the patentees with the degradation of the nation's drama.[65]

Reviewers had fulminated before about what they perceived as specific violations of decorum and rationality at the patent houses. Carlo, the canine hero of Frederic Reynolds' *The Caravan* (Drury Lane, 1803) had provoked some lively satires; in 1804–5, cartoonists laughed at the fashion surrounding appearances of the talented juvenile performer, Master Betty, at Covent Garden. But the outcry over quadruped drama marked a turning-point in the cultural authority of Covent Garden and Drury Lane. *Timour* and *Blue-Beard* (not to mention *Harlequin and Padmanaba*, Covent Garden's oriental pantomime featuring an elephant named Chuny) came to symbolise the decadent triumph of theatrical illegitimacy. The *Dramatic Censor* (February 1811, 156) wrote gloomily of the public's 'resolution to discountenance and proscribe the Legitimate Drama, and establish in its stead a kind of entertainment (forgive the misnomer) recognizable by neither the rules of critics, nor the laws of nature'. Like the anarchic state depicted by Burke in *Reflections*, the rise of illegitimate theatre at the patent theatres now promised the overthrow of order, tradition and hierarchy by barbarism, promiscuity, irrationality and sensation.[66]

This chapter has explored the complex and unstable relationship between the political and generic connotations of illegitimate theatre. To some extent, the category of the illegitimate refers to forms of generic innovation believed to entail, or at least to provide a favourable climate for, political and moral subversion. In other ways, however, the illegitimate alludes more broadly to a set of genres whose production at

---

[64] *Examiner*, 21 July 1811, *LH* 51. In Astley's satire on illegitimate production at the patent houses, Timour and Blue Beard receive a 'just Punishment', while Virtue and Bravery are Triumphant'. See George Male's burlesque, *Baghvan-Ho; or, The Tartars Tartar'd* (Astley's, 1812) and a playbill for 20 January 1812 in HTC. Other burlesques on the subject include *Bipeds and Quadrupeds; or, Blue Beard Travestie* (Sadler's Wells, 1811) and a Surrey prelude entitled *What's a Stage without Horses?* (1811).

[65] Marryatt, Third Theatre Bill; petition of February 1812, reported in *European Magazine*, March 1812, 225, *London Chronicle*, 23 March 1812, *Gentleman's Magazine*, May 1812, 467ff. On the campaign for a third theatre in London, see also Watson Nicholson, *Struggle for a Free Stage*, chapter 9.

[66] See, especially, the *Satirist*'s review of *Timour the Tartar*, May 1811 and the *Theatrical Inquisitor*'s account of *The Forest of Bondy*, October 1814, 5: 264. Cf. the *Morning Chronicle* on *The Cataract of the Ganges*, 28 October 1823 and the *Examiner*'s review of the same play, 2 November 1823, 709, signed 'Q'.

Covent Garden and Drury Lane becomes synonymous with the patentees' cultural treachery. This second definition is important because it
reminds us that plays on very similar subjects might be interpreted in
radically different ways, depending on their place of production. Over
the next few decades, for example, the minor theatres successfully staged
a wide variety of colonial and oriental dramas, including *Alexander the
Great* (Astley's, 1822) and *The Massacre of Rajapoor* (Coburg, 1826). By contrast, however, dramatic orientalism at Covent Garden and Drury Lane
– as we have seen in the furore over *Bluebeard* and *Timour* – had become
inextricable from discourses of patent illegitimacy. So reviewers castigated what they perceived as the spectacular decadence of oriental plays
such as Moncrieff's *Cataract of the Ganges* (Drury Lane, 1823), a piece
dramatising the historic British campaign to abolish the practice of
female infanticide in India. The *Cataract*'s famous dénouement featured
the Princess's escape through a burning forest 'interspersed with clumps
and declivities, in the midst of which the troops engage, horse and foot'
behind which appeared a cataract which seemed to descend from the
roof.[67] Given the expense of this 'painted and gilded balderdash',
declared the *Examiner* in mock despair, the attraction of such spectacles
must eventually wear out; although willing to acknowledge the play's
'most brilliant scenery', 'most magnificent processions' and a 'delightful
confusion' of battles, conflagrations and cataracts, the *Morning Chronicle*
fervently agreed. If the *Cataract* succeeds, wrote the paper's reviewer in
a tone of virtual despair, adieu to Shakespeare.[68] For as these reviews
confirm, oriental drama at the patent houses had come to symbolise the
usurpation of dramatic culture based on language, rhetoric and rationality by a spectacular, illegitimate theatre – a theatre of 'mummeries'.[69]
So was the fall of Covent Garden and Drury Lane, from the theatres of
the nation into its spectacular 'menageries' and 'raree-shows', now irreversible? Certainly, the former defenders of the national drama now

[67] *Examiner* review, 2 November 1823, 709, signed 'Q'. See William Moncrieff, *The Cataract of the Ganges! or, The Rajah's Daughter* (London: Simkin and Marshall, 1823).

[68] Cf. the satirical reception for *Hyder Ali; or, The Lions of Mysore* (Drury Lane, 1831) a *pièce de circon-stance* for M. Martin, the circus trainer, and his troupe of animals. The visual inscription of the Orient within the patent auditoria also provoked controversy. See, for example, Leigh Hunt's satirical description of Drury Lane's new Chinese saloon, *Examiner*, 7 September 1817, *LH* 153–6; cf. a disputatious meeting of the Drury Lane proprietors, reported in the *Theatrical Inquisitor*, September 1817, 11: 197–202, especially 199–200.

[69] On the language of mummery, see the *Morning Chronicle*, 28 October 1823; Taylor's allusions to mummery in the House of Commons debate, reported *London Chronicle*, May 1811, 109: 494. Cf. Elliston's pamphlet, *Copy of a Memorial Presented to the Lord Chamberlain . . . against the Olympic and Sans Pareil Theatres; with Copies of Two Letters, in Reply to the Contents of Such Memorials, Addressed to the Lord Chamberlain by Robert William Elliston, Comedian* (London: John Miller, 1818).

seemed to have become mere commercial traders in the exotic, as sold from Pidcock and Exter Change.[70]

UNMASKING LEGITIMACY

The promotion of illegitimate plays at the patent theatres profoundly undermined the cultural authority of Drury Lane and Covent Garden. During the Regency years, however, another kind of institutional critique began to emerge. In radical discourse, 'legitimacy' had come to refer to its very opposite: the false appearance of constitutional government under the guise of monarchy. For writers such as William Hone and Hazlitt, legitimacy therefore connoted the endemic corruption of the British political system, the 'poor, pettifogging pretext of arbitrary power'.[71] To some extent, the theatrical tropes which pervade Regency radicalism (see the political showman, proprietor of raree shows and political menageries and the production of burlesque state theatricals in the *Black Dwarf*) simply reveal the slow, self-conscious fall of republican idealism into print warfare. But theatre was more than a convenient metaphor through which to imagine the illusions and deceits of Regency government. On the contrary, Drury Lane and Covent Garden theatres had come to be identified as the cultural synecdoche of a corrupt political state.[72]

In these arguments, we can trace a shift in emphasis from the illegitimate repertoire being produced at Drury Lane and Covent Garden to the illegitimate character of the patent institution. Hazlitt's attacks on patent chicanery, for example, were an attempt to alert his readers to the political meanings of cultural organisation and theatrical practices. Such interpretations violently dislodged the traditional image of the patentees as benign cultural stewards: monopoly was now being unmasked as a corrupt system which made possible a cynical disdain for public opinion, and the ruthless crushing of theatrical opposition. In particular, Hazlitt's interpretation of the controversy surrounding Junius Brutus Booth's appearances at Drury Lane and Covent Garden theatres in 1817 provided one of the most elegant and cutting indictments of patent monopoly.

---

[70] On the language of the menagerie, see *The Modern Stage, A Letter to the Hon. George Lamb, M.P. on the Decay and Degradation of English Dramatic Literature* (London: Edwards and Knibbs, 1819); Dramaticus (pseud), *An Impartial View of the Stage . . .* (London: C. Chapple, 1816), 17.

[71] [Leigh Hunt], 'Kings and Coronations', *Examiner*, 22 July 1821, 450.

[72] See T. J. Wooler, *The Black Dwarf*, especially the issues for 5 February, 12 March and 16 April 1817; William Hone, *The Political Showman – At Home! exhibiting his cabinet of curiosities and Creatures – All Alive* (London: Hone, 1821).

The public discontent and anger generated by the Old Price riots echoes through the pages of the *Examiner*. From the earliest issues, Hunt had satirised what he perceived as Kemble's hypocritical imposition of deplorable plays on the public. The production of Colman's burlesque melodrama, *Bonifacio and Bridgetina*, was a good example. Despite universal condemnation, alleged Hunt, Kemble staged the play until it became 'the standing opiate of the season': the managers of the theatres 'prove their affection for public opinion by growing bolder through denial'.[73] In his *Examiner* essays Hazlitt also explored the themes of patent 'quackery' and oppression. In particular, Hazlitt accused Covent Garden and Drury Lane of overturning the democratic rights of audiences and performers by means of censorship, by the suppression of protest and by a tyrannical control over theatrical performance.[74] In these reviews, Hazlitt exposed patent culture as the cultural face of state repression, and the embodiment of that corrupt system of sinecures and placemen characteristic of unreformed government, and known as Old Corruption.

Hazlitt's most startling discussion of these issues can be found in two *Examiner* reviews of 2 and 9 March 1817, published during the furore surrounding Booth's engagements and amid Parliamentary debates over *habeas corpus*.[75] Junius Brutus Booth, who had recently made his London debut at Covent Garden, had marketed himself as a rival to, and dramatic copyist of, Edmund Kean. His face 'is adapted to tragic characters,' remarked Hazlitt, 'and his voice wants neither strength nor musical expression.' But, he continued, 'the imitation of original genius is the *forlorn hope* of the candidates for fame . . . A Kemble school we can understand: a Kean school, is, we suspect, a contradiction in terms.'[76]

When Covent Garden declined to engage him at more than £2 a week, Booth unwisely allowed himself to be persuaded by Kean to appear at Drury Lane. After only one disastrous performance, in which he played Iago to Kean's Othello (Hazlitt was amused by watching Booth's imitations being performed 'in the presence, and as it were with the permission of Mr. Kean'),[77] Booth again broke contract and accepted an engagement at Covent Garden, where his reappearance was greeted by irate spectators incensed to riot by the actor's egregious disloyalty. 'The conduct of this young man is indefensible for his want of

---

[73] *Examiner*, 10 April 1808, *LH* 10–11.

[74] See especially *Examiner*, 5 January, 26 January and 29 October 1817.

[75] My article, '"Fine word, legitimate!"', 223–44, discusses this controversy in more detail.

[76] *Examiner*, 16 February 1817, *Hazlitt* v: 354–5.   [77] *Examiner*, 23 February 1817, *Hazlitt* v: 356.

truth and candour,' declared the *Morning Chronicle* (26 February 1817), 'but that of both Theatres is blameable.' The controversy surrounding Booth, which, as the critic observed, seemed in many ways to recall the Old Price riots, involved a dispute over breached contracts, both by Booth and by the patent houses (by long agreement, Drury Lane and Covent Garden did not attempt to poach actors from the other theatre), with the additional theatrical spice of an alleged *agent provocateur* in the person of Kean, who was said to have lured his rival to Drury Lane in order to humiliate him there, as well as to have orchestrated the subsequent opposition to Booth, through his tavern club, 'The Wolves'. For several days, performances at Covent Garden were inaudible amidst this 'sublime confusion' (*The Times*, 26 February 1817). In the Theatre, rival factions hurled abuse and accusations at each other, placards were raised – 'No Booth!' 'Booth for ever!' only to be destroyed, pugilistic battles took place in the pit, and manager and actor vainly attempted to appease the spectators. For Hazlitt, this theatrical fracas symbolised the abrogation of theatre's function as a democratic forum for the untrammelled expression of public opinion. Monopoly seemed to make possible forms of oppression which precisely corresponded to that being practised in post-Waterloo Britain.[78]

Hazlitt's interpretation of the Booth affair introduces an ideological connection between Drury Lane's determination to suppress public opposition and its unconstitutional authority: 'It seems that the public have nothing to do with the determination of the Managers, but to obey them. This doctrine is not original, but borrowed from high authority. We have here an example of the *imperium in imperio*.'[79] Here, managers casually 'borrow' their methods and strategies from a government which also behaves as if independent of law or established authority. Government and patent managers alike rely on a common stock of despotic tactics, or ideological stage props. Inside the theatre, as at Covent Garden, *habeas corpus* has been suspended, and a Gagging Bill silences the pit critics, 'mak[ing] it sedition to hiss Mr. Booth, and high treason to hoot at the Managers' (XVIII: 222). Hazlitt's description of theatrical repression in Regency Britain emphasises the physical means by which

---

[78] Cp. William Cobbett's indictment of legitimate drama as a school of 'abject slavery' in his essay, 'Decay of the Drama', *Cobbett's Political Register*, 12 June 1830, 69: 769–73. See too Francis Place's argument about theatrical monopoly as a conspiracy by which the political elite cunningly restricted freedom of expression: in [Place] *A New Way to Pay Old Debts* (London: Sherwood, 1812). This pamphlet was published anonymously but later withdrawn, apparently with Place's agreement.

[79] Review of Covent Garden's *The Heir of Vironi*, *Examiner*, 9 March 1817, *Hazlitt* XVIII: 220–2, 221.

the managers achieve their political ends and 'brow-beat and bully' the riotous audiences into submission. In this 'administration of club-law', protesting spectators are expelled for 'disturbing the peace' and the theatre is packed with orders ('those impartial judges and distinguishers between right and wrong, their watermen, firemen, hack authors and box-lobby loungers') so as to intimidate the protestors. Hazlitt paints a disturbing picture of an insidious, seamless continuity between stage and Parliament, where protest – or, in the government's view, a 'treasonable conspiracy' – offers the governing elite a convenient excuse for the suspension of liberty.

The protests over Booth's contract shared certain assumptions and repertoires of crowd behaviour with the Old Price riots at Covent Garden. But the optimism of 1809 about restoring an old theatrical moral economy had been superseded in 1817 by a far more pessimistic and cynical view of the nature and purity of public institutions. Wooler's State Theatricals series, published in the *Black Dwarf*, reveal this change of tone. Here, ministers at the theatre of St Stephen have suspended *habeas corpus*, and banned seditious meetings, in order to thwart disorder and head off the threat of popular insurrection. The prime minister and members of his government appear in Wooler's satires as jugglers who have converted spies into patriots and common liars into truth-tellers. In one especially disturbing piece, these political performers act out their fears about sedition, using live cannon, on the gallery spectators. As Wooler ironically declares, 'the people are to be *really killed*, and *wounded* in the Manchester method: and in all cases nature will be copied as closely as possible'.[80] The State Theatricals series portrays government as an arbitrary sphere where truth and representation can no longer be distinguished; the Peterloo massacre thus becomes the ultimate triumph of the state's talent for appalling dramatic verisimilitude. As in Hazlitt's criticism, and Hone's pamphlets, theatre is a vital pedagogic tool for educating audiences about the political illusions which are perpetrated in the name of government.

For Anti-Jacobin critics, the preservation of monarchy and social hierarchy demanded the defence of the nation's dramatic traditions, and the methodical surveillance of theatrical culture for any signs of cultural and political subversion. In these accounts, illegitimate drama is construed as low, vulgar and worryingly conducive to the production of radical sentiment. Hazlitt's interpretations, by contrast, disrupt this

---

[80] 'Theatricals Extraordinary', *Black Dwarf*, 26 January 1820, 81.

simple correlation between illegitimacy, radicalism and vulgarity. In these arguments, as we have seen, legitimacy and illegitimacy are being mobilised for an impassioned debate about who should be represented in the theatrical and political states.

Illegitimate culture is therefore an unstable category which crosses the boundaries between institutions and indeed between genres. It connotes not only those plays being performed at the minor theatres, but also the controversial production of melodrama and spectacle at the Theatres Royal. As a category, illegitimacy is also crucially implicit in the polemical descriptions of theatrical culture being put forward by writers such as Wordsworth and Coleridge. In many ways, their assumptions about the barbaric and vulgar character of the illegitimate continue to underpin our critical ignorance about this period's theatre. But what kind of political, cultural and theatrical world did illegitimate theatre inaugurate? What did illegitimate genres make representable? Having explored the institutional structures surrounding late Georgian theatre in London, and the politics of cultural monopoly, we can now begin to consider the significance of illegitimate performance.

CHAPTER THREE

Illegitimate production

The dramaturgy, subjects and stage characters of illegitimate theatre constitute a revolution in theatrical representation. What interests me in this chapter are the plots and roles which this physical, visceral aesthetic brings into being. But although illegitimate production deserves attention for its own sake, some of these plays also raise interesting questions about the political character of production at the minor theatres. As we shall see, nervous legislators and horrified reviewers, hearing of the Surrey's dramatisation of the Weare murder (complete with the very gig and shovel used by the murderer) or the 'mania' for *Jack Sheppard* plays, were quick to classify the minor theatres as a transgressive domain. But to what extent is John Stephens right to suspect that playhouses beyond Westminster exercised unchecked 'a degree of political freedom that would certainly have horrified Colman if he ever took the trouble to attend performances'?[1] And what about the production of burlesque and pantomime within Westminster? How could a system of dramatic censorship based on the scrutiny of a dramatic text adequately regulate these spectacular, corporeal forms? Though only a limited number of tropes and characters can be explored here, my argument nonetheless challenges radically the apolitical reputation of the early nineteenth-century theatre.

GENRES

The foreign origins of burlesque, burletta, melodrama and pantomime had ensured their cultural position as genres carelessly dispossessed from definitions of legitimate culture. To some extent, then, illegitimate genres shared a common institutional marginality. A strong argument therefore exists for interpreting melodrama – a genre whose significance

---

[1] John Russell Stephens, *The Censorship of English Drama 1824–1901* (Cambridge University Press, 1980), 52.

as a paradigmatic cultural form in the period has recently attracted much critical attention[2] – in relation to these other theatrical forms, rather than in generic isolation. Moreover, the language of theatrical nomenclature, especially on minor playbills, is often vague, indistinct and gloriously arbitrary: a 'nondescript' gallimaufry of 'melo-dramatic burletta', 'operatic melodrama' and 'serio-comic pantomime' (to name but a few) worthy indeed of Shakespeare's Polonius.[3]

In production too, illegitimate forms frequently overlapped. Panto-mime actors such as Charles Farley (who played the mute role of Francisco in Thomas Holcroft's *A Tale of Mystery*, speaking 'his wrongs without a tongue' with 'an eloquence that was irresistible'),[4] Henry Johnstone (the star of John Fawcett's pantomimical drama, *Pérouse; or the Desolate Island*), Thérèse de Camp (a former pupil of Grimaldi senior at the Royal Circus, who played the dumb Theodore in *Deaf and Dumb*), Dubois (as Orson) and Grimaldi (as the Wild Man) all powerfully shaped the hyperbolic conventions of melodramatic acting. Whereas the patent houses retained separate companies for the production of comedy and tragedy, the mounting of illegitimate theatre was a far more haphazard and improvised business. Throughout the first two decades of the nineteenth century, therefore, pantomime, burletta and melodrama shared, exchanged and borrowed plots, characters and per-formers, jointly forging the conventions and iconography of theatrical illegitimacy.

Illegitimate theatre was never respectful of social and aesthetic dis-tinctions, nor indeed of cultural ownership. On the contrary, cannibal-istic adaptation, piracy and theft pervaded its writing and production. 'We are not over scrupulous', declares George Daniel, with more than a

---

[2] See especially Peter Brooks, *The Melodramatic Imagination: Balzac, Henry James, Melodrama, and the Mode of Excess* (New Haven: Yale University Press, 1976). This study has played a crucial role in revealing the significance of melodrama 'as a mode of conception and expression, as a certain fictional system for making sense of experience' (xii). Christopher Prendergast's monograph, *Balzac: Fiction and Melodrama* (London: Arnold, 1978) also offers a sophisticated and subtle account of melodramatic fiction and highlights in particular melodrama's 'unconscious connivance' with the fantasy of disorder (11). More recently, new historicist and materialist critics have turned their attention to the melodramatic character of public events. See especially Thomas Laqueur, 'The Queen Caroline Affair: Politics as Art in the Reign of George III', *Journal of Modern History* 54 (September 1982), 417–66, and Elaine Hadley, 'The Old Price Wars: Melodramatizing the Public Sphere in Early Nineteenth-Century England', *PMLA* 107 no. 3 (1992), 525–37. For a critique of this melodramatic turn, see my article, 'The Silence of New Historicism: A Mutinous Echo from 1830', *Nineteenth Century Theatre* 22 no. 2 (1996), 61–89.

[3] 'Nondescript' was a favourite ironic term to describe burlesque in this period. See playbills for *Melodrame Mad*, Surrey, 28 June 1819 and *Siamoraindianaboo*, Coburg, 18 January 1830.

[4] *Monthly Mirror*, November 1802, 342.

hint of irony, in his *Remarks* to *The Brigand Chief*, 'whence we derive our entertainment, whether by sly plagiarism, or open theft, – by translation, adaptation, or any other channel accessible to dramatic ingenuity'.[5] At the minor houses, these plays derived their plots from beggar books, recent murders, tales from periodicals (*Tales of my Landlord*), published poems (Southey's *Mary* and *Thalaba*, the spectacular dénouement of the latter featuring 'the Precipitation of Thalaba and Oneiza down the Cataract of Badelmandel, with their Miraculous Escape' and Byron's *Mazeppa*),[6] as well as from contemporary novels (often borrowed from the circulating library in dog-eared copies) by Mary Shelley, Fenimore Cooper, Walter Scott, Edward Bulwer-Lytton and W.H. Ainsworth. France, too, provided a fertile hunting-ground for ambitious minor lessees eager for a new sensation: managers like Astley would travel to Paris to obtain at greatest speed the latest fashionable boulevard play, while lowly hack authors methodically raided the dramas of Guilbert de Pixérécourt and Eugène Scribe.

The impropriety of much illegitimate theatre arises in part from its insouciant disregard for cultural property of all kinds. Such practices, not to mention the prevalence of adaptations from the French and German theatre, only served to confirm the drama's alleged degradation.[7] Yet many of these translations, 'broken remnants' from a French kitchen though they may be, play surprising and disconcerting variations across the plots and ideological design of their parent texts. Appropriation, then, became a process by which the authority of an existing narrative may be implicitly questioned or pointedly reinvented. Rather than castigating illegitimate plays as dully derivative, we need to recognise the sleights of hand which such adaptations often performed in the interstices of narratives not their own.

The devouring, almost bloodthirsty character of illegitimate theatre was not limited to the ceaseless consumption of textual food in the form of plays, poems and narratives. Melodrama and burlesque also delighted in the self-conscious incorporation of recognisable images and

---

[5] J. R. Planché, *The Brigand Chief*, *CBT* xxiv.

[6] Coburg playbill, 14 August 1823. *Mazeppa* was first performed at the Coburg in 1823. Critics and audiences praised the scene in which the wild horse runs off, with Cassimir lashed naked to his back, as 'one of most striking effect; the effect of the platforms, and of the horse's run, produce a unique and interesting *coup d'œil*' (*Drama*, November 1823, 193). Ducrow's hit production of *Mazeppa* (Astley's, 1831), featuring a spectacular panorama, was frequently revived.

[7] On the prevalence of translation as a cause of the drama's 'decline', see the comments about Henry Harris' adaptation, *The Forest of Bondy*, in the *Theatrical Inquisitor*, October 1814, 5: 264. For the impact of translations on the commercial value of original plays, see Douglas Jerrold's remarks, SC 2832–4.

musical sounds from a variety of sources. The realisation of pictures on stage, for example, was one of melodrama's most characteristic devices. Dennis Lawler's play, *Industry and Idleness* (Surrey, 1811) which recreated Hogarth's *Apprentices* and Douglas Jerrold's *Rent Day* (Surrey, 1832), based on Wilkie's eponymous image, are only two instances of those dramatic tableaux, skilfully crafted from the momentary stillness of human bodies, which pervade illegitimate theatre.[8] Moreover, in the introduction of well-known music, from Handel airs to old, familiar ballads, rousing choruses and favourite naval hornpipes, melodrama and burlesque drew attention to their own *pasticchio* construction, representing their dramaturgy as the ingenious improvisation of disparate, often incongruous parts. Moncrieff's *Tom and Jerry*, for instance, cleverly incorporated parlour songs, popular dance tunes and folksong, as well as waltzes and airs, notably from *Don Giovanni*.[9] The realisation and subsequent dissolution of images, like the appropriation and disfiguring of songs, seems to foreground the contingency of cultural order in illegitimate theatre, the susceptibility of images and texts to ironic, even arbitrary quotation and deformation.

The *pasticchio* effects characteristic of this culture often presented audiences with irreconcilable clashes and unresolved dissonances. As Jacky Bratton has observed, plots and subplots in melodrama are frequently intercut and interwoven in melodrama with almost cinematic results.[10] The ambivalent effects which such incongruous juxtapositions produce may account for that dangerous moral agnosticism for which critics obliquely condemned melodrama. 'This order of entertainment,' declared the *Monthly Magazine*, 'pretends to no belief. It has no faith of any kind. It aims to inculcate no truth.' Whereas legitimate drama refines and elevates, melodrama's position as the decadent and degraded antitype of tragedy in British theatrical history can be attributed in part to the sheer moral doubtfulness of its piecemeal aesthetic.[11]

---

[8] See Martin Meisel, *Realizations: Narrative, Pictorial, and Theatrical Arts in Nineteenth-Century England* (Princeton University Press, 1983), chapter 7.

[9] See the persuasive claims made by Janet T. Shepherd in her fine unpublished dissertation, 'The Relationship between Music, Text and Performance in English Popular Theatre 1790–1840', D.Phil thesis, London University, 1991.

[10] See 'British Heroism and the Structure of Melodrama' in *Acts of Supremacy: The British Empire and the Stage, 1790–1830* (Manchester University Press, 1991), 18–61. Bratton persuasively argues that melodrama 'negotiated its ideological positions by the dramatic manipulation of juxtaposition rather than by any more explicit or rationalised process' (23).

[11] 'The English Stage', *Monthly Magazine*, 1842, 2: 199. Cf. the anonymous preface to Arnold's *The Woodman's Hut*, Oxberry IV, which claims that melodrama 'neither exalts nor refines the imagination'.

Melodrama and pantomime also shared other characteristics. As we have seen, the prohibition of dialogue at the minor theatres had encouraged the evolution of a dramaturgy which foregrounded visible and musical signs. This transformation, however, cannot be understood in terms of legal expediency alone. Rather, the iconography of illegitimacy participated in a broader cultural and scientific transformation in which the human body began to be understood as an eloquent compendium of visible signs. Treatises on chironomia, or the art of gesture, for example, presented a radically new perspective on the art of declamation and public speaking, whether in a courtroom or on a stage. Gesture and expression now came to be perceived as indispensable parts of rhetoric; indirectly, such texts also served to legitimate the expressive, physiological language of the body in illegitimate performance. In their emphasis on the physiological basis of gesture (tears of grief, the paleness of fear) and the silent copiousness of the human hands, these treatises defined theatrical performance as the laboratory of gestural expression. According to Gilbert Austin, those who wished to learn the power of gesture to communicate thoughts independently of language should study the silent art of pantomime.[12] The idea of a wordless language of signs which might constitute 'the exterior and visible signs of our bodies' thus underpinned contemporary definitions about the art of modern eloquence;[13] the most dynamic expression of that eloquence could be found in the production of illegitimate theatre.

Psychological theories of the passions, the dissemination of new ideas about physiognomy (as galvanist scientists revealed the body's own corporeal sign system of gasps, blinks, tremors and twitches) and rhetorical treatises promising to reduce 'to scientific principles the art of public speaking', all stimulated public interest in the external, non-verbal expression of human emotion.[14] Practical guides to rhetoric and manuals for performers in this period described gesture as an elaborate, precise and highly codified system. Specific attitudes signified 'fallen greatness', 'hopeless love' or 'vulgar astonishment';[15] writers carefully explained how the body positioned itself in relation to objects of 'desire' and 'aversion'. Manuals of gesture also included advice about the sounds characteristic of intense emotion (choleric speech, for example

---

[12] Revd. Gilbert Austin, *Chironomia; or, A Treatise on Rhetorical Delivery* (London: T. Cadell, 1806), 251.
[13] Henry Siddons, *Practical Illustrations of Rhetorical Gesture and Action, adapted to the English Drama*, adapted from Engel (London: Richard Phillips, 1807), 27.
[14] *Ibid.*, Advertisement. See also Joseph R. Roach, *The Player's Passion: Studies in the Science of Acting* (Newark: University of Delaware Press, 1985), 173–4.   [15] *Practical Illustrations*, 376.

'rolls like an impetuous torrent'),[16] and about the violent effects of feeling on the body. Grief, for instance, 'expresses itself by beating the head or forehead, tearing the hair, and catching the breath, as if choking; also by screaming, weeping, stamping with the feet, lifting the eyes from time to time to heaven, and hurrying backwards and for-wards', whilst vexation 'agitates the whole frame' and malice 'sets the jaws, or gnashes with the teeth'.[17] Though such descriptions also influenced the writing and performance of tragedy and comedy (see for example Joanna Baillie's striking discussion of 'those feelings, whose irregular bursts, abrupt transitions, sudden pauses, and half-uttered sug-gestions, scorn all harmony of measured verse'),[18] it was illegitimate genres – and especially the violent gestures of melodrama – which gave this hyperbolic iconography its most spectacular expression.[19]

The emergence of these genres also brought into being new kinds of dramatic character. Some, like the villainous Romaldi in *A Tale of Mystery*, are in possession of some secret still to be revealed; others like Luke the Labourer, his finger-ends as cold as 'flakes of ice' (ii.ii.33), are driven by a bitter vengeance not yet understood. Psychological pain here acquires a dynamic bodily form: in Buckstone's play, Luke's desire for revenge is represented as a compulsion to express something buried and yet irrepressible – the explosion or physical 'bursting' of a long silent grievance.[20] Not only did these trembling, agitated bodies unwittingly disclose unspoken, unspeakable emotions, but the visceral representa-tion of evil also produced sympathetic physical responses among spec-tators. The reception of Buckstone's drama again provides a good example. Luke's 'harsh and inveterate passion' and unshrinking blood-thirstiness, remarked one reviewer, 'were pourtrayed with a force and truth that frequently made portions of the audience shudder with alarm and dismay'. Such accounts alert us to the way in which a skilled melo-dramatic performer like Daniel Terry might elicit from spectators a

---

[16] *Ibid.*, 266.
[17] *The Thespian Preceptor; or, A Full Display of the Scenic Art* (London: J. Roach 1811), 32–9. See also Leman T. Rede, *The Road to the Stage; or, The Performer's Preceptor* (London: Joseph Smith, 1827).
[18] 'Introductory Discourse', *A Series of Plays; in which it is attempted to delineate the stronger passions of the mind, each passion being the subject of a tragedy and a comedy* (1798–1812, reprinted Oxford: Woodstock Books, 1990), 31.
[19] On the fear of melodramatic violence invading legitimate drama, see Edward Mayhew, *Stage Effect: or, the Principles which Command Dramatic Success in the Theatre* (London: C. Mitchell, 1840). Michael Booth's appendix to *English Melodrama* (London: Herbert Jenkins, 1965) provides a useful introduction to melodramatic acting.
[20] *CMT* ii i.ii 21 and i.iii. Compare the wild language of the 'bursting heart' in John Haines' melo-drama, *The Idiot Witness, DBT* v, iii.i. 23.

visceral mirror of those shocks and bodily jolts characteristic of fear, terror and distress.[21]

The body's usurpation of language as emotional text in illegitimate theatre can be traced in that trope of melodramatic plotting, derived from medieval romance, whereby the body's silent inscriptions, in the form of scars or marks, will prove an individual's biological identity where no language can persuade. Just as identity can be established in melodrama only by visible signs (Eugenia, the mute Unknown Female in Dimond's *The Foundling of the Forest*, for instance, recognises her son Florian by the scars on his hand), so the language of melodrama represents moral qualities as if they were tangible entities: for Paul in Haines' drama, *The Idiot Witness* (Coburg, 1823), innocence is itself a 'cargo'.[22] By the same token, domestic and nautical melodrama follow and also develop the conventions of Gothic in their depiction of the physical vulnerability of the human body, especially the female body, to violation, incarceration and psychological destruction.

Lady Emma Hamilton's fluid, balletic postures, the nineteenth-century craze for *tableaux vivants*, Andrew Ducrow's spectacular *poses plastiques équestres* at Astley's – in which the performer struck attitudes on horseback depicting Mercury, a Roman gladiator or Hercules struggling with the Nemean lion – all confirm that pervasive fascination in late Georgian culture with the wordless depiction of dramatic character.[23] Mute performance is one of illegitimate theatre's most evocative forms of expression. Many of the period's most talented performers – Céline Céleste, Charles Farley, Joseph Grimaldi and indeed Ducrow – were, above all, artists of mime. The silent eloquence of mute performers also provides another interesting link between theatrical culture and Romantic literature (see the language of the inarticulate in Wordsworth's solitary figures, for example).

The description of Ducrow in the role of Mercury, included amongst the sketches which make up *Noctes Ambrosianae*, provides some useful insights into the pleasures of mute production. As Mercury's flight accelerates, Timothy Tickler explains admiringly, Ducrow's horse seems to

---

[21] Unidentified review of J. B. Buckstone, *Luke the Labourer* (Adelphi, 1826), Adelphi cuttings book, Theatre Museum, 22 October 1826.   [22] *Idiot Witness*, III.i. 22.

[23] Ducrow's equestrian scenes, performed in the circle at Astley's, were based on poses from classical statuary. His most famous characters included 'Ajax defeating the Lightning', 'The Vicissitudes of a Tar' (in which he represented his horse as a ship complete with telescopes, window and an anchor) and 'The Death of Othello'. Ducrow also played the mute boy in the Royal Circus production of *The Dog of Montargis*. See A. H. Saxon, *The Life and Art of Andrew Ducrow and the Romantic Age of the English Circus* (Hamden, Conn.: Archon, 1978). On the art of monodrama, see Kirsten Gram Hölmstrom, *Monodrama, Attitude, Tableaux Vivants: Studies on Some Trends of Theatrical Fashion 1770–1815* (Stockholm: Almquist and Wiksell, 1967).

disappear 'if not from the sight of our bodily eye, certainly from that of our imagination, and we behold but the messenger of Jove, worthy to be joined in marriage with Iris'.[24] Watching Ducrow, in other words, allowed the imagination momentarily to transcend the tyranny of the eye. In these skilful juxtapositions of stasis and dynamic motion, Ducrow's 'poetical impersonations' seemed to reveal the capacity for metamorphosis within a single human body.

The primacy of rhetoric and the spoken word in legitimate drama gave way in melodrama and pantomime to a corporeal dramaturgy which privileged the galvanic, affective capacity of the human body as a vehicle of dramatic expression. Jerrold's striking definition of the illegitimate as a drama based on a physical, rather than a mental aesthetic, implicitly recognises the subordinate position of verbal expression in this culture.[25] Again, important parallels and connections exist between illegitimate dramaturgy and the culture of European Romanticism. Rousseau's interpretation of gesture as a form of prelapsarian speech, for example (not to mention his fascination with music as an independent semiotic system and his evolution of a dramatic form which incorporated music, pantomimic gesture, dance and speech), represents a sophisticated and self-conscious precedent for the contingent and untheorised dramaturgy emerging in early nineteenth-century British theatre.[26]

The controversial status of melodrama and pantomime stems in part from their dangerous, questionably effeminate dissolution of language into music. Indeed, the interfusion of music and speech in pantomime, and especially in melodrama, was one important feature of what we might tentatively call an illegitimate aesthetic. As we have seen, John Cross' dumbshow productions had pioneered a style of musical production which became codified in melodrama as a stock expressive repertoire of 'hurry', 'storm' and 'agitato' played by the orchestra.[27] From an

---

[24] *Noctes Ambrosianae* no. 54, *Blackwood's Edinburgh Magazine*, February 1831, 29: 263–84.
[25] SC 2843.
[26] See *Discours sur l'origine et les fondements de l'inegalité* (1754) in Rousseau, *Œuvres Complètes*, 5 vols. (Paris: Gallimard, 1959–95), III. In its interweaving of spoken soliloquy, pantomime and orchestral accompaniment, *Pygmalion* (first performed 1770) puts into dramatic practice Rousseau's theory about the expressive capacity of gesture. Cf. *Fragmens d'Observations sur l'Alceste italien de M. le Chevalier Gluck* (1774) in *Œuvres Complètes*, V: 448, where Rousseau coins the term *melodrame* to describe 'un genre de drame, dans lequel les paroles et la Musique, au lieu de marcher ensemble, se font entendre successivement'.
[27] David Mayer's essay is the best introduction to this subject. See 'The music of melodrama' in James Bradby *et al.*, eds., *Performance and Politics in Popular Drama* (Cambridge University Press, 1980), 49–63 and J. T. Shepherd, 'Music, Text, Performance'.

early stage, melodramatic characters actually spoke their lines accompanied by music.[28] In Peake's dramatisation of *Frankenstein*, Fritz 'speaks through music' his terrified recognition that the monster is alive; De Lacey similarly appeals through music to 'Gracious Heaven' when the monster rescues Agatha from the rivulet.[29] This blending of language and musical sound required performers to adopt a heightened emotional pitch and register, and imbued the dramatisation of extreme psychological states with a peculiar power and quasi-supernatural intensity. In illegitimate production, then, the performer's body had become a complex gestural script to be interpreted through the language of music.

MUTE BUSINESS

The displacement of language in melodrama, its skeletal thinness and scarcity, became a frequent subject of mockery and derision amongst reviewers and critics. The anonymous preface to Samuel Arnold's *The Woodman's Hut* alludes in quietly ironic fashion to the way in which melodrama 'places characters in striking situations . . . and carefully avoids encumbering them with language'.[30] Here, melodrama's corporeal dramaturgy seems to entail a corresponding freedom from the burden of language, as if words might physically inhibit the characters' actions. (The satirical vivacity of Grimaldi's pantomime, as we shall see in chapter 7, depends on the exotic, intense rarity of spoken language.) 'Nothing can be more disagreeable,' declared the *London Magazine* critic, 'than that mixture of talk and dumb show, which we see in some of our Melo-dramas. We wish either the words or the distortions away, and we don't much mind which.'[31] Melodrama's 'mummery' – the apparent usurpation of language and rhetoric by hyperbolic action and expression – epitomised the cultural lowness and aesthetic spuriousness of illegitimate theatre.

In melodrama, language often freezes into apostrophe, deitic claptraps and stiffly formulaic phrases – ''Tis there!'; 'Behold!' with hands

---

[28] On the musical dramaturgy of Holcroft's *Tale of Mystery*, see the *Monthly Mirror*, 342: 'The trees are represented in actual motion from the storm which, with the accompanying music, is well suited to Romaldi's state of mind, whose dreadful guilt has made him a fit object both of earthly and divine vengeance.' The organist Thomas Busby composed the music for Holcroft's play.

[29] R. B. Peake, *Presumption; or, The Fate of Frankenstein*, Dicks 431 I.iii.6; II.v.11, with music by Watson.

[30] [Samuel Arnold], *The Woodman's Hut*, Oxberry IV. Compare Dramaticus (pseud.), *An Impartial View of the Stage* (London: Chapple, 1816), 8; Preface to Moncrieff, *The Ravens of Orléans*, CMT I.

[31] January 1821, 3: 36.

uplifted, or fingers outstretched in fearsome indictments of villainy. *Obi*, John Fawcett's abolitionist serio-pantomime, performed at the Haymarket in 1800, with music by Samuel Arnold, abounds in stylised, mute ceremony. The play opens with a view of an extensive sugar plantation in Jamaica where two female slaves sing of the white man's gold (which buys negro liberty, and separates men from their homeland), but also describe the institution of slavery as a benign form of paternalism which may partly compensate for this painful loss: 'But if white man kind massa be, / He heal the wound in negro's heart.'

The main threat to the plantation's security is represented by Obi, also known as three-finger'd Jack, a vengeful runaway slave. After a rousing chorus, the loyal slaves take solemn oaths to kill three-finger'd Jack and thereby gain their own freedom; after the clergyman has blessed this enterprise, they are solemnly presented with guns and sabres. The dramatisation of slavery in late Georgian drama is a fascinating subject in itself, but what interests me here is why Fawcett should have presented the story of *Obi* as a pantomime. In many ways, the absence of spoken dialogue seems to highlight the danger posed by three-fingered Jack to the plantation's economy (see the silent depiction of the Planter's 'great agitation' when he sees the Captain's hat and gun lying on the ground). Whilst the negroes' songs express gratitude to their paternalist master, Jack's demonic yells create a discordant pattern of anarchic sounds which loudly threatens the plantation's survival.[32] At the same time, however, Obi's muteness helps to make him a figure of inarticulate pathos (see, for instance, his moments of gentleness towards Rosa when he 'observes her youth, pauses, and her entreaties seem to make some impression upon him', II.iii) as well as an anarchic threat. The dramaturgy of pantomime thus transforms the political subject of abolition into a diagrammatic yet highly intense corporeal discourse; what is also noticeable about *Obi* is the way in which pantomime holds in tension, rather than attempting to resolve, these powerful ideological oppositions about the meaning and subjects of slavery.

Pantomime and melodrama invested that which is seen and made visible with a moral power which far outweighed that of words. Moreover, the possession or loss of language often functions as a sign of evil or innocence respectively. Rhetorical skill and linguistic power tend to connote duplicity and deceit, a sophisticated tangle of words which – like the law – the poor and the wronged struggle to unravel. In mute

---

[32] John Fawcett, *Obi; or, Three-Finger'd Jack*, *DBT* LIX.

figures such as the abandoned boy, Theodore, in Holcroft's *Deaf and Dumb* (who communicates by signs 'rapid, almost, as thought itself' 1.ii.12), or Eloi in *The Dog of Montargis*, innocence is pointedly located within the silent eloquence and expressive economy of bodily gesture.

Thomas Holcroft's melodramas provide a fascinating example of this theme. In the last two decades of the eighteenth century, Holcroft, a shoemaker and stable-boy turned journalist and political activist, was one of Britain's leading playwrights; his most successful plays included comedies such as *Duplicity* (Covent Garden, 1781) and his jovial, benevolent play, *The Road to Ruin* (Covent Garden, 1792). But Holcroft's radicalism – he was amongst those prosecuted and acquitted of treason in 1794 – profoundly damaged his career in the theatre. Though audiences had applauded the democratic sentiments expressed in *The Road to Ruin*, Holcroft's later plays, including *Love's Frailties* (Covent Garden, 1794) and especially *Knave or Not* (Covent Garden, 1798), were greeted with suspicion and intense political hostility. Later that year, the disillusioned playwright decided to emigrate to Hamburg, and later went to live in Paris. Whilst in exile, Holcroft tried to make ends meet by preparing translations of two popular French melodramas which subsequently appeared on the British stage.

Both these plays seem to endow the subject of muteness with a powerful political subtext. In *Deaf and Dumb* (Drury Lane, 1801), Holcroft dramatised the story of a dumb boy whose fortune is finally restored to him through the intervention of the Abbé L'Epée (the historical pioneer of a gestural alphabet for the deaf). What is noticeable about this adaptation of Bouilly's play is that muteness becomes a political as much as a semiotic condition.[33] From the beginning, Holcroft reveals Darlemont's palace to be a place of oppressive secrecy, suspicion and deceitful signs. In the very first scene, the audience sees a 'whole length portrait of a boy' which hangs in the centre of the room. Commissioned by Darlemont as a duplicitous sign of affection for the boy whom he abandoned and left for dead in the Parisian night, the picture comes to represent the impossibility of buying silence and keeping even the powerless bound in 'mutual slavery'. 'How dare you hint at what must be eternally concealed?' Darlemont asks Dupré, his servant (1.i.12). Holcroft's use of

---

[33] Thomas Holcroft, *Deaf and Dumb: or, The Orphan Protected* (London: J. Ridgway, 1801), adapted from J. N. Bouilly, *L'Abbé de l'Epée*, first performed in 1800. Kotzebue also produced an adaptation of Bouilly's drama and this was first performed in 1803. Benjamin Thompson's important collection *The German Theatre* (London: Vernor, Hood and Sharpe, 1811), III, includes a translation of Kotzebue's play.

the picture as a visual image of duplicity, like his striking emphasis on Darlemont's slow and paralysing remorse, highlights the psychological burden of murderous secrecy. Through these variations on Bouilly's drama, Holcroft suggests that muteness constitutes a political experience as much as a physical disability. Indeed, Holcroft was no doubt attracted to this play precisely because it offered an idealistic counterpoint to that suppression of political opposition taking place in Britain.

Muteness is also at the heart of Holcroft's *A Tale of Mystery* (Covent Garden, 1802). In this adaptation of Pixérécourt's *Coelina*, Holcroft actually expunges much of the play's original dialogue, and substitutes the silent dramaturgy of pantomime. How can we account for this transformation? Had Holcroft admired the skill and dexterity of mute performers like Mlles Quériau and Soissons whom he had watched performing at the Ambigu and the Gaîté? Might Holcroft's dramaturgy have been influenced by the work of a social theorist and melodramatist such as Rousseau? To what extent was Holcroft attempting to cash in on the vogue for dumbshow performance in London? We know all too little about the impact of continental playgoing on Holcroft's dramatic practice. Nevertheless, as Holcroft pared away the language of *Coelina*, the moral, legal and hereditary order of Pixérécourt's play began to disintegrate.

What seems to have perplexed Holcroft in *A Tale of Mystery* is the retribution of the state. In Pixérécourt's drama, the capture of the villainous Trugelin (whose various crimes and evil machinations include the responsibility for rendering his own brother dumb), provides the catalyst for political and moral restoration. Here, Pixérércourt carefully differentiates the peasants' desire for vengeance from that legitimate punishment which is the prerogative of law.[34] Holcroft's version of moral and political restoration, however, is rather different. In *A Tale of Mystery*, the arrest of Romaldi (the Trugelin character) is carried out not by the French police, but by 'archers'. Though this word is actually a literal translation from the French, the archers also seem to represent a form of political obfuscation, deliberately rendering as vague as possible the state's moral role in the punishment of individuals. The divided sympathies of Francisco and Selina towards Romaldi are also significant. Francisco, the most immediate victim of his brother's treachery, nonetheless tries to help Romaldi to escape; later, he and Selina place them-

---

[34] 'Mes amis, laissez aux lois le soin de nous venger', Dufour tells the peasants, and then instructs the officer, 'Faites votre devoir'. The police duly lead the injured Trugelin away. See Pixérécourt, *Théâtre Choisi*, 4 vols. (Geneva: Slatkine Reprints, 1971), I, III.xi.70.

selves as shields between the fallen, now remorseful, villain and the combatants.

Through these alterations, Holcroft encourages the audience to perceive Romaldi as a figure of pity, as well as a criminal. The final pantomimic scene of *A Tale* therefore resists spectators' desire for moral judgements. Indeed, what fascinates Holcroft about melodrama is the genre's capacity to encode such contradictions. For whereas the conventions of sentimental comedy demanded that benevolence should reign triumphant, melodrama helps to make possible a more dynamic and nuanced view of human nature. Moreover, mute characters such as Theodore enable Holcroft to create what is in fact a political drama about the possession and the loss (or censorship) of speech.

A recurring theme in melodrama, and one of the important subjects dramatised by illegitimate theatre, is the questionable authority of the law, and, more generally, of the state.[35] Mute characters often embody the failure of law to prevent the tyranny of the powerful over the powerless; false accusation is another important trope in these plays.[36] Many nautical and domestic plays also explore the abuse of trust and authority by those in power. Whereas, in *A Tale of Mystery*, the character of Fiametta dramatises the final triumph of 'blunt fidelity and loquacious benevolence',[37] the nature of such recognition is far more doubtful in the ironic dramaturgy of Douglas Jerrold. Here, the dénouements offer no easy reassurance that truthfulness and honesty will finally defeat injustice and oppression. On the contrary, Jerrold exploits the artificiality of melodramatic conventions to draw attention to their sheer, delusory fictionality.

I want to turn now to the wild man, one of the most important mute characters in illegitimate theatre.[38] London fairs in the eighteenth century had already made familiar as a commercial spectacle the wild man's savage primitivism and superhuman strength. Then, during the

---

[35] See for example the sceptical irony expressed by Storm ('What does it avail us that he beats our enemies abroad, while he extends his power to wretches who use it to increase our miseries at home?', i. i) and also by Flutterman, the comic burgomaster, in James Kenney's melodrama, *Ella Rosenberg* (Drury Lane, 1807), *CBT* xxvii.

[36] See for example J. B. Buckstone, *Peter Bell the Waggoner; or, Murderers of Massiac*, Dicks 862 (Coburg, 1826); John Haines, *Alice Grey, The Suspected One* Lacy xliv (Surrey, 1839). Cf. the images of law in Jerrold's *Black-Ey'd Susan* (Surrey, 1829), in which William compares the law to a ship 'of green timber, manned with lob-lolly boys' and 'provisioned with mouldy biscuit' (ii.i).   [37] *Monthly Mirror*, November 1802, 342.

[38] Muteness in British theatre seems to have more varied meanings than is typical of the French melodramatic tradition. On the theme of muteness in Pixérécourt's drama, cf. Peter Brooks, *Melodramatic Imagination*, chapters 1 and 2, and J. Paul Marcoux, *Guilbert de Pixérécourt: French Melodrama in the Early Nineteenth Century* (New York: Peter Lang, 1992).

1790s, this tradition began to be taken up at Sadler's Wells, as we can trace in Thomas Dibdin's *Valentine and Orson* (Sadler's Wells, 1794). In Dibdin's version of the medieval romance about a pair of twin brothers, separated at birth, Orson's violent destructiveness becomes a political threat; see for example the opening scene, where the peasants are pleading for assistance. Another striking feature of this highly successful play – which soon passed into the patent repertoire, and was staged all over Britain for decades – is Orson's willingness to be subjected to human control. At the end of Act I, for instance, Valentine places a cord around Orson's hands and the wild man eventually allows himself to be led away.[39] In Dibdin's play, the story of Orson seems to acquire imperial overtones, to become a political drama in which the savage man meekly consents to European rule in exchange for romantic happiness and the accoutrements of civility.

The patent theatres were quick to recognise the commercial potential of mute savagery. In 1804, Jean Baptiste Dubois, the Sadler's Wells' clown, played the part of Orson at Covent Garden and, according to J. P. Malcolm, 'exhibited very dexterously the rude naïveté, agility, and strength, that should characterise the savage', as well as displaying 'a thorough insight into human nature debased'.[40] Interestingly, the role then passed from one generation of Sadler's Wells clowns to another. Joseph Grimaldi's Orson (strongly influenced by Dubois, who coached him in the role), brought him lavish praise from 'persons ranking high in his own profession, in literature, and in the fine arts'.[41] The role also lay very close to Grimaldi's heart. So wrought up would Grimaldi become during these performances, claimed Charles Dickens, that he would be found between acts in his dressing-room, sobbing in 'violent and agonising' spasms of feeling.[42] Dickens's inclusion of this miniature narrative of histrionic sensibility highlights the way in which the dramatisation of savagery seemed to hold in perilous tension violent tenderness and innocent destructiveness, the gentle and the diabolical.

In Charles Dibdin's aquatic romance, *The Wild Man* (Sadler's Wells, 1809), created as a mute vehicle for Grimaldi, we can trace similar, imperial preoccupations. Dibdin's play also emphasises the creature's savage strength, agility and mute, gestural eloquence. The Wild Man chases

---

[39] Thomas Dibdin, *Valentine and Orson*, *CBT* XXVII, I.iv.19.
[40] Unidentified review, Covent Garden file, Theatre Museum; J. P. Malcolm, *Londinium Redivivum* II: 236.
[41] [Charles Dickens] *Memoirs of Joseph Grimaldi*, edited by 'Boz' (London: William Nicholson, 1884), 136–7.   [42] *Ibid.*

after a boar, and soon reappears, having nonchalantly torn off the animal's leg; his heroic strength is demonstrated by his rescue of Adolphus (the son of Prince Artuff), from being drowned by Muley, the Moorish usurper. In the play's most celebrated scene, the Wild Man silently *consents* to his own submission. First astonished, and then 'quite softened' by the sound of Artuff's silver flute, the Wild Man's emotions mirror the music's successive moods of joy, passion and ferocity. After dancing with delight, he 'throws himself at Artuff's feet, and acknowledges himself subdued by him'.[43]

The subduing of the Wild Man seems to represent the making of empire as a process of benevolent domination: the savage monster consents to the reasoned moral superiority of the imperial state. Moreover, Charles Dibdin also provides a visual correlative for the threat posed by savage anarchy. The opening scene depicts a smoking volcano at daybreak; the volcano's moving lava, reflected in the water, 'exhibits a lurid, igneous hue'. The Wild Man then comes out of the cave, 'seems delighted with the eruption of the Volcano, and expresses his delight by outré antics and a kind of chattering' (i.i). In this scene, the smoking volcano – a characteristic piece of Sadler's Wells trickery – seems to evoke a form of natural ferocity beyond the control of human beings. The volcano's lurking menace, and the Wild Man's delight in its power, silently confirm the moral rightness of subduing his savage violence.

The legacy of the wild man can be traced in a variety of plays. The 'horrible' sublimity of T. P. Cooke's vampires and monsters, for example, has its origins in the dramaturgy of savage muteness. After serving with the Navy in the Napoleonic wars, Cooke had joined the Royalty theatre, and soon became one of London's most famous melodramatic performers. In supernatural plays such as Planché's hit drama, *The Vampyre* (English Opera House, 1820) – in which the Vampyre memorably regrets drawing human blood – and Fitzball's nautical burletta, *The Flying Dutchman* (Adelphi, 1826), the figure of the wild man provided an iconographic blueprint for the dramatisation of supernatural terror.[44] Like the wild man, Vanderdecken and the Vampyre display corporeal agility, tender solicitude and mute expressiveness, especially under the influence of music. Hazlitt particularly admired Cooke's 'spirited and imposing'

---

43 Charles Dibdin, *The Wild Man*, *CMT* II, i.v.22. The wild man is a popular character in illegitimate theatre. See, *inter alia*, Hartland's dance, 'The Wild Boy' (undated Sadler's Wells bill for 1812, Theatre Museum) and Charles Dibdin's pantomime, *Harlequin Wild Man; or, The Rival Genii* (Sadler's Wells, 1814).

44 Edward Fitzball, *The Flying Dutchman; or, The Phantom Ship*, *CMT* II; J. R. Planché, *The Vampyre; or, The Bride of the Isles*, *CBT* XXVII.

portrayal of the Vampire; the *British Stage* also praised Cooke's extraordinary melodramatic vigour.[45] Supernatural monstrosity was depicted in these plays as both human and alien, powerfully destructive and yet poignantly susceptible to tender feeling.

Understanding the ideological contradictions at the heart of illegitimate savagery also enables us better to understand the stage history of *Frankenstein*, for the adaptations of Mary Shelley's novel made by Richard Brinsley Peake and Henry Milner are notable for their appropriation of the wild man's mute eloquence. Not surprisingly, Peake's *Presumption; or, The Fate of Frankenstein* took the English Opera House by storm in 1823. 'The audience crowd to it, hiss it, hail it, shudder at it, loath it, dream of it, and come again to it', wrote a reviewer for the *London Magazine*. 'The piece has been damned by full houses night after night, but the moment it is withdrawn, the public call it up again – and yearn to tremble before it.'[46] Three years later, the Coburg created a similar sensation when it produced Milner's adaptation, a 'Peculiar Romantic Melo-Dramatic Pantomimic Spectacle' entitled *The Man and the Monster! or, The Fate of Frankenstein*, starring the celebrated performer of supernatural roles, 'O' Smith.[47]

According to certain literary critics, the *Frankenstein* plays naively simplify Mary Shelley's novel, portraying the monster as a creature of brute, primitive force, and Frankenstein as a godless, presumptive scientist.[48] But what such arguments tend to neglect is that the iconographic legacy of the wild man complicates these apparent oppositions. The monster's speechlessness (a marked departure from Mary Shelley's novel, of course) is crucial to this production of ambivalence, for the dramaturgy of muteness highlights the creature's capacity for intense feeling and psychological pain. The actor T. P. Cooke obviously succeeded in capturing the subtle combinations of pathos and violence demanded by this part. As the *London Magazine*'s reviewer declared, Thomas Potter Cooke

---

[45] *London Magazine*, September 1820, *Hazlitt* XVIII: 364; *British Stage, and Literary Cabinet*, September 1820, 4: 270.   [46] *London Magazine*, September 1823, 322–3.

[47] *DBT* II. The Coburg play was founded jointly on Mary Shelley's novel and a French piece, *Le Magicien et le Monstre*. On the controversy surrounding the *Frankenstein* plays, see the *Theatrical Observer*, 9 August 1823. The reviewer quotes a placard which warns, 'Do not go to the Lyceum to see the monstrous Drama, founded on the improper work called "Frankenstein".' The plays also spawned a series of burlesques, including *Dr Frankenstein and his Son* (Surrey, 1823) and *Another Piece of Presumption* (Adelphi, 1823).

[48] See especially Albert J. Lavalley, 'The Stage and Film Children of Frankenstein: A Survey', in George Levine and U. C. Knoepflmacher, eds., *The Endurance of Frankenstein: Essays on Mary Shelley's Novel* (Berkeley: University of California, 1979), 243–89, 246–50. Cp. Louis James' fine essay, 'Frankenstein's Monster in Two Traditions' in Stephen Bann, ed., *Frankenstein, Creation and Monstrosity* (London: Reaktion Books, 1994), 77–94.

'has proved himself to be the very best pantomimic actor on the stage. He never speaks; – but his action and his looks are more than eloquent' (September 1823, 8:323).

The monster's abrupt transitions between demonic violence and gentle tenderness, and his susceptibility to the power of music, are also reminiscent of the wild man. According to the *British Stage*, Cooke 'powerfully embodied the horrible, bordering on the sublime or awful'. His exhibition of 'great strength, of towering gait, and of reckless cruelty, contrasted with the fiend's astonishment on hearing a "concord of sweet sounds," and on beholding female forms . . . was masterly and characteristic.'[49] In *Presumption*, the creature delicately attempts to possess the sound of Felix's flute for itself:

> The Monster . . . stands amazed and pleased, looks around him, snatches at the empty air, and with clenched hands puts them to each ear – appears ve his disappointment in not possessing the sound; rushes forward again listens, and, delighted with the sound, steals off, catchi hands. (II.iii.9)

Similarly, in Milner's drama, the sound of Em charms the monster to excitement, tears and then ght. When the music ends, the creature lies down, sub foot of the rock to which, in its bitterness and alienation, it ha ned Emmeline.

To some extent, *The Man and the Monster* transforms Mary Shelley's novel into a quasi-political drama about rebellion against an autocratic power. In the play, the monster storms into the Prince's palace, dismissing armed guards with his bare hands, and laughs exultingly upon the steps of the throne. Again, at the end of Milner's drama, the monster defies capture by the Duke's troops, and then leaps into the crater of Mount Etna, 'now vomiting burning lava' (II.vi.28). The monster's rebellious self-immolation enables the playwright to avoid moral judgements: though the creature is no longer a threat, neither has it capitulated to the power of the state. By contrast, the climax of Peake's play depicts an avalanche whose fall annihilates both the Monster and Frankenstein (III.v.16). Here, Peake solves the moral problem posed by Mary Shelley's story with a *coup de théâtre* which providentially sweeps away both creature and his creator. At one level, both these dénouements simply give dramatic form to the monster's triumphant resolution to ascend its arctic funeral pile, as described by Mary Shelley. But in many ways, the monster's annihilation in these plays also represents the disintegration of

---

[49] *British Stage*, 1823, 5: 30–1.

a theatrical tradition. Whereas once the wild man had become a consenting subject, now the monster and the state are portrayed as having dangerously irreconcilable ambitions.

The confused perplexity discernible in spectators' reactions to the *Frankenstein* plays attests to the conflicting loyalties implicit in savage dramaturgy. Whilst the monster is on the stage, reported the *London Magazine* critic with evident amusement, 'the audience *dare* not hiss, nay – scarcely breathe – but the moment he is well buried under the avalanche, all the good people in the pit feel for their moralities, and give vent to their disapprobation' (September 1823, 8: 323). In this account, the audience's changing sympathies seem to confirm the incommensurable character of wild innocence and savage barbarity. Such evidence suggests that we should no longer regard these dramas as derivative adaptations, mere spectacular shows of blue fire and superhuman strength, in which doors are knocked off hinges and swords peremptorily snapped in two. Rather, we need to be alert to their idiosyncratic transcriptions of monstrosity into the physical aesthetic of illegitimate theatre.

Mute performance, I have argued, dramatises fundamental conflicts about the legitimacy and survival of the state. As we discovered earlier, such roles also contributed to the rise of illegitimate celebrity. The French-born performer Céline Céleste, for example, made her name in a series of mute parts, including the estranged Narammattah in Bayle Bernard's *The Wept of Wish-Ton-Wish* (Adelphi, 1831), Maurice, the mute hero of Planché's *The Child of the Wreck* (Drury Lane, 1837) and Mathilde (successively disguised as a French Spy and as a deranged Arab boy) in *The French Spy* by John Haines (Adelphi, 1837). To some extent, these roles can be seen as having their origins in familiar tropes: the lovesick woman and the amazonian heroine. In many ways, however, the passionate intensity and variety which characterise a mute role such as Mathilde (see especially the scene where she flirts with Marie, and her marked propensity for near-murderous violence) represent a radical departure from theatrical conventions of femininity: mute performance licenses the reimagining of dramatic character by playwrights and performers alike. Then, during the 1840s, J. B. Buckstone created two of Céleste's most celebrated speaking roles: Miami, the graceful, wild, French-Indian huntress of *The Green Bushes* (Adelphi, 1845), and Cynthia, the gypsy heroine of *The Flowers of the Forest* (Adelphi, 1847). In *The Green Bushes*, Miami kills her lover in a moment of jealous passion when she suddenly discovers the existence of his wife; she then spends the rest of her life atoning for her crime. Remorse is also a prominent theme in *The Flowers of the Forest* at the climax of which, forever divided between her loyalty to her tribe, and her love for Alfred, Cynthia silently plunges a knife into her own breast.[50] Through the interpolation of music, as well as through gesture, costume and expression, Buckstone endows the passionate and rebellious Miami and Cynthia with many features of the mute tradition. In particular, Miami's natural grace and sudden violence, like Cynthia's savage, extravagant dancing, recall the wordless, uncivilised passion of Céleste's earlier roles; both characters, like the wild man, seem to exist on the very borders of rationality. What fascinated Buckstone in these plays, it would seem, was the challenge of creating a female character who might be both guilty and innocent, gentle and violent; the most evocative precedents for such a role could be found amidst the expressive conventions of mute performance.

The stage tar, that doughty romantic hero of nautical melodrama, also incorporates certain aspects of the mute tradition. We can trace this dramatic history in plays such as *The Pilot* (Adelphi, 1825) – a hit drama based on the novel by James Fenimore Cooper, but featuring a notable reversal of history in which England's defeat by America curiously disappears – where the imprisoned Barnstaple disdainfully refers to Long Tom Coffin (another starring role for T. P. Cooke) as a 'horrible sea-monster' and 'inhuman cannibal'.[51] A figure of remarkable physical strength, sudden violence and gentle tenderness, the stage tar resembles the wild man in his cultural position on the periphery of civilisation (see for example the character of Philip, the violent, instinctive sailor hero of *Luke the Labourer*). In particular, the sailor's distinctive idiolect (an almost incomprehensible sea jargon of forecastle and frigate, half-tacks and sheet-anchors) draws attention to his cultural strangeness. Ill at ease with language – 'Excuse me if I've lost the steerage of my tongue', Philip apologises – the sailor's inarticulateness reminds us of the muteness of the wild man. For, despite his moral heroism, the sailor remains an unknowable stranger on the very edge of modern civilisation. Indeed, his savage origins help us to understand the extraordinary popularity of nautical drama in this period. In the wake of mass post-war demobilisation, the brave, brusque but unpredictable sailor had usurped the wild

---

[50] *The Green Bushes; or, A Hundred Years Ago, AND* xi; *The Flowers of the Forest, AND* xiii.
[51] Edward Fitzball, *The Pilot; or, A Tale of the Sea, CMT* i. See iii.i.38; iii. ii.41.

man as a theatrical subject precisely because he epitomised contemporary fears about the identity of the civil and the monstrous in late Georgian society.[52]

BLOW-UPS AND THEIR IRONIES

My argument moves now from the figure of the wild man, with all its attendant moral and ideological contradictions, to rather different scenes of violence. Consider the dénouement of *Timour the Tartar* (Covent Garden, 1811), featuring the perilous rescue of Zorilda from the cataract and the destruction of the usurper's castle 'amidst the clash of arms, the braying of trumpets, and the blaze of blue lights'.[53] Imagine the sudden explosion which destroys Grindoff's mill, with the brigands inside, at the end of Isaac Pocock's *The Miller and his Men* (Covent Garden, 1813). Think of the concluding scene of *The Gheber; or, the Fire Worshippers*, a Sadler's Wells aquadrama founded on Byron's *Lallah Rookh*, where the audience witnesses the 'Conflagration of the Temple of the Sun on Real Water'.[54] Or remember the immolation of the tyrant within a burning castle (in defiance of historical fact) in Howard Payne's *Ali Pacha* (Covent Garden, 1822). As George Daniel dryly commented, in his introduction to the play, 'Some licence has been taken with regard to the manner of his death. He was treacherously murdered by an emissary from the sultan; but a *blowing-up* was more dramatic.'[55]

In these spectacular explosions and conflagrations, oriental tyrants seem to merge with evil millers and Napoleonic bogeymen. The political geography of illegitimate theatre, like its genres, was often capacious and indistinct: a composite exotic collection of flats and wings, with scenery, as Skelt's advertisement for Foreign Tree Wings proudly declared, 'to suit all pieces'. Palm trees, moorish arches, and castles with bulbous, onion-shaped towers, concisely evoked a portmanteau dramatic orientalism. By the same token, the archetypal nature of plot and character in these plays encouraged spectators to conflate British and colonial geographies, native and foreign usurpers. Whereas sentimental comedy had portrayed wrongdoing as subject to moral reform within a benevolent universe, illegitimate theatre represented evil as one side of

---

[52] Cf. J. S. Bratton's argument in 'British heroism and the structure of melodrama', in *Acts of Supremacy*, 18–61 and cf. Jim Davis, 'British Bravery, or Tars Triumphant: Images of the British Navy in Nautical Melodrama', *New Theatre Quarterly* 14 (May 1988), 122–43.
[53] *Dramatic Censor*, May 1811, 241–4.   [54] Playbill, 23 March 1818.
[55] Remarks to *Ali Pacha*, *CBT* XI.

an irreducible, manichean opposition. The blow-up, conflagration or cataract therefore provided a visual symbol of evil's incontrovertible defeat by the forces of good; interestingly, contemporary graphic satires, especially those on the subject of Napoleon, share the same visual grammar of volcanic eruption and fiery apotheosis.[56]

'Monk' Lewis' adaptation of the Tamerlane story demonstrates the political topicality of illegitimate orientalism and its spectacular dramaturgy. In this play, Lewis reimagined Timour not as a Marlovian conquering hero, nor as the moral ruler of Rowe's oft-performed Whig play (in which a monarch closely resembling William III goes to war 'To save the weak one from the strong oppressor'),[57] but rather as a petty tyrant and Napoleonic usurper – in other words, as an oriental bogeyman. At the beginning of *Timour the Tartar* (Covent Garden, 1811) Timour is planning to make a political marriage to Zorilda. Though Timour believes her to be the heiress of Georgia, Zorilda is in fact the Queen of Migrelia, bent on avenging her husband's murder and restoring her son, Agib, to the throne. On discovering Zorilda's true identity, Timour immediately imprisons her in the tower, and demands that in order to save her son from death she must consent to be his wife. Whereas Marlowe's Zenocrate is compelled to temporise with her captors, Zorilda, driven by maternal passion and an insatiable desire for vengeance, refuses to submit. In the final, spectacular scene, the Georgians beseige Timour's fortress, which is surrounded by water. Zorilda escapes, only to be flung into the cataract by Timour, from where she is rescued by her son. The Georgians finally overthrow Timour and the legitimate heir is restored.[58]

In Lewis' romantic melodrama, the tragedy of Tamerlane is abandoned in favour of an archetypal confrontation between legitimate heir and evil usurper. One notable feature of this transformation is that femininity becomes simultaneously martial and powerless. The furious, instinctive Zorilda – one unidentified illustration in the Brady collection shows the character on horseback in a pose reminiscent of the mythical Britannia – epitomises heroic, maternal resistance; her imprisonment within Timour's castle, however, highlights her physical vulnerability. As so often in melodrama, the trope of female rescue reveals the precarious character of feminine agency.

---

[56] See, for example, James Gillray, 'Apotheosis of the Corsican-Phoenix', *CPPS* no. 11007, published 1808; George Cruikshank, 'An Eruption of Mount Vesuvius; and the anticipated effects of the [ ] Storm', *CPPS* no. 12555, published 1815.

[57] Nicholas Rowe, *Tamerlane*, first performed 1701, in *Nicholas Rowe: Three Plays*, ed. J. R. Sutherland (London: Scholartis Press, 1929), i.i.58.

[58] M. G. Lewis, *Timour the Tartar* (London: Lowndes, [1811]).

Lewis' play portrays Timour as a Napoleonic bogeyman.[59] The opening scene, for example, evokes that opposition between a great man and a good man (a familiar theme in the discussion of Napoleon's reputation);[60] throughout the play, characters refer to Timour using Napoleonic epithets such as 'usurper' and 'tyrant'. Moreover, Timour's political marriage to Zorilda echoes Napoleon's recent marriage to Marie-Louise. In a tongue-in-cheek review of Lewis' play, the *Examiner* was quick to identify these Napoleonic connections, and ironically described *Timour* as a 'most awful, but at the same time insidious attack on the reputation of BUONA-PARTE'. Buonoparte, suggested the critic, 'is perfectly shocked, no doubt, to hear of these terrible proceedings against him in "the finest theatre in Europe!"'[61]

'Monk' Lewis' *Timour* depicts an oriental world characterised by physical peril and spectacular ideological confrontation. The sheer visual magnificence of such productions can be surmised from Skelt's toy theatre sheet, which depicts some of the play's characters, together with Timour's Grand Car (see plate 7). A recurring theme in stage melodramas such as *Timour* is the glorious (British) liberation of a populace from the barbaric practices and despotic power of the natives.[62] In *The Cataract of the Ganges*, for instance, the British colonel vows to 'dispel the mists of bigotry' (II.i.30) and to enforce religious toleration, while the Rajah of Guzerat proudly acknowledges these 'generous Britons' as the 'greatest of mortal conquerors' (II.i.31). Then, after the libidinous priest has been seen off by a pistol shot from Jack Robinson, the Colonel's comic factotum, the curtain falls 'on the shouts of the Conquerors' (II.vii.50).

It is easy enough to dismiss these plays as populist, racist propaganda. But illegitimate theatre did radically change how the Orient was represented. In particular, the Orient now became a barbaric, despotic place

---

[59] Three years later, in the wake of Napoleon's abdication, Byron would also compare Napoleon to a Timour who broods in 'prisoned rage' recalling that 'The world *was* mine.' See the 'Ode to Napoleon Buonaparte' in *Byron*, The Oxford Authors, ed. Jerome McGann (Oxford University Press, 1986), 252–7.

[60] Cf. Simon Bainbridge, *Napoleon and English Romanticism* (Cambridge University Press, 1995).

[61] *Examiner*, 12 May 1811, 299–300. See also *Morning Chronicle*, 30 April 1811.

[62] Cf. the rhetoric advertising *Tippoo Saib or the Storming of Seringapatam* (Coburg, July 1827), and the language of 'magnanimous intervention' in *Britons at Navarino* (Coburg, December 1827). Compare the dénouement of *The Lion, Chief of Cabul* (Coburg, November 1829), which depicts 'the Stupendous car of the Idol, beneath whose fatal wheels hundreds of the deluded fanatics voluntarily throw themselves and are sacrificed by being crushed under its ponderous burden' (playbill, 2 November). Heidi Holder's essay, 'Melodrama, Realism and Empire on the British Stage' in J. Bratton, ed., *Acts of Supremacy*, 129–49, provides a good introduction to the subject of colonial melodrama.

7. Illegitimate apostasy. *Skelt's Characters in Timour the Tartar.*

to be brought under control by spectacular, quasi-providential physical force.[63] Interestingly, the *pasticchio* structure of melodrama has the effect of duplicating – at the level of social class – Britain's ideological supremacy. In other words, the plays' 'low', comic characters both modify and replicate the imperial values dramatised within the main plot. Hence the colonial authority, 'deep wisdom', and moral seriousness of officers like Colonel Mordaunt in *The Cataract* exist in apposition to the instinctive valour and naive moral certainty of Jack Robinson, who is humorously perplexed by Hindu burial customs, and strongly opposed to the practice of female infanticide, not least on sentimental grounds (for men relive their love affairs in the lives of their daughters, while women are important 'to keep up the stock' (I.ii.8)). Through such duplications and comic juxtapositions, melodrama subtly diffuses the social location of moral authority between officer and factotum. What makes colonial melodrama interesting, then, is the rewriting of empire which it entails:

---

[63] See John Mackenzie's important monograph, *Orientalism: History, Theory and the Arts* (Manchester University Press, 1995), chapter 7.

the moral heroism of the lower classes is crucial to that revisionary process.[64]

The blow-up lies at the heart of ideological conflict in illegitimate dramaturgy. Often, blow-ups become a form of patriotic retribution, an act of dramatic vengeance upon history. The revision which takes place in the Coburg's *Mungo Parke* (1824), for example, demonstrates that ideological triumph which the iconographic conventions of melodrama make possible.[65] In 1795, the Scottish explorer Mungo Parke had been the first European to reach the Gambia; on his second expedition, however, Parke had drowned whilst under attack from the natives.[66] The scenes depicted in the Coburg's *Mungo Parke* drama, including a woody jungle, a landscape with an African hut and the Niger river, were clearly designed to evoke the Gambia as a place of physical danger and cultural strangeness. Through the ideological lens of melodrama, the Coburg playwright also reinvented Parke's death as the triumph of 'British Valour' over 'African Treachery'. The play's last scene features the 'desperate attempt' by Parke and his fellow explorers to force the passage of the river against 'native opposition'; Parke's death in this attack is followed by a 'Tremendous Explosion' of the rock. Such an explosion, together with the deaths of Parke's enemies, provides a form of retrospective vengeance for Parke's death; an African travelogue is rewritten here so as to make history conform to a distinctly melodramatic order of good and evil.

Blow-ups and conflagrations offer visible image of the moral clarity which melodrama often attempts to impose upon the world. But moral clarity in melodrama may also be illusory; sometimes, it is merely a sham. *Swing*, written and performed by Robert Taylor, illustrates the way in which melodramatic conventions can be turned against themselves, whilst Jerrold's *The Mutiny at the Nore* pits the state's justice against our generic expectations of melodrama. In 1831, Richard Carlile, 'the Showman of Free Thought',[67] opened the Rotunda theatre, formerly Cooke's Amphitheatre, at Blackfriars Bridge. By advertising itself as a dissenting chapel, the Rotunda neatly circumvented the licences

---

[64] Cf. the language of liberty as articulated by the sailors Harry Clifton and Mat Mizen in William Barrymore, *El Hyder, The Chief of the Gaut Mountains* (Coburg, 1818), *Lacy* VI.

[65] Cf. Mary Louise Pratt's argument in *Imperial Eyes: Travel Writing and Transculturation* (London: Routledge, 1992), 74ff, that Mungo Parke's travelogue 'exemplifies the eruption of the sentimental mode' into European travel writing.

[66] On Parke's voyages, see his *Journal of a Mission into the Interior of Africa in 1805*, prefixed by Wishaw's life of Parke (London: John Murray, 1815).

[67] E. P. Thompson, *The Making of the English Working Class* (Harmondsworth: Penguin, 1963), 843.

required for theatres or other public meeting-places. The establishment rapidly became a centre of metropolitan radicalism, and its proceedings were minutely observed by government spies.[68] *Swing; or, Who are the Incendiaries?* – a 'politico-monological tragedy' which Robert Taylor performed to enthusiastic audiences before its suppression, offers us a glimpse of a radical, uncensored theatre.[69]

Though notionally set in the reign of James II (history, as so often in melodrama, is the flimsiest of pretexts), *Swing* is in fact a topical republican drama about the incendiary protests by agricultural labourers in rural England; Taylor's play also burlesques the Rotunda's position as a place of political subversion. After the arrest and hanging of one of the Swing brothers (caught whilst stealing pheasants for his friend's wife), mass protest leads to popular revolution and the spectacular triumph of the sovereign people. John Swing then becomes king. But after lecturing the legislature on the needs of the common people, Swing decides to give up his crown and return to the plough.

The rhetoric of incendiarism in this play (and the idea of a 'chymic power', 'more formidable than that of gunpowder') is very striking. It would be fascinating to explore how *Swing* seems to conflate the self-conscious theatricality of Spencean free and easies (radical gatherings, at which convivial singing took place) and the conventions of illegitimate theatre.[70] But what interests me here is that Taylor's drama achieves its subversive effects by burlesquing the melodramatic blow-up and rescue scene. Consider the beginning of Act v, when the mob is up in arms in twenty counties, King James has abdicated, and the Archbishop of Cant's palace is ablaze. According to the conventions of melodrama, the wicked Archbishop would have burned to death in his palace, thus ensuring the triumph of radical reform. But in Taylor's play, the Archbishop is heroically rescued by the republican atheist, John Swing.

---

[68] For reports on the Rotunda, see HO 64/11, fols. 189, 192, 199, 206, 221. Carlile self-consciously advertised the Rotunda's performances as a form of *theatrical* politics. See the *Prompter*, November 1830, 8, where he promises that Taylor's eloquence would combine 'all that can be imagined as to political, moral, and theological instruction, with all that is splendid in theatrical entertainment'. See further I. J. Prothero, *Artisans and Politics in Early Nineteenth-Century London: John Gast and his Times* (Folkestone: Dawson, 1979), 277–82, and especially James Epstein's persuasive account in *Radical Expression: Political Language, Ritual, and Symbol in England, 1790–1850* (Oxford: Clarendon, 1994), 140–4.

[69] Robert Taylor, *Swing; or, Who are the Incendiaries?* (London: Richard Carlile, 1831). By the time of Taylor's performances, Carlile had already been tried and imprisoned for seditious libel.

[70] On radical sociability, and especially the Spencean free and easies, see Iain McCalman, *Radical Underworld: Prophets, Revolutionaries, and Pornographers in London 1795–1840* (Cambridge University Press, 1988), 118–23.

Finally, in a gesture of magnificent improbability, the Archbishop even agrees to join the cause of radical reform.

Taylor's monodrama seems to equivocate between the genres of melodrama and burlesque – between a dramaturgy which moves inexorably towards violent, volcanic confrontation and one which laughingly mocks melodrama's claims of moral legibility and ideological certainty. Indeed, the tension between these two forms may reflect the play's uncertainty about what revolution in Britain might mean. Would radical reform necessarily entail violent upheaval? Or might the power of popular reason itself bring about political change? Whatever the reason for these contradictory generic loyalties,[71] what is remarkable about *Swing* is the play's self-conscious appropriation of burlesque and melodrama for the production of republican laughter.

The Mutiny at Spithead and the Nore (Pavilion, 1830) is another puzzling drama and one whose political loyalties are more subtle than those of *Swing*.[72] Jerrold's play, based on Captain Marryatt's novel, *The King's Own* (1830) dramatises the mutinies which took place at Spithead and the Nore in 1797, and which ended in political compromise between government and mutineers, along with summary punishment for the rebellion's organisers.[73] At the centre of *The Mutiny* is the rash, embittered Richard Parker, a 'striped, heart-broken, degraded man', as he describes himself in the play. Transformed into a 'raging tiger' by his experience of cruelty and injustice on board ship, Parker's leadership of the Nore mutiny is inspired by his angry bitterness about the severity of naval punishments, and by his determination to improve the inhumane conditions of his fellow sailors. In Jerrold's play, this desire for revenge, which finally brings him to the scaffold, can be traced to Parker's wrongful accusation, and subsequent savage punishment, for the theft of a watch.

The final scene of *The Mutiny* shows the preparations for Parker's execution, and the sailor's (traditional) loyal toast to King and country. On the surface, at least, Jerrold's play dramatises the stark and irrevocable consequences of rebelling against the state. In many ways, however, Jerrold's melodramatic design of *The Mutiny* leads its audience to expect

---

[71] Cf. the analogy between classical theatre and republican drama in the Prologue: Taylor reminds his audience that in ancient Greece the purpose of tragedy was 'To speak the people's voice with magic art, / And launch keen satire to the tyrant's heart.'

[72] Pavilion, 7 June to 3 July 1830; Coburg, 16 August to 18 September 1830; Tottenham Street, 27 September to 4 October 1830; Surrey, 3–6 December 1831. For Jeffrey Cox's rather different interpretation of this play, see 'The Ideological Tack of Nautical Melodrama' in Hays and Nikolopoulou, eds., *Melodrama: The Cultural Emergence of a Genre*.

[73] Jerrold's source for his play was Captain Marryatt's novel, *The King's Own* (1830).

some *coup de théâtre* in which Parker will suddenly be proved innocent, and the death sentence suspended. In *Black-Ey'd Susan* (Surrey, 1829), Jerrold had already experimented with the farcical overtones of this melodramatic trope. Here, William, the sailor hero accused of striking his Captain, ascends the scaffold, only to discover by the arrival of a letter (attached most implausibly to a body in the water), that he cannot be guilty of the crime as charged. Parker, however, is not innocent. On the contrary, he is guilty of mutiny, one of the most serious crimes against the state. And yet, as *The Mutiny* is at pains to show, Parker's crime has its own convincing moral teleology: the brutality of naval punishments and – in Jerrold's subtle twist to Marryatt's narrative – a genuine miscarriage of justice.

Jerrold's sympathetic characterisation of the mutineer seems to encourage audiences to desire a sudden intervention which would save Parker's life. Indeed, we may actually be able to hear a little of the audience's surprise and disbelief about Parker's fate as, amidst solemn music, the mutineer walks towards the scaffold, addresses his shipmates, and then drinks a toast: 'Here's health to the King, Confusion to my Enemies, and Peace to my Soul.'[74] For at the Coburg Theatre, Parker's toast apparently met with loud hisses from spectators, who objected to the suggestion that Parker might still nurture patriotic sentiments.[75] Nevertheless, no miraculous piece of fortune or discovery of mistaken identity comes to the aid of the condemned Richard Parker: Jerrold leaves unfulfilled our expectations of a melodramatic reversal. The play's austere justice therefore seems to mock by proving hopeless the audience's earlier sympathies with the mutineer. As if to confirm this view, the magistrates who had been sent by the Home Office to investigate Jerrold's drama duly confirmed that, though 'great interest and sympathy' were produced among the Pavilion spectators when Parker was led out to execution, *The Mutiny* was nonetheless 'perfectly unobjectionable'.[76]

In *The Mutiny*, I believe, Jerrold deliberately undermines his spectators' expectations about the moral certainty of melodramatic dénouements. Just as the end of *The Beggar's Opera* self-consciously encourages its audience to laugh at the theatrical impasse created by the need to hang Macheath in order to instruct the audience, and the conflicting wish to please them by setting him free, so *The Mutiny* mocks the sheer

---

[74] Jerrold, *The Mutiny at the Nore* in *CMT* v, iii.iii.
[75] 'Letter signed 'G.E.' entitled 'Coburg Theatre and Ultra Loyalty' in *Tatler*, 24 December 1831, 3: 603.   [76] HO 59/2 (5 and 7 June 1830).

contingency of melodramatic justice. In his skilful manipulation of those absurdist resolutions and near-farcical scenes of recognition so familiar to contemporary spectators, Jerrold creates a form of generic brinkmanship which seems to reveal the moral hollowness of the state. Far from offering audiences dramatic forms of moral clarity, such ironic dénouements seem designed to question audiences' desires for melodramatic oppositions between good and evil.

TRANSGRESSIONS

Fears about the minor theatres as centres for licentiousness, immorality and sedition preoccupied licensers and reviewers alike. The history of illegitimate production is punctuated by indignant denunciations of certain plays, often accompanied by demands for the intervention of the local magistrates or Examiner of Plays. 'We hereby call on the magistrates of Surrey, in the loudest and most solemn manner, to strip the Coburg Theatre TO-MORROW OF ITS LICENCE', fulminated the *Age* over *Tom Thumb*. Similar protests greeted a range of plays, including *The Tower of Nesle* ('a most licentious drama'), the Adelphi's *Tom and Jerry* ('we really do think the legislature ought to interfere') and the Coburg's production of *George III* ('the magistrates . . . should surely interfere, to prevent violations of decency . . . like the piece in question').[77]

Given the freedom from censorship of the transpontine and East End theatres, the relative scarcity of these controversies might seem surprising. But theatre licences had to be renewed each year at the local Quarter Sessions, and the threat of having a licence revoked clearly concentrated managerial minds; at the Surrey, moreover, Elliston was actually bound by covenant 'not to produce any dramatic pieces of an immoral tendency'.[78] Staging licentious dramas or provoking political excitement would also have endangered that veneer of respectability which managers carefully nurtured through events such as their benefit performances for local charities.

The commercial success of genres such as burlesque and pantomime nevertheless depended to some extent on the inclusion of satire and topical mockery. At patent and minor theatres alike, pantomime proved to be a convenient and flexible genre for introducing such allusions, especially during the political ferment over Parliamentary reform. The Adelphi show, *Grimalkin the Great* (1830), for example, a pantomime

---

[77] *Age*, 3 June 1832 and 30 September 1832; *John Bull*, 10 December 1821, 414; unidentified cutting in Coburg file, 13 September 1824.   [78] George Raymond, *Memoirs of Elliston*, 1: 389.

featuring Luddite cats who destroy machinery, dramatised the victory of a 'radical reformer' (in the shape of a fairy) over an arbitrary, absolute and omnipotent king who has failed to ameliorate his subjects' conditions of work. But this could never have been surmised from the opaque text submitted to the Examiner of Plays. Similarly, in *Harlequin Merman* (Fitzroy, 1833), a 'corpulent plumper' at an election booth was actually torn into a physical split vote. In a variety of ways, pantomime's metamorphic dramaturgy was perfectly suited to the production of mischievous insinuation and satirical visual similes.[79]

Although he seems to have turned a blind eye to many pantomimic violations, John Larpent clearly recognised the transgressive potential of illegitimate laughter. The Examiner of Plays prohibited Charles Dibdin's Bastille pantomime at Covent Garden in 1789, banned *The Two Farmers* (1800), a bold musical entertainment written by Thomas Dibdin on the subject of war, famine and monopoly, and gave a swift and absolute refusal to *The Hustings*, a daring operatic impromptu submitted by the Lyceum in June 1818. Certainly, Arnold must have parted company with his senses to have imagined for a single moment that Larpent would have permitted *The Hustings*. Famine and distress (both incendiary topics in the theatre, as Larpent knew well) are a recurring theme in the play, and the despondent Arable hopes the new Parliament will 'kill the insects that are getting into the ears of our best Crops'. Though the election is eventually won by the heroic Trusty, 'a plan honest John Bull' character, the candidates also feature a number of individuals guaranteed to frighten any Examiner of Plays. These include Chaos (who tells his audiences that radical reform can only be produced by tearing everyone piecemeal, finger by finger, toe by toe: 'it is only tho' destruction & confusion that reformed Liberty can be procured'), and Canvass, a proponent of liberty, everlasting parliaments and free meat, who demands the abolition of taxes, not to mention the end of Church and State.[80]

The Hustings rashly attempted to exploit the carnivalesque freedom often granted by Larpent to burlesques and satirical preludes. Three years later, Moncrieff's burlesque of *Don Giovanni*, produced in the wake of George IV's visit to Ireland during the summer of 1821, also overstepped the mark. Though he did not ban the play, Larpent made extensive cuts to *Giovanni in Ireland* (Drury Lane, 1821). He deleted altogether the scene in which the incorrigible Giovanni flirts with an abbess (in

[79] *Grimalkin or the Cat Wife*, LC Add. MSS 42892 fols. 547–70. For reviews of *Grimalkin the Great*, see *The Times*, 28 December 1830 and *Tatler*, 30 December 1830, 1: 403; on the Fitzroy pantomime, see *The Times*, 27 December 1833. [80] Larpent MS 2031.

defence, Giovanni claims only to be paying his 'Adorations'), and also censored the scene in which a carnival king presides over the farcical trial of Giovanni. Here, the king proposes to dispense entirely with legal procedures 'and proceed with all possible good humour to the Question of hanging' (II.iv).[81] But audiences nonetheless quickly recognised Moncrieff's burlesque as a mischievous satire on George IV: the play attracted 'loud and incessant contention' and was dropped from the repertoire within a week.[82]

The Hustings and Moncrieff's *Giovanni* play remind us how the subject-matter of burlesque and its lively, laughable carelessness, might appear to threaten the dignity of the state and its institutions. Uncensored burlesques of roguery such as Moncrieff's *The Beggar of Cripplegate* (Surrey, 1830) often satirised the corruption of authority from the ostensibly safe distance of history.[83] The Surrey's production of *King, Queen and Knaves; or, The Court of Mary Axe* (1829), a burlesque obliquely mocking Lady Conyngham's political influence on George IV, is a good example of how history at the minor theatres was twisted for contemporary satirical effect.[84] Within Westminster, too, as Planché would confirm in his memoirs, allusions to current events, 'indecent situations' and 'personal insult to those in authority over us' were frequently inserted in burlesques after the texts had been licensed by the Examiner of Plays.[85]

In other ways, too, the subject-matter of illegitimate theatre unwittingly defied decorum and propriety. Naval mutiny, as dramatised by Douglas Jerrold, for example, would never have been permitted by the Examiner. Moreover, given George Colman's anxiety while Examiner about the demonic portrayal of 'our old allies' (the Turks), it seems unlikely that he or indeed his predecessor would have licensed the Coburg plays about the war between Greece and Turkey.[86] By contrast, *George III, the Father of his People* (Coburg, 1824) represented a different kind of transgression. McFarren's drama consisted of a series of melodramatic (and not always historically accurate) anecdotes about the life

---

[81] Larpent MS 2267.   [82] *Examiner*, 30 December 1821, 824.

[83] Moncrieff, *The Beggar of Cripplegate; or, The Humours of Bluff King Hal*, *CMT* VI.

[84] See the bill for 20 May 1829 and a review in *Harlequin*, 23 May 1829, 14.

[85] J. R. Planché, *The Recollections and Reflections of J. R. Planché* (London: Tinsley Brothers, 1872), II: 109.

[86] See correspondence bound with the licensing MSS for *The Revolt of the Greeks* (Drury Lane, June 1824) and *The Suliote or the Greek Family* (Drury Lane, 1829) in BL Add. MSS 42897 fol. 406. The Coburg dramas, in which the Turks were portrayed as a despotic nation devoid of moral principle, included J. Dobbs *Germano or Almanazar the Traitor* (December, 1823), *Latharia the Greek! or the Archon's Daughter* (November, 1823) and Henry Milner's historical drama, *Leonidas, King of Sparta* (October, 1829).

of George III. The play featured the Royal Family at breakfast, the Royal Box at the Handel commemoration in Westminster Abbey, and the King's attempted suicide; *George III* then culminated in monarchical apotheosis, as the King ascended to heaven in a balloon. As one newspaper dryly remarked, the King 'literally talks toasts and sentiments throughout the piece, and performs a thousand affable actions, such as walking out hand in hand with two black footmen, nursing several children, and being in himself a Humane Society to a half-drowned young lady'.[87]

'As for the loyalty of the sentiments,' remarked *The Times* (7 September 1823), 'Heaven knows there is as much of it in the drama at this theatre as the most devoted stomach can bear.' But what made *George III* controversial was its portrayal of living persons, let alone George III and the Regent (the Examiner of Plays routinely censored all such images and allusions in the texts he scrutinised). The conservative press reacted to the Coburg production with opprobrium and indignation: the *John Bull* magazine demanded the intervention of the local magistrates to prevent such 'violations of decency, and exhibitions of mingled falsehood and profligacy'.[88] The real target of critical anxiety, however, would seem to be not so much the impropriety of depicting living individuals such as George IV, but rather a more intangible fear, that the unauthorised and uncontrollable representation of monarchy at a 'low' theatre might actually damage the grandeur and legitimacy of monarchy itself.[89]

Melodrama often capitalised on the iconography of rebellion, whilst morally repudiating that rebellion at the level of plot. In the wake of 'Swing', during which agricultural labourers had attacked justices and overseers, wrecked threshing machines and set fire to ricks and buildings across England, the manager of the Surrey was taking a calculated risk in staging the subject of rural incendiarism. Indeed, the title of George Almar's play *The Fire Raiser; or, The Haunted Tower* (Surrey, February 1831) immediately caught the attention of local magistrates, and had to be swiftly commuted to *The Prophet of the Moor; or, The Fire Raiser* (whether

---

[87] *Morning Chronicle*, 2 September 1824.
[88] Unidentified cutting, Coburg file, Theatre Museum. The *New Times* and *Courier* also expressed horrified amazement about the production of *George III*: see Coburg file.
[89] See cutting from the *Theatrical Observer*, 13 September 1824, in the Coburg file. The reviewer declared that 'the miserable actors belonging to the Coburg cannot be expected to personate nobility and gentry'; 'to see the reigning Monarch ridiculed by a stroller, and the heir presumptive burlesqued by an equally miserable bungler, are things . . . which ought not to be seen'.

the script itself was altered is not clear).[90] This play exploits the dramaturgy of incendiarism whilst simultaneously dismissing fire-raising as a form of political protest.

The play's anti-hero is Marten Gale, an embittered ex-soldier turned fire-raising wizard, who has vowed vengeance against his cavalier colonel. After the failure of various schemes to entrap the colonel, Gale burns down his mansion and imprisons his lover on the haunted moor under the Druid's Stone. But Crazy Ruth (a woman whom he wronged years ago) helps Catherine to escape, and eventually shoots Gale as well; before he dies, Gale even imagines being dragged down by fiends into a fiery hell. According to George Daniel, *The Fire Raiser* was Almar's best play: vigorous, droll, alternately serious and comic, 'often rising into eloquence, and never sinking into low buffoonery'.[91] Far from articulating legitimate political demands, however, the incendiarist's actions are those of an irrational, isolated man in whom bitterness and romantic disappointment have turned to diabolism. Whether or not the Surrey manager commissioned Almar to write a play about incendiarism, we shall never know. But this dramatisation and simultaneous disavowal of transgression in *The Fire Raiser* is typical of melodrama's dense and conflicting political loyalties. Indeed, the ideological mutability of this form is one reason for its enduring power and commercial value.

The most famous episodes of illegitimate transgression concern the adaptations of Pierce Egan's *Life in London* and *Jack Sheppard*, W. H. Ainsworth's Newgate novel about the notorious thief, highwayman, and jail escape-artist. The moral panic which erupted over these plays, first performed at the Adelphi, and swiftly produced at minor theatres all over London, needs to be interpreted in relation to pervasive fears about Newgate culture.[92] Yet the transgressive character of these productions is not limited to their low, criminal subject matter. Reviewers did allege that the Adelphi production featured 'a detailed and elaborate description of all the receptacles of vice, sin, and debauchery . . . in the metropolis', and incited the defiance of beadles and the knocking over of watchmen, 'crowding the theatres with thieves and the streets with brawlers'.[93] But what also disturbed critics was the realisation that

[90] George Almar, *The Fire Raiser; or, The Prophet of the Moor, CMT* IX. On the play's change of title, see unidentified cutting, Surrey file, Theatre Museum. [91] Remarks, *The Fire Raiser*.
[92] On *Jack Sheppard*, see Meisel's helpful discussion in *Realizations*, 265–71. The standard history of the Newgate theme misleadingly portrays Newgate theatre as naively sensational. See Keith Hollingsworth, *The Newgate Novel 1830–1847* (Detroit: Wayne State University Press, 1963), 33ff.
[93] *John Bull*, 10 December 1821, 414; *Examiner*, 3 November 1839, 691–3. Compare William Makepeace Thackeray's belief that 'at the Cobourg, people are waiting about the lobbies, selling Shepherd-bags' (a screwdriver and an iron lever), cited Stephens, *Censorship*, 64–5.

the Lord Chamberlain possessed no practical authority to control the rival productions of *Tom and Jerry* which were springing up beyond Westminster at many of the minor theatres and penny gaffs. (The Astley version, to the horror of the *Drama* critic, featured Cribb and Spring, two celebrated pugilists.) The success of *Tom and Jerry* and *Jack Sheppard* raised the frightening prospect of endless representations at the very theatres patronised by those classes perceived to be most susceptible to immorality.[94]

'AS A PICTURE OF LIFE,' declared the Adelphi playbill of *Jack Sheppard*, 'IT IS UNRIVALLED!'[95] The spectre of adaptation rapidly became synonymous with the impossibility of curtailing illegitimate representation. 'Nothing, for instance, could be more absurd', declared the *Monthly Magazine*, 'than to see the whole rage of official morality cutting and slashing away at Mr Shee's tragedy, the moment when 'Tom and Jerry' was teaching every apprentice, from Westminster to Whitechapel, the whole art and mystery of blackguardism, at sixpence a head.'[96] The *Examiner*'s response to the *Jack Sheppard* craze similarly emphasised the frightening ubiquity of illegitimate representation:

Jack Sheppard is the attraction at the *Adelphi*; Jack Sheppard is the bill of fare at the *Surrey*; Jack Sheppard is the choice example of morals and conduct at the *City of London*; Jack Sheppard reigns over the *Victoria*; Jack Sheppard rejoices crowds in the *Pavilion*; Jack Sheppard is the favourite at the *Queen's*; and at *Sadler's Wells* there is no profit but of Jack Sheppard.[97]

A satirical cartoon entitled 'The March of Knowledge, or Just Come from Seeing "Jack Sheppard"' provides a visual image of this moral danger: a group of young men are depicted in front of a wall on which are posted a collection of playbills advertising productions of *Jack Sheppard* at the Adelphi, Surrey, Victoria, Garrick and Sadler's Wells Theatres.[98] No wonder that legislators were determined to bring the licensing of all the minor theatres within the control of the Lord

---

[94] *Drama*, June 1823, 4: 305. The periodical also cites a correspondent who writes, 'I am certain no lady or real gentleman would attend a theatre to witness such performances, which they must be well aware are only fit for dustmen and costermongers.'

[95] Adelphi playbill, 4 November 1839.

[96] December 1827, 4. Cf. letter from 'J. L. B.' in *Drama*, May 1822, 2: 321–2, noting a variety of *Tom and Jerry* plays: 'This obscene and contemptible production has been already received by at least two hundred distinct London audiences with most 'unqualified' approbation . . . our Minor Theatres are nightly thronged, by means of the lucubrations of Mr. EGAN.' Compare Tomlins, *Brief View*, 339, where the author complains that for three months, eight theatres were performing different versions, 'rendered as attractive as possible, of the life and adventures of a burglar and prison breaker' and that 'sixteen theatres may represent the same morally illegitimate atrocities'.   [97] *Examiner*, 3 November 1839, 691.

[98] The cartoon is reprinted in Meisel, *Realizations*, 266.

Chamberlain. Indeed, once the Theatre Regulation Act of 1843 had become law, the suppression of criminal dramas, especially in the East End, rapidly became one of the Examiner's most pressing concerns.[99]

As reviewers acknowledged, the Adelphi's decision to cast Mrs Keeley as Jack Sheppard seemed to produce a form of criminality which appeared self-conscious and playful, rather than anarchic. 'Nothing could be more exquisite than Mrs. Keeley's acting; the naiveté, the assurance, the humour, and the boldness of Jack were excellently delineated; the slang was given without the least admixture of vulgarity', while the moments of pathos were 'most touching'.[100] In other ways, however, Buckstone's dramaturgy (like that of Thomas Greenwood at Sadler's Wells) actually seemed to celebrate popular disruption and mob rule. In particular, the play's climactic image of Jonathan Wild's smouldering house (conflagrations are a familiar illegitimate trope, as we have seen) is one of real moral ambiguity. 'At the Adelphi,' reported the *Athenaeum* critic with evident disgust, 'Jonathan Wild is burned alive in his house; and as he struggles to escape, the mob dance round in triumph, hurling brick-bats at the suffocating wretch, while Jack Sheppard points with a smile of exultation to the face of his foe!'[101] Moreover, although Jack Sheppard is captured in Buckstone's play, he is never actually executed.[102] In a variety of ways, then, the dénouement of the Adelphi *Jack Sheppard* seemed to demonstrate the anarchic propensity of illegitimate productions to adapt a 'pernicious' text to still more dangerous ends.

Ben Webster's adaptation of *Paul Clifford* (Coburg, 1832), Edward Bulwer-Lytton's Newgate novel, is another interesting example of illegitimate revision. To understand the bitter cynicism of this uncensored Coburg play, performed in the spring of 1832, we need to compare it with Fitzball's melodramatic adaptation, produced at Covent Garden three years later in 1835. In Fitzball's *Paul Clifford*, political conflict is transposed into the private sphere of romantic love.[103] Moreover, Fitzball rejects Bulwer-Lytton's sociological analysis of criminality, and emphasises Clifford's responsibility for his crimes. Whereas, at the end of the novel,

---

[99] On the suppression of the Jack Sheppard plays during the 1840s, see Stephens, *Censorship*, 66–7.

[100] *Morning Chronicle* review, reproduced on Adelphi poster, filed with playbills for 1839, British Library.   [101] *Athenaeum*, 2 November 1839, 830.

[102] Cf. William Moncrieff's adaptation, *Jack Sheppard! or, The Progress of Crime* (Coburg, October 1839) which also featured a 'TERRIFIC CONFLAGRATION' (see the Coburg playbill for 21 October 1839). Compare Thomas Greenwood, *Jack Sheppard; or, The Housebreaker of the Last Century* (Sadler's Wells, October 1839), *CMT* xv and especially the play's last scene in which the soldiers 'fire on the people, who return a volley of stones, and charge them furiously with sticks' (v.iv.68).

[103] Edward Fitzball, *Paul Clifford*, *DBT* xxviii.

Paul abandons England for the new, hopeful land of America, Fitzball depicts his hero departing on a patriotic mission to aid the Queen of Hungary. Here, the reintegration of Clifford into British society also side-steps Bulwer-Lytton's biting social criticism: Fitzball's adaptation dissolves that critique at the heart of this Newgate novel.

By contrast, Webster's *Paul Clifford*, produced amid the anxious stalemate over political reform in March 1832, dramatises a social corruption so endemic that escape becomes impossible. Moreover, the Coburg's cryptic publicity for *Paul Clifford* actually draws attention to the controversy which surrounded the novel's satirical depictions of living politicians.[104] The playbill highlights this political subtext by including ironic comments on these contemporary criminals: Fighting Attie [the Duke of Wellington] is described as 'an old soldier', Scarlet Jem [Sir James Scarlet] as 'a pressman out of work', and Mobbing Francis [Francis Burdett] as 'a Westminster Coney'. The playbill also features a series of epigraphs taken from Bulwer-Lytton's chapter-headings. This polemical collage – 'Can a man doubt whether it is better to be a great statesman or a common thief?' (Fielding's *Jonathan Wild*) and 'The very worst use to which you can put a man is to hang him' (John Wilkes) – encourages spectators to interpret *Paul Clifford* as a drama about power and authority.

At the play's centre is Tomlinson's ironic – and now highly topical – speech to Paul: 'Remember, that nothing is so dangerous to our state as reform: the moment a man's heart grows honest, the gang forsakes him; the magistrate misses his fee; the informer peaches; and the recusant hangs' (III.i).[105] Like *Tom Thumb*, staged a few months later, the Coburg's production of *Paul Clifford* seems to trade on the political uncertainties of the time. Whether or not Davidge was trying to market the theatre as a playhouse dedicated to parliamentary reform, both plays certainly tested the limits of the uncensored stage. Nowhere is this more true than at the trial, where Paul offers a biting indictment of society for 'implanting within me the goading sense of injustice' and then 'submitting me to the corruption of example' (III.v). Moreover, whereas Paul's departure from Britain in the novel holds out the possibility of escape from this corrupt society, Webster's play refuses to share this optimism. So, after the tragic recognition scene between father and son, Paul dies.

---

[104] See Coburg playbill, 19 March 1832. For the novel's reception, see the *Examiner*, 20 June 1830, 387.

[105] Webster, *Paul Clifford, the Highwayman of 1770*, *CMT* VI. Webster himself played the role of Tomlinson.

Does Webster's dénouement offer a moral corrective to Bulwer-Lytton's jauntily burlesque ending? Or, by denying audiences the laughable compensations of burlesque, did the Coburg ending actually compound the satirical bitterness of this novel? In many ways, *Paul Clifford* seems to do both; the play punishes Paul for his transgressions, while at the same time highlighting the arbitrary and corrupt character of the society which judges him. The arch-conservative George Daniel praised Webster for not adopting the dangerous 'wretched and mischievous sophistry' that 'man is the mere creature of circumstance'.[106] Yet, the tragic death of Paul Clifford draws attention to forms of corruption and hypocrisy which are shown to lie at the heart of the British state.

My analysis of Webster's *Paul Clifford* has suggested that we need to look beyond flashpoints of moral and political panic to interpret the nature of transgression in illegitimate theatre. The Surrey production of *Masaniello* (1822, many revivals) also demonstrates the mutant character of illegitimate appropriation, and the fascination of the uncensored minor theatres with the subjects of mutiny and rebellion. The story of Masaniello, the patriot fisherman who led the Neapolitan uprising against the Spanish colonists in 1647, was another controversial subject. Intoxicated by some uncertain combination of power, alcohol and poison, Masaniello went mad, was deserted by his followers and was then killed, only to be posthumously recognised as a Neapolitan hero. The Examiner's censorship of George Soane's play, performed at Drury Lane in 1825, and starring Edmund Kean on horseback, succinctly confirms the perceived danger and potency of the Masaniello narrative as a theatrical subject. In the licensing manuscript, Colman deleted allusions to monarchs treating the people as 'beasts', expurgated the Duke's moral cynicism ('for what are honor, faith, / Love friendship, gratitude, beyond a name?'), and also censored references describing the Spanish colonialists as 'State Caukers'. According to the *Examiner*'s critic, who saw the production at Covent Garden, however, Soane's populace was just too 'contemptible' to make plausible the collision between revolution and reaction in this popular uprising.[107]

The controversy surrounding James Kenney's adaptation of *Masaniello* (Covent Garden, May 1829), a play based on *La Muette de Portici*,[108] illustrates how a plot dramatising the punishment of rebellion

---

[106] See the preface to the published play, signed 'D. G.'

[107] *Masaniello, The Fisherman of Naples* (Drury Lane, February 1825), BL Add. MS 42870, fols. 1–68; *Examiner*, 20 February 1825, 122, signed 'Q'. See also *Theatrical Mince Pie*, 9 February 1825, 69–70.

[108] The libretto was written by A. E. Scribe and G. Delavigne, with music by Daniel Auber. The opera was first performed at Paris in 1828.

may nonetheless be perceived to contain a rebellious counter-narrative. When questioned about the drama at the Select Committee, Kenney defended *Masaniello* as a play with a decidedly 'Tory moral', pointing out that the 'revolutionary fisherman is humiliated, and a lesson is taught very opposite to a revolutionary one'.[109] As if to confirm this view, though from a different perspective, Leigh Hunt suggested to his *Tatler* readers that the melodrama of threatened seduction in Kenney's *Masaniello* had indeed displaced the politics of Neapolitan rebellion. Masaniello thus rises against the government, argued Hunt with evident disappointment, 'not so much because the people are over-taxed (of which very little is said) as because his sister has been ill-treated by the son of the Viceroy'.[110]

In October 1830, however, a royal command performance of Kenney's *Masaniello* at Covent Garden was abruptly cancelled when the *Poor Man's Guardian*, an unstamped radical newspaper, attempted to appropriate the evening's entertainment in order to plead 'the cause of the "*rabble*"'. The newspaper had exhorted its readers to fill the theatre's galleries, and demonstrate to the king that, like the Neapolitan populace, they too 'would hurl any tyrant from his throne who neglected or abused the interests of his people'. The *Poor Man's Guardian* also urged its readers to use these 'spirit stirring songs of liberty' ('Strike home, our chains will sunder! / To vengeance! fire and sword! / Our wrath shall fall in thunder, / And crush the tyrant's horde!', III.ii and III.iv) in order to demand constitutional reform, the abolition of the House of Lords, and the end of public sinecures and monopolies.[111] Such a prospect was enough to make any patent manager instantly withdraw the play from the stage.

Had Colman's jurisdiction as Examiner of Plays extended beyond Westminster, the Masaniello plays performed at various minor theatres during the 1820s would certainly have been censored. The most eclectic of these adaptations was an equestrian play written by Henry Milner for the Surrey in 1822.[112] Advertised as Burroughs' 'first splendid historical melodrama', and starring Henry Kemble in the title role, the Surrey *Masaniello* was clearly designed to compete with historical spectacles at the rival Coburg theatre. The celebration of Neapolitan fishing and seafaring in Milner's play may also have been calculated to appeal to

---

[109] sc 4081. [110] *Tatler*, 27 November 1830, 1: 291.

[111] *Poor Man's Guardian*, 26 October 1830; also see issues for 31 October and 2 November 1830; James Kenney, *Masaniello, or, The Dumb Girl of Portici* (London: Lacy, 1871).

[112] *Masaniello, Fisherman of Naples or Deliverer of his Country* (Surrey, 1822), many revivals. No text is extant: the discussion which follows is based on a Surrey playbill for 26 December 1822. Several playbills, e.g. for 10 February 1825, mention Milner as the author of *Masaniello*.

Surrey-side spectators, many of whom plied their trades on and around the Thames. The play featured Adams' and Woolford's stud of horses, 'elegantly caparisoned', the eruption of Mount Vesuvius by moonlight (displaying 'the Effect of the Liquid Fire pouring in copious Torrents down the Mountain Sides'), and a magnificent procession 'upwards of 100 Feet in Length' of the Viceroy in his State Carriage, drawn by six real horses, with Masaniello on a horse 'in complete armour'. In a striking technical innovation, reminiscent of Astley's equestrian spectacles, this procession formed a '*Line of March upwards of 100 Feet in Length*', and passed through the Surrey audience on a platform which crossed the theatre's pit.[113]

Milner's play also deserves attention for its political revisions of Neapolitan history. In *La Muette*, the Neapolitan populace's savage plunder and uncontrollable butchery are suddenly halted by a volcanic explosion at which the people, 'awe-struck, bend in submission to the will of heaven'.[114] But Milner's dramatisation of Masaniello's betrayal, death and its aftermath is very different. Indeed, the play attributes responsibility for the hero's death to a treacherous Spanish government, 'who caused him to be basely assassinated'. In other words, Milner's play interprets Masaniello's fate as the action of an oppressive colonial power.[115]

As in *Mungo Parke*, Milner rewrites history by inventing a form of popular retribution for Masaniello's death. In the Surrey production, this takes the form of a spectacular equestrian coda starring Leona, Masaniello's wife. After the 'Solemn Funeral Procession' of the hero (complete with the sympathetic death of Masaniello's horse at his grave), Leona addresses the multitude and takes revenge on Julio Genovino, an evil and lascivious priest, for her husband's death. A grand mounted attack on the Citadel follows, from whose burning ruins Leona is dramatically rescued by her horse: 'Total destruction of the Citadel, and final Triumph of the Patriotic Cause. Masaniello's Murder Avenged.'

The Surrey *Masaniello* thus ends with the triumph of popular patriotism; the blow-up of the citadel seems to rehearse the defeat of Spanish power.[116] Whereas the Covent Garden productions of *Masaniello* were subjected to various forms of censorship, the liberty enjoyed by minor

---

[113] Playbill, December 26 1822.

[114] See Milner's later, very different adaptation, *Masaniello; or, The Dumb Girl of Portici* (Coburg, 1829), *CMT* I, III.iii. This version was based on Auber's opera.   [115] Playbill, 26 December 1822.

[116] According to the *Drama*, January 1823, 49, Mrs Pope 'declaimed finely, looked worthy to be the wife of so intrepid a patriot as *Massaniello*, and in the last scene her accomplished *horsemanship* excited universal approbation'.

theatres such as the Surrey included the freedom to stage such controversial narratives on the edge of political representation.

To some extent, then, John Stephens was right to suspect that the minor theatres enjoyed a certain, limited, political freedom. As we have seen, reviewers expressed a variety of fears about the unregulated character of these productions. Nevertheless, illegitimate theatre cannot simply be equated with moral and political transgression. Rather, this chapter has sought to demonstrate that the eclectic dramaturgy of these plays transformed how the contemporary world could be imagined on stage.

CHAPTER FOUR

Illegitimate Shakespeares

ANTIQUARIANISM AND *MAGNA CHARTA*

The year 1823 witnessed two very different theatrical performances of *King John*. As if to shake off the play's propagandist, xenophobic history, Charles Kemble employed the dramatist and antiquarian James Robinson Planché to design his Covent Garden production. Determined to build on Covent Garden's reputation for theatrical antiquarianism, Planché based the visual spectacle of *King John* on Joseph Strutt's *A Complete View of the Dress and Habits of the People of England* (1796–9). The Covent Garden production starred William Macready as King John (played 'perhaps with more vigour than authentic history can countenance') and Charles Kemble as the Bastard.[1]

Planché's highly pictorial design and silvery costumes (though the actors assumed their flat-topped *chapeaux de fer* only with 'sulky' reluctance),[2] confirmed *King John*'s disappearance from political history. Once the quintessential drama of anti-Gallic propaganda, the genteel, decorous antiquarianism of Planché's *King John* suggests the play's meek return to the historical past, weighed down by effigies, seals and illuminated manuscripts. Gone were the anti-Catholic vituperation of Cibber's *Papal Tyranny* (the acting version of *King John* for most of the eighteenth century), the martial fury and withering contempt of Sarah Siddons as Constance and the patriotic fervour of Richard Valpy's adaptation, as performed during the Napoleonic wars.

In Planché's version of theatrical history, the Coburg then attempted to challenge Covent Garden's antiquarian splendour by staging its own history play, *William the Conqueror; or, The Battle of Hastings* (1824). Certainly, the Coburg playbills painstakingly cited the very same authorities on costume and armoury which Planché had consulted for *King John* at Covent Garden. The most amusing aspect of 'this ridiculous and

---

[1] See Planché, *Recollections*, chapter 4; *The Times*, 4 March 1823.　　[2] Planché, *Recollections*, I: 56.

disgraceful exhibition' – according to Planché at least – seems to have been the spectacle of Dr Coombe, Keeper of Medals at the British Museum (attracted to the Coburg, like Planché, by the illusory promise of antiquarian spectacle) vainly trying to preserve his best black suit and immaculate neckcloth amidst the fray in the Coburg pit.[3]

In the wake of the Covent Garden revival, although Planché's memoirs do not mention the event, the Coburg also staged a *King John* play. *Magna Charta; or, The Eventful Reign of King John* opened in April 1823, and ran successfully for about a month. In order to understand the significance of *Magna Charta*, we need to retrace our theatrical steps to the Coburg's first illegitimate production of Shakespeare in 1819–20. Having engaged the celebrated actor Junius Brutus Booth for a short season, William Glossop had staged a series of legitimate plays including John Howard Payne's *Brutus*, John Home's romantic tragedy, *Douglas*, and *Richard III*. Though conspicuously publicised as a melodrama, Moncrieff's adaptation of *Richard III* nonetheless represented an audacious raid on the patentees' Shakespearean capital. Earlier unlicensed productions, notably Elliston's *Macbeth* (Surrey, 1809), had followed the semiotic conventions of illegitimacy, producing Shakespeare in recitative and silent gesture. But with the exception of an occasional, 'almost inaudible' musical accompaniment, the Coburg *Richard III* dispensed with these conventions. Indeed, the only other feature by which the Coburg production could be distinguished from the play as performed at Covent Garden was the murder of the children in the Tower. Whereas, at Covent Garden, these events took place off-stage, the Coburg dramatised the children's murders in full view of the audience, accompanied by music whose purpose the patent informant memorably conjectured was 'to drown the cries'.[4]

Having expended £1500 on *Richard III* (in his own, exaggerated estimate), Glossop's hopes of commercial profit from performing Shakespeare on the south bank were instantly dashed. The patentees immediately prosecuted Glossop for illegally representing legitimate drama, and the manager was fined a total of £100. After his conviction, Glossop must have concluded that future Shakespearean productions should be more comprehensively disguised. Having failed to convince the magistrates about the illegitimate status of Moncrieff's melodramatic *Richard III*, the next two 'Shakespearean' plays performed – *Magna*

---

[3] Planché, *Recollections*, 1: 62.
[4] Testimony of Doobey, an assistant in the Covent Garden box office, reported in *British Stage*, March 1820, 4:140–1.

Charta (1823) and *Wat Tyler* (1825; revived 1831) – omitted Shakespeare's name from the playbills altogether.

Grandiose in scale and visually spectacular, *Magna Charta* confirmed the Coburg's determination to rival the visual antiquarianism and scenic attractions of the patent houses. Wilkins, Pitt, Walker and Jones had painted the 'splendid and characteristic scenery'; the playbill also drew attention to the extravagant costumes and armoury, with pageants arranged by the Coburg's dancing-master, Monsieur le Clercq, and combats – in which real horses appeared for the first time on the Coburg stage – designed by Bradley. The banquet scene, 'embracing the entire extent of the Stage, and the whole of the Company, aided by the Supernumeraries', aimed to recreate a royal banquet 'in times of FEUDAL SPLENDOUR'. In 'The Plain of Runnymede' (painted by Wilkins and Pitt), the bill promised Coburg audiences the 'exact Representation of the Arms, Armorial Bearings, and Warlike Accoutrements of those Ancient times (1215)'.[5]

No text for *Magna Charta! or, The Eventful Reign of King John* survives. Two sources, however, enable us partially to reconstruct the play. In the first of these, a Coburg playbill for 5 May 1823, Henry Milner is named as the play's author; Hodgson's juvenile drama text, also entitled *Magna Charta*, appears to represent a condensed version of the Coburg play.[6] In *Magna Charta*, Milner re-imagined the history of King John through the lens of melodrama. The barons' demand for a Charter, for instance, is intricately woven into a comic subplot of mistaken identities; *Magna Charta* is distinctive too for the moral perspicacity of its plot. King John, therefore, solemnly accepts the justice of his fate. 'Then am I sacrificed at last,' he declares in his final speech, 'I feel the poison working. Well, well, I deserve it. Now, now, Constance – now Arthur, are you satisfied?'[7]

At first glance, *Magna Charta*'s comic subplot, starring two young couples (Céline and Henrique, Louise and Basil), together with O'Shane, Philip Falconbridge's Irish esquire (a typical stage Irishman), merely provides a romantic counterpoint to King John's downfall. During the eighteenth century, the performance of Shakespeare at the London fairs had interpolated comic drolls very similar in style to the subplots of melo-

---

[5] Playbill, 5 May 1823.
[6] The reproduction of texts, scenes and portraits for toy theatres was a profitable line of business in this period for publishers such as Hodgson and Skelt. The popularity of juvenile drama raises many interesting questions about the meanings of theatrical spectatorship; these images also offer the theatre historian a wealth of evidence about costume, gesture and expression, though we need to be cautious about assuming that they provide us with an unmediated historical record.   [7] *Magna Charta*, scene xviii.

drama.[8] But what is perhaps surprising about this narrative of French love, jealousy and loyalty is Milner's inversion of *King John*'s anti-Gallic theatrical history: the subplot of *Magna Charta* presents Frenchmen as the heroic liberators of England's 'persecuted people'.

On closer inspection, *Magna Charta* complicates that 'love of loyalty, order and morality' which Glossop claimed to be producing at the Coburg. For the transformation of *King John* into melodrama also involves the recuperation of that political drama about the making of Magna Charta which Shakespeare's play had repressed. Indeed, the successful demand of the barons for Magna Charta lies at the political centre of Milner's play. Significantly, the two men who make possible the signing of Magna Charta are Baron Falconbridge, an impoverished, virtuous aristocrat, and his faithful French servant, Henrique. Together with Falconbridge, Henrique tries to prevent Hubert from killing Arthur; when Arthur's body is recovered from the moat, Falconbridge presents the dead prince as an almost talismanic political symbol:

See this, ye noblemen of England, and lament for ever! – here is your lawful prince inhumanly murdered! – Follow me, brave Barons, and let us swear never to sheath our swords till John shall grant us a charter to secure our rights and liberties. (Hodgson, scene viii)

The last scene of the play depicts King John, surrounded by the barons, signing 'the great and mighty charter' on the Plain of Runnymede. He is then poisoned, not by an anonymous monk, but by Henrique. As the King drinks from the poisoned goblet, the patriotic chorus rejoices that 'Britain's the land of liberty' (scene xviii). In Milner's melodramatic version of history, the signing of Magna Charta thus becomes the triumphant conclusion of King's John's reign.

For nineteenth-century radicals the barons' rebellion against King John had become a touchstone of legitimate resistance to state power. In certain ways, *Magna Charta* seems to evoke this radical subtext: it is noticeable, for example, that Milner foregrounds the heroism of Baron Falconbridge, 'a poor baron, mean in all but heart, in mind, and title' and Henrique, his loyal and honourable French servant, in the monarch's overthrow. In other ways, however, the patriotism of Milner's play simply dovetails with the chauvinistic rhetoric of popular theatre: *Magna Charta* abounds with patriotic claptraps which celebrate the conviction that 'every English heart would gladly shed its blood to crush

---

[8] See 'A collection of cuttings, playbills, mss. notes, and other material relating to Bartholemew Fair and Pie Powder Court', MS 1514, Guildhall Library.

oppression, and to exterminate the base usurper' (Baron Falconbridge, I.i). Melodrama, as we have seen, characteristically holds in tension such conflicting, even irreconcilable, interpretations. Though the origins of the Coburg *Magna Charta* finally remain ineluctable, it seems probable that Milner's play represents a popular adaptation of Shakespeare's *King John*.

KEMBLE'S MONARCHY: DISSIDENT VOICES

Milner's invention of a justly punished King John reflects the dramatic conventions and ideological loyalties of melodrama. John Philip Kemble's Shakespearean kings, by contrast, represent the crown in a very different light. During a period when the institution of kingship began to be interpreted as vulnerable, even precarious, Kemble designed his Shakespeare productions as the quintessential defence of monarchical legitimacy.[9] Through detailed expurgation of acting texts and the skilful orchestration of majestic images on stage, Kemble created a series of counter-revolutionary productions in which author- ity (whether ducal or monarchical), seemed to become mystically unquestionable. In *Coriolanus* (Drury Lane, 1789), for example, Kemble interpolated an extra speech for Volumnia in order to enhance Caius Martius' majesty. 'He was a thing of blood, whose every motion / Was tim'd with dying cries', Volumnia declares of her son, 'And thrice the Volscians sunk beneath his thunder,/ Bending the knee, as 'twere in ado- ration.' [Flourish of trumpets.][10] Volumnia's description represents her son as a quasi-monarchical individual, awful and inscrutable; the prom- inence of kneeling in these productions helps to signify the divine char- acter of monarchical authority.[11] Huge, statuesque crowds (Kemble was adept at organising his supernumeraries), also helped to define in visual terms the political distance between the ruler and his subjects. The defence and promotion of monarchy underpinned every aspect of

---

[9] On Kemble's productions, see David Rostron, 'John Philip Kemble's Coriolanus and Julius Caesar: An Examination of the Prompt Copies', *Theatre Notebook* 23 (1968), 26–34, and Nicola J. Watson, 'Kemble, Scott, and the Mantle of the Bard' in Jean I. Marsden, ed., *The Appropriation of Shakespeare: Post-Renaissance Reconstructions of the Works and the Myth* (Hemel Hempstead: Harvester, 1991), 73–92.

[10] J. P. Kemble, ed., *Coriolanus, or The Roman Matron*, facsimile text (London: Cornmarket Press, 1970), 1789, II.i.25–6.

[11] Cf. Kemble's much-copied though controversial decision to kneel at the descent of the Ghost in *Hamlet* and, in *Henry V*, his celebrated 'starting up from prayer at the sound of the trumpet' remembered by James Boaden as 'one of the most spirited excitements that the stage has ever displayed'. Boaden, *Kemble*, II: 8.

Kemble's Shakespearean production. Even the richly ornamented heraldic banners used in processions were inscribed with the names of British monarchs: the banner for Alfred the Great proudly proclaimed, 'Founder of the British Monarchy, 872–901!'[12]

In many ways, what Kemble created at Covent Garden was a theatrical monarchy which shored up – even to the extent of standing in place of – the kingship of an incapacitated George III. Indeed, the critical success of this vicarious monarchy can be surmised from the monarchical language which pervades contemporary reviews. A *Times'* critic, for instance, referred to the 'majesty' of Kemble's gestures as Coriolanus (9 May 1814).[13] Kemble's portrayal of King Lear, a king whose madness had now begun to seem so dangerously, topically prescient, also reveals an important shift in emphasis. As one spectator remarked, Kemble's Lear was a 'tranquil, venerable monarch, made shortly after justifiably angry by the conduct of Cordelia'.[14] The genius of Kemble in this part was to forge a plausible and irrefutable emotional logic for Lear's mental disintegration, without ever compromising the king's monarchical authority. Even in the face of 'palsied decrepitude', remarked several critics, Kemble's Lear remained venerable, solemn and dignified.[15]

The dignity, authority and decorum of Kemble's Shakespearean monarchs, however, was precisely what irritated the reviewers of the *Examiner*. To be sure, these critics were quick to acknowledge Kemble's originality as a tragic actor, and to praise his efforts in keeping Shakespeare before the public – were it not for Kemble, declared one critic, the tragedies 'of our most glorious bard would almost be in danger of dismissal from the stage'.[16] But the Shakespearean productions at Covent Garden had also come to represent the patrician complacency of the political establishment, and the moribund moral correctness sweeping through the middle classes.

Kemble's productions, alleged the *Examiner* critics, abounded in fake classicism, 'gorgeous ornament', and gaudy splendour.[17] The managers 'occasionally affect to be classical' commented one reviewer with heavy irony, by introducing 'a fragment of Shakspear' merely in order to

---

[12] T. J. Dibdin, *Reminiscences*, I: 197.

[13] For other references to Kemble's 'majesty', see John Taylor's poem, 'The Stage' and the anonymous pamphlet, 'General Observations on Mr. Kemble's Talents' in John Ambrose Williams, *Memoirs of John Philip Kemble Esq.* (London: I. J.Burn, 1817). On Kemble's 'majestic form', see *A Short Criticism on the Performance of Hamlet by Mr. Kemble* (London: T. Hookham, 1789), 5.

[14] [Edward Mangin], *Piozziana; or, Recollections of the late Mrs. Piozzi* (London: Edward Moxon, 1833), 165.   [15] *Universal Magazine*, May 1808; Dutton, *Dramatic Censor*, 1801, 2: 71–2.

[16] *Examiner*, 3 June 1810, 344.

[17] See for example, [Thomas Barnes], *Examiner*, 19 December 1813, 810.

prevent 'a satiety of farce and pantomime': the revival of *Anthony and Cleopatra* epitomised this 'magnificent raree-show'.[18] Kemble's portentous assumption of Shakespearean majesty soon became a favourite point of reference in these accounts: Leigh Hunt mocked the actor's 'majestic dryness and deliberate nothings' and Hazlitt objected to his 'repulsive stately dignity of manner' in *Cymbeline*.[19] The *Examiner*'s criticism of Covent Garden reveals its reviewers' anxieties about the stultifying influence of respectability, 'methodistical morality' and refinement in contemporary metropolitan culture. 'The Society for the Suppression of Vice,' declared Hazlitt gloomily in his review of Kemble's *Tempest*, only to suppress the comment when he reprinted the piece in *Characters of Shakespeare's Plays*, 'would do well to read Shakespeare'.[20] In parts that suited him, Leigh Hunt joked, Kemble might have been interesting, 'if you could have forgotten that their sensibility, in his hands, was not so much repressed, as wanting'. Hazlitt takes up a similar theme in his review of Kemble as Sir Giles Overreach. If only Kemble would make friends with nature and 'hug her close', Hazlitt laments with genial irony. But perhaps, he continues with an air of resignation, nature has already staged her elopement, and left the actor-manager behind her.[21]

What distinguishes the *Examiner* reviews is their stubborn, rebellious determination to read against the grain of Kemble's legitimate, monarchical productions at Covent Garden. In this way, Hazlitt's subtle and extraordinary Shakespearean readings, like those of Leigh Hunt and Thomas Barnes, become the ideological counter-blast to Kemble's Shakespeare. Thomas Barnes' account of the Covent Garden production of *Coriolanus* represents one of the earliest salvoes in this campaign. In order to appreciate Barnes' argument, let us set his *Examiner* review alongside one published in *The Times* a year later. In 1814, *The Times* praised in fulsome terms Kemble's performance as Coriolanus. With a perceptible hint of nostalgia, the reviewer described Coriolanus as a natural aristocrat, 'deeply imbued with the pride of birth, when the name of a patrician was cherished with an inapproachable and inextinguishable jealousy'. As this account suggests, Kemble's portrayal of

---

[18] *Examiner*, 5 December 1813, 779–80.

[19] *Examiner*, 1 June 1817, 344. Compare the views of the German playwright Ludwig Tieck, who admired Kemble's meticulous arrangement of performers in *Julius Caesar* but concluded that the production suffered from an air of 'pretentious majesty'. See John A. Kelly, *German Visitors to English Theatres in the Eighteenth Century* (Princeton University Press, 1936), 46.

[20] *Examiner*, 11 February 1816, 92.

[21] *Examiner*, 5 May 1816, 286. See also Hunt's review of *Macbeth*, *Examiner*, 9 January 1809, satirising Kemble's 'methodistical artifices of dropt eyes, patient shakes of the head, and whining preachments'. On Kemble's lack of sensibility, see *Examiner*, 5 February 1815, 89.

Coriolanus interlaced patrician pride and bourgeois gentility: the hero's notorious attack on the tribunes was thereby transformed into a triumph of social condescension, 'a model of *refined* and lofty indignation'.[22]

In 1813, during Leigh Hunt's imprisonment for libelling the Prince Regent, Thomas Barnes had taken over the theatre reviews for the *Examiner*. On the night Barnes saw *Coriolanus* Kemble was indisposed, and the leading role was taken by William Conway. (On such occasions, the actor standing in for Kemble was expected to follow precisely the leading actor's interpretation of the role).[23] In this review, Barnes mounts a direct and systematic attack on the conservative values of Kemble's Covent Garden production. In particular, he tries to expose Kemble's transposition of political conflict into genteel domesticity. For, as Barnes quickly recognises, this silent transposition has powerful ideological effects: the 'conjugal fondness', 'filial obedience', and respectability of the Covent Garden Coriolanus serve to legitimate his arrogant disdain for plebeian distress.

Barnes then proposes a distinctive and original counter-reading of the play. Far from being a prototype of domesticity, he argues, Shakespeare's Coriolanus is in fact a savage, a barbarian soldier of primitive Rome: primitive instinct, rather than the dictates of nineteenth-century respectability, shape his behaviour and political choices. Thus Martius' 'attentive submissiveness' to his mother is 'unmixed with affection', whilst his treatment of Virgilia exhibits 'the mere kindness of sexual impulse, unelevated with any noble and rational motive'. How can these 'mere savage virtues' be interpreted in Kemble's production as marks of civilisation? What is more, Barnes argues, Shakespeare engrafts on the savage's pride 'the unnatural and more hateful haughtiness of the social aristocrat, who abhors his inferiors because their "shoes are cobbled," and because their faces are not washed in the scented waters of spruce and perfumed nobility.'[24] For Thomas Barnes, Shakespeare's *Coriolanus* offers us not a historical lesson in gentility, but rather a guide to the barbarous origins of the modern aristocracy.

Having watched Kemble in the title role at Covent Garden, the Irish barrister John Finlay would observe that the moral of *Coriolanus* is 'the conquest of filial duty'.[25] (Finlay does not stop to consider the possibility of a distinction between the domestic, middle-class values of Kemble's interpretation, and those of Shakespeare's play.) Barnes's review, by contrast, confronted and then pointedly undermined the

---

[22] *The Times*, May 19 1814 (my italics).   [23] *Examiner*, 19 December 1813, 810–11.
[24] *Ibid.*, 811.   [25] *Miscellanies*, 280.

political assumptions implicit in Kemble's production. Hazlitt's now famous essay on *Coriolanus*, written three years later, develops and extends Barnes' argument about the Covent Garden show.

By December 1816, of course, the political and theatrical sands had shifted. At Drury Lane, Edmund Kean's portrayals of characters such as Shylock, Richard III and Iago seemed to call into question the monarchical 'religion' as defined by John Philip Kemble. Meanwhile, beyond the walls of the London theatres, Liverpool's government was brusquely confronting mass protest and social disorder. The enactment of the Corn Law in March 1815 had been accompanied by attacks on the houses of MPs. Then, during the spring and early summer of 1816, angry, sometimes violent crowds gathered in rural areas protesting about high food prices and other grievances: the judicial commission sent to the affected areas to suppress this discontent had condemned to death more than twenty men. In November and early December 1816, just before Hazlitt wrote his essay on *Coriolanus*, demonstrations at Spa Fields had raised once more the spectre of mass public disorder.

The version of Hazlitt's argument about *Coriolanus* which is usually reprinted in modern anthologies is taken from *A View of the English Stage* (1818). This essay begins with wry political irony – 'Shakspeare has in this play shewn himself well versed in history and state affairs.'[26] But the *Examiner* review of 15 December 1816 actually opens with the disarmingly factual (and deeply ironic) statement, 'CORIOLANUS has of late been repeatedly acted here.'[27] Hazlitt's formulation is deliberately conventional but, at the same time, double-edged; the repeated acting of Coriolanus refers both to the play's representation on stage, and, by extension, to the political enactment of its underlying conflicts in Regency Britain. And although there is little theatrical detail in this review, Hazlitt's argument can only be understood in relation to the politics of Kemble's production. For the subtle brilliance of Hazlitt's essay consists in its deft, subversive restoration of that Shakespearean language of famine, starvation and human cannibalism which Kemble had resolutely censored in his expurgated production. Having recovered that language of protest, Hazlitt is able to show the disturbing historical connections between the arguments of the Roman plebeians and the rhetoric of political protest and social distress in nineteenth-century Britain. (See in particular the tendentious link Hazlitt makes – and then suppresses in the versions of the review which appear in *Characters* and *A*

---

[26] *Hazlitt* v: 344–50, 347.   [27] Cf. *Hazlitt*, iv: 214–21.

View of the English Stage – between Volumnia's curse on Roman trades, and a newspaper account of Spa Fields). In a variety of ways, then, Hazlitt's interpretation of *Coriolanus* takes the form of a passionate refutation of Kemble's legitimate Shakespeare.

In Kemble's hands, as Barnes recognised, *Coriolanus* had become a modern parable about the rightness of patrician rule.[28] Having removed from his acting text most rhetorical traces of their poverty and distress, Kemble had succeeded in transforming the Roman citizens from articulate, impoverished protestors, critical of luxurious patrician abundance, into dull rebels without a cause. In his essay (and in contrast to his practice elsewhere), Hazlitt does not confront this censorship directly.[29] Rather, what preoccupies him is the cruel, predatory pursuit of the many by the few in human history, and the way in which our experience of reading or watching *Coriolanus* proves our sympathetic complicity with power. Hazlitt then goes on to provide a series of savage analogies for the relationship between Coriolanus and the plebeians. Through these images of a lion hunting a flock of sheep, or the royal hunt of history, 'in which what is sport to the few, is death to the many' (350), he explores our willingness to identify with the powerful at the expense of the powerless, to be entranced by Coriolanus' savage authority rather than sharing in the pain and suffering of the plebeians. By reading against the grain of Kemble's production, Hazlitt thus restores the framework of plebeian protest to *Coriolanus*.

Four years later, Elliston's revival of *Coriolanus* at Drury Lane in 1820 would also stir up contradictory responses in Hazlitt's mind. Here, however, Hazlitt's subject becomes the contradictory claims represented by legitimacy and illegitimacy, Shakespeare and Harlequin. In a variety of ways, Elliston's management marked a cultural and social watershed. The patrician, aristocratic world of patent management – already undermined, nonetheless, during the Regency years, by the 'vulgar' business interests of Samuel Whitbread in the brewing trade – was suddenly faced with the prospect of a lessee who had acquired his capital producing illegitimate drama on the Surrey side. Drury Lane

---

28 Cf. *The Times* review of the 1796 production, 20 April 1796, which celebrates the 'laugh of contempt' from the audience which accompanied 'every appearance of the rabble'.

29 Censorship, whether practised by managers, audiences or the Examiner of Plays, is a frequent theme in Hazlitt's theatre criticism. See his protests over the expurgation of Knowles' *Virginius*: 'is the name of Liberty to be struck out of the English language?' (*London Magazine*, July 1820, *Hazlitt* XVIII, 347). Cf. Hazlitt's ironic references to the political audacity of staging Rowe's *Jane Shore* (*Examiner*, 5 January 1817, *Hazlitt* XVIII:211).

was now in the hands of a watchmaker's son, a ruthless modern cultural entrepreneur.[30]

First performed on 25 January 1820, only a few days before the death of George III, *Coriolanus* was Elliston's second production of Shakespeare at Drury Lane to star Edmund Kean. The manager had examined his acting text for the occasion, and carefully restored a number of speeches expurgated by Kemble, including Menenius' fable of the body politic; at Kean's insistence, the Drury Lane production also included an elaborate storm, made up of hundreds of separate leaves. But the sketchy rehearsal of the supernumeraries, together with Kean's wayward performance (though 'what it wanted in dignity was amply compensated in fire and energy', remarked the *Morning Chronicle*'s reviewer, 26 January 1820), did not impress the critics; according to many spectators, Elliston's revival of *Coriolanus* failed. For Hazlitt, however, Kean's vulgar, anarchic energy in the role, and his indecorous lack of dignified grandeur, made possible a form of political liberation.

In Hazlitt's eyes, Kean thwarted our capitulation as spectators to that aristocratic 'logic of the imagination' by which we tend to fall under the spell of Coriolanus. Rather than colluding with 'the *assumption* of a right to insult or oppress others',[31] Kean's performance revealed these assumptions as contingent and questionable. The Drury Lane production thus offered the chance of momentarily escaping from the identity of poetry and arbitrary power. And so Hazlitt's essay pivots on that now famous remark, 'Mr. Kean's acting is not of the patrician order; he is one of the people, and what might be termed a *radical* performer' (290). With this declamatory comment, the critic quickly evokes, and then threatens to overturn, that binary opposition between the aristocratic principle of poetry and the cause of the people. Whilst acknowledging Kean's inability to portray Coriolanus' 'inordinate self-opinion, and haughty elevation of soul', Hazlitt nonetheless celebrates the social and ideological gulf between character and performer precisely because it exposes the play's savage, primitive poetical justice. Kean's failure of decorum – a failure long associated in Hazlitt's mind with the anarchic, disruptive energy of a Harlequin – thus becomes synonymous with a radical critique of *Coriolanus*:

The intolerable airs and aristocratical pretensions of which he is the slave, and to which he falls a victim, did not seem *legitimate* in him, but upstart, turbulent, and vulgar. (290)

---

[30] See George Raymond, *Memoirs of Elliston*; Christopher Murray, *Robert William Elliston, Manager* (London: Society for Theatre Research, 1975).   [31] *Hazlitt* IV: 215, my italics.

In this word 'legitimate', Hazlitt encapsulates the ideological disintegration of that binary opposition at the heart of the Covent Garden *Coriolanus*. For Kean's performance, argues Hazlitt, lies outside the boundaries of legitimacy (social, political and theatrical) in 'the common arena of man' (290). Whereas Kemble's manner had the air of a conversation with his dinner acquaintances in the boxes, Kean's 'coarse', 'uncouth' performance ('too obtrusive and undisguised a display of nature' to please the boxes),[32] undercuts these aristocratic relations. Rather than making tyranny absolute, the Drury Lane *Coriolanus* evokes a tyranny which is provisional, precarious, half made up.[33] The 'excessive significance' of Kean's performance, his 'studied variations' of scorn and disgust, thus offer a subversive counterpoint which disrupts our wholesale capitulation to arbitrary power.

In other ways, too, legitimacy and illegitimacy spectacularly clashed in the Drury Lane *Coriolanus*. If Kean's transgressions seemed to challenge the ideological legacy of Kemble's production, Elliston's meretricious populism nonetheless disturbingly confirmed the 'illegitimate' appropriation of Shakespeare. Hazlitt's essay is highly critical of the production's tawdry spectacle, including processions, 'some of which were lengthened out as if they would reach all the way to the Circus', 'a sham-fight, of melodramatic effect', and an impression of continuous noise and music (291). In this argument, Elliston is portrayed as a dangerous cultural *parvenu*, careless of the dignity and seriousness of Shakespearean tragedy. For all the radical pleasures of Kean's performance in the leading role, Elliston's *Coriolanus* also evokes that half-acknowledged nightmare of a plebeian *coup d'état*, a vision of imperial dramatic power intent upon the vulgar conversion of Shakespeare into Harlequin.[34]

SHAKESPEAREAN INNOVATIONS

The confusion about a popular Shakespeare which we glimpse in Hazlitt's essay attests to a genuine conflict of cultural values; no other contemporary writer attempts so honestly to acknowledge such contradictory views. For many, indeed, there is no alternative to the theatrical status quo. Take, for example, the memorable evidence provided at the Parliamentary Select Committee on Dramatic Literature by Thomas Morton, reader of plays at Drury Lane. According to Morton, Shakespeare himself had given dramatic support to the theatrical

---

[32] *Examiner*, 18 February 1816, *Hazlitt* V: 285.   [33] Shakespeare, *Richard III*, I.i.21.
[34] *Hazlitt* XVIII: 318.

monopoly. He proceeded to quote the Prologue from *Henry V* to prove
it: 'A kingdom for a stage, princes to act / And monarchs to behold the
swelling scene!' [35] Here was a 'command' from the playwright, declared
Morton, 'that his pieces should be produced only in the noblest temples
of the Muses'. Like other defenders of monopoly who cited
Shakespeare in their evidence, Morton seems blissfully unaware that the
Elizabethan theatre (not to mention the social composition of
Shakespeare's audience) powerfully contradict the political logic of
Shakespearean monopoly. In any case, by 1832, the defence of Drury
Lane and Covent Garden as noble temples of the Muses had become
simply laughable. Jack Palmer's production of *As You Like It*, as we saw
in chapter 1, boldly challenged the patentees' Shakespearean monopoly.
Just over two decades later, in 1809, the Old Price riots would define
Shakespeare as the symbol of a British dramatic tradition now under
siege from effeminate Italian opera and the 'promiscuous' mummery of
melodrama.[36] But the real turning-point in this history, especially in
relation to that presumptuous conviction that Shakespeare's plays were
'but little calculated for the multitude',[37] came late in the summer of
1809, when Robert Elliston, the new actor-manager of the Royal Circus
in St George's Fields, decided to stage his own illegitimate production of
Shakespeare's *Macbeth*.

The Circus play was advertised as 'a Grand Ballet of Action, with recitative, founded on Macbeth'.[38] According to *The Times* (30 September
1809), the crowded audiences were 'altogether as respectable and brilliant as we have ever beheld in the best days of out winter theatres'. By
staging Shakespeare, Elliston was explicitly challenging the exclusive
privileges of the patent houses. But his musical, dumbshow version of
Macbeth also fulfilled all the legal requirements for an illegitimate production, as Busby's opening address wryly confirmed:

> Though not indulg'd with fullest pow'rs of speech,
> The poet's object we aspire to reach;
> The emphatic gesture, eloquence of eye,
> Scenes, music every energy we try

---

[35] *Henry V*, Prologue, lines 3–4. See *SC* 3897.

[36] For the appropriation of Shakespeare by the monopolists, cf. Sheridan's satirical poem, 'Had
Shakespeare when first he took charge of the Stage'. Sheridan portrays the Old Price riots as an
egalitarian, quasi-republican campaign to destroy fashion, beauty, and the stock repertoire.
Whitbread MS 4397, published anonymously in *British Press*, 19 September 1810.

[37] *Theatrical Inquisitor*, December 1814, 5: 403, of *Hamlet* and *Macbeth*.

[38] *The Times*, 25 August 1809. *The History, Murders, Life, and Death of Macbeth*: and a full description
of the Scenery, Action, Choruses, and Characters of the Ballet of Music and Action, of that
name . . . (London: T. Page, 1809).

> To make your hearts for murder'd Banquo melt;
> And feel for Duncan as brave Malcom felt;
> To prove we keep our duties full in view,
> And what we must not *say*, resolve to *do*;
> Convinc'd that you will deem our zeal sincere,
> Since more by *deeds* than *words* it will appear.

In this speech, later printed alongside the published text, the Royal Circus offers an explanation of the terms under which the performers will circumvent the ban on legitimate drama and yet observe the terms of the theatre's licence. To paraphrase this opening address, actions will speak where words may not be spoken. This decision to perform *Macbeth* 'more by *deeds* than *words*' was a tactical as well as a commercial success for Elliston and his company. At a meeting with the Lord Chamberlain, Sheridan did certainly raise the illegality of the Circus production. Whether the Earl of Dartmouth (who was sympathetic to the minor theatres) proceeded to pour cold water on Sheridan's litigious ambitions, we do not know. But, in any case, the patentees took no legal action against *Macbeth*.[39] Elliston – the dramatic Alcibiades of his generation – must have realised that the monopoly of Shakespeare by the Theatres Royal was now in dispute.

Like John Cross' *Circusiana*, the dramaturgy of *Macbeth* is composed from a mixture of dumbshow and recitative in rhyming couplets; the Weird Sisters are the only characters who speak (or rather sing) in the language of Shakespeare. The Surrey band, under the direction of Sanderson, accompanied the characters' recitative with a selection of music attributed to Matthew Locke, but probably by Henry Purcell. Most of the play's scenes were clinched by a single, rhymed couplet, usually taken directly from Shakespeare. But whereas the neat completeness of a couplet often fulfils an aesthetic function in Shakespeare, the doggerel lines spoken at the Surrey had been designed as a form of illegitimate speech ostensibly immune from prosecution.

As in the *Circusiana*, visual signs play an important role in conveying the plot of *Macbeth*: in Act III scene iv, for example, Macbeth uses a picture to explain his orders for the castle's defence. A series of scrolls also supplement the expressive dramaturgy of dumbshow. The silent words written upon these linen banners inform Macduff about the murder of his wife and children, explain the action of the drama (one scroll reads that 'Macbeth ordains a solemn Banquet') and even foreshadow, as if prophetically, the play's dénouement (Malcolm and

---

[39] George Raymond, *Memoirs of Elliston*, I: 437: for the address, see I:403–4.

Macduff's banner at Birnam Wood is inscribed with the words, 'Destruction to the Tyrant').

In its presentation of music as a dramatic language in its own right, the Surrey *Macbeth* prefigures the conventions of silent cinema.[40] In Act I scene vi, for instance, the text states that Macbeth 'appears revolving somewhat in his mind'. But since Macbeth's introspection cannot legally be dramatised in spoken language, a chorus of sprites provides a musical analogy for his revolving thoughts. Conversely, the suspension of music in the dagger scene ('very solemnly and strikingly performed without music') creates a sudden, foreboding silence. As if to express the encroaching evil, only the sound of the bell tolling accompanies the dumbshow scene:

> Lady Macbeth descends and listens at Duncan's door, and finds all quiet, she then enters. Macbeth and attendant descend, Macbeth discharges him, and moves lightly about. Enter Lady Macbeth. A struggle between her and Macbeth, he being afraid to execute the deed. Lady Macbeth then leaves him. An illusion of a spirit holding a dagger appears, which he then endeavours to seize, but it vanishes when he makes the attempt. A bell tolls.
>
> [MACBETH] Hear not that Duncan; for it is a knell
> That summons thee to Heav'n, or to hell.   (I.vii)

The success of Elliston's production, together with the brisk sale of play-texts in cheap copies, demonstrated the commercial profits to be gained from performing Shakespeare on the south bank of the river. In the following year, Elliston staged *Anthony and Cleopatra* (advertised as a 'burlesque Tragic Burletta'), as well as David Garrick's *Jubilee* (based on seventeen of Shakespeare's plays). At the Royalty, Shakespearean productions during the season of 1812–13 included *Richard III*, *King Lear* (a notable event, given the agreement by the Theatres Royal during this period not to stage the play, in order to avoid spectators drawing parallels between the tormented, irrational behaviour of Lear, and the illness of George III), *Othello*, *The Merry Wives of Windsor*, and Garrick's *Catherine and Petruchio*.

The success of the Circus *Macbeth* acted as a spur to other managers of minor theatres to stage their own Shakespearean productions. One delighted spectator at the Surrey wrote to the *Theatrical Inquisitor*, declaring (with ungrammatical enthusiasm) that Elliston was now 'so close . . . upon the heels of the *legitamate* (legitimate) stage, that in spite of the *tinckling* (tinkling) of the piana (piano) and the *jingle* of the rhyme, I can often fancy myself sitting in one of the winter theatres'.[41] Predictably, however, some critics greeted Elliston's *Macbeth* with a mixture of disdain, mockery and condescension. One reviewer ridiculed Elliston for having transformed Shakespeare's tragic hero into 'a musical retailer of eight line verses', and roundly condemned the manager for 'administering to the ignorance or depravity of the multitude'.[42] According to these critics, Elliston's illicit trading in Shakespeare compromised the integrity of England's national playwright; in particular, the spectre of plebeian audiences watching Shakespearean tragedy undermined conventional assumptions about the proper relationships between social class and cultural hierarchy. Now that artisans and small shopkeepers had patronised a dumbshow production of *Macbeth* in St George's Fields, how long could the centre hold?

Over the next two decades, illegitimate productions of Shakespeare took place at almost all the licensed minor theatres beyond Westminster. The Surrey produced a number of Shakespearean burlettas, including *The Mantuan Lovers; or Romeo and Juliet* (1823), and 'a new grand historical spectacle' entitled *The Death of Caesar; or, the Battle of Philippi* (1823) starring Henry Kemble as Brutus. This latter play, whose scenes included 'Field of Mars, with the Olympic Games' and 'Grand Procession to the Capitol' retained Shakespeare's 'principal incidents', although, according to one reviewer, the compiler had apparently abandoned 'all the most beautiful passages of Shakspeare.'[43] The *Times*' dramatic critic was a little more sanguine, and declared that the language of Shakespeare, 'even when delivered by Messrs. Rowbotham and Kemble, is more agreeable than the melo-dramatic stuff which is usually to be found at minor theatres, and we were therefore not displeased to find that *Death of Caesar* . . . was received with considerable approbation' (December 27 1823). The Surrey also staged an eclectic, topical production of *Richard III*. In the Battle of Bosworth Field:

Mr Cooke will (accoutred in a real) French cuirass, stripped from a cuirassier, on the field of battle at Waterloo, and which bears the indenture of several musket shot and sabre cuts go thro' the evolutions of the attack and defence, with a sword in each hand![44]

---

[41] Vol. 1, October 1812, 69, signed 'Veritas'. The words within parentheses are the editor's corrections.

[42] *Theatrical Inquisitor*, April 1813, 2: 136, signed 'H'. For similar condemnations, see the *London Magazine* review in the issue for January 1820, 16: 34.

[43] *Mirror of the Stage*, 5 January 1824, 3:185. The play's scenes are described on a bill for 26 December 1823. The *dramatis personae* include several non-Shakespearean characters including 'Junia' and 'Stingambus'.   [44] Playbill for 11 September 1815.

The interpolation of Cooke's heroic swordsmanship into *Richard III* causes the boundaries between historical and contemporary conflict to disappear. An evening's entertainment at the minor theatres, of course, often interspersed melodrama and burlesque with non-dramatic turns including displays of agility and strength, and the exhibitions of freaks, human and animal. (On March 7, 1818, for example, the Sans Pareil theatre proudly announced the appearance of a 'dwarf woman . . . only the height of a common Tea Table'; other exhibitions included 'the celebrated Esquimaux Indians' at Sadler's Wells in 1823). Cooke's swordsmanship presents the spoils of Napoleonic war as a spectacular exhibit within a Shakespearean battle. Spectators are thus encouraged to interpret the battle of Bosworth Field as a historical event and, simultaneously, as a rehearsal for the nation's military triumph at Waterloo.

Like the Surrey, the Coburg theatre decided to make their own adaptations of Shakespeare's plays. Henry Milner produced several dramas, including *The Three Caskets* (a 'New Tragic Comic Melo-Drama' based on *The Merchant of Venice*, 1827), *The Lovers of Verona; or, Romeo and Juliet* (1826, 1827) and 'at the request of numerous Frequenters of the Theatre,' *Hamlet, Prince of Denmark* (1828).[45] This last play appears to have been based on Jean-François Ducis' neoclassical adaptation, together with a French serio-pantomime. As the playbill declared, 'This Piece is not an alteration or adaptation of Shakspeare's admirable Tragedy of the same name, the Language, Incidents, and in many respects, the Plot, being wholly different' (bill for 4 February 1828). Davidge had recently been fined £100 at the Surrey assizes for illegally representing *Douglas* and *Richard III*, and it seems probable that the manager had decided to protect himself from further prosecutions. No smoke without fire, however: at the same time, Davidge was determined to exploit the commercial potential and dramatic prestige of Shakespeare's *Hamlet*.

Davidge's publicity carefully describes the play as a melodrama ('The Story of Hamlet affords, not only a powerful Interest, but a multitude of powerful Situations, capable of being Melo-Dramatically treated', bill for 28 January 1828.) Reimagined through the lens of melodrama, Shakespeare's *Hamlet* is transformed into a drama about the restoration of justice in a state, rather than a tragedy about Hamlet's tortured subjectivity. To this end, Hamlet becomes a valiant military hero who compels Claudius and Gertrude to acknowledge their guilt and, with the aid of Horatio's 'zeal' and 'loyalty', is finally proclaimed King.

---

[45] Playbill, 28 January 1828.

At the 'Splendid Banquet given in honor of Hamlet's victory' (the Coburg production featured a series of Gothic scenes including 'Cemetery of the Kings of Denmark, by Moonlight' and 'Royal Museum, with the Sarcophagus and Urn of the Late King'), Hamlet presents his mother with the poisoned cup, ordering her to 'Pledge his Father's Memory'; her horror convinces him that she is guilty. Urged on by the spectre, he then takes Gertrude to the elder Hamlet's tomb, and calls on her to 'proclaim her Guilt or Innocence upon his Ashes'. Like the *Circusiana*, Milner's *Hamlet* foregrounds visible proofs of innocence and truth; following the conventions of melodrama, Hamlet's tests of Gertrude also highlight the injustices perpetrated in the name of the state. At the end of the play, Hamlet is put on trial for his father's murder, and the attempted murder of his mother. He is about to be condemned when, at the last minute (a typically melodramatic *coup de théâtre*), the Queen's confession proves her son's innocence, and Hamlet is finally proclaimed King. In this illegitimate production of *Hamlet*, the contingent imposition of melodramatic form leads to a radical transformation in the play's moral and political design.

By the late 1820s, the Pavilion theatre in Whitechapel – where one satirical reviewer noted 'a singular *gout* for the legitimate drama'[46] – was staging more Shakespearean plays than Covent Garden and Drury Lane Theatres put together. In 1829 alone, the Pavilion produced *Richard III, Macbeth, Othello, Hamlet, Cymbeline, Henry IV, Romeo and Juliet, The Merchant of Venice* and *Coriolanus*. Though Elton's impassioned scenes as Othello might occasionally be 'too highly wrought, too vehement', commented one reviewer of the Pavilion production, his performance might nonetheless be classed 'among the best performances of the day'.[47] By this time, most illegitimate productions of Shakespeare had thrown caution to the winds, abandoning even the pretence of staging the plays as melodrama or burletta. Nevertheless, one critic did report as late as 1831 that a Surrey performance of *Othello* had been 'interspersed with melodramatic music, in order to render it legitimately illegitimate'.[48]

The engagement of metropolitan celebrities such as the child prodigy Master Burke and Ira Aldridge represented an important strategy in the marketing of illegitimate Shakespeare. Master Burke's Shylock, reported one critic with evident fascination, 'is a tiny Jew with a six-inch gabardine, and a staff no longer than a crow-quill'.[49] Whereas Ira

---

[46] *Figaro in London*, 13 July 1833, 2: 111.   [47] *Tatler*, ns, 11 August 1832, 358, signed 'S.W.H'.
[48] *Figaro*, 21 January 1831, 82.   [49] *Atlas*, 16 May 1830, 314.

Aldridge, 'the African Roscius' (also known as Keene), was hounded
from the stage with disgust when he played at Covent Garden,[50] he
received a warm reception at the Surrey and the Pavilion Theatres. As
the Surrey playbill proudly declared, 'The circumstances of a MAN OF
COLOUR performing Othello is indeed an epoch in the history of
Theatricals.'[51] Perhaps because audiences at the minor theatres were
more accustomed to the exhibition of race and ethnicity as spectacle,
perhaps because immigrants made up a significant proportion of the
local population, especially in the East End, Aldridge's performances at
the minor theatres were greeted with excitement and sympathetic interest. Moreover, as we shall see, the tragedy of *Othello* had also become
inextricable from the minor theatres' campaign to resist the 'oppressive'
tactics of Drury Lane and Covent Garden; Aldridge's engagement
therefore provided an opportunity to stage prejudice in several guises.

In the summer of 1831, Edmund Kean, now a slightly pathetic figure
whose reputation had been irrevocably tarnished by the effects of alcohol
and a sex scandal, appeared in various Shakespearean roles at the New
City and Coburg playhouses. In an address to the audience, Kean
alluded to the 'monopolising spirit' of Drury Lane and Covent Garden;
he must have delighted local spectators with his vow to make the New
City 'the rival of the large ones in talent, though not in size'.[52] Kean's
choice of Shylock and Othello as his two leading roles may have been calculated to appeal to his audiences' ethnic diversity: in any case, the *Tatler*
reviewer warmly admired the actor's 'masterly identification of himself
with the strongly marked qualities of the malignant Jew'.[53] But at the
Coburg, any hopes that Kean's engagement would mark a new, genteel
chapter in the theatre's history (Davidge had even added a row of stalls
for the occasion), were quickly dashed. Supporters of Cobham, the
Coburg's most popular tragedian and, by all accounts, a vociferous, old-
fashioned ranter, had packed the gallery to watch him play Iago to Kean's
Othello. Kean's obvious inebriation – the *Satirist*'s reviewer described the
performer as 'drenched with good cheer, and sparkling overmuch with
vigorous fermentation'[54] – together with the hostility of Cobham's supporters, produced general uproar. At the end of an almost inaudible
Othello, Kean angrily dismissed the Coburg spectators as 'ignorant,
unmitigated brutes', and 'reeled off the stage amidst the clatter of pewter
pots and ginger-beer bottles, much to the delight of the gods and god-

---

[50] See the rebarbative comments made by *The Times*, 11 October 1825.
[51] Surrey playbill, 22 April 1833.   [52] *Tatler*, 24 May 1831, 2: 900.   [53] *Ibid.*
[54] 3 July 1831, 1:102.

desses'.[55] The Coburg's attempt to market Kean's engagement as an occasion of leisured connoisseurship had failed completely.[56]

Many critics greeted illegitimate performances of Shakespeare with a light-hearted derision which masked a pervasive anxiety about the theatrical disintegration of established cultural and social hierarchies. Reviewers alluded darkly to the 'murdering' of Shakespeare at certain minor theatres, or the 'conspiracy now going on at the Queen's against Shakespeare's immortality' in the presence of 'a selection from the Tottenham Court Road sweeps, and the Saint Giles's vagabonds'.[57] Laughing at plebeian consumption of Shakespeare provided an oblique means by which to confirm the absurdity of granting the theatrical masses beyond Westminster access to legitimate culture. In *A Slap at the Minors or the Beauties of an Unrestricted Drama* (plate 8), the anonymous cartoonist stages the grotesque consequences of plebeian Shakespearean production. The image depicts Shakespeare looking down from the clouds on a scene represented as 'Murder most foul and unnatural'. Here, each of the motley performers is spouting a Shakespearean quotation which ironically exposes the 'trash', rant and 'horrid speech' which are produced once 'every Vile pretender . . . born in the Metropolis' can spit and roar 'the Noblest of our National Poetry.

At the heart of the campaign against patent monopoly lay the symbolic right to stage the works of the national playwright. By insisting that performances of Shakespeare had been 'requested' by audiences (this tactic was almost certainly disingenuous), managers craftily defined themselves as law-breakers, heroically risking prosecution to fulfil the desires and cultural ambitions of their spectators. The frequency with which Shakespeare's plays were performed at benefits in aid of the minor theatres also confirms the playwright's symbolic position in this campaign. *Othello*, declared one playbill, was to be produced in support of the Parliamentary Bill 'to relieve the Minor Theatres from unjust oppression, and thus give the Public an opportunity of seeing the regular Drama performed at other than the Major Houses'.[58] Similarly, John Kemble Chapman staged *Othello* at the New City theatre to pay off the fine he had incurred for illegally performing legitimate drama at Tottenham Street. *Othello*'s dramatisation of prejudice and oppression thus lent a special form of Shakespearean legitimacy to the minor theatres' campaign against Drury Lane and Covent Garden.

[55] John Cole, *The Life and Theatrical Times of Charles Kean*, 2 vols. (London: Richard Bentley, 1859), 1: 162; *Satirist*, 3 July 1831, 1:102.   [56] See playbill, 1 July 1831.
[57] *Figaro in London*, 24 August 1833, 2: 136.   [58] See Surrey playbills, 16 and 27 January 1832.

8. Shakespearean Innovations. *A Slap at the Minors or the Beauties of an Unrestricted Drama.*

Burlesques and travesties represent another form of illegitimate Shakespeare. In these plays, the texts and sounds of elite culture have been rearranged as a collection of absurd fragments and ironic quotations (see, for example, the incongruous inclusion of musical snippets from Rossini and Bellini, as well as numerous parodies of theatrical celebrities). The significance of burlesque as a genre which flatters the cultural knowledge of genteel spectators deserves more critical attention; in this chapter, however, I am concerned simply with burlesque's illegitimate status.

Several years before the famous Circus *Macbeth*, Charles Dibdin wrote a pantomime for Sadler's Wells entitled *Anthony, Cleopatra and Harlequin*.[59] In this burlesque play, Dibdin declared, 'the event and catastrophe, are completely changed, for the purpose of morality'. Thus the 'interference' of the virtuous magician, together with that of Harlequin Nilus, ensures that Cleopatra, 'instead of dying by her own hand, lives to return to virtue; whilst Anthony receives the pardon of Octavia, and recovers the esteem of the Senate' (Argument, 3). Dibdin's pantomime shrewdly combined exotic spectacle (dancing Mummies and Laplanders), magic (in one trick, Puck appears to take off his own head) and patriotism (see various topical allusions to the war against Napoleon). Dibdin's playtext is clearly designed to amuse genteel spectators who could recognise the pantomime's ironic and comprehensive moralisation of Shakespearean history.

Like most pantomimes, *Anthony, Cleopatra and Harlequin* was an occasional show which disappeared almost without trace. By contrast, *Hamlet Travestie* (Regency, 1810), would be performed all over London, as well as becoming an influential model for later travesty-writers. Six editions of John Poole's play appeared between 1810 and 1817; moreover, at Covent Garden in 1813, *Hamlet Travestie* also became the first illegitimate drama to be produced at one of the Theatres Royal.[60] Poole's travesty self-consciously displays the semiotic conventions of illegitimate theatre. The play's composition in rhyming couplets, interspersed with a rich collection of popular songs, ensures that *Hamlet Travestie* falls within the

---

[59] *Songs, and other Vocal Compositions, with a Sketch of the Plot and Description of the Scenery, in the New Comic Pantomime, called Anthony, Cleopatra, and Harlequin* . . . (London: W. Glendinning, 1805).

[60] Apart from the Regency and Covent Garden productions, *Hamlet Travestie* was also performed at the Royalty (September 1811) and Sadler's Wells (August 1819). On *Hamlet Travestie* as a model for later Shakespearean parodists, see the preface to *King Richard III Travestie* (London: Duncombe, 1823). References to the play will be cited from the edition reprinted in Stanley Wells, ed., *Nineteenth-Century Shakespeare Burlesques*, 5 vols. (London: Diploma Press, 1977–8), 1.

definition of illegitimate speech; the play-within-the-play scene features an ironic scroll, on which is inscribed the Duchess's vow: 'No second husband will I take / When I have lost my first' (II.ii.31). The play also alludes with ironic nonchalance to the genres of illegitimate theatre.[61] Hamlet decides, for example, that his father's murder will 'make a charming ballet-pantomime' (I.v.22); in his graveyard song, sung to the popular comic tune of 'Dorothy Dumps', the tragic hero even imagines death as a series of pantomimic changes wrought by Harlequin: 'First his magic displaces / Eyes and nose from our faces, / And like this leaves them ghastly and hollow' (III.ii.47). Hamlet's tender, philosophical meditations on mortality have certainly disappeared, but this burlesque graveyard song has its own poignancy. For, in the words of the song, Poole's Hamlet conjures up through the theatrical anarchy of Harlequin the frightening power of time. Life, like Regency pantomime, the song suggests, is full of violence, lightning changes, unseen powers not understood.

The text of *Hamlet Travestie* is littered with absurd annotations. Here again, this textual paraphernalia serves to highlight the play's burlesque allegiances with illegitimate theatre. In one delightfully ironic note, for instance, Samuel Johnson defines melodrama as 'the climax of theatrical licentiousness'. But Johnson goes on to reassure the reader that, in an age adorned by the performances of John Philip Kemble and Sarah Siddons, there is 'but little cause to fear the re-admission of this monstrous abortion of dramatic libertinism' (62). Through such tongue-in-cheek references to the degraded character of illegitimate culture, *Hamlet Travestie* ingeniously draws attention to its own illicit place in

---

[61] Compare the Shakespearean burlesques staged at the Westminster theatres during the 1830s. These included *Othello, the Moor of Fleet Street* (Adelphi, January 1833), starring John Reeve in a vulgar blackface role as a chimney sweep, Maurice Dowling's burlesques, *Romeo and Juliet, as the Law Directs* (Strand, 1837) and *Othello, according to Act of Parliament* (Liverpool, then Strand, 1838) and Gilbert À Beckett's *King John, with the Benefit of the Act* (St James, 1837). The absurdity of theatrical regulation is a comic theme in many of these Shakespearean burlesques. The two basket-makers' apprentices in Dowling's *Romeo and Juliet*, for example, joke about the prohibition of spoken dialogue at the minor theatres. 'What shall I say?' asks Sampson, who has just fetched a poker from the house. Gregory responds, 'Don't say at all, but sing':

SAMPSON: Is that the law? May I say words that teaze?
GREGORY: So that you sing it, say whate'er you please.

Needless to say, the titles of Dowling's burlesques – 'as the law directs' and 'according to Act of Parliament' – also signal the plays' ironic compliance with theatrical regulation. Compare the licensing MS of Buckstone, *Bad Business* . . . (Adelphi, 1832) in which Charles Mathews (playing himself) explains to other managers how Hamlet must be played 'according to law' (fol. 316, censored by the Examiner of Plays).

Shakespearean reproduction. Though the success of such plays must be attributed to their playful synthesis of grotesque humour, satire and parody (musical, literary and theatrical), burlesques also played a comic role in showing audiences the unrepresentable status of Shakespeare on the minor stage.

'Whenever there is Danger of a Riot,' Kemble advised in his correspondence, 'always act an Opera; for Musick drowns the noise of opposition.'[62] Kemble's cynically pragmatic remark aptly sums up his response to theatrical and political opposition alike. The manager carefully expurgated his acting texts (notably *The Tempest* and *Measure for Measure*), so as to deflect sympathy from characters such as Caliban and Barnadine whose audacious, unlicensed speech otherwise seemed to question the actions of those in power.[63] To some extent, however, Kemble's cautiousness about crowd scenes, and his resolution to prevent 'opposition', was shared by other managers. In the midst of the Corn Law agitation, for example, Sheridan warned Samuel Whitbread about the forthcoming production of *Richard II*, starring Edmund Kean: 'Beware and listen to the wise. Any mischief arising from the allusions I have stated will be laid at your Door.'[64] Sheridan's fears concerned parts of the play, notably the garden scene, 'which if not *judiciously moderated*, are open to application which may produce the most inflammatory effect on the audience at this *peculiar* and perilous Crisis'. Given the widespread anxiety of managers about the incendiary effects of producing *Richard II*, not to mention the heated controversy over the pirated publication of *Wat Tyler*, Southey's republican and allegedly seditious play, I turn now to what appears to be an illegitimate production of *Richard II*.

The most immediate precedent for the Coburg production of *Wat Tyler and Jack Straw; or, The Life and Death of King Richard II* (1825, 1831)[65] would seem to be Richard Cumberland's opera, *Richard the Second*. Despite its utter lack of sympathy for the rebels – 'Fall'n is the foe, Rebellion's leader crush't, / Order prevails, and faction's roar is hush't'

[62] BL Add. MSS 31972, 4 June 1791, fol. 139.
[63] Kemble's casting decisions reflect this strategy of making such characters seem laughable and ridiculous rather than subversive. See especially his decision to cast John Emory, famous for comic portrayals of ignorant stage Yorkshiremen, as Barnadine and also as Caliban. For Hazlitt's objections to this strategy, see *Examiner*, 11 February 1816, *Hazlitt* v: 283.
[64] *Letters of Sheridan*, III: 220, 7 March 1815.
[65] April 1825; January 1831. The playbill discussed here is that for 17 January 1831.

rejoices the chorus in the final scene – Cumberland's play was peremptorily refused a licence. Only after comprehensive revisions, in which the tax-gatherer was transformed into a hearty publican, and Wat Tyler excised altogether, was Cumberland's drama permitted, under the new title of *The Armourer*.[66] Other Wat Tyler dramas either omitted the rebellion altogether, replacing it with a love story, or represented the rebels as a drunken mob in the Shakespearean tradition of Jack Cade's rebellion in *2 Henry VI*.[67]

Like the Coburg *Magna Charta*, *Wat Tyler and Jack Straw* explores the circumstances in which rebellion against the state might be justified. Just as early nineteenth-century radicals cited *Magna Charta* as a political precedent, so too the Peasants' Rebellion had come to represent a turning-point in English history. At the Spa Fields uprising in 1816, for example, a charge led by Watson had rallied his followers by invoking the rebellion of Wat Tyler. During the 1830s, the Chartists would also identify the revolt of 1381 as marking a transformation in the political history of the British people. After the publication of Southey's play in 1817, of course, cheap editions of *Wat Tyler* had become widely available: Richard Carlile claimed to have sold about twenty-five thousand copies of Southey's drama in five years; versions were also published by Fairburn, Hone, Sherwin and Cleave.[68] For a variety of reasons, then, it is safe to claim that the story of Wat Tyler would have been a familiar one for many Coburg spectators. By the mid-1820s, that narrative lay at the heart of contemporary debates about the legitimacy of rebellion and the nature of the modern state.

The Coburg playbill advertising *Wat Tyler* promised to offer a synoptic view of that 'continued scene of tumult and dissension' which characterised Richard's reign:

[66] Larpent MS 963. See further, Conolly, *Censorship*, 42–3; 95–98.
[67] For a romantic version of this political plot see, for example, John Haines, *Richard Plantagenet* (Victoria 1836) *CMT* xiv. In the eighteenth-century comic droll based on the history of Wat Tyler, popular enthusiasm for liberty from the 'Tyrant Dick' seems to arise more from the lure of wealth, gin, and women than from any commitment to political reform. See *Wat Tyler and Jack Straw; or, The Mob Reformers. A Dramatick Entertainment. As it is Perform'd at Pinkethman's and Giffard's Great Theatrical Booth in Bartholomew Fair* (London, 1730). The droll concludes with the stabbing of Tyler, after which the mob commiserate with each other and decide to pledge allegiance to the King.
[68] See R. B. Dobson, *The Peasants' Revolt of 1381* (London: Macmillan, 1970). For the comments of Hazlitt and others in the debate over Southey's politics and *Wat Tyler*, see Frank Hoadley, 'The Controversy over Southey's *Wat Tyler*', *Studies in Philology* 38 (1941), 81–96, and Lionel Madden, ed., *Robert Southey, The Critical Heritage* (London: Routledge, 1972), 233–54. On popular editions of *Wat Tyler*, see Louis James, *Fiction for the Working Man 1830–1850* (Oxford University Press 1963), 74.

ROYAL COBURG THEATRE.

ACTING MANAGER, Mr. HUNTLEY.

THURSDAY, MAY 1st, 1823, and DURING THE WEEK,
Will be presented a New Splendid Historical Drama in Three Acts, to be called,

MAGNA CHARTA!

Or, The Eventful Reign of

KING JOHN.

The Historical Dramas produced at this Theatre, have uniformly been received by the Public with a degree of Enthusiasm highly flattering to the Proprietor, and all those engaged in the undertaking; for strictness of Coincidence with Historical Fact, splendor and correctness of Costume and Decoration, had general impressiveness of Effect, they have been pronounced the most successful efforts of a Minor Theatre to compete with its more imposing rivals. In attempting to represent on the Stage that solemn and important Achievement, the obtaining of Magna Charta, that grand foundation of our Freedom, and guarantee of those invaluable Privileges, which have for Centuries rendered this famed Island the envy of the world; the Proprietor has been most lavish in his Expenditure, anxious, that the celebration of so memorable an Era should receive every degree of Magnificence and Effect that this Establishment can produce, and be so represented, that for correctness of Delineation and gorgeous splendor of Decoration, this Piece has never been equalled in the annals of Historical and Scenic Art.

The whole of the Scenery, entirely New, by Messrs Wilkins, Pitt, Walker, & Co; Jones, Pupil of Mr. Stanfield.—The New & Superb Dresses & Characteristic Armour by Mr. Smythers, Messrs. Cross & Follet.—The Machinery by Mr. Burroughs.—The Music, entirely New, by Mr. T. Hughes.—The Pageants arranged by Ministers Le Clercq.—The Combats by Mr. Bradley.—The Properties by Mr. W. Kelly.—The Piece written by Mr. H. M. Milner.
And Produced under the Direction of Mr. HUNTLEY.

English.

John, King of England, ... Mr. HUNTLEY.
Earl of Salisbury, Mr. COOPER. Hugh de Wells, Chancellor, Mr. HENDERSON. Hubert de Burgh, Chamberlain, Mr. SMITH.
William de Albiney, Mr. WILLIAMS. Gilbert de Maulece, Mr. HONOR. Phillip Falconbridge, Mr. STANLEY.
O'Neale, his Esquire, Mr. DOBBS. Nicholas, Cardinal-Bishop of Frescati, Legate from the Pope, Mr. BOULANGER. Bishop of Ely, Mr. DOWSING.
Roderick de Gilbert, Mr. CALLAHAN. Ladies of the Court, Mesdms. Brook, Dibbin, Davis, Fairbrother, Henderson, Bradley, De Boss, Grisdale, &c.

Barons in Arms for the Charter.
Berda Falconbridge, Mr. ROWBOTHAM; Robert de Fitzwalter, Mr. HOWELL; Earl of Pembroke, Mr. FISHER. Willie de Mareschall, Mr. ROGERS.
Roger Bigod, Earl of Norfolk, Mr. TAYLOR. Gilbert de Clare, Mr. MILLER. Robert de Vere, Earl of Oxford, Mr. PROUD.
Earl of Hereford, Mr. BROWN. Earl of Albermarle, Mr. ATKINS. Earl of Gloucester, Mr. ADAMS. Richard de Piercy, Mr. KEIRNON.
Roger de Montfichet, Mr. WRIGHT. Stephen Langton, Archbishop of Canterbury, Mr. L. BENNETT.

French.
Phillip, King of France, Mr. BARRY. Montmorency, Constable of France, Mr. BRADLEY. Arthur, Duke of Brittagne, Miss PARROCK.
Duke of Maine, Mr. ASBURY. Count of Poitou, Mr. REEVES. Lapierre, Mr. WILSON. Mayor of Anjiers, Mr. HOBBS.
Chatillon, a Herald, Mr. MORRIS. Betrieques, Mr. HILL. Basil, Mr. SLOMAN. Citizens of Anjiers, French Knights, &c.
The Lady Constance, Widow of Geoffroy Plantagenet, Mrs. STANLY. Louise, Mrs. TENNANT. Celine, Miss GASKILL.
Nobles, Knights, Guards, Kings and Pursuivants at Arms, Monks and inferior Clergy, Attendants, Populace, &c. by a numerous Train of Auxiliaries.

SPLENDID & CHARACTERISTIC SCENERY, PAINTED FOR THIS PIECE.

ACT I.
1. Court of the French King, Wilkins & Pitt. 2. Apartment in the Palace of the King of France. 3. Interior of French Cottage, Walker
4. Magnificent Tent of the English King, Walker. Review of the Army by the King in Person,
5. Wood adjacent to the English Camp, Jones. 6. Field of Battle, General Engagement of the Two Armies, headed by the

Respective Kings, Mounted on Superb WAR-HORSES!

DESPERATE COMBAT
Between the Constable of France and Robert de Fitzwalter—Capture of Prince Arthur.
2. THE GATES OF ANJIERS, RETREAT OF THE FRENCH ARMY INTO THE TOWN.——Wilkins & Stanfield.

Combat of Ten.
ATTACK of the English, and SURRENDER of the Keys by the Mayor and Authorities of Anjiers to KING JOHN.

ACT II.
1. FRENCH COTTAGE As before. 2. GRAND HALL in the CASTLE of WINCHESTER. Walker.

GORGEOUS BANQUET

Given by the King of England to his Nobles, commemorative of his Victories in France. In this Scene, embracing the entire extent of the Stage, and the whole of the Company, aided by the Supernumeraries, an attempt will be made, to give a vivid idea of a ROYAL BANQUET, in times of FEUDAL SPLENDOR.
3. Ancient Street in Winchester, Jones. 4. Prison of Prince Arthur in the Castle of Winchester, Wilkins.

Awful Preparations for his Death.
5. EXTENSIVE VIEW OF THE CASTLE WALLS, TURRETS, BATTLEMENTS, MOATS, &c. Wilkins
The Prince meets his Death by being precipitated from the Ramparts into the Moat.—Oath of the assembled Barons to Avenge his Death & obtain the Charter.

ACT III.
1. State Apartment in King John's Palace, Walker. 2. Oratory of Lady Constance, Jones. 3. Camp of the Patriotic Barons, Wilkins & Walker.

THE PLAIN of RUNNYMEDE. Wilkins And Pitt.

Extensive View of the most Picturesque Part of Berkshire, including Windsor, Staines, &c. The advance of the Barons with their whole Military Force, giving an exact Representation of the Arms, Armorial Bearings, and Warlike Accoutrements of those Ancient times, (1215) Approach of the United Clergy of England and Rome, with their PONTIFICAL PARAPHERNALIA;
Grand Entré of the KING with his KNIGHTS and NOBLES Mounted on Superb CHARGERS, splendidly Caparisoned.

PLEDGE OF FAITH BETWEEN THE KING AND THE BARONS;
Solemn, Impressive, and Memorable Ceremonial of Signing MAGNA CHARTA!
AND AWFUL DEATH OF KING JOHN BY POISON.

A COMIC SONG BY MR. SLOMAN.

To conclude with an entirely New Burletta, called,

LORD MANSFIELD's WIG!

OR,

An Anecdote from the Times.

Old Williwig, Mr. LOVEDAY. Lackall, Mr. JONES. Lacklaw, Mr. DOBBS. Miss Williwig, Miss GASKILL.

Boxes 4s. & 3s., Pit 2s. Gal. 1s. Doors open at Half-past 5, begin at Half-past 6. Second Price at Half-past 8.
Places to be taken of Mr. ROBADER, at the New Box Office, in the Grand Saloon of the Theatre, and of whom may be had Private Boxes Nightly, also Free Admissions for the Season, and for the Accommodation of the Nobility and Gentry at the West End of the Town, at the Western Exchange, Old Bond-street, and at No. 192, Piccadilly, opposite Burlington-House. {T. Romney, Printer, Lambeth.}
Ballet-Master, Mons. Le CLERCQ,—Composer & Conductor of the Musical Department, Mr. T. HUGHES,—Leader of the Band, Mr. J. FERON.

9. The Coburg's *Magna Charta*.

The Rebellion of Wat Tyler, occasioned by the tyrannical and oppressive manner in which the exorbitant taxes were extorted; its alarming progress and final determination, by the firmness of the Mayor of London, and the uncommon presence of mind of the young King; the subsequent feuds amongst the Nobles; the return of Bolingbroke from banishment; his usurpation of the power, and unjust deposition of Richard; the murder of that unfortunate Prince in Pomfret Castle.[69]

The language of this bill equivocates between sympathy for the rebels' protest ('tyrannical and oppressive manner in which the exorbitant taxes were extorted') and praise for the rebellion's suppression (the 'firmness' of the Mayor and the 'uncommon presence of mind' of the young King). Moreover, the play's dramatic structure seems to reflect these contradictory judgements about Wat Tyler's rebellion. To a large extent, the Coburg *Wat Tyler* follows the dramatic shape of Shakespeare's play. *Wat Tyler and Jack Straw* opens with the dispute between Mowbray and Bolingbroke in the King's Council Chamber, and incorporates the interrupted combat scene, Bolingbroke's subsequent banishment, the Bristol Castle scene, Bolingbroke's oblique insinuation about Richard's death, and the killing of Richard in Pomfret Castle. Between these scenes, and somewhat anachronistically (as the playbill admits), the rebellion of Wat Tyler takes place.

Is there any evidence to suggest that the Coburg playwright used Southey's drama as one of his sources? Having opened with the famous scene of dissension in the King's Council Chamber, *Wat Tyler and Jack Straw* returned to the scene of 'Rustic Festivity' with which Southey's play begins around Wat Tyler's forge. As in Southey's play, the celebrations are marked by what the playbill calls 'Oppression of the Poor', an allusion which might well refer to Hob and Tyler's conversation in Southey's drama about the new tax which will take away half Tyler's earnings. In both Southey's play and the Coburg piece, tax gatherers then interrupt the festival: the official's lustful behaviour towards Tyler's daughter, Alice, is 'nobly' resented by Tyler, who 'fells the Ruffian to the Earth'. The Coburg playbill also follows Southey in its presentation of the ensuing rebellion as a legitimate popular uprising, with a noble and heroic leader:

The first blow struck for liberty, the Populace take to Arms, determined to shake off the intolerable yoke. – Tyler elected their Chief, prepares to unfurl the Banners of Freedom to the whole Nation.

[69] Playbill, 17 January 1831.

This rhetoric of liberty, freedom and the casting-off of yokes dovetails closely with the language of Southey's drama. On the other hand, the Coburg *Wat Tyler* play bears no trace of Southey's radical agrarian discourse. Most importantly, John Ball, Southey's spokesman for man's inalienable freedom and the oppressive nature of property rights, does not appear in the Coburg play at all.

'When Adam delv'd and Eve span / Where [Who] was then the Gentleman?' This egalitarian epithet is a common topos in nineteenth-century popular literature; again, however, the epigraph on the Coburg playbill echoes the words of Hob and Tyler's song in Act II of Southey's *Wat Tyler*. Similarly, the conference between the King and Tyler in which Tyler 'nobly expostulates on behalf of the People', may well have drawn on the heroic, bitter and also threatening speech which Southey gave his hero: 'The hour of retribution is at hand / And tyrants tremble – mark me, King of England.'[70] In marked contrast to Southey's *Wat Tyler*, however, the rebellion depicted in the Coburg play disintegrates after Tyler's death. Whereas Southey makes clear the betrayal of faith by which the King's promises are overturned and the streets swim with blood, the Coburg playwright escapes this political dilemma by interpolating a formulaic melodramatic scene during which first Piers and then Alice attempt to rescue Tyler's body. With the exception of a scene depicting Jack Straw's sufferings (perhaps modelled on the episode in Act IV of *2 Henry VI*, where Sir Alexander Iden finds, and then kills, Jack Cade), the rebellion then disappears from the Coburg plot. Whereas Southey's play ends with John Ball's heroic and millenarian speech as he goes to his death, the Coburg *Wat Tyler* returns to the power-struggle between Richard and Bolingbroke. We are reminded of Hazlitt's formulation in his essay, 'What is the People?' when he speaks of how the 'hollow profession of good will' hypocritically offered by governments 'dissolves and melts the whole fabric of popular innovation like butter in the sun'.[71]

In the absence of a playtext, it would be unwise to do more than speculate about the politics of *Wat Tyler and Jack Straw*. For the drama's political loyalties appear to be contradictory: how can the legitimacy of rebellion be compatible with the rightness of that rebellion's suppression? And are Shakespeare and Southey the hidden playwrights behind the Coburg *Wat Tyler*? Again, the playbill does not provide

---

[70] Robert Southey, *Wat Tyler*, facsimile reprint (Oxford: Woodstock Books, 1989), 44.
[71] *Hazlitt* VII: 262–3.

sufficient evidence to answer this question with any confidence. Nor does the only extant review offer any assistance: the critic merely commends the Coburg author for combining incidents 'with great ingenuity and strict attention to historical truth', and praises the rousing performance of Gomersal as Wat Tyler.[72] Nevertheless, given the Coburg's practice of staging Shakespeare in various forms of disguise, it does seem likely that *Wat Tyler and Jack Straw* represents a *pasticchio* adaptation of *Richard II* and Southey's *Wat Tyler*. As we have seen, these questionably Shakespearean dramas are distinctive for their revisionary dramatisations of rebellion and for spectacular, yet equivocal vindications of popular opinion.

The early nineteenth century has been portrayed by certain historians of culture as the period which marks Shakespeare's political appropriation as the national poet of monarchy and aristocracy. Annabel Patterson, for example, makes a compelling case for the demise at this time of a 'populist Shakespeare'.[73] As Patterson points out, Coleridge's arguments about Shakespeare's political disinterestedness represent a brilliant attempt to suppress the voice of the people as heard in Shakespeare's plays, and, by extension, to quell the clamour for democratic representation in late Georgian Britain. Yet, despite the interest generated by new historicist critics in the relationships between state power and cultural forms – and the politics of Shakespeare's reproduction in particular[74] – the early nineteenth century has yet to be recognised as the period which brought into being an illegitimate Shakespeare. But performing *Macbeth* at the Surrey or *Richard III* at the Coburg during the 1820s was unquestionably an act of defiance; in these illegitimate productions, the rebellion of the minor theatres against the patent houses merged imperceptibly with discourses of popular representation and dissent in the political sphere. Our knowledge of these plays is fragmentary, and evidence about their reception is extremely scarce. Nevertheless, these adaptations appear to represent a populist rebuff – albeit an unknowing and un-selfconscious one – to that conservative, hierarchical Shakespeare being put forward by writers such as Coleridge. The history I have traced in this chapter also demonstrates Shakespeare's pivotal, symbolic role in the emergence and definition of illegitimate culture. As the prominence of *Othello* in this narrative has confirmed, such productions traded in the contemporary as well as the

---

[72] *Theatrical Rod* no. 2 [1831], 13.
[73] Patterson, *Shakespeare and the Popular Voice* (Oxford: Basil Blackwell, 1989), note 6.
[74] See especially Jonathan Dollimore and Alan Sinfield, eds., *Political Shakespeare: New Essays in Cultural Materialism* (Manchester University Press, 1985).

historical meanings of injustice, prejudice and oppression. The Theatre Regulation Act of 1843 may have permitted all licensed playhouses to perform Shakespeare; ironically, however, the Act destroyed by rendering null and void the peculiar political valency of illegitimate Shakespeare.

CHAPTER FIVE

Reading the theatrical city

Here, I consider how the rise of the minor theatres changed the character of the theatrical city. This chapter locates some of the cultural forms and signs, including playbills, reviews and theatre buildings, through which spectators, managers and critics tried to construe the new cultural metropolis. In addition, I try to show how particular institutional practices at the minor theatres – the burlesque playbill and the emergence of the stock author, for example – altered relationships between playhouses and their publics, and dramatic practice as well. The argument which follows examines the transformation of theatrical production, authorship and spectatorship in the early nineteenth-century city.

PRODUCTION

Whose money built the minor theatres? Whereas the patent theatres had relied for their capital on established traditions of cultural patronage, namely rich and powerful subscribers amongst the aristocracy, the nineteenth-century minor theatres were built, converted and leased by a motley, often evanescent, collection of performers and entrepreneurs.[1] At the Adelphi, Coburg and the Surrey Theatres, the financial control of metropolitan theatrical culture was passing into new hands. To embark on theatre management, however, remained a high-risk business, the susceptibility of theatres to damage, and indeed utter destruction by fire compounding the potentially crippling expenses of production, not to mention rent, taxes, insurance, company wages, advertising, and regular improvements to the building's fabric and

---

[1] Several minor playhouses were built through subscription, including the Royal Brunswick and Coburg Theatres. See Edward Brayley, *Historical and Descriptive Accounts*, 88.

accommodation.[2] Many aspiring lessees gave up their speculations in despair; others persevered, only to end up in the bankruptcy courts.[3]

Actor-managers such as Jack Palmer and Frederick Yates, who had already pursued successful careers as performers at Drury Lane and Covent Garden, no doubt hoped to make their fortunes in theatrical management.[4] Several, including the tenor John Braham (who converted a decrepit hotel in King Street into the St James's Theatre, the first major theatrical concern in the western suburbs) and Eliza Vestris (lessee of the Olympic), had commanded star salaries in their own right: in the autumn of 1829 Vestris was appearing at Drury Lane for £25 a night.[5] Although the star system certainly played a part in the commercial demise of the patent theatres, it also transferred capital to a new generation of performers, several of whom subsequently invested their earnings in the building or leasing of the minor theatres.

Local entrepreneurs, often keen playgoers or amateur performers, recognised the minor theatres' commercial potential. Honeyman, who leased the Surrey, was also proprietor of the Surrey Coffee House; Glossop, a wealthy oil merchant, wax chandler and keen playgoer, advanced a sum towards the lease of the Coburg on behalf of his son, Joseph, who became one of its managers.[6] In the Strand, John Scott invested his profits as an oil and colour merchant (Scott sold and may

---

[2] Brayley, *Historical and Descriptive Accounts*, lists the various rents and taxes payable by the lessees at each theatre. John Scott claimed to have spent £10,000 on improvements at the Sans Pareil; in his *Reminiscences*, II: 112, Tom Dibdin remarks that it cost him £4,000 to renovate the Surrey Theatre. Major fires took place at Astley's (1794, 1803), the Royal Circus (1805), Sadler's Wells (1807), Covent Garden (1809), the East London (1826) and the Brunswick theatre (1828).

[3] According to Brayley, *Historical and Descriptive Accounts*, 88, Philip Astley lost £10,000 at the Olympic Theatre; William Oxberry later gave up the theatre's management after the performers refused to go on stage until he had made good their salary arrears. Minor managers who became insolvent included Tom Dibdin, manager of the Surrey, who allegedly ended up with debts of £37,000 (though according to Brayley, *Historical and Descriptive Accounts*, 74, Dibdin actually owed about £17,000); John Chapman, the manager of the Tottenham Street Theatre (see unidentified cutting at the Guildhall Library reporting the proceedings of the Insolvent Debtors' Court, 20 March 1832); George Davidge (the *Spectator*, January 1838, 3, believed that Davidge had lost between £6,000–£7,000 at the Coburg) and Benjamin Rayner, lessee of the Strand (see SC 621). See the evidence of John Forbes, SC 1863, who complained that he had been unable to extract legal damages from the Adelphi proprietors because the defendants were insolvent. In 1832, magistrates refused a licence to the Garrick on the grounds that the proprietors had only recently been discharged from the Insolvency Act. See *Examiner*, 21 October 1832, 683.

[4] According to Edward Fitzball, Davidge died worth at least £30,000. See *Thirty-Five Years*, I: 113.

[5] *Theatrical Observer*, 7 December 1829.

[6] Thomas Allen, *A New and Complete History of the Counties of Surrey and Sussex*, 2 vols. (London, 1830), I: 307–11, includes a useful history of the Surrey proprietors. On Glossop's investment at the Coburg, see Brayley, *Historical and Descriptive Accounts*, 89.

have invented a dye called 'True Blue'), in the purchase and conversion of the building adjacent to his property which he named the Sans Pareil. He and his daughter Jane Scott ran the theatre for over a decade (Scott was a shrewd businessman, and delighted in squashing his spectators on to the benches) and eventually sold their enterprise, with a very healthy profit, for £25,000.[7]

Several successful managers, including Robert Elliston and Philip Astley, combined theatrical management with other kinds of cultural entrepreneurship. Elliston's financial interests included a circulating library at Leamington and a Literary Association at Bristol;[8] by the time of his death in 1814, Philip Astley was reputed to have erected nineteen amphitheatres in Britain and on the continent.[9] Private companies also hoped to reap profits from a shrewd investment in the minor houses. The London Wine Company had a stake in Sadler's Wells during the 1820s (and sold its own wine at the performances), and the Waterloo Bridge Company maintained a commercial interest in the nearby Coburg Theatre.[10]

The architecture and design of the minor theatres evolved haphazardly from the existing urban fabric – an old clothes factory (the Pavilion), a disused chapel (the New City), a tennis court (the Albion), the Old Savoy Palace (the stones from which were used to build the Coburg), or an old French warship bought from the Admiralty, from whose timbers Philip Astley built his whimsical Olympic Theatre in Wych Street, complete with an elaborate line of horses' heads which ran along the architrave.[11] The Regency Theatre was converted from a concert room; the Strand had housed panoramic exhibitions. Neighbouring taverns provided managers with a residence and, in the early days, a box-office as well: Conquest took the tavern next door to the Garrick, probably the Weaver's Arms, for this purpose; at the Surrey, Elliston used Watney's Equestrian Tavern and Whitbread's Coal Hole. Many performers came to live in the streets around the playhouse in which they worked, so that miniature theatrical neighbourhoods grew up, especially on the south bank of the river.

[7] See E. L. Blanchard, 'History of the Adelphi Theatre' in E. Ledger, ed., *The Era Almanack and Annual* (London, 1887). In 1826, Scott bought the ailing Olympic theatre, together with the wardrobe, scenery, machinery and props, for 4,860 guineas.

[8] Raymond, *Memoirs of Elliston*, II: 35–8.

[9] J. Britton and A. Pugin, *Illustrations of the Public Buildings of London* (London: J. Taylor, 1825), 283.

[10] Brayley, *Historical and Descriptive Accounts*, 90.

[11] Brayley, *ibid.*, 90; N. Whittock, *The New Picture of London, Westminster, and the Metropolitan Boroughs* (London, G. Virtue, [1835]), 396.

The visual magnificence of the minor theatres, together with their spectacular, picturesque scenery, played an important part in defining their reputation as places of modern leisure.[12] Luxurious boxes, burnished chandeliers, lobbies papered in imitation of Siennese marble, intricate naval panoramas designed by Clarkson Stanfield, and Moorish palaces: such forms of persuasive capital soon rivalled the luxurious interiors of the patent houses. So impressed was a Member of Parliament by the Surrey's painters and scene designers that he even commissioned the theatre to make all the flags and 'other showy paraphernalia' for his election campaign.[13]

With the exception of the Pavilion (a 'magnificently dingy' playhouse[14]), managers expended substantial capital on a regular basis to enhance the appearance and the comfort of their playhouses. Even from the cramped confines of the gallery, these interiors, lit by brilliant gas chandeliers of burnished gold,[15] must have seemed like bright palaces of gilt and luxurious velvet, an extraordinary refuge from the dirt, noise and darkness which dominated the daily lives of many spectators. Between seasons, carpenters, painters and seamstresses busied themselves creating private boxes, lined with cushions and decorated in salmon colours, with 'superb patterns of French paper heightened with rich gold mouldings', as well as making lobbies and saloons for the pit and box spectators.[16] In particular, managers believed that lack of comfort at the theatre deterred respectable playgoers, especially women: they therefore installed curtains, partitions and stoves 'at considerable expence'.[17]

The Coburg led its rivals in the production of conspicuous magnificence within the auditorium.[18] In 1822, Glossop commissioned

---

[12] Fitzball, *Thirty-Five Years*, I:64. See in particular *Drama*, March 1824, 36–7, which reported extensive refitting and improvements of the 'utmost taste and liberality' at the Surrey. Critics often drew attention to the elegance and comfort of the newly renovated minor theatres. On improvements at the Royal Circus, see *British Stage, and Literary Cabinet*, January 1817, I: 10; on the Regency, see issue for February 1817, I: 32.   [13] Thomas J. Dibdin, *Reminiscences*, II: 154.

[14] *Columbine*, 25 July 1829, 30.

[15] See bills for Sans Pareil, 10 November 1819 and Coburg, 25 May 1829.

[16] See Coburg bill, 25 May 1829. On the expansion of lobbies and saloons, see *British Stage*, February 1818, 2: 38; bills, 26 December 1817 and 26 December 1821.

[17] See letter, signed 'E. M' entitled 'Hints for Improvements in the Patent Theatres' in *Tatler*, 6 January 1832, 4:19. See also Surrey bills, 8 July 1816, 4 November 1816. An undated Sans Pareil bill (?16 January 1807) reassured spectators that the theatre was 'perfectly Dry, and well aired, the pit being elevated Fifteen Feet from the Ground'. The walls apparently contained upwards of twenty-five flues 'with continual Warmth in them, from Premises adjoining, besides those within the Theatre'. For references to improvements in ventilation, see Coburg bills for 3 April 1820 and 8 November 1833.

[18] Cf. Horace Foote, *A Companion to the Theatres; and Manual of the British Drama*, (London: E. Sanger, 1829), 74, who considered the Coburg's interior to be 'overloaded with ornament'.

an extravagant marine saloon (apparently at a cost of almost £1000) from John Serres. The saloon featured panoramic views by Clarkson Stanfield, representing the recent triumph of the British navy in the bombardment of Algiers (1816), huge mirrors, and statues from casts of Canova, as well as portraits of the theatre's patrons, the Prince of Saxe-Coburg and Princess Charlotte.[19] Having created a saloon which encouraged the Coburg's wealthy spectators to revel in the nation's heroism at sea (battles and combats both historical and imaginary also dominated the theatre's repertoire), the Coburg managers then turned their attention to the pleasures of seeing and being seen within the huge auditorium. Cabanel was therefore commissioned to design a spectacular mirror curtain (based on similar curtains at French theatres) which playbills described as 'the most *NOVAL, splendid, & Interesting Object* ever displayed in a British Theatre' (see plate 10).[20] This enormous mirror consisted of sixty-three plates of glass in a gold frame. Before the evening's performances began, the mirror would be lowered, so that it hung between the auditorium and the stage, reflecting the Coburg spectators in its vast frame. In an address written by George McFarren, the Coburg even presented the mirror's 'truth' as a visual rebuff to the condescending view of minor spectacle, as promulgated by the patentees:

> The giant houses, t'other side the water
> Who give to our humility no quarter,
> Say, nought but nonsense lives within our portals,
> And call our heroes monsters, and not mortals;
> And henceforth to astound these native elves,
> Our portraits must be true, for you'll behold yourselves![21]

Though a handful of reviewers were quick to deride the vulgarity of this Coburg innovation, crowded audiences 'testified their delight at seeing themselves in this immense mirror, and for the first time, "on the stage."'[22] Like plate-glass windows in contemporary arcades, the mirror curtain framed the Coburg's interior as a place of luxury and spectacular experience. At the same time, however, the mirror brilliantly dissolved the boundary between the consumer and the object of consumption, allowing the spectators to become the subject of their own

[19] See bill for 21 November 1822; Brayley, *Historical and Descriptive Accounts*, 92.
[20] Bill for 26 December 1821.   [21] *Drama*, December 1821, 2: 393.
[22] Foote, *Companion*, 75. For attacks on the mirror, see unidentified cutting, Coburg file, 28 December 1821 and *Drama*, January 1822, 2:154.

10. Audiences as spectacle: the looking glass curtain.

spectacle. Indeed, the Coburg's innovation marks a significant step in the transformation of the dramatic spectator into the self-conscious purchaser of cultural goods and visual pleasure.

The playbill represented the most important form of publicity for managers at the minor houses. Far from merely announcing the evening's performances, playbills doubled as programme, miniature review, forum for paper wars between different establishments (see Davidge and Elliston's choice descriptions of each other as an 'illustrious Charlatan' and a 'Vanity-bloated Mountebank' in the controversy over box orders),[23] and dramatic manifesto, ingeniously synthesising fact and puff, jokes and information. New techniques of cheap printing made possible the mass production of minor playbills which spectators might see displayed in shop windows, handed out in the West End (in the case of Astley's Amphitheatre, by Astley himself, to the consternation of the theatre's genteel patrons),[24] or hurriedly plastered on walls by the billstickers. Outside the theatre, playgoers purchased their bills for a penny (buying a bill, Hunt tried to persuade his *Tatler* readers in 1830, is an act of charity, for the playbill-sellers are a pitiful 'care-worn race'); inside the playhouse, fruit-sellers (almost invariably young women) also sold bills, usually for double the price.[25]

How little we know about the reading, purchase and interpretation of playbills. We can imagine many a spectator poring over the contents of a bill by the light of a candle in a gloomy rented two-pair back. But how and in what circumstances did spectators read (or indeed hear read aloud) a playbill? And how did playbill-reading shape spectators' understanding of performance? Leigh Hunt suggests that the *Tatler* might be enjoyed 'to vary the chat between the acts'; the auditorium's bright lights certainly made possible such reading during an evening's entertainment.[26] But practical information on bills, about the hire of opera glasses, or the direction in which coachmen should draw up their horses outside the theatre,[27] was presumably designed to be seen in advance. Having abandoned the stilted conventions of eighteenth-century patent advertising, the minor theatres transformed playbills into ironic and hyperbolic commercial texts.

---

[23] See Surrey bill, 15 June 1829 and Coburg bill for 22 June 1829.
[24] See open letter amongst 'Astley's cuttings', vol. 1, fol. 204a, 11 April 1792, which argues that Astley's practice of handbilling compromises the 'respectability' of the theatre.
[25] *Tatler*, 17 September 1830, *LH* 232. Foote, *Companion*, 138, reports that in Cibber's time, 'starch, married, or matronly women' rather than orange girls sold the bills.
[26] *Tatler*, 17 September 1830, *LH* 232.   [27] See Coburg bill, 6 July 1833.

The manager begs leave to announce; for this night only, a 'new romantic drama of powerful interest',[28] 'Total destruction of the citadel',[29] 'frightful Death in the act of rehearsing his former atrocious crime';[30] 'the obduracy of Human Wickedness'.[31] How seductive, spectacular and sensational are these bills from London minor theatres. Bold, unusual and sometimes gigantic typefaces (with occasional blue titles, blood-red flashes of colour and, from the late 1820s, dramatic woodcuts), eye-catching capitalisation with plentiful exclamation marks, letters 'as tall as lamp-posts, and as reiterative':[32] these eye-catching bills persuasively demanded the attention of urban passers-by. Framed in a punchy rhetoric of sensation and atrocity, minor playbills promised a seductive miscellany of pleasures from a comic dance, bloodthirsty melodrama, freak exhibits and *entr'actes* right up to the concluding farce.

By contrast, let us consider the rhetoric and presentation of a typical Drury Lane bill, prepared by Tabby, the theatre's in-house printer, for performances on 27 October 1825. Here, white space and printed letters in a conventional decorous typeface, with sparing use of a bold font, are neatly balanced. Underneath 'Theatre Royal, Drury Lane', the bill announces that 'His Majesty's Servants will perform (2nd time these 9 years) Congreve's Comedy of Love for Love.' 'To which will be added (3d time these three years) the Melo-drama of The Innkeeper's Daughter.' Here, information is a little more plentiful: music composed by Mr. T. Cooke; a list of characters and performers and four 'New Scenes': 'Sea Coast' and 'Abbey Close' (both by Stanfield), Belfry (Roberts) and Storm at Midnight (Marinam). The time at which the doors open, a list of prices, and performances for the rest of the week, take up the lower part of the bill.

Bland and inscrutable, the Drury Lane playbill seems to exist in a commercial vacuum devoid of rival establishments, prices and competing performances. The implied reader is a culturally literate individual, familiar with the legitimate repertoire, and probably with *Love for Love* as well: author and title therefore appear as a discreet matter of fact. The reference to 'His Majesty's Servants' (a term used exclusively by Drury Lane in this period) confidently proclaims the continuity of royal

---

[28] Coburg bill advertising *The Gamblers; or, The Murderers at the Desolate Cottage*, 17 November 1823.
[29] Surrey bill advertising *Masaniello*, 26 December 1822.
[30] Coburg bill for Milner's *Sanguijela, the Blood-Spiller! or, The Secret Executioner of Charles I*, 12 November 1827.
[31] Coburg bill for McFarren, *Guy Faux; or, The Gunpowder Conspiracy*, 30 September 1822.
[32] *Athenaeum*, 22 September 1838, 700, referring to the Adelphi's bills.

patronage and public service, and also conveniently mystifies the commercial basis of the relationship between theatre and spectators.

If we turn now to a gallimaufry of quotations from minor playbills, it becomes easy to identify the innovations in content, rhetoric and tone pioneered at theatres such as the Adelphi, the Coburg and the Surrey. Given intense rivalry for audiences and a huge expansion in print advertising, the language and appearance of minor playbills was designed to surprise and captivate audiences amidst the sheer razzmatazz of urban typography. To ensure prominent publicity for the Coburg, Davidge was said to give out 600 large bills each week for shops to display in their windows.[33] As the market in playbills grew, so did the number of printers competing for theatrical business: in Southwark, J. H. Cox was even producing unauthorised Surrey playbills in the hope of capturing some of this lucrative market.[34]

Once the playbill had shed its stiff, anonymous, skin, it became a witty instrument of persuasion and commercial rivalry, as well as serving as a skeletal playtext for spectators. Whereas the patent theatres had formerly relied for their puffs on compliant newspaper reviewers and their proprietors, the Adelphi and Coburg managers now provided their own hyperbolic forms of sensational and ironic publicity. Take, for example, the characteristic announcement that 'The New Comic Farcical Burletta of THE ANIMATED EFFIGY, having been received with universal bursts of Applause by crouded Audiences, will be repeated This and Every Evening until further Notice.'[35] Soon, minor playbills abounded with reports of 'Brilliant and overflowing houses', performances put on 'By most Particular Desire', under the 'immediate' patronage of 'several Families of Distinction', and spectacle and novelty 'on a scale of unexampled Magnificence'.[36] The rhetoric of minor playbills helped to forge audience loyalties towards a particular establishment; many bills also took a mischievous pleasure in lampooning the repertoire and cultural pretensions of the Theatres Royal.

Coburg bills specialised in orchestrating sensation even as they claimed to assuage the moral strictures of anxious spectators.[37] Glossop's

---

[33] Thomas J. Dibdin, *Reminiscences*, II: 112. In return the shop received three double orders, each admitting two people to the theatre each week.
[34] For this information I am grateful to the late William Knight.
[35] Sans Pareil bill, 25 January 1811.   [36] Sadler's Wells bills, 9 May 1821, 3 April 1820.
[37] One reviewer imagined the Adelphi managers laughing in their sleeves, 'as they watch the believing looks of smart apprentices of both sexes, who stop to peruse their *argument* at the top of the bills advertising *Tom and Jerry*. The "*morals*" of the thing, are about as laughable, as the *fidelity* of its representation of London manners.' Unidentified cutting, Adelphi file, Theatre Museum, 13 October 1822.

publicity, featuring the prominent use of such adjectives as 'atrocious', 'frightful', 'awful' and 'excessive', craftily promoted criminal sensation under the guise of moral judgement. The Coburg's advertising for *The Gamblers* (1823), a play based on the recent murder at Lyon's Inn of William Weare by John Thurtell, a fellow swindler, is a good example. Lest we are tempted to accuse the Coburg of cashing in on a sensational murder, it is worth remembering that every pamphleteer and puppeteer in the city was capitalising on this notorious event; Thomas De Quincey refers to Thurtell in his essay, 'On Murder considered as one of the Fine Arts', and Carlyle would later coin the expression 'gigmanry' in ironic reference to the apparently 'respectable' nature of a murder committed from a gig.

Since public attention had been 'forcibly attracted' to the fatal consequences of gambling, declared the Coburg playbill, *The Gamblers* would undertake 'to make the Stage the vehicle of those Strong Impressions, which operate most powerfully on the Minds of Youth'.[38] Unfortunately for Glossop, however, the local magistrates had become just as adept as the Coburg's spectators at interpreting minor playbills. Convinced that the Coburg was intending to dramatise this murder before the trial of the accused man had taken place, the justices insisted on the play's withdrawal before its first performance. Not to be deterred, the Coburg decided to capitalise more discreetly on the Weare murder by staging what the playbills described as a French anti-gambling drama entitled *The Inseparables; or, The Spectre of the Desolate Cottage*.[39]

Like insinuation, denial proved to be a useful though not always successful weapon in the production of controversial publicity. The Coburg's advertising for an adaptation of Henry Fielding's burlesque, *Tom Thumb*, performed amidst the tumult over parliamentary reform in May 1832, highlights and simultaneously denies the play's political topicality. Davidge craftily used his publicity to suggest a series of 'connections' between Fielding's characters and 'some late events', namely Queen Adelaide's opposition to creating sufficient peers to ensure the safe passage of the Reform Act in the Lords. According to the bill, any resemblance between 'the good-natured hen-pecked King Arthur' and 'a certain distinguished personage' (William IV), or between the 'termagant breeches-wearing Queen Dollalola' and 'his illustrious consort'

---

[38] Bill, 17 November 1823.
[39] See *The Times*, 18 November 1823; for a review of *The Inseparables*, see *Mirror of the Stage*, 1 December 1823, 3: 138. Davidge gives a somewhat partisan and certainly inaccurate account of the episode in SC 1311.

11. Illegitimate transgressions: staging political reform at the Royal Coburg.

(Queen Adelaide), was 'merely casual'. But, at the same time, the Coburg circulated a large poster. Entitled 'Reform! Reform!', this depicted a King, watched surreptitiously by his wife, refusing to receive petitions (see plate 11). Clearly designed to be viewed alongside each other, the bill and poster marketed the (all-too-ephemeral) *Tom Thumb* as a burlesque about monarchical resistance to parliamentary reform.[40]

The burlesque playbill, another innovation pioneered at the minor theatres, interweaves the inflated conventions of playbill puffing and the hyperbolic dramaturgy of melodrama.[41] Burlesque bills mocked promises of novelty in scenery and costume (the advertising for *Melodrame Mad*

---

[40] The play seems to have been performed on 28 and 29 May, and the playbill discussed here, printed at the theatre's own press (see the Coburg file, Theatre Museum), is dated May 28. After the intervention of the Bow Street magistrates, Davidge withdrew *Tom Thumb*, although the bills remained at large. Davidge (who despite his denials must have authorised this advertising) maintained that any attempt to collect the bills from local shopkeepers would only have fuelled public interest in the play. See SC 1250–8, 1282–5. Davidge's equivocations and denials are unconvincing, and his assertion that the play was not performed is simply untrue.

[41] In his *Reminiscences*, II: 136, Thomas Dibdin claimed to have pioneered the burlesque playbill to advertise his burlesque of *Don Giovanni*.

ironically declared that Helen of Troy's Boudoir would be making 'positively its First Appearance'),[42] and created their own absurd forms of generic nomenclature (see the Adelphi's publicity for a 'Buffo, Terpsichoric, Peripatetic . . . National, Ethical, Pot-Pourrical, Satirical, and strictly loyal and moral Burletta').[43] Many bills burlesqued the extravagant language of dramatic advertising (the bill for a burlesque of *Black-Ey'd Susan* promised each pit visitor a free umbrella to protect against 'inundations of tears', as well as chairs and sofas where ladies might faint 'at pleasure'),[44] as well as mocking the moral concerns of middle-class spectators. The Adelphi bill for *Giovanni the Vampire* (1821) undertook to put 'this atrocious Libertine entirely "*Hors de Combat*", to clap as it were an Extinguisher upon his burning Passions.' This production, declared the playbill, 'will doubtless meet the hearty Concurrence of the Suppressors of Vice, whether publically or privately situated, to whom it is most respectfully dedicated by the Author.'[45]

The burlesque playbill indicates not only the growing sophistication of theatrical advertising, but also a new kind of comic collusion between minor theatres and their audiences. The old fiduciary relationship between patent manager and spectator has disappeared, usurped by a knowing, commercial duplicity. The Coburg's tongue-in-cheek advertising for Buckstone's *Vidocq, The French Police Spy* (July 1829) and *Dominique the Resolute* (see bill for 3 October 1831) exemplifies this transformation. For these playbills take the form of a criminal (or, in the case of *Dominique*, satanic) address to the reader. That address, nonetheless, is cleverly framed as a cautionary tale to impress 'upon the minds of Youth the dangerous evils of bad company' (*Vidocq*).

Vidocq, Buckstone's unpublished drama about the legendary French criminal, convicted of a crime of which he was innocent, only to become a galley slave, a legendary escape artist and then a secret agent to the police (in the course of which he betrays his former companions), was performed at the Coburg soon after the controversial passage of the Metropolitan Police Act. Those who opposed the creation of a national constabulary controlled by the government (notably shopkeepers, artisans and semi-skilled labourers – precisely the occupational groups likely to have made up a substantial proportion of spectators at theatres such as the Coburg) feared that the new police might be deployed as

[42] Surrey bill, June 28 1819. See also the Coburg bill for 20 November 1826 advertising a *Don Giovanni* burlesque.
[43] Adelphi playbill for *Green in France; or, Tom and Jerry's Tour*, 6 January 1823.
[44] Frederick Cooper, *The Elbow Shakers*, Olympic, 7 December 1829.   [45] Bill, 31 January 1821.

agents provocateurs, just like Vidocq, to inform on the populace.[46] To stage a Vidocq play in the summer of 1829, as did both the Coburg and the Surrey Theatres, was to dramatise a narrative with dangerous, even explosive associations about the nature of power and authority within the modern British state. In passing, then, it is interesting to note that the question of belief – can Vidocq ever be trusted? – is a recurring theme in Douglas Jerrold's play, *Vidocq! The French Police Spy* (Surrey, July 1829).

The Coburg's publicity for J. B. Buckstone's *Vidocq* promises to guide the spectator into 'those remote recesses of Society, those dark, mysterious and sometimes appalling transactions, which are only impervious to ordinary means of observation' (bill, 6 July 1829). The existence of an undated poster, entitled 'The Address of an Alarmed Thief to his Brethren', also confirms the Coburg's desire to capitalise on the political controversy surrounding the new police force – a prospect which had raised for many the spectre of government informers in the Placard Plot (in which Castlereagh and his agents had allegedly boosted the supply of published sedition) and the Cato Street conspiracy. Whereas the Surrey bills had attempted (no doubt disingenuously) to market *Vidocq* as a form of ethnography which would inform audiences about the manners and 'peculiarities' of the French, the Coburg advertising exploits both the criminal reputation of its own audience, and the introduction of the new police force. Indeed, the thief even claims that the government has recommended *Vidocq* as an educational drama for the police, who will be required to assemble on Waterloo Bridge before processing to the Coburg; by watching *Vidocq*, they will become 'better Officers, and better Men'.

In his address, the thief describes visiting the Coburg, and his preparations to steal a lady's gold watch. Suddenly

a shout startled me . . . I glanced at the Stage, and there I beheld the renowned *Vidocq*, glaring upon me, like an Eagle upon its prey; my detected fingers crept into my empty pockets, my head fell upon my bosom, and my courage departed.[47]

The only way to defeat Vidocq, declares the thief, will be for all thieves to turn Vidocq: then thieves will have their revenge, for there will be no thieves to take. This burlesque narrative subtly exploits the Coburg's dubious moral reputation. Indeed, the poster cleverly negotiates that theatrical minefield between morality and criminality; its rhetoric

---

[46] See Stanley Palmer, *Police and Protest in England and Ireland 1780–1850* (Cambridge University Press, 1988), 278ff.   [47] Undated poster, Coburg file, Theatre Museum.

exploits public fears about the new police, even as those fears are laughingly dissolved into burlesque. And of course there is a wonderful irony about the prospect of all the thieves around the New Cut getting their revenge on Vidocq by joining the police. Amid the hyperbolic discourse of nineteenth-century print advertising, burlesques such as 'The Address of an Alarmed Thief' reveal the commercial conditions of modern publicity. On the surface, and especially to the unwary reader, they might seem to offer a form of moral reassurance about the nature of theatrical representation; to the knowing playgoer, however, these bills ironically acknowledge themselves as yet another duplicitous text in a highly competitive theatrical city.

The cut-throat character of modern theatrical production also changed the nature of dramatic authorship. The rise of illegitimate theatre transformed contemporary tragedy from the most profitable and prestigious dramatic genre into a minor theatrical form, legally representable at only two London theatres (though permitted to perform tragedy, the Haymarket's repertoire was almost exclusively comic). In the 1790s, tragedies had often fetched £400 – no wonder that Wordsworth and Coleridge had believed that a successful tragedy would transform their finances. By 1820, patent managers rarely paid more than £200, with exceptions only for well-known playwrights such as Sheridan Knowles. But a new opera might easily command £200–£400; at the Haymarket, David Morris had paid £400 outright for *Paul Pry*, John Poole's hit comedy about an endearingly infuriating modern busybody.[48]

The transformation of dramatic authorship was not confined to the commercial value of tragedy. A new generation and, still more important, a new class of dramatic authors, had taken over the theatrical marketplace. Many of the individuals who formed this generation of playwrights – Bayle Bernard, J. B. Buckstone, William Moncrieff and Edward Fitzball – had begun their adult lives as apprentices, or as clerks to solicitors. Several, including Buckstone and Ben Webster, later managed one of the Theatres Royal; others, including Douglas Jerrold, Charles Dance and Charles Dickens would establish themselves as distinguished essayists, journalists and novelists. For many of these men, writing plays for the minor theatres represented the first step on the ladder of the cultural metropolis.

---

[48] For the prices charged for particular genres, see Leman Thomas Rede, *The Road to the Stage*, new edition (London: J. Onwhyn, 1836), 71, and, more generally, John Stephens, *The Profession of the Playwright: British Theatre 1800–1900* (Cambridge University Press, 1992). On the price of *Paul Pry*, see SC 2705.

Why did these playwrights elect to write in the illegitimate genres of burletta, melodrama, farce and burlesque? The simple answer to this question is that they thereby guaranteed for themselves the profits of a growing and greedy market of minor managers, always eager for novelty. Indeed, with the notable exception of Jerrold, who also wrote legitimate comedy (*The Bride of Ludgate*, Drury Lane 1831) as well as historical and domestic tragedy (*Thomas À Beckett*, Surrey 1829; *Martha Willis, the Servant Maid*, Pavilion 1831), most of these dramatic authors ignored legitimate forms altogether. Any plausible account of how theatre represented the hopes, desires, and fears of a modern urban city therefore must be based on an interpretation of the period's illegitimate drama.

The rise of the 'stock author' or 'house dramatist', another illegitimate innovation, also attests to the transformation of dramatic authorship. Philip Astley may have been the first manager to employ a 'stock author' at his Amphitheatre to compose pieces such as *The Siege of Troy*, as well as to devise and deliver puffs and advertisements to the newspapers.[49] At Sadler's Wells, Charles Dibdin combined the roles of stock author and manager, writing 'all the pieces requisite for the Season, of every kind: Burletta, Serious Pantomime, Harlequinade, etc.', as well as inventing the machinery required to stage his plays.[50] Soon, all the minor theatres had their own house dramatists: Moncrieff wrote for the Olympic and the Coburg (where Jerrold would later be hired for £5 a week), while Thomas Dibdin became the stock author at the Surrey. During the early 1820s, Elliston even introduced the stock author at Drury Lane, where Moncrieff was retained at the price of £10 a week to write plays such as the oriental melodrama, *The Cataract of the Ganges* (1823).[51]

According to many critics, the stock author merely confirmed the new, degraded position of playwrights as mere traders or caterers in the dramatic market.[52] As the manager's '*antennae*', the most important skill of a house dramatist lay in his ability to design plays for a particular company and audience (as the preface to Moncrieff's *Giovanni in London* remarked approvingly, 'The author knew his audience, and *catered* for them to a nicety' (my italics)). Unlike house dramatists in Elizabethan theatres, however, the nineteenth-century stock author did not share in the profits of his company; on the contrary, in the language of the day,

---

[49] Charles Dibdin, *Memoirs*, 19.   [50] *Ibid.*, 38.   [51] Moncrieff, SC 3122–29.
[52] Lawrence, *Dramatic Emancipation*, 371. For dramatists as 'tailors', see also Tomlins, *Brief View*, 103. Cf. *Thirty-Five Years*, II: 403–4, in which Fitzball describes how he resigned in disgust from the post of hack writer at the Surrey after having been asked to dramatise the Weare murder.

he was simply a hack, available for hire just like a hackney coach. Moreover, the institutional conditions of stock authorship demanded that the dramatist compose pieces (the plots of which were often based on Newgate tales, poems and French plays, as well as newspaper reports and printed ephemera) at great speed. Writing, in these circumstances, took the form of a theatrical sketch, which would be 'filled up' by a celebrity such as T. P. Cooke or J. B. Buckstone;[53] the practices of stock writing also encouraged various forms of collaborative and joint authorship. According to the *Atlas*, twenty-four hours' notice was all that a good stock author would require to come up with a play, an activity known in the trade as 'cooking' a piece.[54] The commercial demands imposed by spectators' desires for dramatic novelty and sensation, together with the need to provide a succession of vehicles for star performers, required the incorporation, and to some extent, the absorption, of dramatic authorship into illegitimate production.

Publishers soon recognised the commercial potential of the plays being written by these new dramatists at the minor theatres. Several publishers, notably John Lowndes, had taken an interest in some of the early minor dramas.[55] Then, Moncrieff's burlesque, *Giovanni in London* appeared in *Cumberland's British Theatre* (1826–61), the cheapest acting edition ever produced, whilst the publication of *Duncombe's British Theatre* (1828–52) made available a wide selection of plays from the Adelphi, Surrey and Coburg theatres. Both Richardson and Cumberland also devoted special collections to the minor theatre. Moncrieff edited *Richardson's New Minor Drama* (4 volumes, 1828–31), and George Daniel provided the prefaces for *Cumberland's Minor Theatre* (6 volumes, 1828–43), which gathered together an large number of illegitimate plays by authors such as Frederick Fox Cooper, George Almar, Gilbert À Beckett, John Buckstone and Henry Milner.

Until the passing of the Dramatic Copyright Act in 1833, however, the defence of plays as intellectual property was practically impossible.[56] As the evidence of Jerrold, Richard Peake, James Kenney and other dramatic authors at the Select Committee revealed, the position of dramatic authors in the theatrical market remained precarious. Authors had no means of redress – other than a prohibitively expensive legal

---

[53] Mrs Mathews, *The Life and Correspondence of Charles Mathews the Elder*, ed. Edmund Yates (London: Routledge, 1860), 165.

[54] *Atlas*, January 1833, 841; on Thomas Dibdin's facility for rapid composition, see Fitzball, *Thirty-Five Years*, 89.

[55] See *inter alia* Thomas Dibdin, *Melodrame Mad! or the Siege of Troy* (Surrey 1819); [Henry Milner], *The Gamblers* (Surrey, 1823), suppressed.   [56] See Foote, *Companion*, 104–7.

action – if an unauthorised performance took place of an unpublished play. In any case, as Charles Dibdin pointed out, even if an action were successful, publishers often claimed that they were too poor to pay.[57] Nor did dramatic authors receive payment for performances of their plays at provincial theatres. Playwrights also complained bitterly about the creation of unauthorised texts by paid scribblers who transcribed plays directly from a performance. At the Select Committee, for example, Douglas Jerrold alluded darkly to Mr Kenneth, a dramatic agent at the corner of Bow Street, who was said to sell unauthorised texts to country managers.[58] Further evidence of this practice can be found in the memoirs of Charles Mathews the Elder. During his performances of *The Trip To Paris*, Mathews recalls being often distracted by Adelphi spectators 'turning over the leaves' of spurious playtexts which they had purchased at the theatre door.[59]

The campaign by a group of playwrights to introduce legislation to protect dramatic copyright united lowly stock authors (Edward Fitzball and William Moncrieff) and eminent middle-class playwrights (Edward Bulwer-Lytton and Sheridan Knowles). As a result of this, the Dramatic Authors' Society set up a system of registration for the payment of fees by managers to authors (administered by John Miller) but also established prices for various different kinds of dramatic work.[60] Interestingly, this scheme probably contributed to the commercial demise of legitimate drama, for according to the scale of fees listed in Leman Rede's *Road to the Stage*, three-act dramas now commanded the same fees as legitimate tragedies and comedies. In other words, illegitimate plays were now valued in the marketplace at the same price as tragedy and comedy. The Society had simply abandoned any commercial distinctions between the values of tragedy and burlesque, comedy and melodrama in favour of the cold, economic logic of supply and demand; these new prices confirmed the commercial triumph of illegitimate genres.

SPECTATORSHIP

'There is, unquestionably, some magnetic influence pervading "theatres of crowded men:" the attractions of squeezing and suffocation in that hot-air bath, the Adelphi, are duly appreciated by the seekers after excitement. Comfort makes folks fastidious: under high pressure the

---

[57] *Memoirs*, 46.   [58] *SC* 2799; see also Moncrieff's evidence, SC 3149.
[59] Mrs Mathews, *Life of Mathews*, 219.   [60] See Rede, *The Road to the Stage* (1836 edition).

aptitude for fun is mightily quickened; and entertainments must needs be worth seeing, for which people peril ribs and coat-skirts.'[61] Theatre-going in the early nineteenth century began with a journey, whether on foot across the fields to Sadler's Wells, where patrols lined the route with lights to prevent robbery, across the river in a Thames wherry, or by rattling along the streets in a carriage or omnibus. Spectators jostled and pushed to gain entry, perhaps being relieved of a watch by pickpockets around the box-office.[62] Once inside, the heat within the auditorium, especially at the little Haymarket theatre during the summer months, could easily become stifling. Still worse, theatres invariably harboured 'a compound of villainous smells':[63] alcohol, gaslight, as well as hot bodies rarely washed. In the event of the English Emperor or Empress visiting the Coburg, declared Frederick Tomlins, it would be necessary 'to imitate the Roman potentate, by drenching the audience with rose-water to neutralise certain vile odours arising from gin and tobacco, and bad ventilation'.[64] Physical discomfort apart, 'painful feelings' might also be excited amongst respectable theatregoers by the sight of prostitutes (often granted free admission, since they represented a crucial element in the theatrical economy, especially at Drury Lane and Covent Garden) in the upper boxes, and around the saloon areas. Meanwhile, the evening's entertainment, which usually began at 6 pm in the transpontine houses, often lasted for at least four hours. At half price, new spectators arrived, including those whose employment had just ended, as well as leisured Regency bucks taking in the afterpiece: at the Adelphi, the *Examiner* complained crossly about the 'misfortune' of sitting behind 'those half-price hogs'.[65] Theatrical spectatorship certainly required plentiful reserves of stamina and patience.

Many of the spectators at the minor theatres, especially at the East End houses, came from the immediate neighbourhood.[66] Journeymen

---

[61] *Athenaeum*, 22 September 1838, 700.

[62] On pickpockets at theatres, see SC 3375. According to James Grant, many of the youths among the lower classes 'begin their careers as thieves in order that they may have the means of gratifying their *penchant* for theatricals'. See *The Great Metropolis*, 2 vols. (London: Saunders and Otley, 1838), 1:22. On the fear of crime at the minor theatres, see the correspondent in the *Tatler*, new series, 2–4 June 1832, 214, who described the galleries of minor theatres as 'filled with the lowest rabble, and unchecked by any police of any sort'.

[63] *Drama*, April 1822, 2: 386, of the Royalty theatre.

[64] Tomlins, *Brief View*, 60. Compare the *Examiner*'s complains about smells at the Coburg, 12 December 1826, 116.   [65] *Examiner*, 21 February 1830, 116.

[66] Jim Davis and Tracy Davis' seminal analysis of the Britannia audiences asks searching questions about our methodology for describing theatre audiences. See 'The People of the "People's Theatre": The Social Demography of the Britannia Theatre (Hoxton)', *Theatre Survey* 32 (November 1991), 137–65.

mechanics, one of the occupational groups keen to take advantage of education and cheap literature, as well as shopkeepers and provisioners, clerks in public and mercantile offices, artisans, sailors, small gentry and attorneys, made up a significant proportion of the audiences.[67] The East London Theatre, declared one correspondent in 1819, was 'so exclusively frequented by the *Ultra-orientalists*, as to escape the cognizance of us *occidentalists*'.[68] Benefits offer a useful, though atypical guide to the social geography of patronage: for a Royalty benefit, seats could be obtained at a cheesemonger in Whitechapel, a shoemaker in Tower Hill, and a hairdresser's in Grace Alley.[69] East End audiences would have included artisans and many immigrants (especially the Jews who worked in the old-clothes trade around Petticoat Lane and Duke's Place), sailors and others employed in river and sea trades, as well as those involved in industries such as brewing and distilling.[70] Not surprisingly, then, the Royalty, Garrick and Pavilion Theatres all staged a variety of nautical plays, including *The Sailor's Frolic* and *Wapping Old Stairs*, a sombre nautical drama about the eventual vindication of a man falsely accused of being a mutineer. The prominence of plays featuring Jewish heroes and heroines, including *The Benevolent Jew* and Elizabeth Polack's tragedy, *Esther, the Royal Jewess* (Pavilion, 1835) confirms the managers' determination to represent the ethnic make-up of the local community.[71] But the strangest characteristic of East End spectatorship, according to many reviewers, was the popularity of Shakespeare at the Pavilion. In the backwater of Whitechapel, a 'Boetia of thriving black-guardism' whose manners, habits and houses seemed forty years behind the rest of London, how could it be that Shakespeare's plays were performed 'more frequently, and to fuller and more absorbed audiences than the patent theatres can boast'?[72]

In 1807, a false alarm of fire at Sadler's Wells produced such panic that eighteen people died in the ensuing commotion. The dead included

---

[67] Whittock, *New Picture of London*, 31–2. See the disdainful comments of the *Theatrical Inquisitor*, May 1820, 16: 301, which describes theatregoing as 'the favourite recreation of dirty mechanics, of presumptuous shopkeepers, and of ignorant gentry'.

[68] 'Peeping Tom', *Theatrical Inquisitor*, January 1819, 14:21.

[69] Bill for 12 July 1824. A bill for 19 November 1832 also gives a list of shops and public houses at which tickets were available. These included Mulvey's Wine Vaults in Whitechapel Road, the Cheshire Cheese and Grapes taverns in Spitalfields, as well as other taverns in Shoreditch and Mile End Road, a music-seller in Commercial Road, Abraham's Coffee House in Duke's Place and a watch- and clock-maker.

[70] See the statistical evidence offered by L. Schwartz in 'Occupations and Incomes in Late Eighteenth-Century London', *East London Papers* 14 (December 1972), 87–100.

[71] See review published in the *Drama*, October 1821, 1: 303.

[72] Cornelius Webbe, *Glances at Life in City and Suburb* (London, Smith, Elder and Co., 1836), 153.

a gardener's daughter, an apprentice cabinet-maker, a prostitute who had accompanied some sailors to the play, a young wheelwright, a nine-year-old nursery maid who had gone with her mistress, and a boy of eleven who had been visiting the Wells with some neighbours.[73] This sad list offers us very useful information about the nature of early nineteenth-century spectatorship. It reveals the varied forms of commercial, familial and social relationships which existed among different theatre-goers, as well as the large number of children, apprentices and other young people who patronised theatre galleries. Only by delving more deeply into the kinds of sociability entailed by theatrical spectatorship, as well as its characteristic forms of expression, will we begin to understand what it meant to be a theatregoer in early nineteenth-century London.

Local spectators, including many sailors and shopkeepers, also supported transpontine houses such as the Surrey and the Coburg.[74] Indeed, according to Cornelius Webbe, the smoke and fume from the frying of sausages, and preparation of trotters and stewed eel on the New Cut, seemed to permeate the Coburg, and even to obscure spectators' views of the stage.[75] David Osbaldiston, who managed the Surrey Theatre in the early 1830s, confirmed that the majority of his patrons came from the theatre's vicinity.[76] According to Davidge, the Coburg audience even varied according to the day of the week. While 'the working classes generally' visited on Mondays (a legacy of Saint Monday, perhaps), 'the better classes, the play-going public generally' tended to patronise the Coburg in the middle of the week.[77] Nevertheless, theatre critics and graphic satirists always emphasised the 'low' character of the Coburg audience. Given this tendency, what is interesting about 'Royal Victoria. The New Cut Vagabonds Every Night' (plate 12) is the apparent discrepancy between image and text. On the one hand, the caption satirically announces the theatre's audience as a dirty, and even criminal spectacle in its own right. But though the boy towards the left of the picture may indeed be a pickpocket, most of the gallery spectators appear respectable. Yet the vacant expressions of these individuals (there is a deliberate naiveté about the conventions of this image) is clearly designed to provoke laughter about the absurdity of vulgar spectatorship. For the

---

[73] See the unidentified cuttings in 'Collections relating to Sadler's Wells', 3 vols. III, fols. 183–202, British Library.

[74] On the presence of sailors at the Surrey, see *Dramatic Magazine*, September 18 1830, 2: 253. Spectators at the transpontine houses would have included men employed at the docks and in local industries such as brewing and distilling, glass and dye houses, clothing and food supply.

[75] Webbe, *Glances at Life*, 166.   [76] SC 1597.   [77] SC 1270, see also T. P. Cooke, SC 2606–7.

12. Illegitimate spectatorship. *The New Cut Vagabonds Every Night.*

Coburg's location, close to the New Cut and to the morally uncertain neighbourhood of St George's Fields, ensured that the theatre became synonymous with plebeian theatregoing, and all the social and cultural fears which that phenomenon seemed to represent.[78] What is more, Davidge's unwise decision during the theatrical depression of the 1820s to issue box orders at 1s each (thereby making box prices equal to those for gallery admission) only compounded this perception of unrespectability: an ironic *Satirist* reviewer even claimed to have seen chimney sweeps in the boxes.[79]

[78] See Tomlins, *Brief View*, 60; Webbe, *Glances at Life*, 158ff. For a more ironic perspective, compare the *Figaro*'s vitriolic descriptions of the Coburg, e.g. 31 March 1832, 12; 27 October 1832, 186, and 6 July 1833, 107–8.

[79] 10 July 1831, 110; see also *Dramatic Magazine*, September 1829, 208. On the introduction of box orders at Sadler's Wells, see the *Stage*, August 1828, 33 which noticed with displeasure the 'unseemly exhibition' of bonnets and shawls hanging over the front of the boxes. Can it be expected, that 'people of high rank' will fraternise with 'butchers' wives from Whitechapel,' 'whose whole conversation is on the prices of the market, purveyors of milk from Islington, and old clothesmen from Saffron Hill'? Cf. Charles Dibdin, *Memoirs*, 156, where Dibdin declares that the Surrey was the only theatre to have 'preserved its rank; by not adopting the custom, now so general, of admitting the Public to the Boxes, for one shilling each, through the specious subterfuge of an *Order*, or free admission'.

The rapid expansion of neighbourhoods such as Southwark on the south bank, now linked to Westminster by the Waterloo and Blackfriars bridges, as well as the neighbourhoods around Whitechapel, whose populations had been swollen by artisans, sailors and other workers employed at the new docks, created audiences eager to patronise local playhouses. In Southwark, too, a network of houses and public buildings soon covered the old Lambeth marsh land. Plate 13 shows the Surrey Theatre in 1812, just as the neighbourhood's semi-rural position is about to disappear; on the left-hand side of the engraving, we can see a bill-sticker carefully posting a Surrey playbill to the Monument. But many of the new buildings near the theatre, such as the Bethlem and Magdalen Hospitals (the latter for 'penitent' prostitutes, and shown in this engraving to the right of the Surrey), the Indigent Blind School and the Freemasons' Charity School, were dedicated to philanthropic purposes, and could not provide a market for the transpontine theatres. The liberties of the King's Bench prison had originally included the Royal Circus, thereby enabling the debtors confined there to attend performances, but this privilege was swiftly withdrawn after Jack Palmer's notorious performance in John Dent's *Bastille* play.

For a variety of reasons, making the Surrey pay remained a challenge fraught with difficulties. As Tom Dibdin memorably observed, a third of the potential Surrey audience 'are living within certain rules, which proscribe their admission to the theatre', another third 'are living in the odour of sanctity, which proscribes their entering the tents of the wicked ones, unless they can do it with a free admission'. (This would seem to be an ironic allusion to the congregation at Rowland Hill's Rotunda chapel close by in Charlotte Street: Hill delighted in making comparisons between the two institutions, and in one sermon memorably described his chapel and the Surrey Theatre as two ships in sight of a spice island, one 'manned by the elect of heaven', the other 'directed by the devil's crew, and laded with sinfulness'.)[80] 'Of the remainder,' continued Dibdin, 'some go without ever paying for admission, others are too poor to pay, and the remainder choose between the three transpontine minor theatres'.[81] As Dibdin realised, the peculiar social composition of the neighbourhoods around St George's Fields made it imperative that the Surrey should succeed in attracting spectators from beyond the theatre's vicinity.

---

[80] Raymond, *Memoirs of Elliston*, I: 389–90. [81] Thomas Dibdin, *Reminiscences* II: 110.

VIEW of the SURREY THEATRE, MAGDALEN, &c. &c.

Published March 2 1812 by ROBT LAURIE & JAS WHITTLE, No 53 Fleet Street London.

13. View of the Surrey Theatre. Magdalen &c, 1812.

So far I have been exploring the relationship between spectatorship and locality. But it is important to remember that locality also became a dramatic subject at the minor houses. After the introduction of shops and local scenes into Sadler's Wells pantomimes, Thomas Dibdin soon followed suit with *The Dog and the Duck; or, Harlequin in the Obelisk* and *Pedlar's Acre; or, Harlequin in Lambeth* (both Surrey, 1816). The Surrey pantomimes proudly featured views of Lambeth Marsh, Vauxhall Bridge and the new penitentiary. They also illustrated former, dissolute places of local entertainment such as the Dog and Duck, a well-known inn which had been deprived of its licence by local magistrates in 1787. In *The Dog and the Duck*, the eponymous inn appears as a picturesque ruin which is later transformed by Momus into the Regions of Mirth, now happily situated in St George's Fields. Dibdin appropriates the conventions of pantomimic metamorphosis to celebrate the rise of the Surrey theatre as a local, moral 'Pavilion of Pleasure' whose rational entertainments have triumphed over the lewd pleasures of the Dog and Duck.[82] Other local dramas included Thomas Wilks' plays, *The Red Crow* (Sadler's Wells, 1834) and *The Ruby Ring; or, The Murder at Sadler's Wells* (Sadler's Wells 1840), George Almar's *The Clerk of Clerkenwell* (Sadler's Wells, 1834) and Dibdin Pitt's *Wilkins the Weaver; or Bethnal Green in the Olden Time* (Pavilion 1834). Many of these dramas nostalgically memorialise local legends, myths and superstitions; urban conflicts between social classes are displaced on to a romantic, historical past. In a variety of ways, such plays made familiar the cultural geography of an otherwise huge and incomprehensible city. Collective memories and oral narratives seem to become a ballast for human identity in these dramas; the common stock of popular knowledge was passing into new forms as the stuff of modern entertainment.

Many spectators at the minor playhouses, however, may not have been familiar with these local narratives, for they had travelled to the theatre from far beyond their own neighbourhood. Astley's had long been frequented by genteel people, with their children and servants; the *beau monde* had always enjoyed a trip to Sadler's Wells during the summer months.[83] In 1821, as part of her defiant tour of the metropolis, Queen Caroline herself visited not only Drury Lane, but also Astley's Amphi-

---

[82] Playbill for 26 August 1816 in HTC.
[83] See 'Peeping Tom' in *Theatrical Inquisitor*, January 1819, 14, 20–3. A newspaper cutting for 1797 preserved in 'Collections Relating to Sadler's Wells' III, fol. 29, drew attention to the 'brilliancy' of the boxes at Sadler's Wells as proof 'that a well-regulated set of Entertainments will at all times draw the attention of the Beau-monde to a Summer Theatre'.

theatre and the Surrey, to the delight of enthusiastic and noisy crowds.[84] Moreover, by 1817, the Surrey had established a West End box-office to enable theatregoers to purchase tickets in advance; the Coburg also sold seats from the West End, first at Mr Fentum's Music Warehouse in the Strand and at a library in Pall Mall, and later opened box-offices in Whitefriars near the Temple and in Covent Garden (at a Cigar Divan).[85]

Paving, surfacing and 'macadamising' soon made journeys to the theatre faster and more comfortable, whether on foot, carriage or coach. The Metropolitan Pavement Act of 1817 (known as Michael Angelo Taylor's Act) forbade the dumping of 'Slop, Mud, Dirt, Dust, Rubbish, Ashes, Filth' in the street, speeding up the disappearance of that urban detritus which must have deterred many a genteel playgoer from walking to the theatre. Once the deposit of the city's filth, the street was now becoming a neutral thoroughfare for the theatrical traveller.[86] Nor did genteel theatregoers have to step into the damp cold boat of a Thames waterman in order to cross the river; instead they could now speed to Astley's or the Surrey across the new bridges (Vauxhall, 1816; Waterloo 1817; Southwark, 1819).[87] Such was the perceived importance of the Waterloo bridge to the treasuries of the transpontine houses that the event was celebrated with songs and comic sketches. Nevertheless, managers still continued to prize the loyalty of the Thames watermen. In 1820, 'as a reward for their past as well as future attention to the Public', the Coburg Theatre even sponsored a competition, featuring a prize wherry, to be won by the watermen of Blackfriars and Waterloo Bridges.[88]

Improved transport, including omnibuses which took spectators directly to and from the playhouse, also made the Coburg and the Surrey more easily accessible. Coaches for Greenwich and Deptford theatregoers to the Surrey were available by 1819; in 1821, the Surrey advertised a new hackney coach stand, close to the Obelisk in St George's Fields.

---

[84] On the Astley visit, see the *Theatrical Spectator*, 23 June 1821, 86–8. According to the reviewer, the Queen 'met with such a reception, as fully demonstrated the unabated ardour of her popularity'. During the singing of the national anthem, the word 'Queen' was substituted for 'King'; 'rapturous' cheers greeted Gil Blas' reference to the duty of mankind 'to succour women in the hour of peril' and several other passages in the evening's performance were also applauded 'from their apparent reference to her Majesty's cause'. The *Drama* magazine (July 1821, I :155) reported that for her Surrey visit, Queen Caroline had requested a performance of *The Heart of Midlothian*, and commented, 'Many passages were quite applicable to HER MAJESTY's unfortunate situation, and were rapturously caught at by the audience.'

[85] See bills for 4 May 1819, 6 April 1820 and an undated bill, probably October 1831.

[86] See further, James Winter, *London's Teeming Streets 1830–1914* (London: Routledge, 1993), 42ff.

[87] The river crossing cost between 1s 6d and 2s during the early 1820s. See J. Feltham, *The Picture of London for 1822* (London: Longman & Co., [1822]), 428.   [88] Coburg bill, 9 October 1820.

By the early 1830s, the Red Rover Omnibus ferried passengers between Gracechurch Street and the Coburg before and after the evening's performances. According to the *Examiner*, however, the extortionate prices charged by the hackney coaches, poorly co-ordinated stage coach and omnibus timetables, together with the absence of livery facilities for horses, continued to deter many potential spectators.[89]

My exploration of spectatorship began with the *Athenaeum*'s slightly mystified description of the sociable discomfort at the Adelphi. Newspapers and periodicals certainly played a crucial role in advising, cajoling and even warning spectators about particular productions and theatres. Indeed, a favourite comic feature of these accounts is the description of the journey taken to reach the playhouse. Once the theatre has been reached, references to unfamiliar, seemingly remote neighbourhoods then give way to the strangeness, vulgarity or downright dirtiness of local audiences.[90] Reviewing performances at the minor theatres all too often provided critics with an opportunity to rehearse their own gentility (however suspect) and to ridicule the pleasures of poorer spectators: Hazlitt's theatre criticism provides a memorable exception to this general rule.

The rise of the minor theatres was accompanied by a great expansion in dramatic reviewing. Although many drama periodicals soon failed, others, including the *Theatrical Inquisitor* (1812–20), the *Drama, or Theatrical Pocket Magazine* (1821–4) and Leigh Hunt's lively paper, the *Tatler* (1830–2), attracted a wide readership. In addition, leading periodicals such as the *London Magazine*, the *Athenaeum* and the *Spectator* all reviewed performances at the minor theatres, especially from the 1820s onwards, as did newspapers such as *The Times* and the *Morning Chronicle*.

'We saw that independence in theatrical criticism would be a great novelty. We announced it, and nobody believed us; we stuck to it, and the town believed everything we said.'[91] The *Examiner* confirmed Hunt's gleeful declaration of independence by demonstrating a marked disdain for hierarchies of genre or of theatrical institutions. Moreover, the

---

[89] 22 December 1833, 806.

[90] Reviewers caricatured local audiences according to a sensuous lexicon of bad smells, noise, dirt and darkness. See, for example, reports in the *Age*, 23 January 1831, 30; *Figaro*, 24 August 1833, 2:136 and the *Stage*, August 1828, 32–4. For the *Stage*'s response to a request for the inclusion of Pavilion reviews, see the issue of September 1828, 63: 'we candidly avow ourselves incapable of affording ourselves the desired information, never having travelled so far Eastward in our lives, nor feeling any inclination, ever to do so!' Such declarations often provoked responses from indignant theatregoers. Cf. *Stage*, September 1828, 56.

[91] *The Autobiography of Leigh Hunt*, ed. J. E. Morpurgo (London: Cresset Press, 1949), 155, on the principles behind drama criticism in the *News*.

paper's intricate interlacing of theatrical and political examining point-edly gave the lie to that prevailing conviction that theatre somehow existed in a realm beyond contemporary politics.[92] For in the *Examiner*, as Hazlitt observed, '[a] literary criticism, perhaps, insinuates itself under the head of the Political Examiner; and the theatrical critic, or lover of the Fine Arts, is stultified by a *tirade* against the Bourbons'.[93] In the *Examiner*, politics and theatre become interchangeable domains, with shared plots and *dramatis personae*.

At a time of increasing cultural, social and political segregation, the *Examiner* critics presented theatre as an ideal public sphere:

> [Theatres] assemble people smilingly and in contact, not cut off from each other by hard pews and harder abstractions . . . They make people think how they shall best enjoy life and hope with each other, not how they shall be best off indi-vidually and hereafter. They win, not frighten; are universal, not exclusive.[94]

More than any other cultural form, theatre offers a counterpoint to methodistical moral anxieties and the commercial self-interestedness of modern urban life. But this gentle idealism about cultural pleasures which transcend the barriers of class and isolation could not always be sustained in practice. Hazlitt's visit to the minor theatres in 1820 and his ensuing comic debate with Thomas Wainewright reveal some of the fears at the heart of popular spectatorship.[95] As we saw in the discussion of Elliston's *Coriolanus* in chapter 4, Hazlitt's account reveals his contra-dictory views about the desire for cultural democracy and the claims of aesthetic elitism.

The debate was sparked off by Hazlitt's regular dramatic contribution to the March issue of the *London Magazine*. The patent theatres were closed, following the death of the King and the Duke of Kent, and Hazlitt dramatised his visit to the Coburg and the Adelphi as a form of holiday escape from their 'vortex of prejudice and fashion'.

---

[92] Managers of the minor theatres, of course, had their own reasons for making such a claim, espe-cially in the evidence given to the Parliamentary Select Committee: see Davidge's remarks, SC 1254. But the ostensible absence of politics from stage performance was often cited by pamphlet-eers as a cause of the stage's 'decline'. Cf. Edward Bulwer-Lytton, *England and the English*, II: 93–4.

[93] *Edinburgh Review*, May 1823, 38: 349–78, 368.

[94] *Examiner*, 20 July 1817, 456. Cf. Charles Lamb's essay, 'On the Acting of Munden' (*Lamb* II: 149) in which he praised Joseph Munden's comic performances for making 'the pulse of a crowded theatre beat like that of one man'. Compare Jonathan Wooler's discussions in the *Black Dwarf*, e.g. 5 March 1817, 93, in which Wooler presents dramatic spectatorship as the last refuge of popular constitutionalism.

[95] 'Weathercock' was Thomas Wainewright (1794–1852), poisoner, amateur art critic and friend of Lamb, De Quincey, Hazlitt and Macready. See W.C. Hazlitt, *Essays and Criticism by Thomas Griffiths Wainewright* (London: Reeves and Turner, 1880).

Escaped from under the more immediate inspection of the Lord Chamberlain's eye, fastidious objections, formal method, regular details, strict moral censure, cannot be expected at our hands: our 'speculative and officed instruments' may be well laid aside for a time.[96]

Hazlitt's essay opens with excited anticipation. Having escaped from stultified critical duty, he hopes to find at the minor theatres 'a romantic contrast to the presumptuous and exclusive pretensions of the legitimate drama'. In these 'suburbs of the drama', he reflects, no Theatre Royal 'oppresses the imagination, and entombs it in a mausoleum of massy pride' (291). Patent culture is represented here as a form of death: the stiff, grandiose arrogance of Drury Lane and Covent Garden has a deadening effect on audiences and plays alike.

But the Coburg destroyed Hazlitt's hopes of finding a world of dramatic innocence and freedom beyond the patent theatres. On the contrary, the audience seemed to represent a dramatic extension of the coarse and vulgar world of St George's Fields outside, populated by 'Jew-boys, pickpockets, prostitutes, and mountebanks'. In this place of cacophony, familiarity and grotesque physicality, 'our whole scheme of voluntary delusion and social enjoyment was cut up by the roots' (297). During the evening's entertainment, which included Moncrieff's play, *The Judgment of Brutus; or, Tarquin and Lucretia*, the audience laughed and hooted, whilst the physical proximity of spectator and performer entirely banished abstraction. Hazlitt watched with distaste the articulation of Junius Brutus Booth's face, 'with his under-jaws grinding out sentences, and his upper-lip twitching at words and syllables, as if a needle and thread had been passed through each corner of it, and the *gude wife* still continued sewing at her work' (298). Whereas the Theatres Royal had come to represent a form of death-in-life, the Coburg's performers seemed to promise nothing less than the grotesque triumph of the mechanical body. But having escaped from the Coburg to the Adelphi, Hazlitt discovered in the Miss Dennetts' 'easy gracefulness' and 'instinctive gaiety' a redemptive glimpse of sensuousness in motion. Like Hazlitt, the Miss Dennetts were in exile: the performers had left their engagements at the patent houses after a dispute about their contracts. But only those unable to see 'tenderness in the bending of a flower, or liveliness in the motion of a wave of the sea', Hazlitt declares, could possibly fail to be charmed by their performances (299).

Hazlitt's essay equivocates with a refreshing honesty and an endearing

---

[96] *Hazlitt* XVIII: 291–302, 292.

confusion between the wish to define and even celebrate minor culture, and the painful, repulsive experience of visiting the Coburg. Expectation and disappointment rapidly succeed each other; the critic's loyalties oscillate between the claims of an elite theatre characterised by a deathly form of oppression, and a popular, democratic theatre too ebulliently full of life. When he responded to Hazlitt's essay, however, Thomas Wainewright – here writing in the persona of Janus – ironically construed the critic's account as a manifesto for popular culture.[97] According to Janus, Hazlitt's choice of subject represented a daring excess, the 'exuberance of his genius'; at the same time, he gently accused Hazlitt of perversely encouraging the taste of 'what are called the lower orders'. Rather than promoting the cause of 'macaroni and champagne', Hazlitt had expressed an incomprehensible preference for 'boxing and bull beef':

> He affects a liking for *Tatnam*-court-road, rather than for Albermarle-street. He pretends a dislike for lords in the abstract, and would have us imagine that he preferred the noisy rebels in the gallery . . . He entertains serious thoughts of the Royal Cobourg Theatre – which we find, by reference to the picture of London, is situated in the borough of Southwark! (632)

Like so many genteel spectators, Janus insists on mapping theatrical tastes on to social class. In his reply, Hazlitt therefore turns the theatrical tables on his respondent, accusing Janus of making geography the sole criterion for dramatic pleasure:

> We do not hate pathos because it is found in the Borough; our taste (such as it is) can cross the water, by any of the four bridges, in search of spirit and nature; we can make up our minds to beauty even at Whitechapel![98]

Underpinning Hazlitt's argument with Janus is his conviction that since the French Revolution, British spectators have insisted on classifying culture as 'high' or 'low'.[99] So Janus 'swoons at the mention of the Royal Cobourg' and 'is afraid to trust himself at Sadler's Wells, lest his clothes should be covered with gingerbread, and spoiled with the smell of gin and tobacco' (344). Janus's cultural choices thus mirror that genteel tendency to patronise only those entertainments which enable their spectators to distinguish themselves from the lower classes.[100] By contrast,

---

[97] *London Magazine*, June 1820, 625–34.
[98] *London Magazine*, July 1820, *Hazlitt*, XVIII: 343–52, 344.
[99] *Examiner*, May 11 1828, *Hazlitt* XVIII: 400.
[100] Cf. 'The Company at the Opera', *Examiner*, May 1828, *Hazlitt* XVIII: 396, where Hazlitt also repudiates the supposed vulgarity of Sadler's Wells and the East London theatres.

Hazlitt's response daringly questions any fixed relationship between taste and social class.

An amusing *jeu d'esprit* in many ways, the dialogue between Hazlitt and Wainewright confirms the social unease and cultural anxieties which surrounded the transformation of the theatrical city. Having resolved to enjoy the humble pleasures offered by 'the purlieus of taste' which lie beyond Drury Lane and Covent Garden, Hazlitt was nonetheless repulsed by the grotesque sensuousness of playgoing at the Coburg. Such competing and often irreconcilable claims are a recurring theme in Hazlitt's theatre criticism. Dramatic spectatorship, indeed, becomes the crucial test of what cultural democracy might entail.

CHAPTER SIX

Westminster laughter

SCENES FROM THE REJECTED COMEDIES

In 1844, the playwright and journalist Gilbert Abbott À Beckett published *Scenes from the Rejected Comedies*. Like the rejected addresses turned down for the occasion of Drury Lane's reopening in 1812, when Byron had won the prize, À Beckett's collection of miniature burlesques created laughter from the injured pride of disappointed writers. The publicity surrounding these dramas no doubt recalled earlier 'rejections' – the refusal by Drury Lane of Sheridan Knowles' five-act comedy, *The Hunchback* (later warmly received at Covent Garden), or, two decades earlier, Milman's tragedy, *Fazio*.[1] But, by the early 1840s, the *Monthly Magazine* was presenting the rejection of poetic tragedies as irrefutable evidence that the Theatres Royal had simply abandoned literary drama in favour of the shallow, philistine and commercial exigencies of a *manager's* theatre (a theatre they condemned as devoid of capital, both financial and intellectual, hopelessly subservient to arrogant star performers and, above all, manifestly unjust to the ambitions of dramatic authors). The originality of unacted drama, boldly proclaimed its hapless defenders, now proved the corresponding decadence of modern theatrical institutions.[2]

À Beckett's burlesque scenes purport to have been written by contemporary playwrights unsuccessful in winning the £500 prize offered by the Haymarket manager Benjamin Webster, for a new five-act comedy

---

[1] Milman's drama was performed at the Surrey in 1816 under the title *The Italian Wife*.

[2] See 'The Manager's, the Actor's, and the Poet's Theatre', *Monthly Magazine*, August 1840, 4:107–12; cf. 'New Unacted Drama', March 1841, 5: 303–28. In these articles, John Heraud, an aspiring playwright who edited the *Monthly*, together with a group of authors, set out a template for a reformed, poetical theatre. They demanded the creation of an author's joint stock company which would rent Drury Lane and perform new and unacted plays 'of the highest and purest class', together with the foundation of Schools of Theatrical Education 'where a refined and classical taste should be cultivated'. See 'Report of the Dramatic Committee to the members of the Syncretic Association', *Monthly Magazine*, April 1841, 5: 547–52.

'illustrative of British manners'.[3] One year after the passing of the Theatre Regulation Act, by which all licensed theatres in London gained the right to perform tragedy and comedy, Webster's competition aimed to define the Haymarket as the metropolitan centre of legitimate comedy. Ironically, the mocking laughter which greeted the first performance of the winning play, *Quid Pro Quo* (a farcical and satirical drama of social aspiration by Catherine Gore, featuring a boroughmongering peer and a retired tradesman who aspires to take a seat in Parliament), succinctly demonstrated the confusion and perplexity of critics, managers and spectators alike about the nature of modern comedy.

À Beckett's *Rejected Comedies* transformed the controversy over the Haymarket competition into burlesque laughter. This chapter takes the theme of the rejected comedy (and the prevailing discourse of comic 'decline' and 'extinction' which dominates early nineteenth-century criticism of comedy) as a starting-point for exploring the rise of illegitimate laughter. First, however, we might look briefly at the subjects and generic forms chosen by À Beckett for his miniature comedies. The plays include *The Husband* (Sheridan Knowles), a snippet of simmering sexual passion between the Countess of Summerton and John, her footman, and *Credit* (Bulwer-Lytton) in which Stavely, a 'humble member of the middle classes' weighs up the relative merits of Anastasius and Euripides. Meanwhile, in the decorative, leisured world of Planché's *The Absurdity of a Day* (a 'silver fork' drama whose production demands a real Axminster carpet, a sculpture highly scented with eau-de-cologne and three King Charles' spaniels), Lord de Stanville expounds his belief that the British constitution should have been preserved in champagne, whilst À Beckett's own 'rejected' scene, *The School for Sentiment*, hilariously burlesques the language and sentiments of nineteenth-century melodrama. Here, the purity of the female heart 'is brighter than any gem that the proudest noble wears in his glittering but hollow coronet' (iv.37), characters believed dead unexpectedly return to life, and the aristocrat graciously relinquishes his claim to Emily's hand so that she can be married to Herbert, the play's nautical hero.[4]

The pleasures of À Beckett's *Rejected Comedies* are those of absurd comic juxtapositions between legalistic roguery and Latinate puns. The

---

[3] *Dramatic and Musical Review*, 10 June 1843, 281. On questions of gender and politics in the reception of Catherine Gore's play, see Ellen Donkin, 'Mrs. Gore gives tit for tat', 54–74, and Katherine Newey, 'From a female pen: The proper lady as playwright in the West End theatre, 1823–44', 193–211, especially 203–6, in Davis and Donkin, *Women and Playwriting*.

[4] À Beckett's other scenes included *Humbugs of the Hour* (Douglas Jerrold) *A Story of London* (Leigh Hunt), and *Jane Jenkins; or, The Ghost of the Back Drawing Room* (Edward Fitzball).

collection delights too in the sheer incommensurability of its comic settings, from drawing-rooms scented with camellias to a dingy attic where a woman is mending a pair of stockings. Indeed, the glaring incongruities of this burlesque *œuvre* encourage the reader to wonder whether contemporary laughter is properly to be found amongst the new aspirations of the middle classes, in the suspension of conventional gender roles or in gritty confrontations between villainous landlords and the virtuous poor? In a variety of ways, À Beckett's miniature plays reveal the usurpation of traditional 'coat-and-waistcoat' comedy by the fragmented comic world of modern urban laughter.

The desire of newly wealthy members of the middle classes to ape the manners and culture of the aristocracy, the disintegration of genteel laughter into illegitimate forms such as melodrama and farce, the new economics of comic playwriting: these are some of the factors which lie behind the miscellaneous character of À Beckett's scenes, and their apparently incompatible subjects of laughter. In particular, what preoccupied managers, critics and playwrights during this period was the scarcity of new legitimate comedies. No wonder, then, that in his preface to *Floreat Etona* (a burlesque of Boucicault), À Beckett should refer with ironic resignation to 'that almost extinct species – the writer of a successful Five Act Comedy'.[5]

Since the Regency, journalists, pamphlet-writers and playwrights alike had offered a confusing variety of explanations – political, social and, as in À Beckett's account, quasi-biological – for what they perceived as a crisis in comic playwriting.[6] Comedy, acknowledged many reviewers, could no longer be relied upon to amuse and admonish the lower orders. Old comedies, 'which are conversant with artificial manners and with partial follies', declared *The Times* (8 April 1816), 'can take little hold of the attention of the multitude', while 'modern comedies, which deal so largely in fine sentiment, are equally useless to high and low'. In this remark we glimpse an anxious recognition that the purpose of comedy to instruct as well as to amuse (and to instruct in particular that morally vulnerable section of society identified as the lower orders) could no longer be taken for granted. For many reviewers

---

[5] À Beckett, *Scenes from the Rejected Comedies*, 26.
[6] See, for example, Charles Lamb, 'On the Artificial Comedy of the Last Century' in *Lamb* II:141–7; for Hazlitt's concerns about insipidity and decorum in comedy, see *Hazlitt* V:69–70, VI:150, and especially 'On Modern Comedy', IV:10–14. Cf. 'The English Stage' (*Theatrical Inquisitor*, November 1813, III: 201–5, especially 202–3; 'On the Degraded Condition of our Modern Dramatic Literature', *Dramatic Magazine*, April 1830, 2: 76–8, and Francis Place's manuscript notes entitled 'Decline of the Drama', fols. 34–5.

comedy provided a cultural standard against which to measure the 'havoc' produced by 'changes of manners' in British society.[7] Perhaps the most eloquent of all these laments is Charles Lamb's essay about the unrepresentable character of Restoration comedy on the late Georgian stage. For what Lamb explores in this argument is the stubborn, legalistic refusal of contemporary audiences to allow moral licence to the imaginative world of Restoration comedy. 'On the Artificial Comedy of the Last Century' describes those spectators who dread infection 'from the scenic representation of disorder', and who demand that performance should be made commensurable with 'the exclusive and all devouring drama of common life'. In contemporary culture where, Lamb sadly observes, '[t]he standard of *police* is the measure of *political justice*', the speculative pleasures of Congreve and Wycherley's dramas can no longer be staged.

Whereas Elizabeth Inchbald perceived the threat to modern comedy as one of generic competition (where the 'vulgar' attractions of farce overwhelm and finally conquer the 'subtler' pleasures of legitimate comedy), Hazlitt interpreted the crisis of modern comedy as an almost physiological effect of social and political change. The transformation of laughter may be attributed to those 'strange matters' written in men's faces: 'the rise of stocks, the loss of battles, the fall of kingdoms and the deaths of kings'. Such shocks and confusions, argued Hazlitt, deflect dramatic audiences from 'individual caprices, or head-strong passions, which are the nerves and sinews of Comedy and Tragedy.'[8] As these examples indicate, accounts of comedy's demise constitute a virtual subgenre of dramatic criticism in this period. The progress of refinement, the withering influence of the Lord Chamberlain's censorship, the rage for music or the stranglehold of translation over the comic repertoire: writers provided a wealth of often ingenious explanations for the half-empty houses at Covent Garden which greeted performances of a stock comedy, and the disappearance of Restoration plays from the acting repertoire. In the first two decades of the nineteenth century, comedy suddenly seemed to have become an unstable world, its oscillations and proclivities minutely, relentlessly anatomised in the hope that they held the key to the turbulent anxieties of modern life, and indeed the future of British society.

Amidst imperial spectacle and blue-fire melodrama, the Haymarket

---

[7] *Examiner* review of *The Cataract of the Ganges*, 2 November 1823, 710.
[8] *London Magazine*, April 1820; *Hazlitt* XVIII: 304.

Theatre remained the quiet defender of theatrical tradition: a house seemingly impervious to novelty and innovation, a place of 'old plays' and 'old ways'. As one *Examiner* critic declared approvingly in 1835, the Haymarket 'is the only theatre now where we can catch a glimpse of the good old comedy'.[9] Throughout the 1830s, the Haymarket staged dramas by many of the age's leading comic playwrights, including Bulwer-Lytton (*The Sea Captain*, 1839, and his hit play, *Money*, 1840, were both premiered there), Sheridan Knowles (*The Bridal*, 1837) and Dion Boucicault (*A Lover by Proxy, Alma Mater* and, with Charles Mathews, *Used Up*). Ben Webster's competition thus dovetailed perfectly with the Haymarket's institutional policy of producing stock comic plays (*The School for Scandal, She Stoops to Conquer, A New Way to Pay Old Debts*) together with new legitimate comedies, not to mention that procession of bashful, fluctuating bachelors, romantic spinsters and mismatched spouses which populated Buckstone's three-act farcical comedies of modern life: *Second Thoughts* (1832), *Married Life* (1834) and *Single Life* (1839).

When À Beckett invoked the language of extinction to describe the scarcity of successful five-act comedies, he implicitly acknowledged the proto-Darwinian triumph of illegitimate comic forms in early Victorian London. The home of laughter had now moved to the Adelphi and the Olympic – where legitimate comedy was of course prohibited. Here, burlettas, farces, pantomimes and burlesques made up the bulk of the comic repertoire (melodrama also interleaves scenes of farcical low comedy, though this is beyond the scope of my discussion here). A huge and potentially lucrative market now existed in London for illegitimate laughter: no wonder that rising playwrights such as Charles Dance, J. R. Planché, John Oxenford and indeed Charles Dickens (who wrote three farcical burlettas for the St James's Theatre) decided to make their dramatic careers by writing short comedies and farcical burlettas for the minor houses. In a variety of ways, theatrical economics powerfully influenced the direction of early Victorian laughter.[10]

By the 1830s, illegitimate laughter – with the exception of the occasional burlesque – had shed almost all its semiotic signs of marginality; most burlettas performed at the minor playhouses during the 1830s were

---

[9] *Examiner*, 26 July 1835, 469.
[10] On the commercial success of illegitimate laughter, see Place, 'Decline of the Drama', fols. 34–5. Place notes that although Elliston '*takes* the privilege to perform whatever he pleases' at the Surrey theatre, the manager finds 'humorous and pathetic shewy pieces' more advantageous than 'regular Comedies and Tragedies'.

formally indistinguishable from those staged at Covent Garden or Drury Lane. Nevertheless, the institutional position of the minor theatres shaped fundamentally the production of nineteenth-century laughter. At the same time, writers and performers were beginning to forge new characters, languages and forms through which to explore the contradictions and absurdities of urban life.

BURLESQUE AND UNFASHIONABLE FARCE

'[H]ow far it may be proper to permit the Minor Theatres to ridicule the productions of the Major (both being under the same jurisdiction,) is a point of consideration for the Lord Chamberlain only.'[11] So remarked George Colman the Younger, as Examiner of Plays, in a note written to accompany the licensing script for the Adelphi's burlesque, *Hyder Ali; or the Lions of Mysore*. But if Colman hoped to shift the responsibility for such matters of policy on to the Duke of Devonshire, he must have been disappointed: the Lord Chamberlain paid no attention whatsoever to the Examiner's anxieties.

Buckstone's play – 'the most laughable burlesque . . . seen upon the English stage for many years' – satirises Drury Lane's resolution to abandon legitimate drama for the more profitable pleasures of the menagerie.[12] More specifically, *Hyder Ali* parodies an eponymous *pièce de circonstance* starring the celebrated animal trainer, M. Martin, and his troupe of exotic animals, including a lion and a pelican. The Adelphi show ostensibly arises out of a sudden managerial crisis: Drury Lane has lured the 'real' animals away, and so Frederick Yates has to persuade members of his company to take their parts instead.[13] The painters and carpenters are the first to express their scepticism: surely, the introduction of animals will damage the theatre's respectability? 'Money,' declares Yates with ironic aplomb, 'is respectability.' In any case, since the Adelphi is an illegitimate theatre, 'spurious resources' like animals are its 'legitimate property':

[11] MS letter, 20 October 1831, Devonshire. See also Colman's note, 12 October 1831, accompanying the original piece by Alfred Bunn.

[12] For reviews of the Adelphi burlesque, see *Literary Gazette*, 29 October 1831, 701; *Athenaeum*, 29 October 1831, 708. Other burlesques on the same theme include *Learned Lions* (Queen's, October 1831), reviewed *Tatler*, 22 October 1831, 387 and Frederick Cooper, *Loves of the Lions; or Hyder Ali's Squad* (Sadler's Wells, November 1831).

[13] LC MS 42913 fols. 73–94, with scene decorations and a MS prologue in Westminster Public Library.

TOMKINS: You mean to say of the Great Theatres as they are called – were
    to allow of such an exhibition, it would not be in accordance with the
    classic character of those establishments?
YATES: Certainly not – nor in keeping with the excellent taste always
    displayed by them (fol. 76)

Yates then explains to his assembled company that he has been jilted by
the beasts (who prefer 'legitimacy and Drury's boards'), and proceeds to
cast his performers: Buckstone is to play a boa constrictor, John Reeve a
lion, and Mrs Fitzwilliam a cat. Not surprisingly, the Adelphi celebrities
indignantly object to their animal parts: Yates therefore attempts to
suggest that these roles will actually enhance their reputations: Mrs
Fitzwilliam is finally persuaded to perform after Yates has shrewdly presented the part of the cat as a study in the triumph of maternal affection.
But in the chaotic rehearsal scene which follows, the lion is indisposed,
Mrs Fitzwilliam threatens to defect to Drury Lane, after discovering that
her best scene has been cut, the tiger objects to devouring a child, and
the kangaroo's ghost is murdered by actors jealous of its success. The
Adelphi animals prove to be rather less obedient than their live relations
at Drury Lane.

Two years later, the evidence given at the Select Committee on
Dramatic Literature in 1832 provided the Adelphi with the raw material
for a still more audacious rehearsal play: *Bad Business or, A Meeting of
Managers, being a prelude to a Burletta in right Earnest to be called Crimson Crimes
or the Blood Stain'd Bandit* (1832).[14] The drama's original title seems to been
The Dramatic Committee; or, A Burletta According to Law; whether the
Examiner of Plays intervened to suppress this, we do not know.[15] In *Bad
Business*, Buckstone weaves together a satirical commentary on the Select
Committee evidence, and a mock melodrama dramatising the ludicrous
effects of theatrical regulation. The only extant copy of the play is the
licensing script, which includes many deletions, apparently by the
Examiner; again, we have no means of knowing whether these excisions
were actually observed in performance.

The play begins with that familiar burlesque scene – the conference
of managers in distress – featuring Mr Gong, and his brethren,
Puff'emorf, Payorder and Screw. Performers and managers are then
summoned to give evidence. The two major witnesses are Peter Laporte
(then joint lessee of Covent Garden and Drury Lane theatres), and

---

[14] Adelphi 19 November–21 December 1832; LC MS 42919 fols. 307–332; undated bill [1832].
[15] See Colman's MS note accompanying the script, 16 November 1832. Cf. *Age*, 18 November 1832,
    374.

Paganini, the musical celebrity. *Bad Business* portrays both men as swindlers intent upon duping English audiences for their own commercial profit. Laporte, who is already proprietor of twenty-one theatres, hopes to enclose Salisbury Plain for his next establishment (fol. 310–11 deleted), whilst Paganini regards the public as naive dupes: '~~de sheep lead de flock with a bell round his neck~~' (fol. 313, deleted). As if to make his interests perfectly clear, Paganini proceeds to give a short recital on one string, at a salary of a thousand guineas a minute, after which he pockets a collection of cheques, each for one thousand pounds, from his amazed listeners, and promptly disappears (fol. 313, deleted).

The beleaguered managers in *Bad Business* are keen to improve the state of their dramatic treasuries by taking a leaf out of the Adelphi Theatre's book. The witnesses helpfully oblige by providing a description of illegitimate drama – 'Pantomime – explosions – Ghosts & Scrolls' (fol. 316) and then go on to act out how *Hamlet* must be played '~~according to law~~' (fol. 316, references to law and burletta deleted). *Crimson Crimes*, a mock melodrama of 'bloody-minded marauders' and 'pious hermits'[16] is then put into rehearsal. The play includes a series of burlesque dialogues conducted entirely on scrolls (some of which are produced by characters who mysteriously come alive after their dramatic deaths to 'speak' once more);[17] Yates also coaches Mrs Honey (who plays Ogleina, the chief bandit's 'neglected, jealous and treacherous' tenth wife) on how to express her anger 'in the most energetic and ~~legal~~ proper manner possible' (fol. 312). Then, in one of the most absurd episodes, the Adelphi manager Charles Mathews appears in an upper stage box demanding a musical chord in order to prevent Stabberini (who has just stabbed his rival robber) 'going too far'. In this whimsical interlude, the musical accompaniment required by law at illegitimate performances is invoked as if it might actually provide a psychological ballast against melodrama's hyperbolic dramaturgy.[18]

Already disconcerted by the satirical jibes in *Hyder Ali*, George Colman objected strongly to *Bad Business*. In its original form, the play 'appeared to me so highly objectionable that I deferred my application to the Lord Chamberlain for a License, till I had seen the Manager of the Adelphi Theatre, who has, now, very materially altered it.' Although Colman's stated objections were to the play's satires on living persons

---

[16] Unidentified cutting, Adelphi file, Theatre Museum, London.
[17] On the humorous effect of the scrolls, see the *London Literary Gazette*, 24 November 1832, 748.
[18] For other reviews, see *Examiner*, 25 November 1832, 756; *The Times*, 20 November 1832 and *Age*, 18 November 1832.

(i.e. on Laporte and Paganini), his excisions are in fact far more extensive. By deleting references to theatrical regulation and illegitimate performance, Colman attempted to suppress altogether the dramatisation
of theatrical politics in *Bad Business*.

Burlesque was crucial to the minor theatres' reputation for vulgar
laughter, and to the fame of the Adelphi in particular. Audiences
delighted in the plays' grotesque costumes, incongruous snatches of contemporary song, and absurd mock combats fought with bladders,
brooms and vegetables.[19] Throughout this period, playwrights at the
minor houses also appropriated burlesque's 'low' characters and indecorous conventions in order to mock dramatic productions at Drury Lane
and Covent Garden. In these plays, the legitimate becomes dirty, vulgar
and manifestly improbable, a dramatic universe populated by figures
such as master chimney-sweepers. (See the fate of Byron's hero,
Manfred, who is discovered at the Strand Theatre on a 'Disjuncted Pavement' with an 'Awful Precipice overhanging the Drain' in À Beckett's
Man-Fred.)[20] Similarly, in *Gipsy-Jack; or, the Napoleon of Humble Life* (Coburg,
1831), Moncrieff punctures the inflated grandiloquence of Drury Lane's
play about Napoleon's rise and fall.[21] Here, the dramatist rewrites the
trajectory of Napoleonic imperialism as a series of gipsy rebellions
against enclosure and the imposition of rent and taxes, led by Jack, the
Napoleonic carnival king of the Norwood gipsies. The play's elaborate
mock combats on basket horses, together with the summary overthrow
of beadles, and the mock-heroic capture of poultry and stray linen at
Hendon and Barnet, satirise the Napoleonic heroism of Drury Lane's
spectacle, portraying heroic spectacle as unpatriotic nonsense.[22] In such
comic deformations of patent language and spectacle, minor burlesques
cocked a snook at legitimate culture and implicitly questioned the valid-
ity of existing cultural hierarchies.[23]

---

[19] On the attraction of burlesque for plebeian audiences, see [Thomas Wright], *Some Habits and Customs of the Working Classes by a Journeyman Engineer* (London, Tinsley Bros., 1867), 161–2. Cf. a review of *Quadrupeds* in the *Theatrical Observer*, 29 November 1823 (cutting, Theatre Museum) which remarks that the play suited every class, 'for all clearly understood the language in which the sentiments and the story are clothed'.

[20] À Beckett's *Man-Fred*, published in *CMT* IX, parodied a recent dramatisation of Byron's poem at Covent Garden. See also *The Revolt of the Workhouse* (Fitzroy, 1834), *CMT* VIII, in which À Beckett mocked the spectacular orientalism of Covent Garden's fairy-ballet, *The Revolt of the Harem*.

[21] *Napoleon Buonaparte, Captain of Artillery, General, First Consul, Emperor, and Exile* (Covent Garden, May 1831) provided the comic target for the Coburg piece. In his preface to *Gipsy Jack* in *CMT* IX, George Daniel described Lacy's piece as 'a splendid farrago of meretricious buffoonery' and 'grandiloquent fustian'.

[22] George Daniel, Remarks to *Gipsy Jack*; *The Times*, 30 May 1831.

[23] Cp. Linda Hutcheon's definition of parody in *A Theory of Parody: The Teachings of Twentieth-Century Art Forms* (London: Routledge, 1991), 71.

The Adelphi's burlesque productions reflect one aspect of the theatre's talent for trading in vulgarity, blackguardism and the dark underside of modern life.[24] Such a repertoire provoked periodic censure and paternal finger-wagging from dramatic reviewers. 'Knowledge is spreading; refinement with it,' declared the *Tatler*, 'and if the Adelphi wishes to compete . . . with the larger theatres, it should endeavour to lift its audiences, not to lower them.'[25] *Figaro* protested strongly about the tendency of Buckstone's domestic burletta, *Forgery; or, The Reading of the Will* (Adelphi, 1832), a play based on the realisation of Wilkie's paintings 'Reading the Will' and 'Village Politicians'. 'The piece itself is trashy in its language, improbable in its plot, and revolting in some of its situations', the reviewer announced. 'A scene where a man is supposed to be lying dead, is, in our estimation, offensive, and wholly unfit for scenic representation.'[26] Just as critics mocked the Adelphi's fascination with depicting the 'real' or 'natural', so they also deplored the theatre's interest in dramatising the world of blackguardism. In Moncrieff's game of life play, *Up and Down; or, the Road of Life* (Strand, 1838), for example, Lord Montgarvey has set up as an amateur drayman (John Lee, 'who personates one of the first bloods of the day, does it to the life' remarked the *Age*'s reviewer), while ladies' maids abandon domestic service to start businessness and establish genteel societies (Corri's songs for the play included 'Tis woman has the whip hand now, or the ladies are all riding').[27] Though all the characters eventually marry 'in their own station', what disconcerted reviewers about such dramas was their preoccupation with the comic confusions arising from the constant improvisation of new social identities – or, in the words of Mrs Datchett,

---

[24] Many reviewers expressed concern about the vulgarity of Adelphi plays; performances at the unlicensed Strand Theatre also encountered some harsh criticism. The reception of Moncrieff's play, *The Green Dragon* (Adelphi 1819) offers a good example. In an unidentified cutting of 19 October 1819 (Adelphi file, Theatre Museum) a critic described the play's witticism as verging on licentiousness and reported some disapprobation among spectators 'on the delivery of some equivoques not certainly quite congenial to the moral taste of the present age'. Cf. the *Examiner*'s objections (18 October 1829, 664) to a song in Hook's farce, *York and Lancaster* (Adelphi, 1829) which 'evidently disgusted the female well-bred part of the audience' and 'would not have been endured for a moment at either of the great houses'. Attitudes towards women playing male roles were also changing. Elizabeth Yates' breeches roles, remarked an *Examiner* critic, were 'revolting to delicacy' and 'repugnant to good taste' (see 19 October 1828, 678–9 and 26 October 1828, 694). [25] *Tatler*, 8 December 1830, 1: 327.
[26] *Figaro in London*, 10 March 1832, 56. Jerrold's play, *The Rent Day*, based on Wilkie's painting, had been staged at Drury Lane two months earlier.
[27] 'To us it seems *all low*', commented *Figaro in London*, 8 September 1838, 142. Cf. *Morning Chronicle*, 4 September 1838, which thought the play 'very coarse' and, more favourably, *Age*, September 9 1838, 286. For other game of life plays, see Moncrieff, *The Heart of London; or, A Sharper's Progress* (Adelphi, 1830), Edward Stirling, *The Rubber of Life; or, St James's and St Giles* (Strand, 1841) and *The Scamps of London, or The Cross Roads of Life* (Sadler's Wells, 1843).

landlady at the Queen's Arms, the collapse of 'the proper order of things'.[28] For what the Adelphi drama had begun to explore was a new and confusing world where social roles and forms of business were no longer fixed and immutable, but might be assumed and exchanged, just like parts in a play.

Westminster laughter, especially at the Adelphi and the Strand Theatres, dispensed with the representation of gentility and decorum, and turned instead to the dramatisation of urban vulgarity and blackguardism. Unfashionable farce represents an important subgenre in this emerging category of illegitimate laughter. In these plays, identity has become a matter of entrepreneurship. The empirical world is not simply beyond the protagonists' control, but uncertain, almost nonsensical: bacon mysteriously disappears and matches are unaccountably used up, as if in a 'steady increase of evaporation' (*Box and Cox*, Lyceum 1847); scarcity, especially of clothes, constantly jeopardizes the survival of the protagonists' illusory, respectable identity.

In *Dissolving Views; or, the Lights and Shadows of Life* (Strand, 1844) Lothario Larkins, 'an unfortunate gentleman', opens the curtains of his garret bed to discover that the washerwoman has failed to return his only suit; Brown, meanwhile, the medical student who inhabits the next room, has borrowed his trousers. How can he sustain the illusion that he is a 'gentleman of independent property' at the West End party with Caroline Jones? Physical danger in these plays provides a dramatic analogy for the precarious character of social identity. Larkins finally succeeds in reaching his garret, though his coat has split up the back and his face is smeared with blood.[29] Such risks and hazards often threaten the stars of unfashionable farce: Grimes, the beleaguered lawyer's clerk in *The Man with the Carpet Bag* (Strand, 1835) is all but arrested as a criminal, the Strange Gentleman in Charles Dickens' eponymous burletta (St James, 1836) is in receipt of a death warrant, while the hapless Perkins in Oxenford's farce, *What have I done?* (Olympic, 1838) virtually ends up in a duel. In *Box and Cox*, of course, this experience of jeopardy verges on absurdity: having pretended to commit suicide in order to avoid marrying Mary Ann (proprietor of bathing machines at Margate), Box and Cox live in a shadowy world of non-being as two interdependent, inseparable halves of a single life in the same room.

The apprentices, clerks and shopmen who are the unheroic stars of unfashionable farce inhabit an existence forever divided between a

---

[28] *Up and Down*, BL Add. MS 42948 fols. 232–343, fol. 289.
[29] *Dissolving Views*, BL Add. MS 42972, fols. 279–290b.

claustrophobic lower middle-class world of trade and frugality (in unfashionable farce, identity is inextricable from a line of *work*; compare the leisured world of Vestris' Olympic plays) and a fantastic, invariably futile world of aspiration.[30] To early Victorian audiences, this was the world of the 'gent', a character whose distinctive social and cultural world Charles Dickens explored in *Sketches by 'Boz'* (1836) and Albert Smith mocked in his satirical pamphlet, *The Natural History of the Gent* (1847). According to Smith, the gent is a despicable character who vainly attempts to escape his lowly social position on the outermost borders of the middle class by a 'futile aping of superiority'.[31] But what fascinates Dickens about these individuals on the borders of respectability is the way in which theatre and performance define and shape the gent's fantasy life.

Gents eagerly patronised theatres at half price, bought dramatic texts in the sixpenny and threepenny editions 'as fast as they appear', and sported extravagantly patterned theatrical clothes like the distinctive, large checked patterns 'of the true light comedian pattern' sold by cheap tailors. They delighted in identifying actors in the street, and invariably possessed an encyclopedic knowledge of the 'private manners and customs' of comic performers.[32] The heroes and sartorial models of these young men were London's leading low comedians such as John Buckstone; the unfashionable laughter being staged at theatres like the Adelphi sought to dramatise the fears, aspirations and desires which characterised this world of urban masculinity.

Unfashionable farce transformed the life of the gent into a form of dramatic celebrity. In particular, farce's physical aesthetic seems to evoke the experience of a city running at breakneck speed without providence, order or causality. Identity, here, is uncertain, often on the verge of exposure, especially from women.[33] Charles Selby's play, *Dissolving Views*, again offers a good example. The farce's title probably refers to a form of magic lantern first shown at the Adelphi in 1837. At one level, the theme of 'dissolving views' alludes to the pleasures of watching visual images which appear and disappear, just like a magic lantern, as in scene iii, during which the audience watch the farcical confusions simultaneously

---

[30] Unfashionable farce represented a large proportion of the comic repertoire at the Westminster minor theatres. Apart from the plays discussed here, see *inter alia*, *The Bricklayers' Arms* (Adelphi, 1830), Charles Selby, *The Unfinished Gentleman* (Adelphi, 1834) and Tyrone Power, *How to Pay the Rent* (Haymarket, 1840).

[31] Albert Smith, *The Natural History of the Gent* (London: David Bogue, 1847), 2.

[32] See especially Smith, *ibid.*, chapter 4; 'Boz', *Sketches*, 532, 537.

[33] See, for example, the characterisation of women such as Mary Ann in *Box and Cox* and Mary, the laundress, in Joseph Stirling Coyne, *How to Settle Accounts with your Laundress* (Adelphi, 1847).

unfolding in three rooms of a West End house. At another level, however, 'dissolving views' also refer to the illusions by which Larkins passes himself off as a gentleman of independent property. The image of the magic lantern thus provides a spectral analogy for the confusions and dissolutions implicit in the experience of identity in the nineteenth-century metropolis.

In unfashionable farce, gentility is always improvised and social roles contingent.[34] In À Beckett's farce, *The Man with the Carpet Bag* (Strand 1835), the unscrupulous lawyer Grab decides to conceal certain dishonestly obtained papers vital to his success in the case of Fleece *v.* Pluckwell in a gentleman's carpet-bag. Slyly chosen in preference to a lawyer's blue bag as an unequivocal sign of respectability, Grab believes that the carpet-bag will guarantee his freedom from suspicion. But when his clerk Grimes arrives at the Hat and Hatband, the carpet-bag attracts instant attention because Wrangle, Grab's legal opponent, has recently published a hoax story warning landlords against a notorious thief distinguished by the carpet-bag which he carries. Instead of connoting respectability, Grab's bag now signifies criminality and impostership.

Grimes finds himself in a nightmarish version of that modern world where the signs of respectability have lost their persuasive power. Even the coachman is unconvinced by his assumed identity: 'I makes a point of never speaking to them as an't respectable' (27). In the wake of Wrangle's hoax, the language and objects of respectability only provoke suspicion: despite all Grab's attempts to prevent disclosure, the talismanic carpet-bag is finally opened and his dishonesty uncovered. Though the legal profession's fraudulence is the play's immediate satirical target – as George Daniel remarked, 'considerable mirth is elicited at the expense of the law . . . the hard hits against the legal profession are truly subtle and searching' – *The Man with the Carpet Bag* also stages the farcical breakdown of those contemporary signs through which individuals discern and judge each other's social identities.[35]

---

[34] The essays of Michael Booth and Jim Davis in James Redmond, ed., *Farce*, Themes in Drama no. 10 (Cambridge University Press, 1988) offer an excellent introduction to this period's farce. See Booth, 'Early Victorian Farce: Dionysus Domesticated', 95–110 (which interprets farce as an inherently conservative genre), and Davis, 'His Own Triumphantly Comic Self: Self and Self-Consciousness in Nineteenth-Century English Farce', 115–30. On the later period, cf. Jeffrey Huberman, *Late Victorian Farce* (Ann Arbor: UMI Research Press, 1986), 16, who presents farce as a 'quick, one-act assault on the middle-class ideals of Victorianism'.

[35] Remarks, *CMT* XIII. Compare the complaint of an *Examiner* correspondent (8 February 1829, 83), '[I]f a man is convicted of forgery, he is not to be hanged now-a-days *because he is a highly respectable man* . . . This word salves all sores, smooths all difficulties . . . Power naturally thinks it has a right to grasp whatever, by direct or indirect means, it can lay its sleek, well-bred hands on.'

In early nineteenth-century farce, individuals and objects alike seem to conspire against the protagonist. The financial and social contingency of the gent's world – where the desperate struggle to appear respectable manifests itself in the living of double lives, and indeed the doubling of human identities – is a new variation on this conspiracy. Moreover, in unfashionable farce, the gent emerges as a modern version of that age-old comic trope, the social imposter. The comic theatre of this period abounds with imposters, from Dandolo, the aristocratic Oyster Devil, who threatens to consume an East End alderman's entire stock of oysters, and Jem Wheedle, the cunning, roguish adventurer, who plays on the assorted weaknesses and foibles of the Docker family, to the tallow-chandler Jack Brag, who has forged for himself an aristocratic pseudo-identity.[36] In these plays, identity has become inseparable from speculation, for modern imposters seek to profit from the willingness of their victims to interpret dress, manners and language as stable and unequivocal signs of social class and moral integrity. By contrast, the heroes of unfashionable farce comically fail to exert any kind of authority over their environment. In their celebration, and simultaneous exposure, of the illusions and deceptions at the heart of lower middle-class urban life, such farcical dramas made unfashionable laughter out of masculine identities in social and economic jeopardy.

MATHEWS' BUDGET

With the exception of these unfashionable farces, most successful forms of illegitimate laughter in early nineteenth-century London married generic innovation with the appearance of social delicacy. By appropriating the rhetoric and visual accoutrements of genteel domesticity, managers and performers hoped to woo audiences who might otherwise have forsaken theatre for opera, concerts, or – in the case of middle-class spectators in particular – readings and parlour entertainments.[37]

On definitions of respectability, see Peter Bailey's seminal article, '"Will the Real Bill Banks Please Stand Up?": Towards a Role Analysis of Mid-Victorian Working-Class Respectability', *Journal of Social History* 12 (1979), 336–53.

[36] In Edward Stirling's play, *Dandolo; or, The Last of the Doges* (City, 1838), *DBT* xxxv, the imposter is a leisured, insatiable seducer-consumer who insinuates himself into an Aldgate back parlour. Leading comedians like Buckstone, Tyrone Power and Harley played many of these imposter roles. In his farce *Weak Points* (Haymarket, 1838), *AND* iv, Buckstone took the part of Jem Wheedle, whilst Harley played Jack Brag in À Beckett's eponymous farce, based on Theodore Hook's novel (St James, 1837), *Dicks* 534. See also Buckstone's farce, *The Irish Lion* (Haymarket, 1838), *Dicks* 822, which starred Tyrone Power as a journeyman tailor believed to be Tom Moore, the celebrated poet and songster. [37] See, *inter alia*, SC nos. 3070, 3089.

Charles Mathews' *At Homes*, for example, converted the budget, a mere standby of provincial performance, into an entertainment whose social location and dramatic structure brilliantly dispelled middle-class anxieties about theatrical representation. An irresistible mixture of satirical caricature and delicate pathos, the *At Homes* soon became one of the highlights of the theatrical season. Mathews was even invited to perform at Hampton Court and Carlton House, in gratitude for which the King granted him 100 guineas from the Privy Purse. He also appeared at numerous fashionable parties, where Albina, the Countess of Buckinghamshire, nurtured a desperate and unrequited passion for the actor. Memoirs, prints and countless admiring reviews attest to Mathews' fame; Coleridge even composed an extempore poem in which the actor's comic versatility is transformed into a form of theatrical pantheism:

> If, in whatever decks this earthly ball,
> 'Tis still great mother Nature – *one in all!*
> Hence Mathews needs must be her genuine son,
> A second Nature, that acts ALL IN ONE.[38]

But perhaps the greatest tribute offered to Mathews was that penned by 'Q' in the *Examiner*. Mathews' comic genius, declared the reviewer, lay in his capacity to invent individual characters who were, at the same time, representative. 'The personation of Mathews is doubtless of the very highest order,' the critic resoundingly declared, 'for it individualises classes of character, and so far is Shakespearean'.[39] 'Q'´s remarks are not only a comment on the subtlety of Mathews' imitations, but also a typically polemical intervention in contemporary debates about legitimate and illegitimate theatre. For the *Examiner* critic controversially suggests that Mathews' characters might actually be compared with those created by Britain's national playwright.

By 1818, Charles Mathews the Elder was already a well-known comic actor at Covent Garden and at the Haymarket. He had captivated audiences with his performances of 'officious valets' and 'humourous old men', including Sir Fretful Plagiary in Sheridan's *The Critic*, Mawworm in *The Hypocrite* and Dick Cypher, member of the Four-in-Hand Club, in Pocock's satirical comedy, *Hit or Miss*. Disillusioned, however, by the failure of the patent managers to cast him 'in the legitimate shape of a regular comedian',[40] Mathews was persuaded by the canny Samuel Arnold in 1818 to join the Lyceum, an establishment licensed at that time

---

[38] *Life of Mathews*, 247.   [39] 17 March 1822, 171.   [40] *Life of Mathews*, 204.

to perform musical theatre.[41] In a revealing comparison, Mathews later declared that he had abandoned professional practice (the patent theatres) to sell medicines, like contemporary quacks, on his own account. Indeed, Mathews now began to create a form of laughter based on what we might define as social quackery – the duplicities, deceptions and social alchemies characteristic of modern life.

Mathews' success at the Lyceum annoyed the patentees, who made 'very serious efforts' to put an end to the *At Homes*.[42] But Mathews comically exploited this opposition: as he boldly declared in the farewell address to *Mail-Coach Adventures*, 'I am contending in the cause of the public, who ought not to be curtailed of their lawful amusements'.[43] In various ways the *At Homes* self-consciously foregrounded their institutional position in the shadow of theatrical monopoly: even the punning nomenclature of the 'mono-poly-logues' reminded Lyceum audiences that monopoly had forced Mathews into producing monologues.

The *At Home* entertainments consisted of miscellaneous imitations (especially of opera singers, legendary performers such as George Frederick Cooke and Charles Macklin and, in *The Youthful Days of Mr Mathews*, theatrical characters like Tate Wilkinson (with his distinctive 'motley-coloured plaid-pattern'd discourse'), ventriloquism and recitations. Between the various parts of the entertainment, 'favourite rondos' were played on the piano by Mr Knight, who also accompanied Mathews' songs. Having woven these characters together into a loose 'conversational web',[44] Mathews concluded his shows with the famous Mono-poly-logues. In these songs, interspersed by 'patter' speech (the equivocation between speech and song recalls the ruse of burletta as well as Grimaldi's patter songs), Mathews rapidly imitated in quick succession a collection of characters who might be found in such places of modern sociability as a mail coach, on the Polly Packet (*Adventures in Air, Earth, and Water*), in a Brighton boarding-house (*The Youthful Days*) or at a public house (*Memorandum Book*).

In the *At Homes*, as Hazlitt observed, Mathews became his own

---

[41] *Ibid.*, 207–11. Arnold, one of the age's great theatrical entrepreneurs, drew up a ten-year contract with Mathews and proceeded to pocket thousands of pounds from the success of the *At Homes*. Since the shows did not fall within the definition of a dramatic performance, they were never submitted for licensing to the Examiner of Plays. When the Lord Chamberlain called on Arnold to request a manuscript of one of the *At Homes*, Mathews admitted that his performances had 'never yet been committed to writing'. But the actor succeeded in mollifying the Lord Chamberlain by offering to perform one of his entertainments in front of the duke and his family. See *Life of Mathews*, 318.

[42] Mathews, *Mail-Coach Adventures* in *The New Budget of Fun*, 62. [43] *Ibid.*

[44] *Examiner*, 17 March 1822, 171.

'prompter, manager, and performer, orchestra and scene-shifter'.[45] Through his innovations in language, props and costume, Mathews also redefined the Lyceum stage as the extension of a private drawing room. Lyceum playbills therefore invited spectators not to a theatrical perfor- mance, but to a quasi-domestic entertainment: a 'lecture', 'memoran- dum', 'invitation' or 'annual'. As the Lyceum playbill announced, 'The public are respectfully informed, that they will find Mr. Mathews 'At Home,' this evening, Thursday, April 2nd, 1818 . . . when he will have the honour of presenting his visitors with an entertainment called MAIL-COACH ADVENTURES.' At the beginning of the entertainment Mathews would appear in his 'private dress' 'just as he would have entered any evening party';[46] the Lyceum's stage would become a private room for the occasion, complete with table, chair and lamps. Richard Dighton's etching (plate 14), which depicts a commanding and elegantly dressed Mathews, with a grand, high-backed chair and table lamps, highlights the transformation of actor and public institution into the host of a private party. The success of the *At Homes* was due not only to Mathews' remarkable skills as a mimic, but also to his revision of the implied social contract between performer and audience.

Mathews' entertainments carefully avoided that 'vulgarity', 'broad- ness' and coarseness which spectators and reviewers frequently con- demned in the satirical comedies of Theodore Hook and John Buckstone.[47] Indeed, one of Mathews' greatest skills was in portraying a character of enormous vulgarity without himself being perceived as vulgar.[48] In his praise for the famous portrait of the Scotch lady mourn- ing for her late husband in *Mail-Coach Adventures* – 'you might really think you were sitting with her in an inn, and attending to the calm old gos- siping of a grey-haired Scotch-woman, with her failing memory, her kindly noddings', remarked Leigh Hunt,[49] – Hazlitt summed up the comic subtlety of Mathews' caricature: 'It was a portrait of common

---

[45] [Hazlitt], *London Magazine*, May 1820, *Hazlitt* XVIII:320.   [46] *Life of Mathews*, 201.

[47] See for example Hazlitt's objections to the 'offensive morality' and low comedy in Hook's *Exchange No Robbery; or, The Diamond Ring* (Haymarket, 1820), *Hazlitt* XVIII: 365. For other moral animadversions on Hook's drama, see the *Examiner's* review, 18 October 1829, 664 of *York and Lancaster*. On the coarseness of Buckstone's drama, see *Morning Chronicle* review of *Married Life*, 21 August 1834; *Morning Post* review of *Weak Points*, 30 April 1838, *Atlas* review of *The Dream at Sea*, 29 November 1835, 757 and *Morning Chronicle* review of *Up and Down; or, The Road of Life*, 4 September 1838.

[48] The *Drama* critic drew readers' attention to the absence of 'vulgar prejudice' and 'national antipathy' in Mathews' impersonation of American characters. One *Examiner* reviewer, 18 March 1821, 172, did, however, object to 'an excess of representations of vulgar cockneyisms' in *Adventures in Air, Earth, and Water*.   [49] *Examiner*, 12 April 1818, 236.

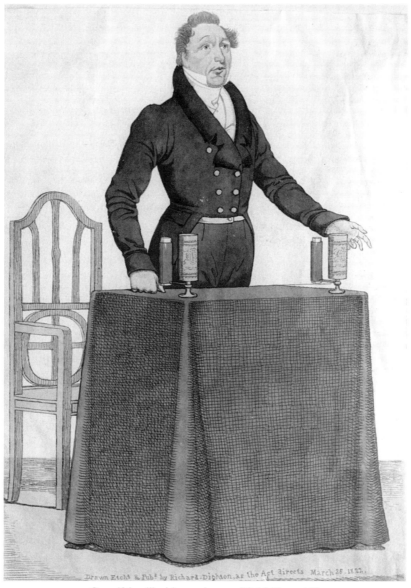

14. Gentrifying illegitimate theatre. *Mr Matthews at Home.*

nature, equal to Wilkie or Teniers – as faithful, as simple, as delicately humourous . . . but without one particle of caricature, of vulgarity, or ill-nature.'[50]

Mathews' entertainments shared with the novels of Charles Dickens a rich and subtle combination of family caricature, social satire (including topical references to such subjects as 'the pecuniary *crisis*' and the bubble mania)[51] and delicate pathos. His caricatures – nervous valetudinarians, jealous apothecaries, gossipy old Scotch ladies, young bloods from Saville Row and Yorkshire gamesters, literary butchers and ignorant 'cits' – dramatised the aspirations, anxieties and embarrassments of an age fascinated by its boundless social mobility. One of the ladies in the *Trip to Paris* even wishes for a bill 'to prevent the vulgar being seen at any of the places of fashion': 'it really is quite intolerable . . . we shall not have a place shortly, to hide our heads in'.[52] Other characters, like Mr Verjuice (who dislikes everything contemporary), are perplexed and confused by the pace of social and technological change. In *Mr. Mathews' Comic Annual for 1833*, Verjuice sings a song called 'Modern Innovations' which nostalgically evokes a time when 'young ladies on politics, their minds did not fix', and when books and newspapers 'were fewer, and not known to the poor'.[53] Mathews' world also included many eccentrics and social misfits (Mr Sillylynx, a conspiracy theorist, Dr Prolix, 'whose talent lies in being fatigued',[54] and Mr Llewellyn ap Lydd, a plump and cheerful Welshman in *The Youthful Days* who frequents spas and springs in the vain hope of growing thinner).

Mathews' *At Homes* delighted in malapropism and linguistic mistake.[55] These shows burlesqued genteel embarrassment (Lady Dawdle hosts a picnic in the *Invitations* to which all fourteen guests have brought a leg of mutton), social condescension (Major Longborn 'finds everything extraordinary abroad, and nothing worth attending to at home';[56] and middle-class domesticity (the Dilberry family invite Mathews to dine amid nursery ballads and a smoking chimney, accompanied by a 'Brilliant Sonata on the Pianoforte by Miss Jane Dilberry'). But these satirical caricatures also featured sentimental vignettes of disappointment and loss. Mathews' portrait of the bereaved Scotch lady, and his impersonation of M. Mallet, the French emigré father in America who visits the Boston

---

[50] [Hazlitt], *London Magazine*, May 1820, *Hazlitt* XVIII: 322.
[51] *Examiner*, 11 March 1827, 152, signed 'Q'.
[52] *Trip to Paris*, in *The New Budget of Fun*, 71.
[53] *Mr. Mathews' Comic Annual for 1833* (London: W. Holmes, n.d.), 6–7.
[54] *Examiner*, 9 April 1820, 235–6.
[55] Cf. *The Vulgarities of Speech Corrected* (London: James Bulcock, 1826), 3.
[56] *Examiner*, 11 March 1827, 152, signed 'Q'.

post-office hoping to collect a letter from his beloved daughter in France, became two of his most celebrated impersonations:

Few, although laughing the previous moment, can avoid shedding tears at the powerful display of anxiety and distress of the poor French emigrant father, and his look of horror and consternation when he discovers that he had destroyed the letter for which he had been waiting for so long – the best tragedian in London could not have produced a greater effect.

'This is not only good acting – it is more,' continued the reviewer warmly, 'it is good feeling.'[57] Again, the reference to tragedy is instructive: Mathews' impersonations seemed to offer his audiences the pleasures and emotions associated with legitimate performance within an illegitimate dramatic form.

Mathews' *At Homes* cleverly balanced the illusion of a genteel drawing-room with the cyclopaedic variety, speed and excitement of domestic and international tourism. The opening of the *Mail-Coach Adventures* brilliantly captures the sound of voices competing for the attention of the waiter, the cracking whip and bustle as the mail coach departs, the physical jostling of people and their snatches of conversation and command ('Set me down at the butcher's shop; I should not like to be seen getting out of a coach').[58] Just as, in 'On Modern Comedy', Hazlitt had secretly longed for a stage coach journey straight out of Lawrence Sterne, complete with 'odd accidents' and 'ludicrous distresses', rather than suffer the tedium of unexceptional journeys on a modern stage coach,[59] so Mathews presented his spectators with a theatrical place (free from dirt, obnoxious smells, physical discomfort or moral danger) from which to enjoy the social variety and chaotic proximity of modern travel. No wonder then, as the *London Magazine* admiringly remarked, '[s]enators unbend themselves in Mr Mathews's company; dowagers, old maids, young maids, recent widows, citizens' wives, clumps of daughters, all abandon themselves to joy and jollity'.[60] Through his extraordinary comic inventiveness, versatility and eccentric sense of fun, Mathews had transformed the Budget into a highly successful entertainment about the social quackery of metropolitan life.

PETTICOAT GOVERNMENT AT THE OLYMPIC

Just as Mathews recreated the Lyceum stage as a genteel private drawing-room, so Eliza Vestris marketed the Olympic Theatre as a luxurious

---

[57] *Drama*, March 1824, 5: 93–95.   [58] *Mail-Coach Adventures*, 17.   [59] *Hazlitt* IV: 12.
[60] *London Magazine*, February 1825, 2: 81.

house, full of rich fabrics, beautiful costumes and picturesque scenery. Like Mathews, Vestris also presented herself to her audiences in a multiplicity of often contradictory guises: as Restoration soubrette, Venus, Cleopatra, Julius Caesar, an omnibus manager, the 'Captain of Invincibles' and as a modern woman longing for a home of her own.[61] Although theatre historians have been quick to identify Vestris as a dramatic reformer (shorter bills, the abolition of visits by spectators to the green room, elegant and historically correct scenery and costumes), far less attention has been paid to the illegitimate forms which she pioneered at the Olympic. The striking thing about these comic productions, especially the Christmas extravaganzas written for her by Planché and Charles Dance, is their equivocal representations of Vestris herself. Extravaganza, in particular, became a genre through which one of the capital's leading performers, now a female actor-manager, attempted to dramatise the conflicting aspirations at the heart of modern femininity.

Like Mathews, Vestris' lessee-ship of the Olympic theatre was the result of growing disillusionment with the practices and policies of the Theatres Royal. In the late 1820s, Vestris had quarrelled with Elliston over his refusal to permit her appearance at the Opera House whilst she was still engaged at Drury Lane. Vestris promptly retaliated by refusing to appear in cross-dressed parts such as Don Giovanni and Macheath, and Elliston was forced to relent.[62] Two years later, however, Vestris declined to renew her engagement (the perilous financial position of Drury Lane only serving to confirm her restlessness and dissatisfaction), and decided instead to perform in a short season at the Tottenham Street theatre. As we saw in chapter 1, Vestris' appearance there in various legitimate roles led to the managers' prosecution. Indeed, one of the posters advertising her engagement proudly proclaimed Vestris' support for the cause: 'this lady has determined to become the *first* to resist the coalition entered into by the *Major* Theatres.'[63]

The débâcle at Tottenham Street must have alerted Vestris to the dangers of illegally producing legitimate drama, but it also demonstrated that she could make her living beyond the Theatres Royal.

---

[61] For these images, see reports in the *Dramatic Magazine*, 1 April 1831, 3: 90–1; *New Monthly Magazine* (1834), 40: 531–2, as well as Vestris' dramatic roles in *The Paphian Bower; or, Venus and Adonis* (Olympic, 1832) and T. H. Bayly's *The Grenadier* (Olympic, 1831). Cf. Kathy Fletcher's argument about Vestris' 'emigration to distinctly masculine territory' in 'Planché, Vestris, and the Transvestite Role: Sexuality and Gender in Popular Theatre', *Nineteenth Century Theatre* 15 no. 2 (1978), 8–33, 21.

[62] William Appleton, *Madame Vestris and the London Stage* (New York: Columbia, 1971), 23.

[63] 'Charles Kemble's Mercies or the "999" Increasing' in HChK.

Shortly afterwards, Vestris succeeded in acquiring the lessee-ship of the Olympic theatre, originally built by Philip Astley, in the still insalubrious neighbourhood of Wych Street. Again, this development was immediately construed by certain critics as an act of rebellion. According to the *Age*, Vestris' management represented a 'a bold experiment against the anti-national monopoly of patent rights . . . A woman has raised the standard of rebellion against King Kemble and his tyrannical edicts.'[64]

Whereas the Adelphi had built its reputation on performances of blue-fire melodrama, vulgar burlesque and diabolical spectacle, Eliza Vestris eschewed such 'transparent plots for eloping frustrated by transparent obstacles, and prudent impediments overthrown by impudent stratagems'.[65] Instead, she created an illegitimate repertoire based on farcical comedies of manners, elegant historical plays often set in Restoration London or other court societies (Princess Victoria saw Vestris' lavish production of *The Rape of the Lock* and made various sketches of the play), and mythological extravaganza, a genre whose sexual equivocations seemed to celebrate and yet simultaneously to dissipate the phenomenon of female managerial power.

When spectators took their seats at the refurbished Olympic, they were delighted by the theatre's new-found elegance and grace: flying Cupids on the ceiling, light crimson drapery, and boxes delicately ornamented by Bartolozzi.[66] Reviewers were quick to applaud Vestris' managerial 'reforms' including the abolition of playbill puffs (thus raising, according to the *Athenaeum*, 'a fair laugh at the expense of the great advertising practitioners of Drury Lane and Covent Garden')[67] and the introduction of elaborate *mise-en-scène*, together with 'scrupulously correct costumes'.[68] But Vestris' management was also distinctive for its preoccupation with images of femininity which seemed to dramatise the actress' new institutional authority.

Vestris' management was founded upon the erotic capital of transvestism. Born in London into an artistic professional family, originally from Italy, she had soon shown early talent as a singer and musician. Having married Armand Vestris, the leading French dancer in 1813, she made her operatic debut as a mezzo-soprano at the King's Theatre. By the early 1820s, Vestris was being romantically linked with a number of men, including the MP Thomas Duncombe, Horatio Clagett and Montague Gore; from the last two of these she received annuities of

---

[64] *Age*, 9 January 1831, 14.   [65] *Atlas*, 5 October 1834, 634.
[66] *Athenaeum*, 24 September 1831, 621.   [67] 21 April 1832, 260.
[68] Planché, *Recollections*, I: 237.

several hundred pounds. Scandalous unauthorised memoirs soon appeared concerning what were advertised as her 'public and private adventures' as well as bawdy songs, verses and titillating broadsides; in 1825 the so-called Siren of Mayfair sued one publisher and was awarded £100 in damages, although she was unable to prevent the secret memoirs' publication.[69] Even as the Olympic opened, an Italian modellist working in London was prosecuting a rival sculptor for having stolen her plaster cast of Vestris' leg, a disembodied image of the performer which had soon become a sensational metropolitan icon.[70]

Vestris reluctantly agreed to play the breeches role in Drury Lane's production of *Giovanni in London; or, The Libertine Reclaimed.* According to the *Theatrical Inquisitor*, the part of Giovanni was one which 'no female should assume till she has discarded every delicate scruple by which her mind or person can be distinguished';[71] the playwright himself later confessed to having been amazed that his burlesque had actually received a licence.[72] In many ways, the role of Giovanni further compromised the performer's already dubious moral reputation, for the act of cross-dressing stimulated fantasies which its producer could neither intercept nor interdict, and Vestris became the subject of a miniature erotic cult, conducted in reviews and scandalous memoirs.[73] Nevertheless, Vestris' brilliance lay in her skill to chasten or even censor her travesty roles. Leigh Hunt, for example, delighted in her transformation of Giovanni's 'heartless rakery' into harmless laughter, passing over 'the least pleasant features of it with a well-bred air of unconsciousness'.[74] 'She so divests *Macheath* of his blackguardism', wrote another *Examiner* reviewer, 'renders him so unlike himself and his sex, converts him into some thing so taking and genteel . . . in short, makes him such a gentlewomanly sort of man, that he and this three wives seem like three females playing a frolic in a masquerade.'[75]

Vestris' celebrity in roles such as Don Giovanni also enabled her to become lessee, at £1,000 per annum, of the Olympic theatre. The few women who managed British theatres before Vestris were usually widows who had taken over the business after the death of their hus-

---

[69] See Appleton, *Madame Vestris* 42. Iain McCalman argues that courtesan confessions or *chroniques scandaleuses* became associated with the interests of the radical cause during the 1820s. See *Radical Underworld*, 222–4. [70] *Examiner*, 23 January 1831, 61.
[71] *Theatrical Inquisitor*, January 1818, 16: 394. [72] SC 3177–8.
[73] Scandalous accounts included *Memoirs of the Public and Private Life, Adventures and Wonderful Exploits of Madame Vestris* . . . (London: Chubb, [?]1830); *Memoirs of the Life, Public and Private Adventures of Madame Vestris* (London, 1839). [74] *Examiner*, 4 June 1820, 363.
[75] *Examiner*, 30 July 1820, 363–4.

bands; lack of capital had excluded women from running theatres in their own right.[76] With lower rents, and smaller running costs, the London minor theatres offered women – notably performers such as Harriet Waylett and Louisa Nisbett who had acquired capital through their celebrity in cross-dressed roles – their first opportunity to own 'their own house'.[77] Indeed, by the early 1830s, female management had become a fashionable bandwagon as male reviewers competed with each other to declare the imminent triumph of 'Female management for ever!'[78]

As in Mathews' entertainments, the pretensions and absurdities of vulgar-genteel society became a favourite subject at the Olympic; in particular, the social betrayals implicit in language fascinated leading playwrights such as Charles Dance and John Oxenford. Characters like Mrs Figgins, a grocer's wife in Dance's farce, *The Water Party* (Olympic 1832), open their lips, only to be discovered 'like the daw in the fable, that was tricked out in peacock's feathers' as the 'mere ape of gentility';[79] Similarly, Clementina Moss, seller of artificial flowers in the Burlington Arcade, vainly attempts to cast off her lowly social origins by adopting a 'superlatively delicate' form of speech, full of absurd, vulgar-genteel malapropisms.

During this period, contemporary manuals of etiquette painstakingly distinguished between 'vulgar' and 'genteel' idioms and expression, and offered ominous warnings about the linguistic vulgarities of 'mercantile pedantic' as spoken by nineteenth-century tradesmen. Etiquette, declared an anonymous manual, is 'the barrier society draws around itself as a protection against offences the "law" cannot touch – a shield against the intrusion of the impertinent, the improper, and the vulgar'.[80] Vestris' comic productions delighted in exposing the clumsy deceptions, practised in the name of respectability, by the vulgar-genteel. At the same time, however, the ingenious verisimilitude of the Olympic's *mise-en-scène* encouraged its audiences to abandon themselves to the pleasures

[76] See the female managers mentioned in the *Dramatic Magazine*, 1 February 1831, 3:11.

[77] See Vestris' opening address in *Dramatic Magazine*, 1 February 1831, 3:26–7. Other female managers included Fanny Fitwilliam who ran the Royal Clarence in 1832 with W. H. Williams and then Sadler's Wells, Harriet Waylett, who managed the Strand with Benjamin Rayner, and Louisa Nisbett at the Queen's Theatre.

[78] On female management, see *Satirist*, 17 and 24 June 1832, 2: 198, 206; *Athenaeum*, 16 June 1832, 389. After her success at the Olympic, Vestris became the joint lessee of Covent Garden with her second husband, the actor Charles James Mathews (whose father had invented the *At Home* entertainments), although she was forced to declare herself bankrupt only a few years later.

[79] *The Vulgarities of Speech Corrected*, 3; cf. K. C. Phillips, *Language and Class in Victorian England* (Oxford: Blackwell, 1984).   [80] *Hints on Etiquette* (London, 1834), 5.

of visual illusion. There was a pleasing opposition, then, between the production of genteel life (see, for example, the famous set for Charles Dance's *The Burlington Arcade* (1838), complete with wigged busts, perfume bottles and artificial flowers; according to the *Spectator*, the illusion of perspective had been so skilfully created that 'we almost expected to see some of the actors go right through . . . and disappear in the street')[81] and the *contrived* and spurious gentility of the plays' vulgar characters.

Vestris marketed the Olympic as a company of female stars. As reviewers observed, 'The men are just sufficient in number and quality to fill up the necessary coadjuting parts.'[82] Her own roles included a number of soubrette characters who skilfully outwitted kings, duped libertines and upstaged arrogant coxcombs (often played by James Vining).[83] As Lucy, the malapert star of Planché's *Court Favour, or 'Private and Confidential'* (1836), Vestris played a tormenting, tantalising coquette who is also a political schemer, and a 'perfect Machiavel in petticoats' (she has heard it said that 'women are the best politicians'). Similarly, as Catherine Ormsdorf in William Bayle Bernard's *The Conquering Game* (1832), Vestris delivered a comprehensive lesson on government to the misogynistic Charles XII (who intends to subdue and discipline a wife as fully as he would his military troops), and then proceeded to humiliate the king by compelling him to dress in women's clothes. Though Charles XII's monarchical authority is finally reinstated (he rewards Catherine by giving her in marriage to her childhood sweetheart), Bernard's emphasis on Vestris' 'conquering' role seems to draw attention to the actress's managerial conquest of a London theatre.

The evolution of Olympic extravaganza, a genre which simultaneously capitalised on, and made respectable, the eroticism of transvestite roles like Don Giovanni, highlighted these fantasies of feminine power. At a time when pantomime was falling into disrepute, Olympic extravaganza emerged as a luxurious, genteel alternative.[84] As the *Examiner* had wryly remarked a few years earlier, 'The roguery, robbery, and

---

[81] 22 December 1838, 1208.
[82] *Spectator*, 8 January 1831, 31; see also *Athenaeum*, 8 January 1831, 29.
[83] Apart from the dramas discussed below, see also Planché's *The Court Beauties* (1835). The play featured full-length portraits reproduced from those at Hampton Court and a scene showing the Mall in full perspective, complete with trees, singing birds and King Charles spaniels. Cf. J. F. Smith's *The Court of Old Fritz* (Olympic, 1839). See further, Planché, *Recollections* 1: 237 and Matthew Mackintosh, *Stage Reminiscences* (Glasgow, J. Hedderwick, 1866), 80–3.
[84] See, for example, *Theatrical Inquisitor*, December 1814, 5: 402; *London Magazine*, February 1823, 195. Vestris' pantomimes also carefully avoid the lewd and vulgar connotations of earlier mythological burlesques such as Kane O'Hara's *The Golden Pippin*, a play banned by the Lord Chamberlain in its original form.

cruelty of *Clowns* – the imbecile and incapable rascality of *Pantaloons* – the easy seductiveness of *Harlequins* – the amorous surrenders of *Columbines* . . . all these things are supposed to be immoral and unfit for young people in this advanced age of the world. In other words, reality has taken the place of fiction, and we cannot afford to be spectators of both.'[85] To be sure, the romantic entanglements of Olympic gods and goddesses can hardly be said to correspond to contemporary moral 'reality'; nevertheless, extravaganza did indeed substitute for the anarchic, upside-down world of pantomime an arch, self-conscious worldliness about nineteenth-century finance, sociability and moral values.

Taking for their plots episodes from classical mythology, Planché and Charles Dance created a genteel burlesque entertainment, spoken in absurd doggerel verse, and featuring spectacular mythological scenery (including Mount Olympus and the imperial palace of Pluto), elaborate burlesque costumes, and comic parodies of contemporary songs, ballads and airs (especially from operas such as *Masaniello, Der Freischütz* and *The Marriage of Figaro*). In many ways, these leisured mythological worlds offer a delicious escape from work, domesticity and moral delicacy. Moreover, while offering audiences the illusion of respectability (for all their verbal wit and ingenuity, these plays carefully avoid vulgarity and bawdiness), Olympic extravaganza created a fantastic, sexually ambiguous world populated by semi-chaste heroes and epicene princes. At a time of increasing anxiety about women's political demands – in 1832, MPs refused to consider a petition for women's suffrage; three years later they ridiculed the proposal that women should be admitted to a special gallery to view parliamentary proceedings – extravaganza enabled Vestris to market herself, and by extension the Olympic Theatre, as a realm of luscious sexuality and female power.

The extravaganzas I discuss here are the early mythological pieces: *Olympic Devils; or Orpheus and Eurydice* (Christmas 1831); *The Paphian Bower; or, Venus and Adonis* (Christmas 1832) and *The Deep, Deep Sea; or Perseus and Andromeda* (Christmas 1833).[86] In these plays, Planché and Dance seem to have reinvented in mythological form the prevailing image of subservient 'coadjuting' males in thrall to dominant women at the Olympic, and the bitter, much publicised rivalry between Vestris and her fellow actresses.[87] Extravaganza represents henpecked husbands in thrall to

---

[85] *Examiner*, December 30 1828, 821.

[86] *The Extravaganzas of J. R. Planché* ed. T. F. D. Croker and S. Tucker, 5 vols. (London: Samuel French, 1879). Scene references will be given within the text.

[87] On Vestris' disputes with Maria Foote and with her sister Josephine Bartolozzi, see *Theatrical Observer*, 9 March 1832; *National Omnibus*, 18 November 1831.

their domineering, cacophonous, high-spending wives; women constantly suspect their husbands' fidelity and shrewish goddesses disrupt men's work, leisure and sleep. In *Olympic Revels*, Juno takes revenge on the rival for her husband's attention by bestowing upon Pandora the fatal gift of curiosity ('Woman's dear passion'). Similarly, *The Deep, Deep Sea* begins with Neptune, played by James Bland, taking a nap in his submarine villa 'in the blissful absence of his shrewish lady', who spoils his sleep and makes him seasick.[88] This mythological world of cacophonous domestic strife serves to highlight the sensuality and half-celestial allure of Vestris' own characters.

In *Olympic Revels* Vestris played the innocent but disingenuous Pandora; as Venus and Calypso she portrayed mythological women whose love is comically unrequited. Like the wonderful American sea serpent, part man, part horse, part alligator, who agrees to eat up Ethiopia in order to satisfy Amphitrite's demands for revenge against Queen Cassiope, these mythical women threaten the men who cross their path with romantic annihilation. Vestris' characters carefully differentiate the manager's sexual charisma from that of her company, and they also self-consciously capitalise on spectators' knowledge of Vestris' scandalous past. When Venus expresses her wish to marry Adonis, for example, he, with proper nineteenth-century prudery, manifests anxiety about Venus' marital status: Venus swiftly admits to 'a flirtation with a chap named Mars' and 'a proper deed of separation' from Vulcan (scene i, 101). Such allusions encourage the Olympic spectators to perceive Vestris as a woman with a notorious sexual past, but also seem to license her transgressions as a corollary of her mythological celebrity.

In Olympic extravaganza, cross-dressing becomes a role assumed and then rescinded – an act of sexual and sartorial ventriloquism. As Orpheus and Perseus, Vestris acquires the traditional attributes of masculine identity: heroism, physical strength and political power. In the characters of Calypso and Venus, by contrast, Vestris epitomises viraginous womanhood in her fierce pursuit of either a man who is played by a woman or, its figurative version, an epicene hero who seems to hover between masculinity and femininity.[89] As Perseus, for instance, Vestris succeeds in killing Medusa, and releasing Andromeda from the rock; here, her actions appear to be those of the warrior woman in man's

[88] See *Morning Chronicle*, 27 December 1833.
[89] On the demise of the warrior woman in nineteenth-century culture, see Dianne Dugaw's persuasive argument in *Warrior Women and Popular Balladry, 1650–1850* (Cambridge University Press, 1989).

clothes – a dramatic Joan of Arc, as she had described herself to Olympic audiences. But at the heart of this drama is a sexual taboo, for what the ghostly plot of the extravaganza encourages spectators to imagine is a same sex union between Vestris-as-Perseus, and Andromeda. That possibility, however, is swiftly averted when Vestris proceeds to renounce the clothes, weapon and gender of the warrior hero. (Compare Shakespeare's romances which also evoke, if for only for a split second, the threat of an incestuous union between fathers and daughters.) For, in the play's concluding tag, Vestris throws away 'her manly courage with her manly part' (scene iv, 68) and chastely presents herself to her Olympic audience as a humble woman manager. The play's transgressive subtext silently dissolves, and with it the half-seductive, half-threatening connotations of female power. But what is remarkable, perhaps, is that such power was being imagined at all.

Olympic extravaganzas offer the cultural historian a wealth of insights into nineteenth-century nonsense. These plays delight in jokes about commercial products and brands (Amphitrite's mother revives her with Barclay's double stout); illegalities of various kinds (in *Telemachus; or, The Island of Calypso*, performed in December 1834, the spirit of whisky declines to appear on stage lest it is required to pay duty to the excise man), and burlesque modes of transport (in *The Paphian Bower*, the Muses arrive in a blue omnibus, while the boat designed by Minerva for Telemachus' escape from Calypso's island is a modern steamer). In these absurd and incongruous clashes between ancient and modern characters, mores and narratives, those middle-class values of work, marriage and respectability can be temporarily suspended.

The prominence of metamorphosis in Olympic extravaganza helps to represent identity as fluid and mutable: Perseus turns his rival Phineus to stone, whilst Orpheus makes trees and animals dance. At the close of *The Paphian Bower*, Venus herself alludes to these changes of identity when she reassures the audience, 'Though metamorphoses I've here a few, / I never wish to metamorphose you!' (scene iii, 112). In certain ways, the theme of metamorphosis offers a counterweight to the transgressions represented by Vestris' cross-dressed roles, licensing the manager's shape-changing as nothing more than a light-hearted mythological game. Nevertheless, during a period of confused hostility about women's roles in public life (see the cartoons vilifying Queen Adelaide's attempts at petticoat government in the early 1830s), Olympic extravaganza provided a mythological mould for the contradictory desires and fears implicit in female management.

REJECTED COMEDY AND THEATRE HISTORIOGRAPHY

We began this chapter by exploring À Beckett's *Scenes from the Rejected Comedies* as a text concerned with the fragmentation of laughter in early Victorian London. Rejection, I have suggested, is a recurring theme in the interpretation of comic performance. Hazlitt's essay 'On Modern Comedy', and Lamb's discussion of Restoration plays, both present contemporary laughter as a powerful index of social change. What preoccupies Hazlitt is the idea that political and economic upheaval ('the rise of stocks, the loss of battles, the fall of kingdoms, and the death of kings') has damaged our physiological capacity to enjoy legitimate theatre (the 'individual caprices, or head-strong passions, which are the nerves and sinews of Comedy and Tragedy'). For Charles Lamb, the disappearance of Restoration comedies from the stock repertoire represents the dismal triumph of that complacent, fireside morality which refuses to distinguish between the world of the imagination and that of social life.

The career of John Liston, the most famous face-changer and gestural contortionist of his age, aptly sums up the metamorphosis of theatrical laughter. Like Harley and Joseph Munden, Liston originally belonged to that generation of late Georgian comedians who had delighted audiences with their facial ticks and grotesque movements. As Hazlitt recalled, Liston's drollery 'oozes out of his features, and trickles down his face: his voice is a pitch-pipe for laughter'.[90] Such was 'the exquisite comicality' of Liston's face, the critic remarked, that it constituted a national calamity: playwrights, audiences and managers alike abandoned legitimate comedy in order to enjoy the pleasures of watching Liston performing in farce. But by the end of his career, even Liston had been compelled to change with the times. As the busybody Paul Pry (Haymarket, 1825), Liston transformed the familiar figure of the gossip and scandalmonger into a distinctly modern character whose insatiable curiosity represented both a laughable and also an insidious threat to the integrity of private life. Later, at the Olympic, Liston would be cast by Eliza Vestris in a series of vulgar-genteel roles as a cowardly lover, a retired hairdresser and a 'gentleman in difficulties'. By the 1830s, Liston had relinquished the pleasures of the grotesque in favour of a comic trade in social knowledge and contemporary manners.

The rise of the minor theatres, and the expanding market for illegitimate forms, is one important factor in the crisis of legitimate comedy

[90] *Hazlitt* XVIII: 279.

described by writers such as Lamb, Hazlitt and Bulwer-Lytton. Romantic theatre criticism, I have suggested, reflects on what social and political changes lie behind the banishment of certain dramatic characters and subjects from the stage; the subject of laughter thus becomes intricately connected with questions of censorship and taboo. At the minor theatres, burlesques and other comic productions such as Mathews' *At Homes* often drew attention to their illegitimate status. But these plays are also fascinating for their own sake. They have much to tell us, for example, about definitions of class and respectability, and about the perplexing experience of technological change. As we have seen, leading performers such as Charles Mathews and Eliza Vestris made their reputations by dramatising the chameleon-like character of identity and social roles in the early nineteenth-century metropolis. In different ways, both Vestris and Mathews can be seen as modern ventriloquists whose comic performances self-consciously exposed how contingent were the boundaries and distinctions which now separated genders, classes and nations.

Laughing comedy vs sentimental comedy
give way to the debate
that both are no longer playable
because lack of agreed upon
culture. (They still exist)

Societal roles are fictive
Class is mutable
Pastiche to rewrite masterpieces
Identity as a matter of intrepreneurship

CHAPTER SEVEN

Illegitimate celebrities

The historiography of early nineteenth-century theatre has been dominated by descriptions of tragedy and comedy, as performed at the
Theatres Royal. We have already explored how such an approach has
distorted our understanding of illegitimate theatre. What is more, many
of the age's most famous performers – Eliza Vestris, John Buckstone,
Charles Mathews and Elizabeth Yates – spent a large part of their
careers working in the minor theatres. Other well-known figures, including Céline Céleste and Thomas Potter Cooke, became celebrated not for
their tragic or comic parts, but because of their leading roles in illegitimate genres, whether in extravaganza, pantomime, melodrama or burlesque.

Theatrical celebrity in this period is a fascinating subject, and it would
be tempting to devote this chapter to an exploration of role, narrative
and image (both on stage and off, in prints and toy theatre portraits, for
example) in its production. But my subjects here are two illegitimate performers – Joseph Grimaldi and Edmund Kean. The history I sketch
moves between the patent and minor theatres, and crosses the threshold
which divides legitimate and illegitimate genres. The relationship
between illegitimacy and celebrity is also different in each case. Whereas
Grimaldi's stage career took the form of a single, illegitimate role – that
of the Clown – Kean's illegitimacy had to do with his performances of
Shakespearean tragedy. Though Kean's interpretations inspired adula-
tion, scornful disdain and fierce controversy, Grimaldi's whimsical,
lawless Clown seems to have been greeted with almost universal delight.
But having captivated and fascinated audiences during the Regency
years, the stars of both men quickly faded. Kean's notorious addiction
to alcohol was compounded by sexual scandal: when news broke in 1825
of his affair with Mrs Charlotte Cox (the episode received voyeuristic
coverage in countless lewd prints and pamphlets), furious audiences peremptorily hounded the performer off the Drury Lane stage. Meanwhile,

debilitated by the violent exertions of the Clown's role over many years, Grimaldi's health soon declined, the audience's convulsions of laughter at the Clown's tricks on stage matched only by the agonising pain which the performer was seen to suffer in the wings.[1] By the end of the Regency, however, Joseph Grimaldi and Edmund Kean had defined the terms of illegitimate celebrity. Both performers changed the boundaries of theatrical expression on the late Georgian stage, and profoundly shaped that culture's experience of disorder, violence and pain. Their influence is especially tangible amidst the period's theatre criticism, and also, in the case of Edmund Kean, in Romantic playwriting.

GRIMALDI, THE URBAN ANARCHIST

For a quarter of a century, Joseph Grimaldi was the unquestioned King of English Clowns. Admired by leading critics such as Hazlitt and Leigh Hunt, watched by thousands, from nameless apprentices packed shoulder to shoulder in the galleries at Sadler's Wells to the Lord Chancellor and Lord Byron, Grimaldi became a quintessential Regency celebrity.[2] The vogue for pantomime in early nineteenth-century London, of course, cannot be attributed solely to the 'irresistible' fascination of Grimaldi's Clown. In many ways, pantomime revealed the theatrical triumph of spectacular connoisseurship, technical brilliance and mechanical virtuosity. These shows invited playgoers into an alluring visual world featuring intricate panoramic landscapes by famous scene painters such as Grieve and Roberts, luxurious images of magic gardens and oriental palaces, and subtle realisations of old and new London scenes, from Greenwich Hospital and Charing Cross to Waterloo Place, Westminster Hall and Vauxhall Gardens. At pantomimes, audiences revelled in the optical ingenuity of early nineteenth-century culture, delighting in the illusionistic representation of vast spaces, moving

---

[1] Charles Dickens, *Memoirs of Joseph Grimaldi*, 231.

[2] On Byron's acquaintance with and patronage of Grimaldi, see Richard Findlater, *Grimaldi, King of Clowns* (London: Macgibbon and Kee, 1955), 167–70. Findlater, p. 113, quotes Lord Eldon's famous praise for the 'sublime impudence' with which the Clown stole a leg of mutton. His book also includes contemporary poetic tributes to Grimaldi; see, for example, James Smith's 'Tributary Stanzas' (pp. 230–1). Cf. Hazlitt's comments in 1815 on the 'ugly rumour' that Grimaldi had died: 'We would not believe it; we did not like to ask any one the question, but we watched the public countenance for the intimation of an event which "would have eclipsed the gaiety of nations"' (*Hazlitt* XVIII: 208). Grimaldi's celebrity spawned a miniature industry in images and souvenirs, including many famous prints of particular pantomime scenes and transformations as well as images of the performer's face which appeared on domestic objects such as cruet jugs. Many of these can be seen in the Raymond Mander and Joe Mitchenson collection.

pictures, subtly changing lights and colours. But by the Regency, that archetypal pantomimic narrative in which two lovers, their union frustrated by the opposition of a cantankerous father-figure, are transformed into Harlequin and Columbine, had become no more than a thinly veiled pretext for magnificent scenic display. In these shows, the dizzying, awe-inspiring world of Romantic travel – from the towering magnificence of the Alps to the icy landscapes of the North Pole – found its first, enchanted mass audience. But the star of Regency pantomime, nevertheless, whether in his satirical burlesques of Regency dandies or his absurd transformations of cheeses and wheelbarrows into boats and patent safety coaches, was Joseph Grimaldi.[3]

My argument acknowledges, though does not explore, pantomime's importance as a genre of popular visual knowledge. Rather, I am interested in the emergence of pantomime as a theatrical form which dramatised the pleasures, fears and absurdities of urban life. At Sadler's Wells, I want to argue, Grimaldi, Charles Dibdin, and his company transformed the rustic landscapes and magical universe of John Rich's pantomimes into a satirical, whimsical entertainment which took as its subject the entrepreneurial and illusory character of the early nineteenth-century city. Indeed, my discussion here presents the Sadler's Wells shows as the theatrical blueprint for the more famous Regency pantomimes. For by the time Grimaldi played the Clown at Covent Garden in 1806, the metamorphosis of Richian pantomime was all but complete. What is more, the innovations pioneered at Sadler's Wells had laid the foundation for pantomime's new status amongst radical theatre critics as a lively, anarchic counterpoint to a stultified and repressive political culture.

Having inherited control of Lincoln's Inn Fields after the death of his father in 1714, John Rich began to devise a spectacular form of entertainment, based on the Italian *commedia dell'arte*, which would display his own skill in mime.[4] Rich's pantomimes featured magnificent scenery painted by designers from Italian theatres, as well as music, dance and tricks of construction, and ingenious technical effects. Most importantly, Rich had invented the English Harlequin, a silent figure of wit and

---

[3] My discussion here is indebted to David Mayer's definitive and compelling account of the structure, evolution and political significance of early nineteenth-century pantomime in *Harlequin in His Element*. See especially chapters 6, 'Aspects of the Economy' and 8, 'Censorship and Political Expression'.

[4] On Rich's pantomime, see R. J. Broadbent, *A History of Pantomime* (New York: Benjamin Blom, 1964), chapter 15; Allardyce Nicoll, *A History of Early Eighteenth Century Drama, 1700–1750* (Cambridge University Press, 2nd edition 1929), 251–8.

magic who performed picturesque transformations in which palaces and temples turned into huts and cottages, men and women into wheelbarrows and joint-stools, and colonnades into beds of tulips.[5] Rich became celebrated, too, for his intricate mimes, the most famous of which showed the birth of Harlequin, painstakingly emerging from a huge egg by the heat of the sun in *Harlequin Sorcerer* (1717). Yet although Rich's Harlequin was presented as a romantic figure of larceny, his crimes did not go unpunished: the dénouement of *Harlequin Sorcerer*, for example, featured a characteristic scene of divine retribution in which four devils carried Harlequin off to the infernal regions.

At the end of the eighteenth century, pantomime played a crucial part in the repertoire of minor theatres such as Sadler's Wells. Since pantomime was classified as an illegitimate genre, managers at the minor playhouses could devise and stage these entertainments without fear of prosecution (the furore over Delpini's unlicensed speech, discussed in chapter 1, is an important exception). Moreover, pantomime's seductive combination of scenic spectacle, mechanical trickery and acrobatic virtuosity invariably attracted large and profitable houses.[6] At Sadler's Wells in particular, the popularity of pantomime must also be attributed to the remarkable collection of performers, many originating from France and Italy, who had found employment at the theatre during the 1780s and 1790s as dancers, acrobats and clowns. They included Jean Baptiste Dubois, an actor, tumbler and juggler, soon to become London's leading clown at Drury Lane, and Jack Bologna, son of the posture master Pietro Bologna. Bologna senior had brought a troupe of Italian tumblers to England in the mid-1780s, and performed tricks and feats of strength, along with his wife, a slack-wire dancer, and his two sons. Another important member of the Sadler's Wells company was Giovanni Battista Belzoni ('the celebrated Patagonian Sampson') an extraordinary strongman who starred in the Sadler's Wells show of skulduggery, *Jack the Giant Killer* (1803), in which Grimaldi played the dwarf. Other continental performers in the company included Grimaldi senior (a Pierrot and notorious low humorist), the clown Paulo Redigé (known as the 'Little Devil'),

---

[5] Thomas Davies, *Memoirs of the Life of David Garrick*, 2 vols. (London, printed for the author, 1780), I: 92.

[6] The commercial value of pantomimes compared to other entertainments is borne out by the prices offered to Charles Dibdin the Younger by the Astleys. See Charles Dibdin, *Memoirs*, 18–19. Newspapers and periodicals often marvelled at the costs incurred by patent and minor theatres alike in the production of pantomimes. See the *Examiner*, 6 January 1828, 9, which reported that Drury Lane and Covent Garden had each expended £1,000 on the Christmas pantomime. The Surrey had spent £500, whilst other minor theatres had incurred costs of £100–200.

whose family had played at the French boulevard theatres, together with his father (a Pierrot), Placido Bussart (Signor Placido), a Parisian Harlequin, and Jack Richer ('Charming Richer'), one of the age's most famous and elegant rope dancers.[7] Richer, of course, would later be immortalised in 'The Indian Jugglers', where Hazlitt warmly praised him as 'matchless in his art', a man who added to his 'extraordinary skill exquisite ease, and unaffected natural grace'. Indeed, the essay is a joyful and self-deprecating description of the miraculous skills and 'mechanical excellence' characteristic of illegitimate culture.[8]

What might be significant about this hotchpotch of nationalities and dramatic traditions amongst the company at Sadler's Wells? As Charles Dibdin's memoirs make clear, the informal, collaborative practices of the Sadler's Wells company helped to make possible the eclectic cross-fertilisation of tricks, dramatic characters and gestural traditions.[9] The originality of early nineteenth-century pantomime, then, can be partly accounted for in terms of its capacious assimilation of miscellaneous popular entertainments including swordsmanship, clowning in the ring and the exhibition of postures and feats of strength.

Dubois – a performer who 'bears away the palm from all without exception, to whom speech is denied'[10] – laid the foundations for the transformation of Richian pantomime. Before being engaged at Sadler's Wells, Dubois had played clown during the horsemanship in the ring at Jones' Equestrian Amphitheatre in Whitechapel. It is not surprising, therefore, that Dubois began to incorporate into pantomime the conventions of amphitheatrical clownsmanship. And the time was certainly ripe for a clowning revolution, for the pantomime Clown had long been portrayed as a dull buffoon character, a mere vestige of the *zanno* in *commedia*. So Dubois started to experiment by representing the Clown as a character with a distinct national or ethnic identity (Dutch or Jewish, for example); on one occasion, he even cast himself as a hunchback Clown. As Dubois conducted these experiments, the Clown's character and appearance started to become uncertain, mutable, subject to change and metamorphosis. In particular, Dubois' study of the Clown's identity introduced into the character a malicious, sinister undertow: the Clown now became notable for sudden and 'masterly' transitions from pleasure

---

[7] Charles Dibdin, *Memoirs*, chapters 4 and 5, includes a detailed account of the Sadler's Wells' company and repertoire. On Richer, see Dibdin, *Memoirs*, 41; J. P. Malcolm, *Londinium Redivivum*, III: 235.   [8] *Hazlitt* VIII: 80.

[9] Findlater, *Grimaldi*, 53, compares the 'bustling democracy' of Sadler's Wells with the hierarchical discipline characteristic of a royal theatre such as Covent Garden.

[10] Malcolm, *Londinium Redivivum*, III: 235–6.

to menace, approbation to abhorrence. In these transformations, we can glimpse the mutation of that savage iconography discussed in chapter 3. Once a witless buffoon, the Clown was changing into a morally ambivalent character, neither entirely civilised nor wholly savage.[11]

Grimaldi's portrayal of the Clown blended the variations introduced by Dubois, and certain aspects of the Pierrot figure, with the criminality of Rich's Harlequin. Having eschewed the conventional representation of Clown as a slow, unfeeling, victim, incapable of discernment or recognition, with vacant eyes, dangling arms and open mouth, Grimaldi created an earthier, more anarchic character: 'half-idiotic, crafty, shameless, incorrigible' and an emblem of 'gross sensuality'.[12] In certain ways, Grimaldi's Clown became a stage character inextricable from an age of European warfare in which print and oral cultures alike traded energetically in patriotic propaganda. The Clown's stolid, earthy corporeality and patriotic songs ('O give me little England, where a man's head is his own freehold property, and his house is his castle') clearly evoked the loyal, patriotic commonsense of that archetypal Englishman, John Bull.[13] But at the same time Grimaldi's Clown evoked those dastardly *sans culottes* and demonic villains of patriotic serio-pantomimes.[14] In such contradictions, perhaps, lay the theatrical brilliance and satirical topicality of Grimaldi's clown, a character by turns treacherous and loyal, cowardly and patriotic, grotesque and pathetic, ridiculous and graceful.

Though we might be tempted to interpret the Regency Clown as Grimaldi's peculiar and idiosyncratic creation, writing, acting and pantomime production at the Wells were in practice inextricable. Performers such as Jack Bologna, who composed many of the ballets, and Grimaldi, who invented numerous transformations, shared the business of mounting pantomimes with Charles Dibdin and other arrangers.[15] Interestingly, Dibdin clearly perceived his role as the arranger to

[11] Malcolm, *Londinium Redivivum*, III: 236.
[12] Charles Dibdin, *Memoirs*, 89. On the predecessors of the Clown, see Findlater, *Grimaldi*, 145–6.
[13] Grimaldi's song is from the opening night of the 1811 season at Sadler's Wells, and no doubt provided a patriotic contrast to his demonic portrayal of Napoleon in the evening's pantomime, *Dulce Domum: or England the Land of Freedom*. Grimaldi appeared as John Bull in Charles Dibdin's prelude, *New Brooms; or, The Firm Changed* (Sadler's Wells, 1803).
[14] Grimaldi played a desperado in Charles Dibdin's serio-pantomime, *The Great Devil; or, The Robber of Genoa* (Sadler's Wells, 1801) and Rufo the Robber in *Red Riding Hood* (Sadler's Wells, 1803). See too Grimaldi's role as the necromantic monster, Hag Morad, in [Thomas J. Dibdin], *The Talisman; or Harlequin Made Happy* (Sadler's Wells, 1796).
[15] For Bologna's ballets, see Charles Dibdin, *Memoirs*, 56. As manager and stock author from 1800, Charles Dibdin not only wrote and produced the Wells pantomimes but was also responsible for inventing the pantomime machinery. On his famous and much-imitated mechanical ship, designed for *The Aethiop, or The Siege of Granada* (Sadler's Wells, 1801), see *Memoirs*, 46.

involve notating the 'peculiar whimsicality' which he observed in Grimaldi at Wells rehearsals.[16] In a variety of ways, then, the technical virtuosity and satirical ingenuity of early nineteenth-century panto-mime at Sadler's Wells represented the fruits of a genuine partnership.

As Clown usurped Harlequin as the star of Sadler's Wells pantomimes, the moral structure of Richian pantomime began to disintegrate. The theatrical atrophy of Harlequin can be traced in metatheatrical form within the plot of *Wizard's Wake; or Harlequin and Merlin* (Sadler's Wells, 1802), where an enfeebled Harlequin is made to ascend a funeral pyre in order that he may be reborn, just like the phoenix.[17] From the late 1790s, too, the Sadler's Wells Clown begins to emerge as a lawless figure, utterly careless of human pain.[18] In *The Talisman* (Sadler's Wells, 1796), for example, the Clown ingeniously outwitted Harlequin by enclosing him in a sugar hogshead, and throwing him into the Thames river, whilst in *Goody Two Shoes; or Harlequin Alabaster* (1803), Goody Two Shoes purchased a raven from the Clown 'to prevent his tormenting it'.[19] The pantomime universe was already becoming a stage for the Clown's half-malicious, half-playful experiments in the inflicting of pain. In later pantomimes, these forms of persecution become still more pronounced: Clown drops hot lead on Pantaloon's feet (*Broad Grins; or Harlequin Mag and Harlequin Tag*, Olympic, 1815, scene iii), and imprisons Lover in a sack of flour (*Harlequin and the Dandy Club*, Drury Lane, 1818, scene vi). In these shows, Clown acted as the punisher of the 'libidinous, miserly' Pantaloon. Whereas Richian pantomime had been careful to underline the punish-ment of Harlequin, its larcenous star, now only the shadowy, ethereal Harlequin could mitigate or punish the Clown's urban anarchy, for jus-tices, constables and other figures of human authority were almost invari-ably unsuccessful.[20]

The lawlessness of Grimaldi's Clown might have been expected to produce suspicion, not to say alarm, amongst genteel audiences and middle-class critics troubled by fears about the character's effects on dis-cipline and social order amongst the lower classes. But with the excep-tion of a letter received by Charles Dibdin, castigating him 'in the most

[16] Charles Dibdin, *Memoirs*, 43.
[17] *Plots, Songs, Chorusses, &c. in the comic pantomime, called Wizard's Wake; or, Harlequin and Merlin* (London: W. Glendinning, [1803]).
[18] See *Sketch of the Story, Scenery, &c. with the Songs, and Recitatives, in the new serio-comic entertainment of The Talisman; or Harlequin Made Happy* (London: W. Glendinning, [1796]), scene iv.
[19] *Ibid.*, scene xix; *Songs, Chorusses, Leading Features, in the new comic pantomime, called Goody Two Shoes; or, Harlequin Alabaster* (London, [1803]). Hazlitt saw a revival of this pantomime at Sadler's Wells in 1820. See *Hazlitt* XVIII:326.   [20] See Charles Dibdin, *Memoirs*, 89.

virulent manner' for the Clown's criminality and 'moral turpitude', moral opposition to Grimaldi's character was remarkably scarce. The performer's skill, we must therefore surmise, lay in his capacity to banish any hints of vulgarity and coarseness from the Clown's criminality.[21] In any case, this half-innocent, even naive, character, on the mysterious threshold between human sentience and subhuman savagery, somehow obviated questions about responsibility and punishment. As the writer in *Oxberry's Dramatic Biography* commented of Grimaldi, 'robbery became a science in his hands . . . he seemed so imbued with the spirit of peculation, that you saw it in him, merely as a portion of his nature, and for which he was neither blameable nor accountable'.[22] The bewitching impudence of Grimaldi's Clown converted 'moral delinquency' into a form of hedonism, substituting for moral judgement an 'irresistible' collusive pleasure on the part of the spectator.[23] The Clown's compulsive theft of letters, statues or bread, and the anarchic world of the early nineteenth-century harlequinade, were allowed to exist because of pantomime's perceived status as a theatrical genre beyond rationality.[24] Grimaldi's Clown, therefore, was presumed to inhabit an imaginary space outside ordinary human morality.[25]

Grimaldi transformed the Clown into a character remarkable for his eloquent gestural and bodily expressiveness. From those globular, winking eyes, a vivacious nose 'capable of exhibiting disdain, fear, anger, even joy' to his artful, infinitely varied repertoire of grimaces, the Clown seemed to celebrate the articulate power of the unspeaking human body.[26] Each sneeze, yawn and grin seemed to have been precisely calibrated for a particular comic, whimsical or pathetic effect; spectators marvelled at the mobility of Grimaldi's face, the lightning speed and verve with which the Clown's emotions changed, the way in which a single facial feature seemed to carry its own peculiar cargo of emotion. In an attempt to find a critical language for this wordless eloquence,

---

[21] Compare the low humour of Grimaldi senior, whose satirical song about the Quakers was banned by local magistrates. Henry D. Miles, *The Life of Joseph Grimaldi* (London, 1838), 17.

[22] 'Memoirs of Joseph Grimaldi', 1827, 1: 119.

[23] For the Clown's 'moral delinquency' see 'Some Recollections of Grimaldi', *New Monthly Magazine* (1837), part 2, 374–84, 384. On the language of the 'irresistible', a recurring theme in reviews of Grimaldi, see *The Times*, 24 April 1810 and 27 December 1814.

[24] On pantomime's irrationality, see the letter signed 'A Friend to Rational Amusement' printed in *The Times*, 30 December 1807 and similarly *The Times*, 28 April 1807.

[25] But compare the extensive fracas about Bradbury's 'offensive' behaviour as Clown. The controversy began during a performance of the Drury Lane pantomime, *Harlequin and the Dandy Club; or 1818*, and is discussed at length in the *European Magazine*, January 1819, 75: 48–51.

[26] *New Monthly Magazine* (1837), part 2, 383.

reviewers frequently compared Grimaldi's body to a silent text. In 1828, for example, *The Times*' critic recalled how, in his ridicule of contemporary fashions, Grimaldi 'became a *living epigram*, so terse and pointed, as to set translation entirely at defiance'.[27] This imagery is striking for, though not entirely silent, the Clown did indeed treat spoken language as a precious commodity. Words seemed to represent peculiarly valuable forms of expression which the Clown introduced on occasions of unusual intensity, when overwhelmed by a particular sensation. For the Clown, as for Rousseau's primitive man, language existed primarily as a form of expression, rather than for the negotiation of conflict and dispute. When the Clown did break his silence – to say 'nice' (when eating gingerbread) and 'don't' (to someone about to torture him), 'the necessity with which he was delivered of his exclamation was made apparent to everybody, and contained a world of concentration'.[28] In these expressive monosyllables, language became a rare, sensuous form of expression, as if the illicit status of the spoken word at Sadler's Wells had suddenly acquired its own unique aesthetic logic.

The corporeal expressivity of Grimaldi as Clown is just one example of the way in which illegitimate theatre privileged gesture and non-verbal sounds over spoken language and rhetoric. At Sadler's Wells, of course, the virtual absence of language in pantomime constituted not simply a dramatic convention but rather a legal necessity.[29] In order to circumvent this prohibition, as well as to exploit to the full Grimaldi's whimsical, ironic stage persona, Sadler's Wells pioneered the tradition of the Clown's patter song. Here, sung verses are interspersed with snatches of absurd and incongruous dialogue; the patter song exists in that intermediate domain of illegitimate culture, suspended in a no-man's-land between song and speech. But the songs' legal contingency did not stand in the way of their popularity. On the contrary, the sneezing song, 'A Typitywitcket: or Pantomimical Paroxysms' in *Bang Up! or, Harlequin Prime* (Sadler's Wells, 1810) and 'Hot Codlins' in *The Talking Bird* (Covent Garden, 1819), turned into such favourites that they continued to be performed long after the pantomime's run had ended.

Satirical, sometimes pathetic, and invariably absurd, Dibdin's patter songs endowed the Clown with his own form of comic illegitimate

---

27 *The Times*, 27 December 1828, my italics. Cf. the account given in the *New Monthly Magazine*: 'Speech would have been thrown away in his performance of Clown; every limb of him had a language' (383).   28 [Leigh Hunt], *Tatler*, December 28 1831, 3: 613.

29 The opening scene of *Broad Grins* in which the Prompter successfully obtains a place for his mute girlfriend in the pantomime ironically invokes the belief that pantomime was devoid of speech. As Mayer points out, *Harlequin in His Element*, 20–1, we cannot be certain how much of Regency pantomime was actually silent.

speech. In the interlude between verses, Grimaldi would interpolate a piece of spoken dialogue. This was usually made up of apparently arbitrary snatches of disembodied conversation, full of nonsense and rich in malapropism and *double entendre*. One good example is the song, 'What'll Mrs Grundy Say?' (from *Bang Up*, words by Charles Dibdin, with music by William Reeve). Here, Grimaldi dramatises the competing voices heard in tea-time conversation at the house of Mrs Mag, mantua-maker:

Pray ladies is the tea to your liking? – Dear Mrs. Mag you've made mine too sweet. – La, Mem, you're not like Miss Muzzlemump fond of the grocer – aye, and if report speaks true there's no love lost between 'em – he! he! he! – I purtest Miss, you're quite scandalous – pray ladies how long has the invisible girl opened shop? dear me Mem that's a queer question – I suppose the lady deludes to the adwertisement about inwisible peticoats – Dear me, aye, Mrs. Roundabout bought one, – she'd no occasion, her peticoats were always inwisible . . . [30]

There is a wonderful comic disjunction here between the Clown's corporeal solidity and the dizzying succession of incongruous voices which he assumes as part of the patter. Indeed, the Clown seems to present himself in these songs as a dramatic mouthpiece of metropolitan speech, a body scarcely in possession of his own voice. In this way, the Clown's songs reveal that characteristic tension in illegitimate theatre between silence and (ventriloquised) speech, articulation and muteness.

Grimaldi's songs, however, are important for another reason, for they enabled Charles Dibdin to reinvent Richian pantomime as an entertainment dramatising metropolitan mania, or the irrational, unstoppable pursuit of fashion. Visual satire appears to have been a feature of pantomimes at the Wells from Dibdin's earliest shows. In 1803, J. P. Malcolm noted with approval that the Sadler's Wells pantomimes 'afford many temporary allusions to the follies of the times, in the pads, false breasts, false calves, and transparent dresses'.[31] Two years later, in *Harlequin and Aesop; or Wisdom versus Wealth* (Sadler's Wells, 1805), Dibdin created for Grimaldi a whimsical patter song caricaturing female dress which the actor performed dressed as a *femme de modes*.[32] Thereafter, arrangers began to use a satirical subject – the craze for antiquarian pursuits, the new sport of four-in-hand driving, the fashion for gentlemen jockeys, and the absurdities of Regency dandyism – as a pantomime's unifying theme.[33]

---

[30] Cited Mayer, *Harlequin in His Element*, Appendix B, 352–3.   [31] *Londinium Redivivum*, III: 235.
[32] Charles Dibdin, *Memoirs*, 67.
[33] See, for example [Charles Dibdin], *Bang Up: or, Harlequin Prime* (Sadler's Wells, 1810), burlesquing the craze for four-in-hand driving and *Fairlop Fair: or, The Genie of the Oak* (Sadler's Wells, 1812) which satirised the rage for antiquarianism.

Metropolitan mania fulfilled a useful structural role in the Wells pantomimes because it lent thematic coherence to the otherwise episodic
scenes of the harlequinade. More importantly, Dibdin's innovation also
helped to transform pantomime into an urban genre. The picturesque
cottages and village scenes of John Rich's shows now gave way to views
and scenes of the modern city, a city characterised in pantomime as a
place of contagious irrationality, constant mobility and compulsive
social improvisation. Of course, it was the wave of *Tom and Jerry* plays in
1821–2 which really defined London as a hedonistic, panoramic stage of
pleasure. But Moncrieff's drama was careful to represent Tom and
Jerry's cultural journey, from Tattersalls to low dives in the East End, as
a carnivalesque form of comic education. By contrast, the pantomime
metropolis features neither the contrasts of leisure and poverty depicted
in the *Tom and Jerry* plays, nor the linguistic richness of contemporary
London. Nor did pantomime attempt to legitimate itself as a vicarious
form of cultural education (the Clown, indeed, never learns anything).
Rather, pantomime dramatised the city as an unstable, contingent, spectacular world, as a place of metamorphosis, innovation and relentless
self-fashioning.

The transformation of pantomime into a metropolitan genre was
already discernible at the Wells shows being performed in the late 1790s.
The Talisman (1796) featured many city scenes including a caricature print
shop, a gunsmith's and a tobacconist's, as well as a metamorphic gallery,
an exhibition of waxworks, and a view of the Thames. At the waxwork
exhibition (scene xvi), where Harlequin and Columbine are posing as
wax figures in order to elude their pursuers, Clown takes a sabre to the
head of a waxen Harlequin, and triumphantly carries off the waxwork.
In *The Talisman*, the harlequinade starts to become a city spectacle. The
prominence of exhibitions in this play also foreshadows pantomime's
fascination with the illusory boundaries between life and representation
in the modern metropolis.

By the late 1820s, the business of realisation on stage – whether this
was a realisation of a Hogarth print, a Tudor procession or that fashionable innovation in London shopping, the Burlington Arcade – was starting to dominate the production of illegitimate drama.[34] But the
harlequinade's inclusion of recognisable shops, and their sudden metamorphosis (see in particular the celebrated transformation of Ward's
Medicine shop to Jarvis' Coffin shop in *Peter Wilkins; or, The Flying World*,

---

[34] On the pictorial dramaturgy of early nineteenth-century theatre, see Meisel, *Realizations*, chapters 3 and 6.

performed at the Wells in 1800) anticipates by several decades this craze for realisation, and is remarkable too for its more sceptical and ironic view of the 'world of goods'.[35] In many ways, however, the prominence of shops in the Regency harlequinade can simply be ascribed to Charles Dibdin's shrewd business sense. Having successfully introduced the Cornhill Lottery Office as one of the harlequinade shops in *Thirty Thousand; or, Harlequin's Lottery* (Sadler's Wells, 1808), Dibdin was besieged by local tradesmen clamouring to have their own 'Show-Shops' included in the Sadler's Wells pantomime.[36] Of course, the Wells shows provided local business with a convenient form of free advertising; in so doing, pantomimes no doubt played a part in nurturing the thriving local economy. But Dibdin's evidence also suggests that this innovation provided a form of benefit in kind, because the tradesmen whose shops were being featured then purchased tickets for their employees to see the pantomime.

Although the inclusion of these shops suggests a certain pride in the local economy, the Clown's behaviour, and in particular his compulsive thefts, entirely subvert that economy's fundamental principles. For the gluttony of the Clown, delightfully incorporated into the dramatic structure of *Peter Wilkins* – a pantomime which featured Dubois as Gobble, the eating Clown, and Grimaldi as Guzzle, the drinking clown,[37] – seems to mirror the city's greed in its consumptive, competitive excess. Here, the Clown's irresistible fondness for food and drink offers a physical corollary for oversupply, mimicking the uncontrolled character of purchase and desire in the modern city. The unexpected metamorphosis of urban goods and shops in pantomime, as hat-boxes turn into watch-houses, and apple-stalls to printer's shops, seems to transform into laughter the experience of endless change and social mobility.[38]

The activity of consumption (whether food, domestic or cultural goods such as images and exhibitions) created a collusive, imaginative alliance between the Clown and the spectator. In the eyes of the Clown, London simply provided a glorious, inexhaustible miscellany of objects, both from nature and from culture, to be consumed or reimagined through acts of comic reconstruction (pantomime tricks). In the famous

---

[35] For reviews of *Peter Wilkins*, see 'Collections Relating to Sadler's Wells', III, fol. 62. On the cultural history of consumption, see further, Colin Campbell, *The Romantic Ethic and the Spirit of Modern Consumerism* (Oxford: Blackwell, 1987) and especially John Brewer and Roy Porter, eds., *Consumption and the World of Goods* (London: Routledge, 1993).   [36] Charles Dibdin, *Memoirs*, 101.
[37] For *Peter Wilkins* as a turning-point in the history of pantomime, see Dibdin, *Memoirs*, 43; 48; Findlater, *Grimaldi*, 74.
[38] *Harlequin Horner; or, The Christmas Pie*, Larpent MS 1947, scene xvi; *The Valley of Diamonds; or, Harlequin Sinbad* (Drury Lane, 1814), Larpent MS 1837, scene xiv.

song, 'Once a man ran away with the monument' from *London, or Harlequin and Time* (Sadler's Wells, 1813), the Clown tells a delightfully nonsensical story about the city itself being consumed. The song concerns a larcenous character (a version of the Clown himself, perhaps) who, having run away with the monument, decides to swallow it, in order to escape detection by the watchman. When he is captured, the man is found to have acquired an entire collection of London sights, including Aldgate Pump (in his hat) and the clock of St Paul's (in his fob for a watch). But the thief finally defeats his pursuers by spitting out the monument, which promptly (and conveniently) knocks to the ground the Lord Mayor and the aldermen.[39] Throughout this pantomime, set in 'Modern London' (see the stage direction for scene ii), the city is represented as if it were a collection of goods which might be eaten, stolen and acquired just like food in a shop.

In his history of puffing and quackery, J. D. Bunn would nostalgically recall how the silent language of advertising on London walls compulsively arrested the attention of the passer-by.[40] Pantomime, too, was fascinated by that competitive array of shop signs, placards and bill-boards which jostled for view in the early nineteenth-century city. Hats changed into shop signs, houses appeared plastered with placards, and the Clown would amuse himself by making up songs from music titles, or pasting a bill boy to the wall beneath his own bills. The mute appeals scattered across the city (appeals whose delusory rhetoric signifies the disintegration of printed words as fiduciary promises) became a silent alphabet for the Clown's infinite comic improvisation.[41] Whereas for a poet such as Wordsworth, the 'blank' illegibility of London represented a form of cultural alienation, the Clown's tricks and improvisations celebrated the infinite mutability of the metropolis and its susceptibility to playful reinterpretation.[42]

[39] [Charles Dibdin], *Songs, and Other Vocal Compositions, in the Pantomime called London; or Harlequin and Time* (London: W. Glendinning, 1814).

[40] [J. D. Bunn], *The Language of the Walls: and, A Voice from the Shop Windows. Or, The Mirror of Commercial Roguery. By One who Thinks Aloud* (London, 1855), 3–4.

[41] For the metamorphosis of hats, see [Thomas J. Dibdin], *Harlequin and Fancy* (Drury Lane, 1815), Larpent MS 1896, scene xiv, and for the house plastered with placards at Walker's Advertising Office, see *Harlequin Harmonist* (Drury Lane, 1813), Larpent MS 1790, scene xiii. The Clown's wonderfully surreal song made up from music titles can be found in *Harlequin Tom* (Olympic, 1820), Larpent MS 2195, scene iv, and Clown's pasting of a bill-poster boy in the Coburg show, *Harlequin and the Royal Ram; or, The Brazen Dragon* (1832), HTC, cited Mayer, *Harlequin in His Element*, 228.

[42] See *The Prelude*, 1805 text, Bk 7, especially lines 696–713. Wordsworth was captivated, however, by the delusory sign, 'Invisible', inscribed upon the chest of Jack the Giant Killer, in a pantomime at Sadler's Wells. See Bk 7: lines 301–10. Cf. Steven Marcus' argument in 'Reading the Illegible' in H. J. Dyos and Michael Wolff, eds., *The Victorian City*, 2 vols. (London: Routledge, 1973), 1: 257–76.

The Wells pantomimes dramatised the city as a place of masquerade, improvisation and perpetual image-making.[43] The caricature print shop scene in *The Talisman*, for example, exposed professional men as hypocrites and corrupt double dealers. In this scene, the principal necromancer (played by Dighton), now transformed into a ballad singer, performs a satirical song entitled 'The Picter Shop'. Though doctors, lawyers, MPs and other 'great men' may cut 'a mighty swell' in all their finery, explains the ballad singer, they are in fact like pictures which, once turned round, reveal themselves as 'paper-skulls':

> Your Doctors and Attorneys are honest men enough,
> And always do their best – to be touching of the stuff,
> But they're like Picters too, for while the world is in a bustle,
> While Patients die and Clients fail, they never move a muscle.   (scene vi)

The ballad's satirical effect arises from the devastating simplicity of its organising image, and the deftness of its slowly mocking logic. Like portraits in a print shop, parliamentary orators 'are oft put up to sale'; surely, then, it would make no difference 'If all such pretty Picters were hung up in a frame.' The satirical relationship between pictures and deceivers here acquires a shocking final twist by which the hanging of pictures evokes the hanging of men at the gallows – the proper punishment for professional paper-skulls.[44] Yet the ballad's conclusion deflates the song's derision with a patriotic appeal to king and country: 'May Britons true to Britain's King be neither bought nor sold.' Within the satirical logic of 'The Picter Shop', loyalty to George III provides a reassuring counterpoint to the delusory representation of pretty Picters.

For all the mockery in 'The Picter Shop', the Sadler's Wells shows also celebrated the showmanship of the modern city. The image-maker's song in *The Talisman*, performed by the celebrated Wells actor, William ('Jew') Davis, epitomises this theme. 'I've *doctors* out of *plaister* form'd, and landlords made of *chalk*', with a Buonaparte 'all made up of *plaister* of *paris*', declares the image-maker, gleefully promoting his own miniature

---

[43] For later examples, see the statuary scene at a plumber's shop in [Thomas J. Dibdin], *Harlequin and Humpo* (Drury Lane, 1812), Larpent MS 1750, scene xi; the Masquerade Warehouse scenes in [Thomas J. Dibdin], *Harlequin in his Element; or, Fire, Water, Earth, and Air* (Covent Garden, 1807), scene ix, as well as *Harlequin and Fancy*, scene ix, and [J. R. Planché], *Rudolph the Wolf; or, Columbine Red Riding Hood* (Olympic, 1818), Larpent MS 2065, scene ix.

[44] The gallows is a recurring topos in pantomime. See, for example, *Harlequin and Humpo* (Drury Lane, 1812), Larpent MS 1750, scene viii, in which Clown sees a gallows through his stolen telescope and [George Fox], *The House that Jack Built; or, Harlequin Tattered and Torn* (Olympic 1821), Larpent MS 2270, in which a seed shop and nursery are transformed into a distant view of ploughed land with a gallows. Cf. review in the *Morning Post*, 27 December 1821.

universe in which life and representation have become indistinguish-able.[45] The Camera Obscura man's song in Farley's pantomime, *Harlequin and the Red Dwarf* (Covent Garden, 1812) shares the same ironic perspective. Come and peep, he invites his audience, "Twill show you the whim of this bustle and strife, / It will, sure as Death, and as Natural as Life'.[46] Substance, as the Camera Obscura man ruefully acknowledges, 'has long ceased the fashion to be'. Like so many pantomime songs (compare the duet between the auctioneer and the clown in scene xii of this pantomime), the Camera Obscura man's promises skip with lightning irony between the deceptiveness and seductiveness of metropolitan illusionism.

In Rich's pantomimes, Harlequin's supremacy as a theatrical magician, capable of transforming objects with a slap of his bat, had remained undisputed. At Sadler's Wells, however, Grimaldi's famous tricks of construction created a new kind of rivalry between the Clown and Harlequin. For what distinguished the Clown's inventions was their incongruous and implausible composition from the urban miscellany of the street. Whereas Harlequin is above all a magician, Grimaldi humorously presented himself as an entrepreneurial inventor. Many of Grimaldi's tricks therefore involved the building of new vehicles, from patent safety coaches, steam carriages and balloons to steam packets. Each of these vehicles was assembled from a collection of unlikely materials: placard boards, bonnet-baskets, cleavers, a barber's pole, meat chops and a washing-tub.[47] In Charles Farley's pantomime, *Harlequin and Padmanaba; or, The Golden Fish* (Covent Garden, 1811), for example, the Clown mocked the driving mania in Regency London. In what became one of his most famous tricks of construction, the Clown proceeded to build a tandem in imitation of the curricle driven by the notorious dandy, Romeo Coates (see William Heath's etching, plate 15). Having assembled his tandem from a wicker cradle and four large cheeses, plus a whip made out of a collection of garters, Grimaldi mounted the cradle (topped by a live cock), and triumphantly steered his dog-coach off the stage.

In Grimaldi's tricks of construction, the conventional pattern of pursuit and escape in the eighteenth-century harlequinade seems to acquire the modern, technological absurdity of science-fiction. At the

---

[45] Farley, *Talisman*, scene xii. Compare the song by an image man in *Harlequin's Hour Glass; or, Time Works Wonders*, Larpent MS 1897, scene ix.

[46] *Harlequin and the Red Dwarf; or, The Adamant Rock* (Covent Garden, 1812), Larpent MS 1749, scene iv. [47] See further, Mayer, *Harlequin in His Element*, 210 ff.

15. The modern entrepreneur. *Grimaldi's Tandem in the Comic Pantomime of the Golden Fish.*

same time, the (literal and metaphorical) instability of these vehicles is part of a clownish critique about the dangers implicit in modern technology. Indeed, the propensity of Grimaldi's pantomimic steam-packets to explode on stage even prompted a complaint from the *Morning Post* reviewer, who suggested that the blow-up under Vauxhall Bridge 'might by possibility excite a feeling opposed to the interests of those concerned, in improving a discovery of great importance to the world of science, and to mankind in general'.[48] But what is interesting about these tricks of construction is that Grimaldi represents the Clown as a modern inventor in his own right: an ingenious urban entrepreneur for whom technological change merely constitutes another delightful form of consumption.

Grimaldi's tricks included the famous Vegetable Man in Farley's *Harlequin and Asmodeus; or, Cupid on Crutches* (Covent Garden, 1810) whom he assembled from the melons, turnips and carrots garnered from Covent Garden market. Having come to life, the Vegetable Man proceeded to do battle with his own creator; many of the Clown's other

[48] 27 December 1816.

tricks of construction also feature characters who come to galvanic life from clay and tallow.[49] Here, as in his famous satires on contemporary fashion, the Clown subverted the boundaries separating nature and culture, destroying spectators' assumptions about the distinction between that which is alive, and that which has been manufactured. In *Harlequin and the Red Dwarf*, too, Grimaldi notoriously mimicked the modish dress of the Hussars as worn by the Prince Regent and many of his circle. He dressed himself on stage (an act of preparation involving a pose of embarrassed modesty) in a pair of red pantaloons, two black varnished coal scuttles (as boots), together with a white bearskin, a muff and a black tippet. In this act of sartorial improvisation, the exquisite precision and dramatic hauteur of Hussar costume suddenly disintegrates into an collection of objects arbitrarily collected from everyday life.

In *Harlequin Gulliver* (Covent Garden, 1817) Grimaldi developed the satire on female fashions which he had originally presented at Sadler's Wells. The incongruous ingredients for the Clown's female dress in this trick consisted of a plum pudding, a coal scuttle and an iron stovepipe. Again, Grimaldi's attire conspicuously contaminated the delicacy and luxurious narcissism of contemporary dress.[50] By appropriating objects associated with the servants' quarters to parody the world of salons, clubs and elegant drawing-rooms, Grimaldi comically revealed fashion's dark underside of sweat, dirt and industry.[51] At the same time, the Clown's burlesque construction of genteel clothes from items of food questioned those classifications which demarcate what we eat from what we wear. In all Grimaldi's sartorial satires, fashion is cleverly represented both as a form of excessive physical consumption, and also as an activity entailing grotesque bodily contortion.

According to many reviewers, pantomime constituted no more than spectacular, irrational entertainment for children and simple holiday folk. There is a precise, and largely unquestioned correlation, then,

---

49 A version of this trick seems to have been performed by Grimaldi in [Charles Dibdin the Younger], *Harlequin and the Water Kelpe* (Sadler's Wells, 1806). See also [Thomas J. Dibdin], *Harlequin and Fancy*, scene xii, in which Clown builds a man out of earthenware. Cf. *The Times*, 27 December 1828 of Grimaldi, 'He was a sort of Shakspeare in his way, – he exhausted natural monsters, and then "imagined new". *Frankenstein* was nothing to him.'

50 [Charles Farley], *Harlequin Gulliver; or, The Flying Island*, Larpent 2003, scene v.

51 Compare the scene in [Charles Farley], *Harlequin and Friar Bacon; or, The Brazen Head* (Covent Garden, 1820), reviewed *The Times*, 27 December 1820, in which the Clown invades the boudoir of a lady of quality in the costume of a chimney sweeper, and cf. *Humpty Dumpty; or Harlequin and the Fairy of the Enchanted Egg* (Sadler's Wells, 1832), scene vi, in which Clown and Pantaloon ruin the clothes of dandyish characters by covering them with shoe-blacking.

between the lowly cultural status of pantomime,[52] and its alleged patronage by unsophisticated, infantile audiences.[53] The pantomime season did of course coincide with the public holidays of Boxing Day and Easter Monday, days on which 'holyday' audiences eagerly and clamorously packed the galleries of patent and minor theatres alike. But the innovations pioneered at the Wells, not to mention the celebrity of Grimaldi, had transformed pantomime into an entertainment at the cultural and financial heart of London theatrical life. Hence the enthusiasm of leading writers such as Coleridge and Byron, both of whom hoped to capitalise on pantomime's commercial lure. Coleridge's uncompleted dramatic sketches, for example, included a plan for a pantomime 'from a Story in the Tartarian Tales';[54] despite his satirical jibes about pantomime in 'English Bards and Scotch Reviewers' (see line 597), Byron was quick to incorporate its cultural capital into his pantomimic poem, *Don Juan*. For in the hands of Grimaldi and Charles Dibdin, pantomime had emerged as a versatile and virtuosic form whose visual wit, mechanical ingenuity and satirical license seemed to capture the desires and nightmares of a modern metropolis.

As I suggest in chapter 3, pantomime's illegitimate status permitted a certain satirical licence which made possible the theatrical defeat of beadles and constables, or the self-aggrandisement of military men. The skeletal character of pantomime texts, which usually consisted of no more than a brief compendium of scenes and songs, gave away little or nothing to the Examiner of Plays about a pantomime's satirical visual similes and grotesque tricks of construction. For though explicit political comment was avoided, pantomimes nonetheless delighted in the production of oblique, yet telling visual satires: the transformation of a policeman into a scarlet soldier (a jibe at the introduction of the new police force), or the metamorphosis of a roulette wheel into a treadmill

---

[52] Charles Dibdin the Younger bravely attempts a defence of pantomime, arguing that the harlequinade is no less rational than most of 'those indescribable fooleries . . . now commonly exhibited under the name of Farces; and which have done more towards degrading what is called the *legitimate* Stage, than almost any other species of Extravaganza ever produced.' See *Memoirs*, 89. The exclusion of patent pantomimists, with the notable exception of Grimaldi, from the social benefits of the Theatrical Fund established by the patent theatres is one example of pantomime's perceived institutional marginality. See [Charles Dickens], *Memoirs of Joseph Grimaldi*, 249. On the problems of Carlo Delpini, another pantomimist, gaining access to the benefits of the Theatrical Fund, see Findlater, *Grimaldi*, 217.

[53] On pantomime as nursery entertainment, see for example, *The Times*, 28 April 1807 (review of the Wells show) and 5 January 1813 (review of the Covent Garden pantomime). In its account of the Covent Garden pantomime, *The Times*, 27 December 1815, mentions various categories of pantomime spectator, including 'tradesmen freed from labour, busy men from employment'.

[54] Coleridge, *Letters*, in Kathleen Coburn, ed., *Collected Works*, IV: 606.

(a mocking allusion to a recent judgement in which gaming-house owners had been arrested and sentenced to punishment on the tread-mill, before their trial had actually taken place).[55] In a variety of ways, the physical instability of objects and characters in these shows – the sheer uncertainty of its corporeal aesthetic – created the conditions for pantomime's unlicensed retributive laughter.

Leading eighteenth-century critics had dismissed Rich's pantomimes as spectacular mummery. But Grimaldi's satirical verve and corporeal eloquence fascinated contemporary writers. In his satirical remarks about Southey's political apostasy Hazlitt wryly remarked that panto-mime tricks 'often bear a striking resemblance to real life', a theme which Leigh Hunt skilfully developed in the *Examiner*.[56] In these accounts, there is often a sense of contradiction between pantomime's lowly, marginal status and, on the other hand, Grimaldi's expressive genius as a per-former. Take, for example, the comparison between Grimaldi and Edmund Kean in the radical *Champion*. What Grimaldi shares with Edmund Kean, suggests the critic, is the capacity to express feeling and thought in the body rather than through speech. 'He is as facile in expression as that gentleman, and his eye as fully seconds his thoughts; – we think, also, that he is as energetic, and perhaps even excels the tra-gedian in trick and activity.' The writer's slightly hesitant tone here seems to question that hierarchy of genres which assumes that the expressive pleasures of pantomime necessarily pertain to an inferior cul-tural domain from those of tragedy.[57]

Grimaldi's performances, argued several critics, licensed a form of sensuous, psychological release amongst his audiences. His acting com-bined exquisite sentiment – the absurd duet between the Pythagorean Clown and the oyster crossed in love '*moves every muscle* in the house', reported Hazlitt – and a magical innocence, like a child 'waking to per-ception, but wondering at every object he beholds'.[58] In the Clown's alluring naiveté (compare Grimaldi's portrayal of the wild man, as dis-cussed in chapter 3), the world seemed to become new, strange and won-derful, as if for the first time. Similarly, the uncontrollable laughter which broke out at these performances seemed to represent a kind of emotional regeneration:

---

[55] See further, Mayer *Harlequin in His Element*, 266–7.
[56] *Morning Chronicle*, 11 January 1814, *Hazlitt* XIX: 118. Hazlitt compared Southey to a Harlequin who, though cut to pieces and 'nailed piece-meal to the wall, again starts into life, and leaps upon the stage once more'. The article also refers to that famous transformation, first seen in Charles Dibdin's pantomime, *Chaos; or Harlequin Phaeton* (Sadler's Wells, 1800) in which a young chimney sweep was thrown into a cauldron only to emerge as a 'little dapper volunteer'.
[57] *Champion*, 31 December 1815, 421.　　[58] Oxberry, 'Memoirs of Joseph Grimaldi', 119.

all parties seem convulsed with laughter, and their arms, shoulders, features, and whole body, are at once set bustling with delight. In the pit, there immediately appears a sea of pleasure; and the people roll backwards and forwards like waves.[59]

This spontaneous energy exists in vivacious apposition to the political repression and social segregation taking place elsewhere in Regency Britain, widely anatomised in the *Champion* and other radical newspapers. Leigh Hunt's *Examiner* essays develop this theme of pantomime's regenerative character into a mischievous fantasy of political retribution.

Hunt's first article, which appeared in January 1817, began by invoking that familiar topos of dramatic 'decline': 'There is no such thing as modern comedy, tragedy, nor even farce, since Mr. Colman has left off writing it, but Pantomime flourishes as much as ever, and makes all parties comfortable.'[60] But having alluded to generic hierarchies, Hunt then turns the assumptions which underpin them upside down. He admires the 'animal spirit' of pantomime and the pleasurable rhythms of the genre's music, which, 'gay and eternal', run 'merrily through the whole piece, like the pattern of a watered gown'. The pantomime clown, Hunt remarks with evident satisfaction, 'is very stupid, mischievous, gluttonous, and cowardly', and Harlequin, 'perpetual motion personified' (142).

A few weeks later, in his second article, Hunt returns to the theme of pantomime's animal spirit and musical energy:

The stage is never empty or still; either Pantaloon is hobbling about, or somebody is falling flat, or somebody else is receiving an ingenious thump on the face, or the Clown is jolting himself with jaunty dislocations, or Columbine is skimming across like a frightened pigeon, or Harlequin is quivering hither and thither, or gliding out of a window, or slapping something into a metamorphosis.[61]

The jaunty bustle of pantomime – and especially its independence from spoken language – then begins to acquire political connotations. A pantomime, declares Hunt, 'is also the best medium of dramatic satire'. The virtual absence of dialogue in pantomime, he suggests, offers a form of imaginative, and by implication, satirical freedom, leaving the spectators 'to imagine what supplement they please to the mute caricature before them'. The illegitimacy of pantomime, in other words, provides the semiotic preconditions for the genre's imaginative licence. And here, Hunt gradually and craftily envelopes the reader within his radical

---

[59] *Champion*, 31 December 1815, 421.   [60] *Examiner*, 5 January 1817, *LH* 140.
[61] *Examiner*, 26 January 1817, *LH* 144.

fantasy. Harlequin's bat, he continues, makes us think of 'what precious thumps we should like to give some persons' and he imagines

a whole train of them go by at proper distances, like boys coming to be confirmed, – the worldly, the hypocritical, the selfish, the self-sufficient, the gossiping, the traiterous, the ungrateful, the vile-tempered, the ostentatious, the canting, the oppressing, the envious, the sulky, the money-scraping, the prodigiously sweet-voiced, the over-cold, the over-squeezing, the furious, the resenter of inconvenience who has inconvenienced, the cloaker of conscious ill by accusation, the insolent in return for sparing.[62]

Hunt's satirical procession, like those catalogues of political abuses listed in radical pamphlets, disconcertingly juxtaposes the treasonous and the trivial. Indeed, this arbitrary collection of the ostentatious and the oppressive reminds us of the chaotic, episodic quality of the pantomime city. Hunt then proceeds to appropriate pantomime's dramaturgy of benign transformation for his imaginative political manifesto. If only we could place looking-glasses before his patients, he suggests, 'they might know themselves when transformed into their essential shapes, after which they might recover' – and turn the glass on Hunt himself.[63] A familiar pantomimic trope (a scene featuring a plate of cut-glass), is suddenly transformed into a form of moral and political diagnosis.[64] Out of the sheer, contingent disorder of the Regency harlequinade, Leigh Hunt creates an ironic fantasy of England's political regeneration.

In Hunt's description, pantomime is presented as a genre of extraordinary dynamic vitality. The innovations in structure and character pioneered at Sadler's Wells, I have suggested, lie behind this transformation. In Grimaldi's hands, the conventions of pantomime had acquired a powerful satirical dimension as well as a new kind of sentimental eloquence. As Leigh Hunt's interpretation confirms, pantomime's near wordless dramaturgy made possible a special kind of imaginative and political freedom.

ROMANTICISM, ILLEGITIMACY AND EDMUND KEAN

Audiences besieged the doors of Drury Lane for Edmund Kean's performances as Hamlet and as Richard III. The free list had been

---

[62] *LH* 144–5.

[63] Cf. *The Times*, 21 December 1825, 'If comedy holds the mirror up to nature, it is pantomime, with her concave glass, that should, peculiarly, caricature the deformities of the town.'

[64] See especially the temple of cut-glass in [Thomas J. Dibdin], *Harlequin in his Element; or, Fire, Water, Earth, and Air* (Covent Garden, 1807), discussed in detail in Mayer, *Harlequin in His Element*, 207–8. Clown also runs through a mirror in *The Valley of Diamonds; or, Harlequin Sinbad* (Drury Lane, 1814), Larpent MS 1837, scene viii.

suspended, the streets were blocked with crowds and carriages. Bruised, squashed and dishevelled, spectators fought for places in the theatre to watch the actor who had become the metropolitan sensation of 1814.[65] The dark-haired, swarthy Edmund Kean would be lionised at elegant parties where he was taciturn, off-hand, and skulked uncomfortably in corners, eager to escape to a tavern. He would soon be invited to Holland House and fêted by men such as Byron, who presented him with a handsome Turkish sword, by Sir George Beaumont, who made the actor the gift of a Spanish cloak and by Sir Edward Tucker, who bestowed upon him a pet lion. But Kean despised elite sociability, preferring the wilder excitements of prize-fighting, heavy drinking and the disreputable companionship of the Wolf Club, a group of performers, dramatists and camp-followers who met at the Coal Hole Tavern. Then, at night, Kean would be seen galloping furiously out of London on one of his magnificent black horses. Well might Thomas Grattan compare Kean with Byron and Napoleon, describing all three men as '[r]eckless, restless, adventurous, intemperate; brain-fevered by success, desperate in reverse; seeking to outdo their own destiny for good; and rushing upon dangers and difficulties, which they delighted first to make, and then to plunge within . . .'[66]

On 30 March 1814, the diarist Joseph Farington had company for dinner. His guests included John Taylor and Robert Smirke, architect of the new Covent Garden theatre. The conversation soon turned, as it would on several occasions over the next few months, to 'the new popular actor', Edmund Kean. Taylor promptly declared, 'He is an *Humbug*: His acting is often false, & without anything like classical taste, He is a *Pot-House* Actor.'[67] Robert Smirke also dismissed Kean's celebrity and claimed that, in its determination to make the actor popular, the Drury Lane management had simply been packing the theatre with orders. But as the dinner guests conceded, many critics and spectators in London were marvelling at this 'original' and 'extraordinary' performer. On subsequent evenings that spring, the artist Sir Thomas Lawrence acknowledged the power of Kean's acting, and Sir George Beaumont praised Kean's 'bewitching' smile, his fire and electricity. John

---

[65] On the reception of Kean, see the biographies by F. W. Hawkins, *The Life of Edmund Kean* (London: Tinsley Brothers, 1869) and Harold N. Hillebrand, *Edmund Kean* (New York: Columbia University Press, 1933). Leigh Wood's essay, 'Actors' Biography and Mythmaking: The Example of Edmund Kean' in Thomas Postlewait and Bruce McConachie, eds., *Interpreting the Theatrical Past: Essays in the Historiography of Performance* (University of Iowa Press, 1989), 230–47, offers an important cautionary note.

[66] Thomas Colley Grattan, *Beaten Paths; And Those Who Trod Them*, 2 vols. (London, 1862), II: 195.

[67] Joseph Farington, *The Farington Diary*, 8 vols. (London: Hutchinson & Co, 1922–8), VII:228–9.

Taylor, however, remained adamant: 'Kean has art in His acting in attempting to give touches of nature, but it is low, vulgar art, without dignity or elevated conception of character.'[68]

In the controversy about Kean's Shakespearean performances, the language of fire, electricity, lightning and savagery clashed against a rhetoric of dignity, taste, elevation and decorum.[69] For many contemporary observers, Kean's celebrity proved the triumph of 'originality' 'genius' and 'nature' over the stately, classical dignity of the Kemble school. He is a 'wonder', declared Byron, 'his style is quite new – or rather natural – being that of Nature'.[70] From a modern perspective, the language of originality and genius suggests that Kean was a quintessentially *Romantic* performer. As Tracy Davis has argued, Coleridge's famous dictum that seeing Kean act was like 'reading Shakespeare by flashes of lightning', has now acquired the status of an unquestionable verdict.[71] But the danger of romanticising Kean is that we lose sight of his distinctly *illegitimate* revolution.

Kean's 'revolution' in acting, declared a *Blackwood's* critic, was all the more extraordinary 'from its having happened quite unconsciously and unintentionally on the part of its creator, and quite unexpectedly by every one else'.[72] The popular comparison of Kean's acting to electricity similarly assumes his unexpected brilliance and unconscious virtuosity. Such interpretations, however, wilfully misrepresent Kean's deliberate and self-conscious artistry. Far from being a wild, unstudied genius, Kean's theatrical revolution was the work of an iconoclastic actor who defined himself in opposition to the traditions of legitimate performance.

Contemporary reviews of Kean often invoke the discourse of illegitimacy. Pantomime, for example, is a frequent point of reference. Writing

---

[68] See Farington's entries for 23 April 1814, 241, 3 May 1814, 243 and 19 May 1814, 249.

[69] According to Crabb Robinson, Kean's 'most flagrant defect' was 'want of dignity'. See *Diary, Reminiscences and Correspondence of Henry Crabb Robinson* ed. Thomas Sadler, 3 vols. (London, Macmillan & Co., 1869), I: 426. For Hazlitt's views on Kean's detractors, see *Champion*, 8 January 1815, *Hazlitt* 5: 208, and his Preface to *A View of the English Stage*, 5: 176.

[70] Byron, *Letters*, IV: 67. On the language of genius and originality in Hazlitt's reviewing of Kean, see *Hazlitt* IV: 300, V:212; V:225.

[71] '"Reading Shakespeare by Flashes of Lightning": Challenging the Foundations of Romantic Acting Theory', *ELH* 62 (1995), 933–54. Davis argues that the divided opinions about Kean's performance can be explained to a large extent by the 'physical and optical circumstances' of watching by gaslight. Coleridge's comment is recorded in Henry Nelson Coleridge, *Specimens of the Table Talk of Samuel Taylor Coleridge*, 2nd edition (London: John Murray, 1836), 13. On Kean as a 'typical "Romantic"', see Jonathan Bate, *Shakespearean Constitutions: Politics, Theatre, Criticism 1730–1830* (Oxford: Clarendon, 1989), 141.

[72] Cited F. W. Hawkins, *The Life of Edmund Kean* (London: Tinsley Brothers, 1869), I: 201.

about a performance of Edward Young's *The Revenge*, in which Kean had played the part of Zanga, Hazlitt stoutly objected to Kean's 'pantomimic exaggeration'.[73] According to Hazlitt, Kean's hyperbolic gestures in the role were ostentatious and incongruous, a too-self-conscious ploy for quick theatrical effect. Indeed, as Hazlitt later complained in his review of Kean's Richard II, the 'pantomime part of tragedy' told on the stage simply because it provided the greatest opportunity for 'inexpressible dumb-show and noise'.[74] But other critics invoked the genre of pantomime in admiration rather than in rebuke: Henry Crabb Robinson praised Kean's 'fine pantomimic face and remarkable agility'.[75]

The language of illegitimacy – 'extravagance', 'agitation', and 'excess' – pervades the reviewing of Kean.[76] In particular, reviewers were fascinated by the corporeal intensity of Kean's Shakespearean heroes. Hazlitt eloquently recorded the 'convulsed motion of the hands and the involuntary swelling of the veins in the forehead' in Kean's Othello, and Kean's early biographers recalled the actor's 'quivering blood-stained hands' and the 'shuddering agony with which he refused to carry back the daggers' as Macbeth.[77] Kean had translated that tremulous, agitated body at the heart of melodramatic performance into the interpretation of Shakespearean tragedy.

Kean had served his dramatic apprenticeship as acrobat, swordsman, Gothic villain and as Harlequin (in which role he was famous for his dying scenes, and his acrobatic leaps through hoops of fire). In contemporary dramas such as George Colman's *Blue-Beard* and *The Iron Chest*, James Kenney's domestic melodrama, *Ella Rosenburg* and Holcroft's *A Tale of Mystery* (in which he played the aristocratic villain, Romaldi), as well as in his 'savage' roles in pantomimical ballets, Kean had perfected those hyperbolic gestural codes, expressive signs and muscular postures which characterised illegitimate performance.[78] As we have seen, sudden, extreme transitions between emotions – from rage to pathos, from psychological torment to farcical laughter – dominated melodramatic

[73] *Hazlitt* V: 228.

[74] *Examiner*, 19 March 1815, *Hazlitt* V: 222. On Kean's 'pantomimic evolutions', see also IV: 298.

[75] Henry Crabb Robinson, *Diary*, 7 March 1814, I:426.

[76] On Kean's 'extravagance', see Hazlitt, *Champion*, 9 October 1814, *Hazlitt* V: 201 and also V: 223, V: 271, V: 258. For the language of 'agitation', see Old Playgoer, An (pseud.), *Desultory Thoughts on the National Drama, Past and Present* (London: Onwhyn, 1850), 48. On Kean's 'excess', see *Hazlitt* IV: 299.   [77] *The Times*, 27 October 1817, *Hazlitt* XVIII: 263; Hawkins, *Life of Edmund Kean*, I:273–4.

[78] On Kean's early career, see *William Cotton, The Story of the Drama in Exeter, during its best period, 1787 to 1823. With Reminiscences of Edmund Kean* (London: Hamilton, Adams and Co., 1887), 26–9.

acting; many of Kean's most celebrated innovations in Shakespearean performance similarly featured virtuosic transitions of mood. In the scene where Othello is baited by Iago, for example, 'the alternations of excruciating suspicion, and tender recollection, were depicted with a force, a pathos, and a power of expression that were perfectly electrical'.[79] Kean's sudden, jeering laughter at the speech, 'Chop off his head' in *Richard III* became another famous theatrical 'point'.[80] But reviewers also expressed displeasure about the self-conscious fracturing of dramatic illusion which these transitions often produced. Kean, declared Leigh Hunt, 'is much farther gone in stage trickery than we supposed him to be, particularly in the old violent contrasts when delivering an equivoque, dropping his voice too consciously from a serious line to a sly one, and fairly putting it to the house as a good joke'.[81] Whereas such juxtapositions helped to define melodrama's distinctive clashes of emotion, almost as if performer and actor self-consciously colluded in the excess of feeling, critics deplored their appearance in Shakespearean tragedy.

In action, rather than language, lay the poetic intensity of Kean's most successful tragic characters. As Hazlitt declared, 'Mr. Kean affects the audience from the force of passion instead of sentiment, or sinks into pathos from the violence of action, but seldom rises into it from the power of thought and feeling.'[82] This combination of pathos and emotional violence gave Kean's Shakespearean characters their strangely impassioned fervour; the psychology of Kean's tragic heroes, like that of the tormented villains of Gothic melodrama, seemed to arise from the bodily passions which spring from pain.[83] Similarly, Kean's mastery of mute business – his long melodramatic pauses and wordless sounds, apparently suspended between silence and speech – also confirms his awareness of illegitimate stage effects. Reviewers often remarked how Kean's body seemed to speak words without saying them: his characters appeared to cross over into a world where, as if prohibited or tran-

[79] *Theatrical Inquisitor*, May 1814, 4: 307. Cf. *Hazlitt* IV: 299 on Kean's Richard III, 'The frequent and rapid transition of his voice from the expression of the fiercest passion to the most familiar tones of conversation was that which gave a peculiar grace of novelty to his acting on his first appearance.'   [80] [Thomas Barnes], *Examiner*, 27 February 1814, 138.

[81] Review of *Richard III*, *Examiner*, 26 February 1815, *LH* 113.

[82] Hazlitt on Kean's Romeo, *Champion*, 8 January 1815, *Hazlitt* V: 210. On the death scene in *Richard III* as 'a piece of noble poetry, expressed by action instead of language', see Barnes' review, *Examiner*, 1814, 138.

[83] Compare *Hazlitt* V: 209, 'Mr Kean's imagination appears not to have the principles of joy, or hope, or love in it. He seems chiefly sensible to pain, or the passions which spring from it, and to the terrible energies of mind or body, which are necessary to grapple with, or to avert it.'

scended, speech had disappeared.[84] The actor's most famous pieces of mute business were the lines drawn on the ground, with the point of his sword, in *Richard III*, and also his impulsive return in *Hamlet*, 'from a pang of parting tenderness', to press his lips to Ophelia's hand, at the end of the nunnery scene. Like the kiss he bestowed as Bertram on Imogen's child, the poignancy of Kean's gestural epilogue arose from a sudden, melodramatic transition from angry vitriol to wordless gentleness. This moment of unspoken emotion, Hazlitt remembered, 'had an electrical effect on the house'; the prince's kiss became 'the finest commentary that was ever made on Shakespear.'[85] And here is Hazlitt's elegant sleight of hand: the finest commentary ever made is one made without language at all.

Illegitimate performance, as we have seen, privileged the expressive silence of mute characters. Stylised postures and dramatic tableaux highlighted contrasts between movement and stasis, silence and speech. To a large extent, the uneven, jerky rhythms of Kean's verse represented a self-conscious rejection of that smooth, decorous, articulation characteristic of Kemble and his followers. Indeed, as a young actor, Kean had made his living from staging one-man shows at such venues as the Great Room in Bedford Square in which he parodied the stiff hauteur of leading metropolitan performers. In his Shakespearean interpretations, Kean appears to have introduced into blank verse that musical articulation which was characteristic of illegitimate diction. Take, for example, two descriptions of Othello's farewell, one of Kean's most celebrated roles. To Hazlitt and George Vandenhoff, Kean's speech seemed to dissipate language into music: the apostrophe '*struck* on the heart and the imagination like the swelling notes of some divine music'.[86] According to Vandenhoff, Kean ran 'on the same tones and semitones' with 'the same rests and breaks, the same forte and piano, the same crescendo and diminuendo, night after night, as if he spoke it from a musical score.'[87] The pace and emotional pitch of Othello's farewell suggest that

---

[84] On Kean's dissolution of speech into feeling, see Hawkins, *Life of Edmund Kean*, 1: 288 and Hazlitt's review of *Romeo and Juliet*, *Champion*, 8 January 1815, *Hazlitt* v:210: '[I]n the midst of the extravagant and irresistible expression of Romeo's grief, at being banished from the object of his love', Hazlitt recalled, Kean's voice 'suddenly stops, and faulters, and is choaked with sobs of tenderness, when he comes to Juliet's name. Those persons must be made of sterner stuff than ourselves, who are proof against Mr. Kean's acting, both in this scene, and in his dying convulsion at the close of the play.'   [85] *Morning Chronicle*, 14 March 1814, *Hazlitt* v:188.

[86] *Morning Chronicle*, 6 May 1814, *Hazlitt* v:189, my emphasis.

[87] *Dramatic Reminiscences*, cited Harold N. Hillebrand, *Edmund Kean* (New York: Columbia University Press, 1933), 128. Cf. Crabb Robinson's diary entry, 1: 430, recording his own wordless response to Othello's farewell as spoken by Kean: 'I could hardly keep from crying: it was pure feeling.'

melodrama's musical orchestration had migrated into Shakespearean tragedy.

'Mr. Kean's style of acting,' declared Hazlitt boldly, 'is not in the least of the unpremeditated, *improvisatori* kind: it is throughout elaborate and systematic, instead of being loose, off-hand, and accidental.'[88] Hazlitt, I think, is right to reject the description of Kean as an unstudied genius; as his comments suggest, Kean's savage energy and muscular vitality represent the outward signs of an illegitimate revolution in tragic performance. For many critics, however, that revolution seemed to threaten the plebeian invasion of Shakespearean tragedy. Reviewers and versifiers therefore closed ranks, dismissing Kean as a vulgar actor whose class and education rendered him incapable of even understanding elite culture. In the words of these detractors, Kean was an actor merely bred 'to tumble for his meat / To act the monkey in plebeian street', to grin in barns 'as Harlequin or droll'.[89] The performer's illegitimate birth, uncouth body, hoarse voice (which Leigh Hunt comically compared to that of 'a hackney-coachman's at one o'clock in the morning'), poor education, scant knowledge of literature and social gracelessness all proved his absolute unfitness to perform Shakespearean tragedy.[90]

An interesting parallel exists between the mockery of Edmund Kean's lowly social origins and illegitimate apprenticeship in the role of Harlequin, and the critical disdain which greeted John Keats. In both cases, the language of vulgarity neatly encompasses accusations of stylistic uncouthness and social pretension, as well as charges of unjustified aesthetic innovation. Recently, scholars have begun to investigate more closely the use of the term 'Cockney' in the definition of Keats' alleged aesthetic, moral and political deviance.[91] Indeed, the ideological connotations of Keats' Cockneyism – vulgarity, radicalism, profanity and lack of gentility – demonstrate the unacknowledged similarities between the reception of Keats' poetry and that of Edmund Kean's performances. For the arguments which were being sociably waged at the house of John Farington and in the pages of the *Examiner* over Kean's 'vulgarity' and 'originality' during 1814 and 1815 in many ways anticipate the ideological and aesthetic terms of the Cockney debate. Edmund Kean came

[88] *Hazlitt* v: 202.
[89] *Literary Gazette*, cited Giles Playfair, *Kean* (New York: E.P. Dutton, 1939), 240; on Kean's humble origins, see *Blackwood's Edinburgh Magazine*, September 1824, 16: 272.
[90] *Examiner*, 26 February 1815, *LH* 114.
[91] See Nicholas Roe, *John Keats and the Culture of Dissent* (Oxford: Clarendon, 1997), 60.

to represent the (splendidly flawed) theatrical hero of the Cockney School.[92]

The critical home of the Cockney writers was of course Leigh Hunt's newspaper, *The Examiner*. Scholars of Cockneyism, however, seem to have neglected the crucial and exciting role played by dramatic spectatorship and theatre criticism in Cockney culture.[93] For in Kean's illegitimate performances, these reviewers began to explore what a radical modern dramaturgy might mean. No wonder, then, that one of the *Blackwood's* reviewers was determined to dismiss Kean's celebrity as no more than the theatrical sideshow of Cockneyism. Kean, declared this reviewer, was simply a vulgar actor puffed up by a 'knot of numskulls'. 'The whole tribe puffed Kean, and silenced the voice of common sense. We of this Magazine glorify ourselves for having put an end for ever to such folly.'[94]

Kean's celebrity threatened to dissolve the generic and, by implication, the social and political distinctions between Shakespearean tragedy and illegitimate theatre.[95] His performances seemed to challenge the myth of Shakespeare's aristocratic politics (as defined by critics such as Coleridge), and indeed the playwright's unquestioned position as the cultural symbol of the political establishment. In Hazlitt, Kean found a reviewer eager to show how illegitimate performance violently disrupted the decorous traditions and moral certainties of Shakespearean character criticism. Indeed, Hazlitt's most polemical interpretations originate from a set of questions and amiable quarrels with Kean about the politics of Shakespearean character. In one of his *Examiner* reviews, for instance, Hazlitt slides almost imperceptibly from a discussion of Kean's Iago ('one of the most extraordinary exhibitions on the stage') to a sly and tendentious description of Shakespeare's villain as 'a true prototype

---

[92] As recent monographs by Jeffrey Cox and Nicholas Roe have shown, the 'Cockney School' represented a crucial site of political and literary opposition dedicated to the radical reform of England through poetry and criticism. What we call the second generation of Romantic poets, suggests Cox, 'is not merely a temporal gathering, but a self-consciously defined group' at the centre of which were Leigh Hunt, Keats and Hazlitt. See Jeffrey N. Cox, *Poetry and Politics in the Cockney School: Keats, Shelley, Hunt and their Circle* (Cambridge University Press, 1998), 4. On Kean's followers constituting a 'critical religion', see Leigh Hunt, *Autobiography* I: 173. Hazlitt, however, was as quick to point out Kean's defects as he was to admire his genius. See especially *Hazlitt* V: 204; on Kean's cold, tame, lifeless Romeo, see V: 209.

[93] See, for example, 'Cockney Contributions for the First of April', *Blackwood's*, July 1824, 16: 67–71, 69–70 which parodies Leigh Hunt's theatrical criticism.

[94] Review of the *Biography of the British Stage*, *Blackwood's*, September 1824, 16: 271–6, 275.

[95] On Kean's habit of *levelling* Shakespeare into *'conversational* form', see Finlay, *Miscellanies*, 209–14.

of modern Jacobinism'.[96] In this account, Kean's portrayal of Iago's gay demonism provides the theatrical script for Hazlitt's dangerously revisionist interpretation of Shakespearean morality.

For Hazlitt, Kean represented a radical performer who was above all 'the antithesis of a court-actor'.[97] Whereas the object of the court, and the Kemble school, was 'to suppress and varnish over the feelings', Kean's acting gave way to feeling. 'His *overt* manner must shock them,' Hazlitt reflects, with an air of solemn portent, 'and be thought a breach of all decorum.'[98] In the sly irony of 'all decorum', Hazlitt delightedly evokes a fantasy of theatrical disorder being suddenly unleashed on the world. For what made Kean's performances subversive was precisely that his breaches of theatrical decorum might in some way be proleptic of a wider, still more unpredictable, collapse. Hazlitt's criticism of Kean thus takes the form of playful sedition: these illegitimate performances dare to imagine the disintegration of the British political and cultural state.

Kean's performances in Shakespearean roles, as well as in melodrama and revenge tragedy, captivated a generation of playwrights. In the final section of this chapter, I want to consider one example of Kean's illegitimacy, as inscribed within contemporary tragedy. Like Maturin's *Manuel* (Drury Lane, 1817), Shelley's *The Cenci* (1819, unperformed during Shelley's life), and Byron's *Sardanapalus* (1821, performed Drury Lane, 1834), *Otho the Great* is a tragedy imagined for Edmund Kean.[99] Although the relationship between Kean, dramatic text and theatrical performance is different in every case, all these plays (together with *Bertram*, in which play Kean starred in the Drury Lane production) can usefully be defined as illegitimate tragedies. In other words, each play attempts to re-imagine tragedy in the wake of Edmund Kean's illegitimate revolution.

---

[96] *Examiner*, 21 July 1814, *Hazlitt* V: 212. On this point, see Jonathan Bate's subtle and persuasive argument in *Shakespearean Constitutions*, 160–2. [97] On Kean's radicalism, see *Hazlitt* XIX: 257.

[98] 'On the Spirit of Monarchy', *Liberal*, January 1823, *Hazlitt* XIX: 257.

[99] Published in 1848, *Otho* was not performed during Keats' lifetime. On *Sardanapalus*, see Peter Manning, 'Edmund Kean and Byron's Plays', *Keats–Shelley Journal* 21–2 (1972–3), 188–206. According to Manning, 'The acting of Edmund Kean is as much part of the genealogy of *Sardanapalus* as Dryden's *All for Love*, or as Otway's *Venice Preserv'd* is of Byron's *Marino Faliero*' (201). On Maturin's plays, see John B. Harris, *Charles Robert Maturin: The Forgotten Imitator* (New York: Arno Press, 1980). Bertram's fiend-like glory and amoral demonism provided an important theatrical precedent for Count Cenci, a role designed by Shelley for Edmund Kean to perform. See *The Letters of Percy Bysshe Shelley* ed. F. L. Jones, 2 vols. (Oxford: Clarendon, 1964), II: 8; *Shelley's Poetry and Prose*, eds. Donald H. Reiman and Sharon B. Powers (New York: Norton, 1977), 391.

What I want to suggest is that the much-maligned *Otho the Great* is Keats' dramatic experiment in notating the moral and political landscape of illegitimacy. The critic Francis Jeffrey robustly castigated the 'puerile extravagance and absolute bombast' of Ludolph's passionate speeches; twentieth-century scholars have also been quick to deride Keats' sub-Shakespearean dramaturgy.[100] But Ludolph's sensuality, hyperbolic intensity, and romantic bewitchment should more properly be interpreted as Keats' attempt to translate Edmund Kean's passionate indecorum into the idiom of contemporary tragedy. Moreover, Ludolph's disdainful opposition to court politics seems to mirror Kean's own position as a theatrical and political dissenter. In our 'unimaginative days', Keats had written two years earlier in his review of Kean, 'Habeas Corpus'd as we are out of all wonder, curiosity, and fear', we feel grateful for the passion and excitement of Kean's performances. 'He is a relic of romance; a posthumous ray of chivalry.'[101] For John Keats, the actor's illegitimate excess came to represent a redemptive, imaginative counterweight to the deadening pressures of a tyrannical political state: Ludolph's romantic extravagance converts this rhapsodic interpretation of Kean into dramatic poetry.

In Maturin's *Bertram*, a play which offers some interesting parallels with *Otho*, the hero's thwarted romantic passion mutates into that fiery, convulsive anarchy in which 'each upstart humour, or phrensy of the moment, is struggling to get violent possession of some bit or corner of his fiery soul and pigmy body'.[102] But in *Otho the Great*, set amid the tenth-century court of the Roman Emperor during the Hungarian wars, what fascinates Keats is the incommensurable character of political dissent and sexual passion. Like Maturin, Keats chooses to highlight the corporeal nature of Ludolph's passion, his shadowy existence on the borders of bodily disintegration. When I dream of you, 'my brain will split', Ludolph tells Otho (iii.ii. lines 203–4); the prince becomes suddenly violent, as in iii.ii when he orders his lover Auranthe, and Conrad, to be thrown from the windows, momentarily jocular (a famous characteristic

---

[100] Letter to R. M. Milnes, 15 August 1848, in G. M. Matthews, ed., *Keats: The Critical Heritage* (London: Routledge, 1971), 209. On the play's critical history, see R. S. White's helpful remarks in *Keats as a Reader of Shakespeare* (London: Athlone Press, 1987), 204–8. For *Otho* as a drama about the theatrical character of personal identity, see Charles J. Rzepka, '*Theatrum Mundi* and Keats's *Otho the Great*: The Self in Society', *Romanticism Past and Present* 8 (Winter 1984), 35–50.

[101] 'On Edmund Kean as a Shakespearian Actor', *Champion*, 21 December 1817, in *The Poetical Works and Other Writings of John Keats*, ed. H. B. Forman, revised M. B. Forman, 8 vols. (London, 1938–9), v: 229–30.   [102] *London Magazine*, February 1820, *Hazlitt* xviii: 284, of Kean's acting.

of Kean's Shakespearean roles), and susceptible to internal convulsions (iv.ii. line 598). He is possessed, too, by a love which dangerously exceeds courtly decorum: 'He soars!' declares the First Lady, and the Second responds with satirical amazement, 'Past all reason' (iii.ii. line 37). Later in the play, Ludolph disturbingly imagines Auranthe's alleged betrayal of him as the preying and 'gnawing' of a scorpion upon his brain (v.v. lines 155–8). Amidst the fen-like stupor of Otho's court, then, Ludolph's passion is vital, dynamic, transgressive.[103]

The rhythms of Ludolph's passion – discontinuous and jerky, full of hesitation and exclamation – mirror the whirlwind pace and lightning transitions which marked Kean's illegitimate iconography. In the speech, 'Must I stop here? Here solitary die?' Ludolph muses on how Auranthe's death has forestalled his own revenge:

> Silent – without revenge? – pshaw! – bitter end –
> A bitter death – a suffocating death –
> A gnawing – silent – deadly – quiet death!
> Escaped? fled? vanished? Melted into air?
> She's gone! – I cannot clutch her! No revenge!   (v.i. lines 21–5)

Auranthe's death is imagined here in grotesque language which is strongly reminiscent of the terrible, consumptive mortality depicted in *The Eve of St Agnes*. But what is also noticeable about this speech is its intense disjointedness. Silence and quiet are juxtaposed against the painful sounds of gnawing and suffocating; Ludolph is torn between construing Auranthe's death as gentle disappearance, or as violent, sensory dismemberment. And what Keats seems to be noting here are the inchoate, trembling sounds of Kean's speech – interrogative, full of doubtful pauses and sudden, explosive exclamations.

In *Otho the Great*, Keats attempt to portray passion as a form of political opposition in its own right. Before the play begins, Ludolph has joined the Red Duke, Conrad of Lorraine, in fermenting rebellion, only to change sides quite suddenly in order to fight on behalf of his father, Otho, in the final battle. Later in the play, Ludolph dismisses his involvement in the rebellion and refers pityingly to his fellow rebels as 'self-deceivèd wretches' (i.iii. line 76). But though Ludolph portrays himself as the victim of plotting men, he nonetheless seems utterly divided between the contradictory impulses of passionate protest and filial subordination. For Daniel Watkins, *Otho* reveals the contradiction between

---

[103] References to *Otho the Great* are cited from *The Poems of John Keats*, ed. Miriam Allott (London: Longman, 1970).

'ideological representation' (the ability of the state to incorporate and absorb dissidence) and 'material reality' (the instability of feudal relations in the play, notably of religion and marriage).[104] Certainly, the endless references by Ludolph and others to Otho's 'noble' nature and paternal kindness dovetail uneasily with the political stalemate and atmosphere of imminent conspiracy at Otho's court. But for all his magnanimous behaviour towards Gersa (the leader of the Hungarians), and his pious decision to liberate the 'holy sisterhood' kept in thraldom by the enemy, Otho nonetheless appears in the play as an imperious figure, intemperate and arbitrary in his judgements. Possessive and manipulative, the Emperor actually seems to rule his people as if they were animals rather than citizens. In Act v, for example, he summons the knights to the banqueting hall and keeps them there indefinitely, 'grievously' tantalised, 'Swayed here and there, commanded to and fro, / As though we were the shadows of a dream / And linked to a sleeping fancy' (First Knight, v.v. lines 2–4). In Otho, political and familial tyranny seem to have become disturbingly synonymous.

The marble columns and imperial domes of Otho's power evoke the Emperor's hollow paternalism. Otho's benevolent, yet suffocating relationship with his son exemplifies the opposing imperatives of liberty and imprisonment. For Ludolph's passion seems to arise from both a yearning desire for romantic autonomy (his father initially opposes his marriage to Auranthe) and also an incipient political rebellion against imperial power. 'Disobedience, / Rebellion, obstinacy, blasphemy, / Are all my counsellors' (II.i. lines 105–7), he tells Otho in a tone of repentant irony; elsewhere, however, in his recognition of Conrad's political opportunism, and especially in his description of Otho's courtiers – 'prodigious sycophants' who plot and gossip, disturbing '[t]he soul's fine palate' like he who breathes 'the discoloured poisons of a fen' (II.i. line 22) – Ludolph appears all too aware of the systemic hypocrisy and murky cynicism which lie at the heart of empire. Just like his theatrical model, Edmund Kean, the princely Ludolph refuses to be a 'court-actor'.

Keats' declared ambition was to bring about 'as great a revolution in modern dramatic writing as Kean has done in acting'.[105] His collaboration on *Otho* with Charles Brown, in the summer of 1819, had aimed to

---

[104] Watkins, *A Materialist Critique of English Romantic Drama* (Gainesville: University of Florida Press, 1993), 209.

[105] Letter to Benjamin Bailey, 14 August 1819, in H. E. Rollins, *The Letters of John Keats, 1814–1821*, 2 vols. (Cambridge, Mass.: Harvard University Press), II: 139.

transform his reputation ('My name with the literary fashionables is vulgar – I am a weaver boy to them – a Tragedy would lift me out of this mess'[106]), as well as the perilous state of his finances.[107] Keats' correspondence also reveals the poet's contradictory desires – to become 'a popular writer' and, at the same time, to avoid being contaminated by 'the poisonous suffrage of a public'.[108] And what Keats produced from this confusion of desires, I think, was an experiment in the writing of Cockney tragedy. Hazlitt's and Hunt's reviews, of course, had already defined Edmund Kean as a Cockney hero; in his *Champion* essay, Keats himself had portrayed the performer as a symbol of romantic freedom amidst political oppression. To imagine Ludolph as a role for Kean was thus to evoke a powerful dissenting history. Moreover, the writing of *Otho* took place at a time when Keats was deeply preoccupied with the historical and contemporary tensions between monarchical power and the rights of the common people, an issue which also underpins the struggle for power within *Otho the Great*.[109] In a variety of ways, Keats' tragedy thus seems to provide a dramatic bridge between the sensuous expansiveness of his early poetry, and the political world of Cockney theatre criticism.

Whilst rehearsing the betrayal which leads to his own tragic disintegration, Ludolph's passion for Auranthe provides the opportunity to construct an alternative, ideal world of Keatsian chivalry and romance: 'Though heaven's choir / Should in a vast circumference descend / And sing for my delight, I'd stop my ears!' (III.ii. lines 38–40). In the face of betrayal, however, Ludolph's inchoate political opposition disintegrates into love's madness. Overwrought by the 'tight-wound energies of his despair,' and frustrated in his attempts to practise 'fine-spun vengeance' on Auranthe, Ludolph dies, still seeking out his father's hand, and poignantly exclaiming about the sultriness of the air. A relic of chivalry and

---

[106] *Ibid.*, Letter to George and Georgiana Keats, 17–27 September 1819 II: 184–218.

[107] The plot seems to have been proposed by Brown, though Keats rejected the 'melodramatic' incidents proposed for Act v in favour of his own denouement. Brown MS, cited in *The Poems of John Keats*, ed. E. de Sélincourt (London: Methuen and Co, 1926), 552.

[108] Keats, *Letters* II: 144, 146.

[109] Keats, *Letters* II: see the long journal letter to George and Georgiana Keats, 17–27 September 1819, in which Keats alludes to his tragedy and includes a miniature history of monarchical power. In his account, Keats describes the 'gradual annihilation of the tyranny of the nobles, when kings found it their interest to conciliate the common people, elevate them, and be just to them'. This period was followed, he suggests, by a time during which kings colluded with the nobles against the people, and a long struggle took place 'to destroy popular privileges' (193). Contemporary social and economic distress in Britain, he suggests, will now provide a catalyst for popular rebellion.

passion (as Keats had written of Edmund Kean), Ludolph nonetheless leaves the earth as 'Habeas Corpus'd' as his father's courtiers. His passion ultimately nullifies his political dissent.

My reading of Keats' *Otho the Great* has attempted to establish a framework for interpreting the illegitimate genealogy of those 'Romantic' tragedies written for Edmund Kean. The composition of such plays, I have argued, entailed far more than cashing in on London's leading theatrical celebrity, or dully capitulating to the 'tyranny' of acting over authorship.[110] On the contrary, Kean's dramatic iconoclasm actually made imaginable characters such as Ludolph. Ironically, however, Kean's departure for America ('the worst news I could have had', reported Keats, dolefully)[111] ensured that actor and character were never united; having received a summary rejection from Covent Garden, Keats gave up the hope that his tragedy would ever reach the stage.

Regency audiences never had the opportunity to watch Edmund Kean as the princely, incurably romantic, tragic Ludolph. Yet Kean exerted a great influence over contemporary playwriting and reviewing. In particular, his wild, indecorous characters radically changed the direction of Shakespearean criticism. Few contemporary performers – let alone actors who had made their name as Harlequin, leaping through hoops of fire – could have claimed as much. Just as Joseph Grimaldi had reinvented the cultural status and political meanings of pantomime, so Edmund Kean reimagined the heroes of Shakespearean tragedy. At the heart of this revolution lay the genres and iconography of illegitimate theatre.

---

[110] For Keats' and Brown's deliberations about theatrical effect in *Otho*, and especially for Brown's suggestion that an elephant might be introduced, presumably as a sop to popular taste, see Keats' letter to C. W. Dilke, 31 July 1819, *Letters* II: 135. On the tyrannical usurpation of authorship by stage celebrity (a frequent theme in contemporary criticism), see Timothy Webb, 'The Romantic Poet and the Stage' in *The Romantic Theatre: An International Symposium*, Richard Allen Cave ed. (Gerrard's Cross: Colin Smythe, 1986), 9–46, 37.

[111] Letter to George and Georgiana Keats, *Letters* II: 186. See also *Letters* II: 241.

Epilogue

Illegitimate theatre was a culture of spectacular conflagration, urban entrepreneurship and social metamorphosis. The genres of extravaganza, pantomime, melodrama and burletta staged dramatic characters and theatrical subjects never before represented on the London stage: farcical heroes like Lothario Larkins who inhabit a proto-absurdist universe on the edge of dissolution, vengeful slaves such as three-fingered Obi and the bitter Negro of Wapping, Grimaldi's wily, anarchic Clown, and the mute eloquence of Céleste's forsaken women. From a collection of miscellaneous entertainments – swordsmanship and slack-rope dancing, comic songs and circus acts – arose a lively, original culture whose commercial success and dramatic vitality all but usurped legitimate drama.

The predominance of language and rhetoric in tragedy and comedy gave way in illegitimate culture to a corporeal dramaturgy which highlighted the expressive body of the performer. The benevolent reconciliations characteristic of sentimental comedy were overturned by violent clashes between nations and social classes, for illegitimate plays are preoccupied with the idea that the world – and especially the Orient – has become a place of intense ideological conflict. Melodrama and pantomime, however, also question the nature of political authority, especially the authority of the state. By utterly changing how the world could be imagined on stage, these plays and performers also radically shaped the politics and dramaturgy of Romantic playwriting.

Illegitimate genres transformed the characters and dramatic subjects being represented on the British stage. Sounds, images and narratives are woven together to create incongruous, *pasticchio* effects; subversive dramaturgy is confounded by moral plotting, sometimes with ironic consequences. Moreover, certain plays staged at the minor theatres beyond Westminster dramatise savage, diabolical or criminal subjects which would certainly have been censored, if not actually forbidden, by the

Examiner of Plays. These occasional violations and illicit acts of trespass were nonetheless cautious, calculated and disingenously wrapped in sugary moral publicity; shrewd managers knew all too well the dangers of alienating their audiences, or indeed the local magistrates.

By removing the institutional distinction between the patent and the minor theatres, the Theatre Regulation Act abolished the category of illegitimate theatre. Melodrama, burletta, extravaganza and pantomime did not vanish, of course, but their position as genres on the cultural margins of the metropolis changed for ever; now the Pavilion, the Surrey and the Coburg theatres were licensed to stage Massinger, Sheridan and Shakespeare, without the subterfuges of music, scrolls and doggerel verse. Following the views of early nineteenth-century commentators and pamphleteers, theatre historians often describe the Theatre Regulation Act as a triumphant victory for dramatic free trade. In many ways, this is true; at the same time, however, the abolition of monopoly also brought about the political disappearance of a once irrepressible theatrical culture. Apart from overturning the conventions of British drama, the phenomenon of illegitimate theatre had also revealed to dramatic audiences the deeply political character of cultural institutions. Even after 1843, however, the concept of dramatic illegitimacy was not lost entirely. For in many ways, arguments about the morality of illegitimate plays, and about the relationship between art and entertainment, would re-emerge in the classification and reception of British music-hall. The novelist Angela Carter evocatively recalls these cultural hierarchies in *Wise Children* (1991), when Dora Chance explains to the reader, '[N]ot only are Nora and I, as I have already told you, by-blows, but our father was a pillar of the legit. theatre and we girls were illegitimate in every way – not only born out of wedlock, but we went on the halls, didn't we.' 'Romantic illegitimacy,' she observes ruefully, 'always a seller.'[1]

Far from being an invisible or incidental structure, the institution of patent monopoly powerfully determined the nature of dramatic authorship, the conditions of theatrical production, and the experience of spectatorship. As I have shown, the politics of monopoly – and especially Shakespeare's position as a legitimate playwright – lie at the heart of Romantic theatre criticism. At the centre of debates about theatrical regulation in this period are a set of difficult questions about the meaning and consequences of cultural democracy. How should the cultural state be regulated? Which theatres should be licensed to perform

---

[1] *Wise Children*, first published 1991 (London: Vintage, 1992), 11.

Shakespeare? Should public taste be allowed to determine the dramatic repertoire? How might the state encourage and support dramatic literature? Late Georgian culture was a period marked by profound anxieties about theatre as a potential site of political excitement and social disorder; it is remarkable too for the questions raised about who should be held responsible for the vitality of a nation's drama.

The political and dramatic clash between legitimate and illegitimate culture defined the terms of cultural debate in late Georgian London. What is more, many of the critical values disputed there still haunt our modern judgements about cultural hierarchy, Shakespearean politics, and the nature of the imagination. Having abandoned our idealistic Romantic assumptions about dramatic audiences and institutions, and set aside nineteenth-century judgements about the (legitimate) drama's 'decline', we can now begin to recognise the revolution brought about by illegitimate theatre.

Select bibliography

This bibliography is divided into the following sections:
(i)   Theatre manuscripts
(ii) Plays
(iii) Newspapers and journals
(iv) Other primary sources
(v)   Secondary sources

Note on playbill collections and theatrical ephemera

Unless otherwise mentioned, the playbills cited in this book are from the collections in the British Library. Other major archives consulted for this study include the Harvard Theatre Collection, Harvard University; the John Johnson collection of printed ephemera in the Bodleian Library, Oxford; the Noble collection in the Guildhall Library, London; and the archives held at the Theatre Museum in London. For playbills of Shakespearean performances, I have also referred to the archives at the Birmingham Shakespeare Library and the Folger Shakespeare Library. London libraries with useful collections of bills and cuttings include the Southwark Local History Library, the Tower Hamlets Public Library and the Victoria Library in Westminster. For toy theatre, I have used the Jonathan King Collection of Juvenile Drama at the Museum of London and the Brady Collection, Christ Church, Oxford.

The Theatre Museum archives for this period contain many reviews which are filed with the playbills for individual theatres. I have also referred to the various scapbooks held in the British Library (see the Place Newspaper Collection, set 59, 2 vols., 'Astley's cuttings from newspapers', 3 vols., 'Collections relating to Sadler's Wells', 3 vols., and the scrapbook of press cuttings on London theatres, c. 1780–1825). Other reviews can be found in the archives of the Garrick Club, the Guildhall Library (see especially J. P. Kemble, 'A Collection of Gleanings from Periodicals and Newspapers 1711–1768; consisting principally of Advertisements respecting Theatrical Performances, Fairs, etc. etc., in London and the Provinces', 2 vols., and 'A collection of cuttings, playbills, mss notes and other material relating to Bartholemew Fair and Pie Powder Court') and the Harvard Theatre collection (Adelphi Theatre Scrapbook; Theatrical Cuttings 1785–1818; the Old Price scrapbook, and Frederick Burgess' scrapbook, 'Penny Theatres, Illustrated with Views, Bills, Advertisements etc.').

(I) THEATRE MANUSCRIPT COLLECTIONS

Bedfordshire Record Office: Whitbread MS 4397.

British Library: Add. MS 29643 Covent Garden Theatre. Letter Book of H. Robertson, 1823–1849; F. Latreille MSS. Add MS 32252 (Fairs); Place Add. MSS 27789; 27831; 27833; 35144; Add. MS 31972 (correspondence of J. P. Kemble).

Duke of Devonshire's Collections, Chatsworth House: George Colman, Plays (box); MS Diary of William Spencer Cavendish, 6th Duke of Devonshire; MS Correspondence of the 6th Duke.

Guildhall Library: Noble Collection; MS correspondence of Francis Place; 'A collection of cuttings, playbills, mss notes, and other material relating to Bartholomew Fair and Pie Powder Court', MS 1514.

Harvard Theatre Collection: Adelphi Theatre and Covent Garden Financial Papers; bMS Thr 267 boxes 1–3; Drury Lane Letters and Documents. fMS Thr 12. no. 23; 'Charles Kemble and the Minor Theatres' (bound volume of broadsides, newspaper cuttings, affidavits, & MS correspondence).

Home Office Papers; HO 59. 2 (Police courts and magistrates); HO 60. 2 (Police courts entry books); HO 65. 1 (Entry books); HO 119/4; Historical MSS. Commission Report XIII (v), 1892; Report XVI, Appendix 1 (Dartmouth II, 1896).

Public Record Office: Lord Chamberlain's Papers, LC 7/4.

Staffordshire Record Office: Dartmouth papers, D (W) 1778 I. ii (1734).

(II) PLAYS

Almar, George. *The Rover's Bride; or, the Bittern's Swamp. CMT* XI.
The Fire Raiser; or, The Prophet of the Moor. CMT IX.
[À Beckett, Gilbert A.] *The Revolt of the Workhouse. CMT* VIII.
Man-Fred. CMT IX.
The Man with the Carpet Bag. CMT XIII.
Jack Brag. Dicks 534.
King John, with the Benefit of the Act. Reprinted in Wells, *Nineteenth Century Shakespeare Burlesques*, 1.
Scenes from the Rejected Comedies by some of the competitors for the prize of £500, offered by Mr. B. Webster, lessee of the Haymarket Theatre, for the best original comedy, illustrative of English manners. London: Punch, 1844.
[À Beckett, Gilbert A.] *Another Piece of Presumption.* Larpent MS fiche 254/16.
The Parish Revolution. LC MS 42939 fols 2–25.
Arnold, Samuel J. *The Woodman's Hut. Oxberry* IV.
[Arnold, Samuel J. and R. B. Peake] *Patent Seasons.* Larpent MS 2166.
Baillie, Joanna. *A Series of Plays; in which it is attempted to delineate the stronger passions of the mind, each passion being the subject of a tragedy and a comedy.* First published 1798–1812, reprinted Oxford: Woodstock Books, 1990.
Barrymore, William. *Trial by Battle; or, Heaven Defend the Right. DBT* XX.
El Hyder, The Chief of the Gaut Mountains. Lacy VI.

[Barrymore, William and J. Raymond] *The Suliote or the Greek Family*. LC 42897 fols 405–444b.

Bayly, Thomas Haynes. *A Gentleman in Difficulties*. Dicks 545.

Bernard, William Bayle. *The Wept of Wish-ton-Wish*. Dicks 546.

The Conquering Game. *DBT* XXXVI.

[Bernard, William Bayle] *The Bricklayers' Arms*. LC MS 42899 fols. 226–60.

Bouilly, J. N. *L'Abée de l'Epée*. Paris, 1800.

Buckstone, John Baldwin. *Luke the Labourer*. *CMT* II.

A New Don Juan! *RMD* I.

Peter Bell, the Waggoner; or, The Murderers of Massiac. Dicks 862.

Victorine; or, 'I'll Sleep on it.' *AND* VIII.

Second Thoughts. Dicks 839.

Henriette the Forsaken. *AND* VIII.

Isabelle; or, A Woman's Life. *AND* VIII.

Weak Points. Dicks 845.

The Irish Lion. Dicks 822.

Jack Sheppard. *AND* VII.

The Green Bushes; or, A Hundred Years Ago. *AND* XI.

The Flowers of the Forest. A Gipsy Story. *AND* XIII.

Weak Points. *AND* IV.

[Buckstone] *The Pilot; or, A Tale of the Thames*. LC MS 42905 fols 123–46.

[Buckstone] *Grimalkin or the Cat Wife*. LC MS 42892 fols 547–70.

[Buckstone] *Hyder Ali; or, The Lions of Mysore*. LC MS 42913 fols. 73–94.

[Buckstone] *Bad Business or, A Meeting of Managers, being the prelude to a Burletta in right Earnest to be called Crimson Crimes or the Blood Stain'd Bandit*. LC MS 42919 fols. 307–322.

Byron, Lord George. *Mazeppa* (vol. IV); *Manfred* (vol. IV) and *Sardanapalus* (vol. VI) in *Lord Byron: The Complete Poetical Works* ed. Jerome J. McGann. 6 vols. Oxford: Clarendon, 1980–6.

[Canning, George and John Frere] *The Rovers; or, The Double Arrangement*. *Anti-Jacobin* 1798, reprinted in Trussler, *Burlesque Plays of the Eighteenth Century*.

Colman, George, the Elder. *The Manager in Distress*. London, 1780.

Colman, George, the Younger. *New Hay at the Old Market*. London: T. Cadell and W. Davies, 1795.

Feudal Times; or, the Banquet Gallery. London: T. Cadell and W. Davies, [1799].

The Iron Chest. London: T. Cadell and W. Davies, 1796.

Blue-beard; or, Female Curiosity! First published 1798. London: T. Cadell and W. Davies, 1800.

John Bull; or, The Englishman's Fireside. Dublin: O'Brien, 1803.

The Quadrupeds of Quedlinburgh; or, The Rovers of Weimar. Larpent MS 254/502.

Cooper, Frederick Fox. *The Elbow-Shakers; or, Thirty Years of a Rattler's Life*. *RMD* I.

Black-Eyed Sukey; or, All in the Dumps! *RMD* III.

Coyne, Joseph Stirling. *How to Settle Accounts with your Laundress*. Dicks 955.

Cross, John. *Circusiana; or A Collection of the most favourite Ballets, Spectacles, Melo-Dramas, &c. performed at the Royal Circus, St George's Fields*. 2 vols. London: T. Burton, 1809.

Cumberland, Richard. *Richard the Second*. Larpent MS fiche 253/308.

The Death of Don Giovanni; or, The Shades of Logic, Tom and Jerry. Larpent MS fiche 254/76.

Dance, Charles. For *Olympic Revels*, *Olympic Devils*, *Telemachus*, and *The Deep, Deep Sea*, see under Planché.

The Water Party. Dicks 563.

The Burlington Arcade. *AND* 6.

Dent, John. *The Bastille*. London: W. More, 1789.

Dibdin, Charles Isaac Mungo (Charles Dibdin, Jr). *The Great Devil; or, The Robber of Genoa*. *CMT* xiv.

[Charles Dibdin, Jr] *Plots, Songs, Chorusses, &c. in the comic pantomime, called Wizard's Wake; or, Harlequin and Merlin*. London: W. Glendinning, [1803].

[Charles Dibdin, Jr] *Plots, Songs, Chorusses, &c. in the comic pantomime, called Jack the Giant Killer*. London: W. Glendinning, 1803.

[Charles Dibdin, Jr] *Songs, Chorusses, Leading Features, in the new comic pantomime, called Goody Two Shoes; or, Harlequin Alabaster*. London, [1803].

[Charles Dibdin, Jr] *Songs, and other Vocal Compositions, with a Sketch of the Plot and Description of the Scenery, in the New Comic Pantomime, called Anthony, Cleopatra, and Harlequin*; Performing at the Aquatic Theatre, Sadler's Wells. London, 1805, bound in the Theatre Museum's copy of *The Writings for the Theatre of Charles Dibdin*. 2 vols. London: 1919, 1.

[Charles Dibdin, Jr] *The Wild Man; or, The Water Pageant*. *CMT* xi.

[Charles Dibdin, Jr] *Songs, Duets, Trios, Chorusses, &c. with a description of the scenery in the new comic pantomime, called Bang up! or, Harlequin Prime*. London: W. Glendinning, 1810.

[Ch. Dibdin] *Songs, and Other Vocal Composition, in the Pantomime called London; or Harlequin and Time*. London: W. Glendinning, 1814.

[Dibdin, Thomas J.] *Valentine and Orson*. *CBT* xxvii.

Don Giovanni; or, A Spectre on Horseback. *CMT* ii.

Melodrame Mad! or, The Siege of Troy. London: John Miller, 1819.

[Dibdin, Thomas J.] *Sketch of the Story, Scenery, &c. with the Songs, and Recitatives, in the new serio-comic entertainment of The Talisman; or Harlequin Made Happy*. London: W. Glendinning [1796].

[Th. Dibdin] *Harlequin in his Element; or, Fire, Water, Earth, and Air*.

[Th. Dibdin] *Harlequin and Humpo*. Larpent MS 1750.

[Th. Dibdin] *Harlequin and Fancy; or, the Poet's Last Shilling*. Larpent MS 1896.

Dickens, Charles. *The Strange Gentleman*. Dicks 466.

Dimond, William. *The Foundling of the Forest*. London: Longman, 1809.

Dowling, Maurice. *Othello, according to Act of Parliament*. Reprinted in Wells, *Nineteenth Century Shakespeare Burlesques*, 1.

Romeo and Juliet, As the Law Directs. Reprinted in Wells.

Ducis, J. F. *Hamlet*, Tragédie en cinq actes. Paris, 1769, new edition, 1815.

D'Urfey, Thomas. *The Famous History of the Rise and Fall of Massaniello*. 2 vols. London, 1699–1700.

[Farley, Charles.] *Harlequin and Asmodeus; or, Cupid on Crutches*, LA 1651.

[Farley, Charles.] *Harlequin and the Red Dwarf; or, The Adamant Rock*. Larpent MS 1749.

[Farley, Charles] *Harlequin Gulliver; or, The Flying Island*. Larpent MS 2003.

Fawcett, John. *Obi; or, Three Finger'd Jack*. *DBT* LIX.

Fielding, Henry. *Tumble-Down Dick; or, Phaeton in the Suds*; *Pasquin*; *The Historical Register for the Year 1736*; *Eurydice Hiss'd*, in *The Works of Henry Fielding*, 14 vols. London: J. Johnson, 1808, V.

Fitzball, Edward. *Thalaba the Destroyer; or, The Burning Sword*. *CMT* V.

The Floating Beacon; or, The Norwegian Wreckers. *CMT* II.

The Pilot; or, A Tale of the Sea. *CMT* I.

The Flying Dutchman; or, The Phantom Ship. *CMT* II.

The Inchcape Bell; or, The Dumb Sailor Boy. *CMT* I.

The Red Rover; or, The Mutiny of the Dolphin CMT VI.

Jonathan Bradford; or, The Murder at the Road-Side Inn. *DBT* XII.

Paul Clifford. *DBT* XX.

The Negro of Wapping; or, The Boat-Builder's Hovel. *DBT* XXIX.

[Foote, Samuel] *Piety in Pattens*. Larpent MS 467.

[Fox, George] *The House that Jack Built; or, Harlequin Tattered and Torn*. Larpent MS 2270.

Garrick, David. *Harlequin's Invasion*. In *Three Plays* ed. Elizabeth P. Stein. New York: W. H. Rudge, 1926.

Gay, John. *The Beggar's Opera*. In *The British Theatre; or, A Collection of Plays, which are acted at the Theatres Royal . . .* 25 vols. London: Longman, Hurst, *et al*, 1808, XII.

Green in France; or, Tom and Jerry's Tour. Larpent fiche 254/133.

[Greenwood, Tom.] *Death of Life in London; or, Tom and Jerry's Funeral*. LC MS 42866 fols 2–12b.

[Greenwood, Tom.] *Jack Sheppard; or, the Housebreaker of the Last Century*. *CMT* XV.

Haines, John T. *The Idiot Witness; or, A Tale of Blood*. *DBT* V.

The Ocean of Life; or, Every Inch a Sailor. Dicks 634.

The French Spy; or, The Siege of Constantina. Dicks 680.

Alice Grey, the Suspected One; or, The Moral Band. Lacy XLIV.

Richard Plantagenet. *CMT* XIV.

Harlequin Harmonist. Larpent MS 1790.

Harlequin Horner; or, The Christmas Pie. Larpent MS 1947.

Harlequin's Hour Glass; or, Time Works Wonders. Larpent MS 1897.

Harlequin Tom, the piper's son stole a pig and away he ran. Larpent MS 2195.

The History, Murders, Life, and Death of Macbeth: and a full description of the scenery, action, choruses, and characters of the Ballet of Action, of that name, as performed with enthusiastic Applause, to overflowing Houses, a Number of Nights, at the Royal Circus, St George's Fields, London; with the Occasional Address, spoken by Mr. Elliston; And every Information, to simplify the Plot; and enable the Visitors of the Circus, to comprehend this matchless Piece of Pantomimic and Choral Performance. London, 1809.

Holcroft, Thomas. *Duplicity*. London: G. Robinson, 1781.
  The Road To Ruin. Dublin: T. Wilkinson, 1792.
  The German Hotel. London: G. C. J. and J. Robinson, 1790.
  Love's Frailties. London, 1794.
  Knave or Not? London, 1798.
  Deaf or Dumb; or, The Orphan Protected. London: J. Ridgeway, 1801.
  A Tale of Mystery. CBT VIII.
[Holcroft, Thomas] *The Rival Queens, or Drury Lane and Covent Garden*. Larpent MS
  fiche 253/615.
Hook, Theodore. *Killing No Murder*. London: G. H. Davison, n. d.
The House that Jack Built; or, Harlequin Tattered and Torn. Larpent MS 2270.
The Hustings. Larpent MS 2031.
Inchbald, Elizabeth. *Lovers' Vows*, from the German of Kotzebue. London, 1798.
  Every One Has His Fault. London: G. C. J. and J. Robinson, 1793.
Jerrold, Douglas. *Vidocq, the French Police Spy*. DBT VIII.
  John Overy, the Miser; or, The Southwark Ferry. RMD II.
  Black-Ey'd Susan or, 'All in the Downs.' DBT IV.
  The Flying Dutchman; or, The Spectral Ship. RMD III.
  Thomas À Beckett. RMD III.
  The Mutiny at the Nore; or, British Sailors in 1797. CMT V.
  Martha Willis, the Servant Maid; or, Service in London. Lacy XXXIII.
  The Rent Day. 2nd edition. London: C. Chapple, 1832.
Keats, John. *Otho the Great*. First published 1883. In *The Poems of John Keats*, ed.
  Miriam Allott. London: Longman, 1970.
Kenney, James. *Ella Rosenberg*. London: CMT, 1807.
  Masaniello, or, The Dumb Girl of Portici. Lacy XCIII.
Lewis, M. G. *The Castle Spectre*. London: J. Bell, 1798.
  Adelmorn, the Outlaw. London: J. Bell, 1801.
  Timour the Tartar. London: Lowndes, [1811].
McFarren, George. *Guy Faux; or, The Gunpowder Conspiracy*. CMT IV.
Magna Charta; or, The Eventful Reign of King John. Juvenile drama text published by
  Hodgson [1823].
[Mathews, Charles the Elder] *Mail-Coach Adventures* and *The Trip to Paris* in *The
  New Budget of Fun*, no date.
  Mr Mathews' Comic Annual for 1833. London: W. Holmes, no date.
Maturin, Charles Robert. *Bertram; or, The Castle of Aldobrand*. CBT XLIII.
Milner, H. M. *The Man and the Monster! or, The Fate of Frankenstein*. DBT II.
  Mazeppa; or, The Wild Horse of Tartary. CMT V.
  Lucius Catiline, the Roman Traitor. London: J. Lowndes, n. d.
  Masaniello; or, The Dumb Girl of Portici. CMT I.
[Milner, H. M.] *The Gamblers*. London, n. d.
Mitford, Mary. *Charles the First*. London, 1834.
Moncrieff, William. *Giovanni in London; or, The Libertine Reclaimed*. CBT XVII.
  Tom and Jerry; or, Life in London. RMD I.

The Cataract of the Ganges! or, The Rajah's Daughter. London: Simkin and Marshall, 1823.

The Heart of London; or, The Sharper's Progress. Dicks 430.

The Beggar of Cripplegate; or, The Humours of Bluff King Hal. CMT XI.

Reform; or, John Bull Triumphant. RMD IV.

Gipsy Jack; or, The Napoleon of Humble Life. CMT IX.

Eugene Aram; or, Saint Robert's Cave. CMT X.

[Moncrieff, William] *Giovanni in Ireland.* Larpent MS fiche 254/2267.

[Moncrieff, William] *Up and Down; or, the Road of Life.* LC MS 42948 fols 232–343.

Morton, John Maddison. *Box and Cox. DBT* LX.

Oxenford, John. *The Rape of the Lock. DBT* XXXIII.

Doctor Dilworth. Dicks 558.

English Etiquette. Dicks 658.

Payne, John Howard. *Brutus, or the Fall of Tarquin.* London, 1818.

Ali Pacha. CBT XI.

Peake, Richard Brinsley. *Presumption; or, The Fate of Frankenstein. Dicks* 431.

Pixérécourt, Guilbert de. *Coelina, ou l'enfant du mystère.* In *Théâtre Choisi.* 4 vols. Geneva: Slatkine reprints, 1971, I.

Planché, J. R. *Rudolph the Wolf; or, Columbine Red Riding Hood.* Larpent MS 2065.

The Vampyre; or, The Bride of the Isles. CBT XXVII.

The Brigand Chief. CBT XXIV.

Court Favour, or 'Private and Confidential'. London: Chapman and Hall, n. d.

The Child of the Wreck. Lacy XXXIX.

[and Charles Dance] *Olympic Revels, Olympic Devils, The Deep, Deep Sea; or, Perseus and Andromeda* and *Telemachus; or, The Island of Calypso.* In *The Extravaganzas of J. R. Planché, Esq. 1825–1871* eds. T. F. Dillon Baker and Stephen Tucker. 5 vols. London: Tinsley Bros, 1879.

Pocock, Isaac. *The Miller and his Men, CBT* XXVI.

Poole, John. *Hamlet Travestie.* Reprinted in Wells, *Nineteenth Century Shakespeare Burlesques*, I.

Power, Tyrone. *How to Pay the Rent. AND* IX.

Rede, William L. *Cupid in London; or, Some Passages in the Life of Love. DBT* XVII.

[Rede, William L.] *The Conquest of Cupid; or, Lucre against Love.* LC MS 42962 fols 77–96.

Selby, Charles *Frank Fox Phipps, Esq. Dicks* 959.

The Unfinished Gentleman. DBT XV.

[Selby, Charles] *Dissolving Views; or, the Lights and Shadows of Life.* LC MS 42972 fols. 279–290b.

Shakespeare, William. *Coriolanus, or The Roman Matron* ed. John Philip Kemble. Facsimile text. London: Cornmarket Press, 1789.

Shelley, P. B. *The Cenci.* First published 1819. In *Shelley's Poetry and Prose* ed. Donald H. Reiman and Sharon B. Powers. New York: W. W. Norton, 1977.

Sheridan, R. B. *Pizarro.* First published 1799. In *The Dramatic Works of Richard Brinsley Sheridan* ed. Cecil Price. 2 vols. Oxford: Clarendon, 1973.

Smith, John F. *The Court of Old Fritz*. London: Chapman and Hall, 1839.
[Soane, George] *Masaniello, the Fisherman of Naples*. LC MS 42870 fols 1–68.
Stirling, Edward. *Dandolo; or, The Last of the Doges*. London: W. Strange. 1838.
　The Rubber of Life; or, St James's and St Giles's. DBT XLIII.
Southey, Robert. *Wat Tyler*. London, 1817 (facsimile reprint, Oxford: Woodstock Books, 1989).
Taylor, Robert. *Swing; or, Who are the Incendiaries?* London: Richard Carlile, 1831.
Thompson, Benjamin. *The Stranger*, translated from Kotzebue in *The German Theatre*. London: Vernor, Hood and Sharpe, 1811, I.
The Valley of Diamonds; or, Harlequin Sinbad. Larpent MS 1837.
[Walker, C. E.] *The Revolt of the Greeks*. LC MS 42867 fols. 69–93b.
Walker, John. *The Factory Lad. DBT* XI.
Wat Tyler and Jack Straw; or, The Mob Reformers. A Dramatick Entertainment. As it is Perform'd at Pinkeytham's and Giffard's Great Theatrical Booth in Bartholomew Fair. London, 1730.
Webster, Benjamin. *Paul Clifford, the Highwayman of 1770. CMT* VI.
[Westmacott, Charles.] *Othello, the Moor of Fleet Street*. LC MS 42920 fols 77–95.
Wilks, Thomas. *Sudden Thoughts. Dicks* 407.

(III) NEWSPAPERS AND JOURNALS

For full bibliographic details of theatrical journals, see James F. Allerton and John W. Robinson, *English Theatrical Literature 1559–1900: A Bibliography*. London: Society for Theatre Research, 1970.

Age
Anti-Jacobin
Athenaeum
Atlas
Black Dwarf
Blackwood's Edinburgh Magazine
British Stage, and Literary Cabinet
British Stage; or, Dramatic Censor
Champion
Cobbett's Political Register
Cobbett's Parliamentary Debates
Courier, and Evening Gazette
Drama, or, Theatrical Pocket Magazine
Dramatic and Musical Review
Dramatic Censor, or, Critical and Biographical Illustrations of the British Stage
Dramatic Gazette; or, Weekly Record of the Stage, Music, Public Exhibitions, &c.
Dramatic Magazine
European Magazine and London Review
Examiner
Figaro in London

Fraser's Magazine
Gentleman's Magazine
Hansard's Parliamentary Debates
Harlequin. A Journal of the Drama
John Bull
Literary Chronicle and Weekly Review
Literary Gazette
London Chronicle
London Magazine
Mirror of the Stage; or, New Dramatic Censor
Mirror of Parliament
Monthly Magazine; or, British Register of Literature, Science, and the Belles Lettres
Monthly Mirror
Monthly Review
Monthly Theatrical Review
Morning Chronicle
Morning Herald
National Omnibus, and General Advertiser
New Monthly Magazine and Literary Journal
Nic-Nac; or, Oracle of Knowledge
Political Review
Poor Man's Guardian
Prompter
Quarterly Review
Satirist; or, Censor of the Times
Stage; or, Theatrical Inquisitor
Statesman
Surrey Dramatic Spectator; or, Critical Remarks, on the Daily Performances, with the Bills of the Play
Tatler, The, A Daily Journal of Literature and the Stage
Theatre
Theatre; or, Dramatic and Literary Mirror
Theatrical Inquisitor, or Literary Mirror
Theatrical Mince Pie, entirely original. Containing a Correct Account of the Several Appearances of Mr. Kean and Miss Foote
Theatrical Mirror; or, Daily Record of Public Amusements, Bills of the Play, and Minute Observations on the Performances
Theatrical Observer; and Daily Bills of the Play
Theatrical Recorder
Theatrical Rod! A Weekly Journal of The Stage, Literature, and General Amusement
Theatrical Spectator
Thespian Sentinel; or Theatrical Vade-Mecum
The Times
True Briton
Westminster Review

(IV) OTHER PRIMARY SOURCES

À Beckett, G. A. *The Quizziology of the British Drama*. London: Punch, 1846.

Ackermann, R[udolph]. *The Microcosm of London; or London in Miniature*. 3 vols. London: R. Ackermann, 1808–10.

Allen, Thomas, *The History and Antiquities of London*. 5 vols. London: Cowie and Strange, 1828.

A New and Complete History of the Counties of Surrey and Sussex. 2 vols. London: I. J. Hinton, 1830.

Answers to all the Objections which have been raised against . . . the Royalty Theatre. [?]1794.

Austin, Rev. Gilbert. *Chironomia: or, A Treatise on Rhetorical Delivery*. London: T. Cadell, 1806.

Bamford, Francis and Duke of Wellington (eds). *The Journal of Mrs Arbuthnot 1820–1832*. 2 vols. London: Macmillan, 1950.

Bedford, Arthur. *The Evil and Mischief of Stage-Playing . . . occasioned by the erecting of a Playhouse in the Neighbourhood*. 2nd edition. London: J. Wilford, 1735.

Blanchard, E. L. 'History of the Adelphi Theatre', in E. Ledger, ed., *The Era Almanack and Annual* (London: 1887).

Boaden, James. *Memoirs of the Life of John Philip Kemble*. 2 vols. London: Longman, 1825.

Brayley, Edward W. *Historical and Descriptive Accounts of the Theatres of London*. 3 vols. London: J. Taylor, 1826.

[Britton, John] *Sheridan and Kotzebue*. London: J. Fairburn, 1799.

Britton, J. *The Original Picture of London, Enlarged and Improved*. Revised ed. London: Longman, [1826].

Britton, J. and A. Pugin. *Illustrations of the Public Buildings of London*. London: J. Taylor, 1825.

Bull, John (*pseud*.) *Covent Garden Theatre!! Remarks on the Cause of the Dispute . . .* London, 1809.

Bulwer-Lytton, Edward. *Paul Clifford*. 3 vols. London: H. Colburn and R. Bentley, 1830.

England and the English. 2 vols. New York: Harper, 1833.

Bunn, Alfred. *The Stage: Both Before and Behind the Curtain, from 'Observations Taken on the Spot.'* 3 vols. London: Bentley, 1840.

[Bunn, J. D.] *The Language of the Walls: and A Voice from the Shop Windows; or, The Mirror of Commercial Roguery. By One who Thinks Aloud*. London, 1855.

Burke, Edmund. *Reflections on the Revolution in France*. First published 1790. London: Penquin, 1968.

Byron, Lord George Gordon. *Letters and Journals* ed. Leslie A. Marchand. 8 vols. London: John Murray, 1973.

Byron. The Oxford Authors ed. Jerome McGann. Oxford University Press, 1986.

Case of the Renters of the Royalty Theatre. n. d.

Cole, John William. *The Life and Theatrical Times of Charles Kean*. 2 vols. London: Richard Bentley, 1859.

Coleridge, S. T. *The Collected Letters of Samuel Taylor Coleridge*, ed. E. L. Griggs. 6 vols. Oxford: Clarendon, 1956–1971.

The Collected Works of Samuel Taylor Coleridge, gen. ed. Kathleeen Coburn. 16 vols. Princeton University Press, 1971– .

Coleridge. The Oxford Authors, ed. H. J. Jackson. Oxford University Press, 1985.

Coleridge, Henry Nelson. *Specimens of the Table Talk of Samuel Taylor Coleridge*. 2nd edition. London: John Murray, 1836.

[Colman, George, the Elder] *A Very Plain State of the Case, or the Royalty Theatre versus the Theatres Royal . . .* London: J. Murray, 1787.

Considerations on the Past and Present State of the Stage. London: C. Chapple, 1809.

Considerations upon how far the Present Winter and Summer Theatres can be Affected by the Application to Parliament for an Act to enable his Majesty to License . . . the Royalty Theatre . . . London [1794].

Cotton, Henry. *The Story of the Drama in Exeter, during its best period, 1787 to 1823. With Reminiscences of Edmund Kean.* London: Hamilton, Adams and Co., 1887.

Covent Garden Theatre!! Remarks on the Cause of the Dispute . . . London: J. Fairburn, 1809.

Cutspear, W., (*pseud.*) *Dramatic Rights: or, Private Theatricals, and Pic-Nic Suppers, justified by Fair Argument.* London: T. Burton, 1802.

Davies, Thomas. *Memoirs of the Life of David Garrick.* 2 vols. London: printed for the author, 1780.

Decastro. *The Memoirs of J. Decastro*, ed. R. Humphreys. London: Sherwood, 1824.

Denman, John. *The Drama Vindicated.* Cambridge: W. H. Smith, 1835.

Dibdin, Charles Isaac Mungo (Charles Dibdin the Younger). *History and Illustrations of the London Theatres.* London: The Proprietors of the 'Illustrations of London Buildings', 1826.

Memoirs of Charles Dibdin the Younger ed. George Speaight. London: Society for Theatre Research, 1956.

Dibdin, Thomas J. *The Reminiscences of Thomas Dibdin.* 2 vols. London: H. Colburn, 1827.

[Dickens, Charles] *Memoirs of Joseph Grimaldi*, edited by 'Boz'. First published 1830. London: W. Nicholson, 1884.

Doran, Dr [John] *'Their Majesties' Servants'. Annals of the English Stage from Thomas Betterton to Edmund Kean.* 2 vols. London: W. Allen, 1864.

Dramaticus (*pseud.*) *An Impartial View of the Stage, from the days of Garrick and Rich to the present period; or the causes of its degeneration and declining state, and shewing the necessity of a reform in the system . . .* London: C. Chapple, 1816.

Drury's Resurrection: or, The Drama versus the Menagerie. London: G. Shade, 1812.

The Eastern Theatre Erected. An Heroic-Comic Poem in Three Cantos. London: W. Brown, 1788.

Elliston, Robert W. *Copy of a Memorial Presented to the Lord Chamberlain . . . against the Olympic and Sans Pareil Theatres; with Copies of Two Letters, in Reply to the Contents of Such Memorials, Addressed to the Lord Chamberlain by Robert William Elliston, Comedian.* London: J. Miller, 1818.

Farington, Joseph. *The Farington Diary*. 8 vols. London: Hutchison and Co., 1922–8.

Feltham, J. *The Picture of London for 1822*. London: Longman and Co., [1822].

Finlay, John. *Miscellanies*. London: Whittaker, Treacher and Co., 1835.

Fitzball, Edward. *Thirty-Five Years of a Dramatic Author's Life*. 2 vols. London: T. C. Newby, 1859.

Fitzgerald, Percy. *A New History of the English Stage from the Restoration to the Liberty of the Theatres*. 2 vols. London: Tinsley Bros, 1882.

Foote, Horace. *A Companion to the Theatres; and Manual of the British Drama*. London: E. Sanger, 1829.

Friend of the People, A., (*pseud.*) *A Private Peep into the Treasury of the Theatre-Royal, Covent-Garden, and the Exposition of the Engagement of Madame Catalani*. London: G. Shade, [1809].

Frost, Thomas. *The Old Showmen, and the old London Fairs*. London: Tinsley Bros, 1874.

Genest, John. *Some Account of the English Stage, from the Restoration in 1660 to 1830*. 10 vols. Bath: H. E. Carrington, 1832.

A Genuine Collection of OP Songs . . . London, n. d.

Gilliland, Thomas. *Elbow Room, a Pamphlet; containing Remarks on the Shameful Increase of the Private Boxes of Covent Garden* . . . London: printed for the author, 1804.

Goede, C. A. G. *The Stranger in England; or, Travels in Great Britain*. 3 vols. London: Mathews and Leigh, 1807.

Grant, James. *The Great Metropolis*. 2 vols. London: Saunders and Otley, 1836.

Sketches in London. London: Orr and Co., 1838.

Grattan, Thomas Colley. *Beaten Paths; And Those Who Trod Them*. 2 vols. London, 1862.

Hawkins, F. W. *The Life of Edmund Kean*. London: Tinsley Brothers, 1869.

Hazlitt, William. *The Complete Works of William Hazlitt*. Centenary Edition, ed. P. P. Howe. 21 vols. London: Dent, 1930–34.

Hazlitt, William C. *Essays and Criticism by Thomas Griffiths Wainewright*. London: Reeves and Turner, 1880.

Hindley, Charles. *The True History of Tom and Jerry; or, The Day and Night Scenes, of Life in London from the Start to the Finish!* London: Reeves and Turner, 1888.

Hints on Etiquette. London, 1834.

Hone, William. *The Political Showman – At Home! exhibiting his cabinet of curiosities and Creatures – All Alive*. London: Hone, 1821.

The Every-Day Book and Table Book; or, Everlasting Calendar of Popular Amusements. 3 vols. London: Tegg, edition of 1831.

Howard, Frederick, Earl of Carlisle. *Thoughts upon the Present Condition of the Stage, and upon the Construction of a New Theatre*. London, 1809.

Hunt, J. H. L. *Leigh Hunt's Dramatic Criticism 1808–1831*, ed. Carolyn Houtchens and Lawrence Houtchens. New York: Columbia University Press, 1949.

The Autobiography of Leigh Hunt. ed. J. E. Morpurgo. London: Cresset Press, 1949.

Impartial Observations on the Proceedings Instituted by the Proprietors of the Theatres Royal,
Drury Lane and Covent Garden, against the Minor Establishments. London: T.
Boys, 1820.

An Inhabitant of the Tower hamlets, (*pseud.*) *The Tendency of Dramatic Exhibitions.*
[?]1794.

[Jackman, Isaac] *Royal and Royalty Theatres.* Letter to Philip Glover, Esq . . .
London: J. Murray, 1787.

Keats, John. *The Poetical Works and Other Writings of John Keats* ed. H. B. Forman,
revised M. B. Forman. 8 vols. London: Hampstead edition, 1938–9.

The Poems of John Keats, ed. E. de Sélincourt. London Methuen and Co., 1926.

The Poems of John Keats ed. Miriam Allott. London: Longman, 1970.

Lamb, Charles. *The Works of Charles and Mary Lamb*, ed. E. V. Lucas. 7 vols.
London: 1903–5.

Lawrence, James. *Dramatic Emancipation; or Strictures on the State of the Theatre, and*
on the consequent degeneration of the Drama. In *The Pamphleteer* vol. 2, no. 4.
London, 1813.

A Letter . . . on the Statutes for the Regulation of Theatres, the Conduct of Mr. Palmer, of
Mr. Justice Staples, and the Other Justices [1787].

A Letter to a Member of Parliament on the Impropriety of Classing Players with Rogues and
Vagabonds . . . London: J. Murray, 1824.

The Life of John Philip Kemble. London: J. Johnston, 1809.

Macarthy, Eugene. *A Letter to the King on the Question now at Issue between the 'Major'*
and 'Minor' theatres. London: Effingham Wilson, 1832.

[Mackintosh, Matthew] An Old Stager, *Stage Reminiscences: being recollections, chiefly*
personal, of celebrated theatrical and musical performers during the last forty years.
Glasgow: J. Hedderwick, 1866.

Malcolm, J. P. *Londinium Redivivum; or, an Ancient History and Modern Description of*
London, etc. 4 vols. London, 1802–7.

[Mangin, Edward] *Piozziana; or, Recollections of the late Mrs. Piozzi.* London:
Edward Moxon, 1833.

Mansel, Robert. *Free Thoughts upon Methodists, Actors, and the Influence of the Stage*
. . . Hull: printed for the author, 1819.

Mathews, Mrs. *The Life and Correspondence of Charles Mathews the Elder*, ed.
Edmund Yates. London: Routledge, 1860.

Mayhew, Edward. *Stage Effect: or, the Principles which Command Dramatic Success in*
the Theatre. London: C. Mitchell, 1840.

Memoirs of the Public and Private Life, Adventures and Wonderful Exploits of Madame
Vestris . . . London: W. Chubb, [?1830].

Memoirs of the Life, Public and Private Adventures of Madame Vestris . . . London, [1839].

Miles, Henry D. *The Life of Joseph Grimaldi.* London: C. Harris, 1838.

Miller, David Prince. *The Life of a Showman: to which is added Managerial Struggles.*
London: Lacy, 1849.

The Modern Stage, A Letter to the Hon. George Lamb, M. P. on the Decay and Degradation
of English Dramatic Literature. London: Edwards and Knibbs, 1819.

More, Hannah. *Strictures on the Modern System of Female Education.* First published
1799. 2 vols. London: Cadell, 1826.

The National Drama; or the Histrionic War of the Majors and Minors. London: E. Muers, 1833.

Old Playgoer, An, (*pseud.*) *Desultory Thoughts on the National Drama, Past and Present.* London: Onwhyn, 1850.

Old Prices: Comprising an Answer to the Pamphlets in Favour of the Imposition, entitled Theatrical Taxation, and The Statement of a Few Facts, and an Impartial Appeal on the Subject at Issue between the Public and Covent Garden Theatre. London: Gale and Curtis, 1809.

One Who Dares to Think For Himself, (*pseud.*) *Reason versus Passion; or, an Impartial Review of the Dispute between the Public and the Proprietors of Covent Garden Theatre* . . . London: Wilson [1809].

O. P. *The Interesting Trial at Large of Henry. Clifford, Esq. Barrister at law, against James Brandon, Box-Keeper of the Theatre Royal, Covent Garden* . . . London: J. D. Derwick, 1809.

Oulton, W. C. *A History of the Theatres of London* . . . 3 vols. London: C. Chapple, 1818.

Oxberry's Dramatic Biography, and Histrionic Anecdotes. [Ed. Catherine & William Oxberry]. 5 vols. London: G. Virtue, 1825–26.

[Palmer, John] *Case of the Theatre in Well Street.* 1790.

A Paper having been distributed, called 'Reasons why the Bill for licensing the Royalty Theatre should not pass into a law,' the following analysis . . . ?1794.

Parke, Mungo. *Journal of a Mission into the Interior of Africa in 1805*, prefixed by Wishaw's life of Parke. London: John Murray, 1815.

Parliamentary Papers, *Reports from Committees, 1831–2.* 18 vols. Vol. vii, *Report and Minutes of Evidence of the Select Committee on Dramatic Literature*, House of Commons, August 1832, 9–252.

[Philo-Dramaticus (*pseud.*)], *A Letter to C. Kemble and R. W. Elliston on the Present State of the Stage* (London: Marsh 1825), 730.

Pindar, Peter, jun. (*pseud.* of George Daniel). *The Plotting Managers, a Poetical Satyrical Interlude: to which is prefixed A Letter to Lord S–D.N–Y, on his recommending the Suppression of the Royalty-Theatre.* London: J. James, 1787.

[Place, Francis] *A Brief Examination of the Dramatic Patents.* Extracted from the *Monthly Magazine*, March 1834.

[Place, Francis] *A New Way to Pay Old Debts.* London: Sherwood, 1812.

Planché, James R. *The Recollections and Reflections of J. R. Planché.* 2 vols. London: Tinsley Brothers, 1872.

Plumptyre, James. *Four Discourses on Subjects Relating to the Amusement of the Stage.* Cambridge: J. Hodson, 1809.

A Letter to the Author of a Tract entitled The Stage: Three Dialogues between Mr. Clement and Mr. Mortimer. Cambridge: J. Hodson, 1819.

A Letter to the Most Noble Marquis of Hertford . . . *on the subject of a Dramatic Institution.* Cambridge: J. Hodson, 1820.

A Poetical Epistle to Henry Clifford, Esq. on the late disturbances in Covent Garden Theatre. Edinburgh: J. Moir, 1810.

Polydore, Augustus, (*pseud.*) *The Trial of Mr. John Palmer, Comedian* . . . *Tried in the*

Olympian Shades before the Right honourable Lord Chief-Justice Shakspear . . . . John Milton, Joseph Addison, Thomas Otway . . . London: J. Ridgeway, 1787.

Pope, Alexander. *The Poems of Alexander Pope*, ed. John Butt. London: Methuen, 1965.

Pythagoras (*pseud.* of Jesse Foot?). *A Vindication of a Right in the Public to a One Shilling Gallery either at the New Theatre Royal in Covent-Garden, or somewhere else.* London: J. Own, 1792.

Raymond, George. *The Memoirs of Robert William Elliston.* 2 vols. London: John Mortimer, 1844.

Reasons why the Bill now about to be Presented to the House of Commons, for Licensing the Royalty-theatre, should not now pass into a law. [?1794].

The Rebellion; or, All in the Wrong. A serio-comic-hurly-burly, in scenes, as it was performed for two months at the new Theatre Royal, Covent-Garden . . . London: Vernon, Hood and Sharpe, 1809.

Rede, Leman T. *The Road to the Stage*, new edition. London: J. Onwhyn, 1836.

Renter, A, (*pseud.*) *A Short Address to the Public on Raising the Prices at Covent Garden Theatre.* London, 1809.

A Review of the Present Contest between the Managers of the Winter Theatres, the Little Theatre in the Hay-market, and the Royalty Theatre . . . London: Charles Stalker, 1787.

Reynolds, Frederic. *The Life and Times of Frederic Reynolds.* 2 vols. London: Henry Colbourn, 1826.

Robinson, Henry Crabb. *Diary, Reminiscences and Correspondence of Henry Crabb Robinson* ed. Thomas Sadler. 3 vols. London: Macmillan and Co., 1869.

The London Theatre 1811–1866. [Selections from the diary of Henry Crabb Robinson] ed. Eluned Brown. London: Society for Theatre Reseach, 1966.

Rousseau, J. J. *Discours sur l'origine et les fondements de l'inegalité.* First published 1754. In *Oeuvres Complètes.* 5 vols. Paris: Gallimard, 1959–95, III.

Fragmens d'Observations sur l'Alceste italien de M. de Chevalier Gluck. First published 1774. In *Oeuvres Completes*, V.

Savage, W. H. *The Vulgarisms and Improprieties of the English Language.* London: T. Porter, 1833.

Scott, Walter. 'An Essay on The Drama'. *The Complete Works of Scott.* 30 vols. Vol. VI: 219–395. Edinburgh, 1870.

Shelley, Mary. *Frankenstein; or, The Modern Prometheus.* First published 1818. London: J. M. Dent, 1959.

Shelley, P. B. *The Letters of Percy Bysshe Shelley* ed. F. L. Jones. 2 vols. Oxford: Clarendon, 1964.

Sheridan, R. B. *The Letters of Richard Brinsley Sheridan* ed. Cecil Price. 3 vols. Oxford: Clarendon, 1966.

A Short Criticism on the Performance of Hamlet by Mr. Kemble. London: T. Hookham, 1789.

Siddons, Henry. *Practical Illustrations of Rhetorical Gesture and Action, adapted to the English Drama,* adapted from Engel. London: Richard Phillips, 1807.

Smith, Albert. *The Natural History of the Gent.* London: David Bogue, 1847.

Smith, Rev. George. *Dreadful Catastrophe. Destruction of the Brunswick Theatre, Wellclose Square.* 3rd edition. London: W. K. Wakefield, [1828].

Stockdale, J. J., ed., *The Covent Garden Journal.* 2 vols. London: J. J. Stockdale, 1810.

Tegg, Thomas. *The Rise, Progress, and Termination of the O. P. War in Poetic Epistles.* London: T. Tegg, 1810.

Thackeray, Thomas James. *On Theatrical Emancipation; and the Rights of Dramatic Authors.* London: C. Chapple, 1832.

Theatrical Monopoly; being an Address to the Public on the Present Alarming Coalition of the Managers of the Winter Theatres. London: Fielding and Walker, 1779.

Theatricus, (*pseud.*) *Theatrical Taxation; which embraces Reflections on the State of Property in the Theatre-Royal, Covent-Garden, and the Engagement of Madame Catalani . . .* London: G. Hughes, [1809].

Thelwall. *The Life of John Thelwall.* By His Widow. London: John Macrome, 1837.

Thelwall, John. 'On the Political Prostitution of our Public Theatres.' In *The Tribune* III, 279–318. London, 1796.

Thespian Preceptor; or, A Full Display of the Scenic Art. London: J. Roach, 1811.

Thirlwall, Rev. Thomas. *A Solemn Protest against the Revival of Scenic Exhibitions and Interludes at the Royalty Theatre . . .* London: T. Plummer, 1803.

Timbs, John, *London and Westminster: City and Suburb.* 2 vols. London: R. Bentley, 1868.

Curiosities of London. 2 vols. London: D. Bogue, 1855.

Tomlins, F. G. *A Brief View of the English Drama, from the earliest period to the present time: with suggestions for elevating the present condition of the art, and of its performers.* London: C. Mitchell, 1840.

The Past and Present State of Dramatic Art and Literature; addressed to authors, actors, managers, and the admirers of the old English drama. London: C. Mitchell, 1839.

The Nature and State of the English Drama. London: C. Mitchell, 1841.

[Tomlins F. G] One of the Public (*pseud.*) *Major and Minor Theatres. A Concise View of the Question . . . with remarks on the decline of the drama, and the means of its restoration . . .* London: W. Strange, 1832.

True Briton, A (*pseud.*) *Strictures on the Engagment of Madame Catalani at Covent-Garden Theatre, and on the Italian Opera.* London: Cox and Baylis, 1809.

Vandenhoff, George. *Leaves from an Actor's Notebook; with Reminiscences and Chit-Chat of the Green- Room and the Stage, in England and America.* New York: D. Appleton, 1860.

Versus Amicus (*pseud.*) *A Letter to John Kemble, Esq. upon the Present Disturbances at the Theatre Royal, Covent Garden; with some hints for the better accomodation of the public.* London, [1809].

Vidocq, Eugène François. *Memoirs of Vidocq, Principal Agent of the French Police until 1827 . . .* 4 vols. London, 1828–9.

The Vulgarities of Speech Corrected. London: J. Bulcock, 1826.

Wade, J. *History of the Middle and Working Classes.* London: Effingham Wilson, 1833.

Webbe, Cornelius. *Glances at Life in City and Suburb.* London: Smith, Elder and Co., 1836.

'*What-Do-You-Want?*' *explained in a Poetical Epistle from O. P. to All the Aitches with notes illustrative.* London: Tegg, n. d.

Whittock, N. *The New Picture of London, Westminster, and the Metropolitan Boroughs.* London: G. Virtue, [1835].

Wilkinson, Robert. *Londina Illustrata: graphic and historic memorials of monasteries, churches, chapels, schools . . . and modern and present theatres, in the cities and suburbs of London and Westminster.* London: Wilkinson, 1819.

Williams, John Ambrose. *Memoirs of John Philip Kemble Esq.* London: I. J. Burn, 1817.

Winston, James. *Drury Lane Journal.* Selections from James Winston's Diaries 1819–1827, ed. Alfred L. Nelson and Gilbert B. Cross. London: Society for Theatre Research, 1974.

Wordsworth, William. *William Wordsworth* ed. Stephen Gill. The Oxford Authors. Oxford, 1984.

The Prelude 1799, 1805, 1850 ed. Jonathan Wordsworth, M. H. Abrams and Stephen Gill. New York: W. W. Norton, 1979.

[Wright, Thomas] *Some Habits and Customs of the Working Classes by a Journeyman Engineer.* London: Tinsley Bros, 1867.

Wyndam, Henry Saxe. *Annals of Covent Garden Theatre from 1732 to 1897.* 2 vols. London: Chatto and Windus, 1906.

(V) SECONDARY SOURCES

Agnew, Jean-Christophe. *Worlds Apart: The Market and the Theatre in Anglo-American Thought.* Cambridge University Press, 1986.

Altick, Richard. *The Shows of London.* Cambridge, Mass.: Harvard University Press, 1978.

Anderson, Patricia. *The Printed Image and the Transformation of Popular Culture, 1790–1860.* Oxford: Clarendon, 1991.

Appleton, William. *Madame Vestris and the London Stage.* New York: Columbia University Press, 1974.

Arac, Jonathan and Harriet Ritvo, eds. *Macropolitics of Nineteenth-Century Literature.* Pennyslvania University Press, 1991.

Arundell, Dennis. *The Story of Sadler's Wells 1683–1964.* London: Hamish Hamilton, 1965.

Backscheider, Paula R. *Spectacular Politics: Theatrical Power and Mass Culture in Early Modern England.* Baltimore and London: Johns Hopkins University Press, 1993.

Baer, Marc. *Theatre and Disorder in Georgian London.* Oxford: Clarendon, 1992.

Bailey, Peter. *Leisure and Class in Victorian England: Rational Recreation and the Contest for Control, 1830–1885.* London: Routledge, 1978.

'"Will the Real Bill Banks Please Stand Up?" Towards a Role Analysis of Mid-Victorian Working-Class Respectability.' *Journal of Social History* 12 (1979), 336–53.

Popular Culture and Performance in the Victorian City. Cambridge University Press, 1998.

Bainbridge, Simon. *Napoleon and English Romanticism*. Cambridge University Press, 1995.

Ball, Robert Hamilton. *Shakespeare on Silent Film: A Strange Eventful History*. London: Allen and Unwin, 1968.

Barish, Jonas. *The Antitheatrical Prejudice*. Berkeley: California University Press, 1981.

Barker, Clive. 'The Chartists, Theatre, Reform and Research'. *Theatre Quarterly* 1 (1971), 3–10.

Barker, Francis *et al. 1789: Reading, Writing, Revolution*. Proceedings of the Essex conference on the sociology of literature. Colchester: University of Essex, 1982.

Barrett, Michèle, *et al. Ideology and Cultural Production*. London: Croom Helm, 1979.

Bate, Jonathan. *Shakespearean Constitutions: Politics, Theatre, Criticism 1730–1830*. Oxford: Clarendon, 1989.

Bayley, C. A. *Imperial Meridian: The British Empire and the World, 1780–1830*. Harlow: Longman, 1989.

Bell, Ian A. *Literature and Crime in Augustan England*. London: Routledge, 1991.

Bennett, Susan. *Theatre Audiences: A Theory of Production and Reception*. London: Routledge, 1990.

Biggs, Murray. 'Staging *The Borderers*: Dragging Romantic Drama Out of the Closet'. *Studies in Romanticism* 27 no. 3 (1988), 411–71.

Bishop, Conrad Joy. 'Melodramatic Acting: Concept and Technique in the Performance of Early Nineteenth-Century English Melodrama.' (unpublished doctoral thesis, Stanford University, 1967).

Black, Joel. *The Aesthetics of Murder: A Study in Romantic Literature and Contemporary Culture*. Baltimore: Johns Hopkins University Press, 1991.

Bogorad, Sameul N. and Robert Gale Noyes. '*Samuel Foote's Primitive Puppet-Shew* featuring *Piety in Pattens: A Critical Edition*'. *Theatre Survey* 14 no. 1a (Fall 1973).

Booth, John. *A Century of Theatrical History 1816–1916: The Old Vic*. London: Stead's, 1917.

Booth, Michael R. *English Melodrama*. London: Herbert Jenkins, 1965.
    English Plays of the Nineteenth Century. 5 vols. Oxford: Clarendon, 1969–76.
    'East End and West End: Class and Audience in Victorian London'. *Theatre Research International* 2 (1977), 98–103.
    Prefaces to English Nineteenth-Century Theatre. Manchester University Press, [1980].
    'Early Victorian Farce: Dionysius Domesticated', in *Farce*, no. 10, ed. James Redmond. Cambridge University Press, 1988, 95–110.
    'Melodrama and the Working Class' in *Dramatic Dickens* ed. Carol Hanbery Mackay. Basingstoke: Macmillan, 1989.

Bourdieu, Pierre. *Distinction: A Social Critique of the Judgement of Taste*. Trans. Richard Nice. First published Paris, 1979. London: Routledge, 1984.

Brantlinger, Patrick. *The Spirit of Reform: British Literature and Politics, 1832–67.* Cambridge, Mass.: Harvard University Press, 1977.
Bread and Circuses: Theories of Mass Culture as Social Decay. Ithaca: Cornell University Press, 1983.
Rule of Darkness: British Literature and Imperialism, 1830–1914. Ithaca: Cornell University Press, 1988.
Bratton, J. S. 'British heroism and the structure of melodrama'. In Bratton, *et al.*, eds. *Acts of Supremacy: The British Empire and the Stage, 1790–1830.* Manchester University Press, 1991, 18–61.
'The Contending Discourses of Melodrama'. In Jacky Bratton, Jim Cook and Christine Gledhill, ed., *Melodrama: Stage, Picture, Screen.* London: British Film Institute, 1994, 38–49.
Bratton, J. S. and Jane Traies. *Astley's Ampitheatre.* Cambridge: Chadwyck-Healey, 1980.
Bratton, J. S. 'Jane Scott the writer-manager'. In Davis and Donkin, *Women and Playwriting,* 77–98.
Brewer, John and Roy Porter, eds. *Consumption and the World of Goods.* London: Routledge, 1993.
Bristol, Michael. *Shakespeare's America, America's Shakespeare.* London: Routledge, 1990.
Broadbent, R. J. *A History of Pantomime.* New York: Benjamin Blom, 1964.
Bromwich, David. *Hazlitt: The Mind of a Critic.* Oxford: Oxford University Press, 1983.
Brooks, Peter. *The Melodramatic Imagination: Balzac, Henry James, Melodrama, and the Mode of Excess.* New Haven: Yale University Press, 1976.
Burroughs, Catherine B. *Closet Stages: Joanna Baillie and the Theater Theory of British Romantic Women Writers.* Philadelphia: University of Pennsylvania Press, 1997.
Butler, Marilyn. 'Telling it Like a Story: The French Revolution as Narrative'. *Studies in Romanticism* 28 (1989), 345–364.
'Plotting the Revolution: The Political Narratives of Romantic Poetry and Criticism'. In Kenneth Johnston *et al*, eds., *Romantic Revolutions: Criticism and Theory.* Bloomington: Indiana University Press, 1990.
Calhoun, Craig. 'Class, Place and Industrial Revolution' in Nigel Thrift and Peter Williams, eds., *Class and Space: The Making of Industrial Society.* London: Routledge, 1987, 51–72.
Campbell, Colin. *The Romantic Ethic and the Spirit of Modern Consumerism.* Oxford: Blackwell, 1987.
Carlson, Julie. 'An Active Imagination: Coleridge and the Politics of Dramatic Reform'. *Modern Philology* 86 (1988), 22–33.
Carlson, Julie A. *In the Theatre of Romanticism: Coleridge, Nationalism, Women.* Cambridge University Press, 1994.
Carlson, Marvin. *The Theater of the French Revolution.* Ithaca: Cornell University Press, 1966.
'The Old Vic: A Semiotic Analysis'. In Carlson, *Places of Performance: The Semiotics of Theatre Architecture.* Ithaca: Cornell University Press, 1989, 56–74.

Theatre Semiotics: Signs of Life. Bloomington: Indiana University Press, 1990.

Carter, Angela. *Wise Children*. First published 1991. London: Vintage, 1992.

Carter, Rand. 'The Architecture of English Theatres 1760–1860'. 2 vols. (unpublished doctoral thesis, Princeton University, 1966).

Cave, Terence. *Recognitions: A Study in Poetics*. Oxford: Clarendon, 1988.

Chandler, Frank. *The Literature of Roguery*. 2 vols. London: Archibald Constable, 1907.

Chartier, Roger. 'Culture as Appropriation: Popular Culture Uses in Early Modern France'. In Steven L. Kaplan, ed., *Understanding Popular Culture: Europe from the Middle Ages to the Nineteenth Century*. Berlin and New York: Mouton, 1984, 229–53.

Cultural History: Between Practices and Representations. Trans. Lydia G. Cochrane. Cambridge: Polity, 1988.

'Texts, Printings, Readings'. In Lynn Hunt, *The New Cultural History*.

Christie, Ian R. *Stress and Stability in Late Eighteenth-Century Britain: Reflections on the British Avoidance of Revolution, etc.* Oxford: Clarendon, 1984.

Colley, Linda. 'The Apotheosis of George III: Loyalty, Royalty and the British Nation, 1760–1820.' *Past and Present* 102 (1984), 94–129.

Britons: Forging the Nation, 1707–1837. Yale University Press, 1992.

Collick, John. *Shakespeare, Cinema and Society*. Manchester University Press, 1989.

Conolly, Leonard W. *The Censorship of English Drama 1737–1824*. San Marino, California: The Huntington Library, 1976.

Copley, Stephen and John Whale, eds. *Beyond Romanticism: New Approaches to Texts and Contexts 1780–1832*. London: Routledge, 1992.

Cowan, Anita. 'Popular Entertainment in London 1800–1840: The Relationship between Theatre Repertoire and Theatre Location' (unpublished doctoral thesis, University of Washington, 1978).

Cox, Jeffrey N. *In the Shadows of Romance: Romantic Tragic Drama in Germany, England and France*. Athens, Ohio: Ohio University Press, 1987.

'Ideology and Genre in the British Antirevolutionary Drama of the 1790s.' *English Literary History* 58 (1991), 579–610.

'The Ideological Tack of Nautical Melodrama'. In Hays and Nikolopoulou, *Melodrama*, 167–89.

Poetry and Politics in the Cockney School: Keats, Shelley, Hunt and their Circle. Cambridge University Press, 1998.

Craton, Michael. *Testing the Chains: Resistance to Slavery in the British West Indies*. Ithaca: Cornell University Press, 1982.

Cunningham, Hugh. *Leisure in the Industrial Revolution*. London: Croom Helm, 1980.

Davis, Jim. 'British Bravery, or Tars Triumphant: Images of the British Navy in Nautical Melodrama'. *New Theatre Quarterly* 14 (1988), 122–43.

'His own Triumphantly Comic Self: Self and Self-Consciousness in Nineteenth-Century English Farce.' In *Farce:* Themes in Drama no. 10, ed. James Redmond. Cambridge University Press, 1988, 115–30.

Davis, Tracy. *Actresses as Working Women: Their Social Identity in Victorian Culture*. London: Routledge, 1991.

'Reading Shakespeare by Flashes of Lightning: Challenging the Foundations of Romantic Acting Theory'. *ELH* 62 (1995), 933–54.

Davis, Jim and Davis, Tracy C. 'The People of the "People's Theatre": The Social Demography of the Britannia Theatre (Hoxton)', *Theatre Survey* 32 (1991), 137–65.

Davis, Tracy C. and Ellen Donkin, eds., *Women and Playwriting in Nineteenth-Century Britain*. Cambridge University Press, 1999.

Davison, Peter *et al.*, eds. *Literary Taste, Culture and Mass Communication*. 14 vols. Vol. I: *Culture and Mass Culture*; vol. VIII: *Theatre and Song*. Cambridge: Chadwyck-Healey, 1978–80.

Deane, Seamus. *The French Revolution and Enlightenment in England, 1789–1832*. Cambridge, Mass.: Harvard University Press, 1988.

Dobson, Michael. *The Making of the National Poet: Shakespeare, Adaptation, and Authorship, 1660–1769*. Oxford: Clarendon, 1992.

Dobson, R. B. *The Peasants' Revolt of 1381*. London: Macmillan, 1970.

Dollimore, Jonathan and Alan Sinfield, eds. *Political Shakespeare: New Essays in Cultural Materialism*. Manchester University Press, 1985.

Donkin, Ellen, *Getting into the Act: Women Playwrights in London, 1776–1829*. London and New York: Routledge, 1995.

'Mrs Gore gives tit for tat'. In Davis and Donkin, *Women and Playwriting*, 54–74.

Donohue, Joseph W. Jr. 'Burletta and the Early Nineteenth-Century English Theatre'. *Nineteenth Century Theatre Research* 1 (1973), 29–51.

Theatre in the Age of Kean. Oxford: Basil Blackwell, 1975.

Dramatic Character in the English Romantic Age. Princeton University Press, 1976.

Douglas, Mary and Baron Isherwood. *The World of Goods: Towards an Anthropology of Consumption*. Harmondsworth: Penguin, 1980.

Drakakis, John, ed. *Alternative Shakespeares*. London: Methuen, 1985.

Dugaw, Dianne. *Warrior Women and Popular Balladry, 1650–1850*. Cambridge University Press, 1989.

Easton, Susan, *et al. Disorder and Discipline. Popular Culture from 1550 to the Present*. Aldershot: Temple Smith, 1988.

Elam, Keir. *The Semiotics of Theatre and Drama*. London: Methuen, 1980.

Epstein, James. *Radical Expression: Political Language, Ritual, and Symbol in England, 1790–1850*. Oxford: Clarendon, 1994.

Evans, Bertrand. *Gothic Drama from Walpole to Shelley*. Berkeley: University of California Press, 1947.

Evenden, Michael. 'Inter-mediate Stages: Reconsidering the Body in "Closet Drama"'. In *Reading the Social Body*, ed. Catherine B. Burroughs and Jeffrey David Ehrenreich. University of Iowa Press, 1993, 244–69.

Fahrner, Robert. *The Theatre Career of Charles Dibdin the Elder (1745–1814)*. New York: Peter Lang, 1989.

Fenner, Theodore. *Leigh Hunt and Opera Criticism: The 'Examiner' Years, 1808–21*. Lawrence: University Press of Kansas, 1972.

Ferris, Lesley. *Crossing the Stage: Controversies on Cross-Dressing*. London: Routledge, 1993.

Findlater, Richard. *Grimaldi, King of Clowns*. London: Macgibbon and Kee, 1955.

Fletcher, Kathy. 'Planché, Vestris, and the Transvestite Role: Sexuality and Gender in Popular Theatre'. *Nineteenth Century Theatre* 15 no. 2 (1978), 8–33.

Fraser, Derek and Anthony Sutcliffe, eds. *The Pursuit of Urban History*. London: Edward Arnold, 1983.

Fulford, Roger. *Samuel Whitbread 1764–1815: A Study in Opposition*. London: Macmillan, 1967.

Galperin, William H. *The Return of the Visible in British Romanticism*. Baltimore: Johns Hopkins University Press, 1993.

Gans, Herbert J. *Popular Culture and High Culture: An Analysis and Evaluation of Taste*. New York: Basic Books, 1974.

Ganzel, Dewey. '"Patent Wrongs and Patent Theatres": Drama and the Law in the Early Nineteenth Century' *PMLA* 76 (1961), 384–96.

Geertz, Clifford. *The Interpretation of Cultures: Selected Essays by Clifford Geertz*. New York: Basic Books, 1973.
  Local Knowledge: Further Essays in Interpretative Anthropology. New York: Basic Books, 1983.

George, M. D. *English Political Caricature 1793–1832*. Oxford: Clarendon, 1959.

Gilmartin, Kevin. *Print Politics: The Press and Radical Opposition in Early Nineteenth-Century England*. Cambridge University Press, 1996.

Golby, J. M. and A. W. Purdue. *The Civilization of the Crowd: Popular Culture in England 1750–1900*. London: Batsford, 1984.

Goodlad, J. S. R. *A Sociology of Popular Drama*. London: Heinemann, 1971.

Grady, Hugh. *The Modernist Shakespeare: Critical Texts in a Material World*. Oxford: Clarendon, 1991.

Grimstead, David. *Melodrama Unveiled: American Theater and Culture 1800–1850*. Chicago University Press, 1968.

Hadley, Elaine. 'The Old Price Wars: Melodramatising the Public Sphere in Early Nineteenth Century England'. *PMLA* 107 no. 3 (1992), 525–37.
  Melodramatic Tactics: Theatricalized Dissent in the English Marketplace, 1800–1885. Stanford University Press, 1995.

Harris, John B. *Charles Robert Maturin: The Forgotten Imitator*. New York: Arno Press, 1980.

Harrison, Brian. 'State Intervention and Moral Reform in Nineteenth-Century England,' in *Pressure from Without in Early Victorian England*, ed. Patricia Hollis. London: Edward Arnold, 1974.

Harrison, Mark. *Crowds and History: Mass Phenomena in English Towns, 1790–1835*. Cambridge University Press, 1988.

Hay, Douglas *et al.*, eds. *Albion's Fatal Tree: Crime and Society in Eighteenth-Century England*. London: Allen Lane, 1975.

Hays, Michael. *The Public and Performance: Essays in the History of French and German Theatre 1871–1900*. Ann Arbor: UMI Research Press, 1981.

Hays, Michael and Anastasia Nikolopoulou, eds. *Melodrama: The Cultural Emergence of a Genre*. New York: St. Martin's Press, 1996.

Hayter, Alethea. 'Coleridge, Maturin's *Bertram*, and Drury Lane'. In Donald Sultana, ed., *New Approaches to Coleridge: Biographial and Critical Essays*. London: Vision Press, 1981, 17–37.

Hemmings, F. W. J. *Theatre and State in France, 1760–1905.* Cambridge University Press, 1994.

Henkle, Roger B. *Comedy and Culture: England 1820–1900.* Princeton University Press, 1980.

Hillebrand, Harold N. *Edmund Kean.* New York: Columbia University Press, 1933.

Hoadley, Frank. 'The Controversy over Southey's *Wat Tyler*'. *Studies in Philology* 38 (1941), 81–96.

Holder, Heidi. 'Melodrama, Realism and Empire on the British Stage'. In Bratton, *Acts of Supremacy*, 129–49.

Holderness, Graham, ed. *The Shakespeare Myth.* Manchester University Press, 1988.

Hollingsworth, Keith. *The Newgate Novel 1830–1847.* Detroit: Wayne State University Press, 1963.

Hölmstrom, Kirsten Gram. *Monodrama, Attitude, Tableaux Vivants: Studies on Some Trends of Theatrical Fashion 1770–1815.* Stockholm: Almquist and Wiksell, 1967.

Hone, J. Ann. *For the Cause of Truth: Radicalism in London 1796–1821.* Oxford: Clarendon, 1982.

Huberman, Jeffrey. *Late Victorian Farce.* Ann Arbor: UMI Research Press, 1986.

Hume, Robert D. *Henry Fielding and the London Theatre: 1728–1737.* Oxford: Clarendon, 1988.

Hume, Robert D., ed. *The London Theatre World, 1660–1800.* Carbondale: Southern Illinois University Press, 1980.

'Texts within Contexts: Notes towards a Historical Method'. *Philological Quarterly* 71 (1992), 69–100.

Hunt, Lynn A. *The New Cultural History.* Berkeley: University of California, 1989.

Hutcheon, Linda. *A Theory of Parody: The Teachings of Twentieth-Century Art Forms.* London: Routledge, 1991.

Hyslop, Gabrielle. 'Deviant and Dangerous Behaviour: Women in Melodrama'. *Journal of Popular Culture* 19 (1985), 65–77.

Innes, Joanna. 'Politics and Morals: The Reformation of Manners Movement in Later Eighteenth-Century England' in Eckhart Hellmuth, ed., *The Transformation of Political Culture: England and Germany in the Late Eighteenth Century.* Oxford University Press, 1990, 57–118.

Jackson, Russell. 'Before the Shakespeare Revolution: Developments in the Study of Nineteenth-Century Shakespeare in Production'. *Shakespeare Survey* 35 (1982) 1–12.

Jacobus, Mary. '"That Great Stage Where Senators Perform": Macbeth and the Politics of Romantic Theater.' *Studies in Romanticism* 22 (1983), 353–87.

James, Louis, *Fiction for the Working Man 1830–1850.* London: Oxford University Press, 1963.

James, Louis, ed. *Print and the People 1819–1851.* London: Allen Lane, 1976.

'Taking Melodrama Seriously: Theatre and Nineteenth-Century Studies'. *History Workshop* 3 (1977), 151–8.

'Frankenstein's Monster in Two Traditions'. In Stephen Bann, ed., *Frankenstein, Creation and Monstrosity*. London: Reaktion Books, 1994, 77–94.

Jones, Stanley. *Hazlitt, a Life: From Winterslow to Frith Street*. Oxford University Press, 1989.

Kabbani, Rana. *Europe's Myths of Orient: Desire and Rule*. London: Pandora, 1986.

Kalikoff, Beth. *Murder and Moral Decay in Victorian Popular Literature*. Ann Arbor: UMI Research Press, 1986.

Kelly, John A. *German Visitors to English Theatres in the Eighteenth Century*. Princeton University Press, 1936.

Kelly, Linda. *The Kemble Era: John Philip Kemble, Sarah Siddons and the London Stage*. London: Bodley Head, 1980.

Klancher, Jon P. *The Making of English Reading Audiences, 1790–1832*. Madison: University of Wisconsin Press, 1987.

Knight, William. *A Major London 'Minor': the Surrey Theatre 1805–1865*. London: Society for Theatre Research, 1998.

Kwint, Marius. 'Astley's Amphitheatre and the Early Circus in England, 1768–1830' (unpublished doctoral thesis, Oxford University, 1994).

LaCapra, Dominick and Stephen L. Kaplan, eds. *Modern European Intellectual History: Reappraisals and New Perspectives*. Ithaca: Cornell University Press, 1982.

Laqueur, Thomas. 'The Queen Caroline Affair: Politics as Art in the Reign of George III'. *Journal of Modern History* 54 (September 1982), 417–66.

Lavally, Albert J. 'The Stage and Film Children of Frankenstein: A Survey'. In George Levine and U. C. Knoepflmacher, eds. *The Endurance of Frankenstein: Essays on Mary Shelley's Novel*. Berkeley: University of California Press, 1979, 243–89.

Leask, Nigel. *British Romantic Writing and the East: Anxieties of Empire*. Cambridge University Press, 1992.

Leppert, Richard. *The Sight of Sound: Music, Representation, and the History of the Body*. Berkeley: University of California Press, 1993.

Levine, Lawrence W. *Highbrow / Lowbrow: The Emergence of Cultural Hierarchy in America*. Cambridge, Mass.: Harvard University Press, 1988.

Levinson, Marjorie *et al.*, eds. *Rethinking Historicism: Critical Readings in Romantic History*. Oxford: Blackwell, 1989.

Liesenfeld, Vincent. *The Licensing Act of 1737*. Madison: University of Wisconsin Press, 1984.

Linebaugh, Peter. *The London Hanged: Crime and Civil Society in the Eighteenth Century*. London: Allen Lane, 1991.

Lougy, Robert E. *Charles Robert Maturin*. Lewisburg: Bucknell University Press, 1975.

Lowenthal, Leo. *Literature, Popular Culture and Society*. California: Prentice Hall, 1961.

McCalman, Iain. *Radical Underworld: Prophets, Revolutionaries, and Pornographers in London 1795–1840*. Cambridge: Cambridge University Press, 1988.

McConachie, Bruce A. *Melodramatic Formations: American Theatre and Society, 1820–1870*. University of Iowa Press, 1992.

McGracken, Grant. *Culture and Consumption: New Approaches to the Symbolic Character of Consumer Goods and Activities*. Bloomington: Indiana University Press, 1988.

Mackenzie, John. *Orientalism: History, Theory and the Arts*. Manchester University Press, 1995.

Mackenzie, John, ed. *Imperialism and Popular Culture*. Manchester University Press, 1986.

Macmillan, Donald. *Catalogue of the Larpent Plays in the Huntington Library*. San Marino, California: Henry E. Huntington Library, 1939.

Madden, Lionel, ed. *Robert Southey: The Critical Heritage*. London: Routledge, 1972.

Magnuson, Paul. *Reading Public Romanticism*. Princeton University Press, 1998.

Malcolmson, R. W. *Popular Recreations in English Society 1800–1850*. Cambridge University Press, 1973.

Mander, Raymond and Joe Mitchenson. *Lost Theatres of London*. London: New English Library, 1976.

Manning, Peter. 'Edmund Kean and Byron's Plays'. *Keats-Shelley Journal* 21 no. 2 (1972–3), 188–206.

Marcoux, J. Paul. *Guilbert de Pixérécourt: French Melodrama in the Early Nineteenth Century*. New York: Peter Lang, 1992.

Marcus, Steven. 'Reading the Illegible'. In H. J. Dyos and Michael Wolff, eds., *The Victorian City*. 2 vols. London: Routledge, 1973.

Mayer, David III. *Harlequin in His Element: The English Pantomime 1806–1836*. Cambridge, Mass.: Harvard University Press, 1969.

'The Music of Melodrama'. In Bradby, James, *et al.*, eds. *Performance and Politics in Popular Drama: Aspects of Popular Entertainment in Theatre, Film, and Television, 1800–1976*. Cambridge University Press, 1980. 49–63.

Meisel, Martin. *Realizations: Narrative, Pictorial, and Theatrical Arts in Nineteenth-Century England*. Princeton University Press, 1983.

Mekeel, Joyce. 'Social Influences on Changing Audience Behaviour in the London Theater' (unpublished doctoral thesis, Boston University, 1983).

Melling, Joseph and Jonathan Barry, eds. *Culture in History: Production, Consumption and Values in Historical Perspective*. Exeter University Press, 1992.

Mellor, Anne K. 'Joanna Baillie and the Counter-Public Sphere'. *Studies in Romanticism* 33 (1994), 559–67.

Miles, Dudley. *Francis Place, 1771–1854: The Life of a Remarkable Radical*. Brighton: Harvester, 1988.

Moody, Jane. '"Fine word, legitimate!": Towards a Theatrical History of Romanticism'. *Texas Studies in Literature and Language* 38 nos. 3 and 4 (1996), 223–44.

'The Silence of New Historicism: A Mutinous Echo from 1830'. *Nineteenth Century Theatre* 22 no. 2 (1996), 61–89.

'Illusions of Authorship'. In Davis and Donkin, eds. *Women and Playwriting*, 99–124.

'Suicide and Translation in the Dramaturgy of Elizabeth Inchbald and Anne

Plumptre'. In Catherine Burroughs, ed., *Women in British Romantic Theatre*. Cambridge University Press, 2000, pp. 257–84.

Moore, John David. 'Coleridge and the "Modern Jacobinical drama": *Osorio, Remorse* and the development of Coleridge's critique of the stage, 1779–1816'. *Bulletin of Research in the Humanities* 85 (1982), 443–64.

Moretti, Franco. *Signs Taken for Wonders: Essays in the Sociology of Literary Forms*. Trans. Susan Fischer *et al.* London: New Left Books, 1983.

Morris, R. J. 'The Middle Class and British Towns and Cities of the Industrial Revolution, 1780–1870' in Fraser and Sutcliffe, *Pursuit of Urban History*, 286–306.

Murray, Christopher. *Robert William Elliston: Manager*. London: Society for Theatre Research, 1975.

Napier, Elizabeth R. *The Failure of Gothic: Problems of Disjunction in an Eighteenth-Century Literary Form*. Oxford: Clarendon, 1987.

Newey, Katherine. 'From a Female pen: the Proper Lady as Playwright in the West End Theatre, 1823–44' in Davis and Donkin, *Women and Playwriting*, 193–211.

Nicholson, Watson. *The Struggle for a Free Stage in London*. London: Constable, 1906.

Nicoll, Allardyce. *A History of English Drama 1660–1900*. 6 vols. Cambridge University Press, 1952–9.

Nikolopoulou, A. 'Artisan Culture and the English Gothic Melodrama' (unpublished doctoral thesis, Cornell University, 1990).

O'Gorman, Frank. *Voters, Patrons and Parties: The Unreformed Electoral System of Hanoverian England 1734–1832*. Oxford: Clarendon, 1989.

Otten, Terry. *The Deserted Stage: The Search for Dramatic Form in Nineteenth-Century England*. Ohio University Press, 1972.

Ozouf, Mona. *Festivals and the French Revolution*. Translated by Alan Sheridan. Cambridge, Mass.: Harvard University Press, 1988.

Palmer, Stanley. *Police and Protest in England and Ireland 1780–1850*. Cambridge University Press, 1988.

Patterson, Annabel. *Shakespeare and the Popular Voice*. Oxford: Basil Blackwell, 1989.

Perkin, Harold. *Origins of Modern English Society*. London: Routledge, 1969.

Pfister, Manfred. 'Reading the Body: The Corporeality of Shakespeare's Text' in Hanna Scolnicov and Peter Holland, eds. *Reading Plays: Interpretation and Reception*. Cambridge University Press, 1991.

Phillips, K. C. *Language and Class in Victorian England*. Oxford: Blackwell, 1984.

Playfair, Giles. *Kean*. New York: E. P. Dutton, 1939.

Postlewait, Thomas and Bruce McConachie, eds. *Interpreting the Theatrical Past*. University of Iowa Press, 1989.

Pratt, Mary Louise. *Imperial Eyes: Travel Writing and Transculturation*. London: Routledge, 1992.

Prendergast, Christopher. *Balzac: Fiction and Melodrama*. London: Arnold, 1978.

Prothero, I. J. *Artisans and Politics in Early Nineteenth-Century London: John Gast and his Times*. Folkestone: Dawson, 1979.

Ranger, Paul. *'Terror and Pity Reign in every Breast': Gothic Drama in the Patent Theatres, 1750–1820*. London: Society for Theatre Research, 1991.

Rees, Terence. *Theatre Lighting in the Age of Gas*. London: Society for Theatre Research, 1978.

Reid, J. C. *Bucks and Bruisers: Pierce Egan and Regency England*. London: Routledge, 1971.

Richardson, Alan. *A Mental Theater: Poetic Drama and Consciousness in the Romantic Age*. University Park, Pennsylvania: Pennsylvania State Unniversity Press, 1988.

Richardson, David, ed. *Abolition and its Aftermath: The Historical Context, 1790–1916*. London: Frank Cass, 1985.

Ritvo, Harriet. *The Animal Estate: The English and Other Creatures in the Victorian Age*. Cambridge, Mass.: Harvard University Press, 1987.

Roach, Joseph R. *The Player's Passion: Studies in the Science of Acting*. Newark: University of Delaware Press, 1985.

Roberts, M. J. 'The Society for the Suppression of Vice and its Early Critics'. *Historical Journal* 26 (1983), 159–76.

Roe, Nicholas. *John Keats and the Culture of Dissent*. Oxford: Clarendon, 1997.

Root-Bernstein, Michèle. *Boulevard Theater and Revolution in Eighteenth-Century Paris*. Michigan: UMI Research Press, 1981.

Rosenfeld, Sybil. *The Theatre of the London Fairs in the Eighteenth Century*. Cambridge University Press, 1960.

Rostron, David. 'John Philip Kemble's *Coriolanus* and *Julius Caesar*: An Examination of the Prompt Copies'. *Theatre Notebook* 23 (1968), 26–34.

Russell, Gillian. 'Playing at Revolution: The Politics of the O. P. Riots of 1809'. *Theatre Notebook* 44 (1990), 16–26.

The Theatres of War: Performance, Politics, and Society, 1793–1815. Oxford: Clarendon Press, 1995.

Rzepka, Charles. '*Theatrum Mundi* and Keats's *Otho the Great*: The Self in Society'. *Romanticism Past and Present* 8 (1984), 35–50.

Samuel, Raphael. *People's History and Socialist Theory*. London: Routledge, 1981.

Samuel, Raphael, and Gareth Steadman-Jones, eds. *Culture, Ideology and Politics: Essays for Eric Hobsbawm*. London: Routledge, 1982.

Patriotism: The Making and Unmaking of British National Identity. 3 vols. London: Routledge, 1989.

Saxon, Arthur H. *Enter Foot and Horse: A History of Hippodrama in England and France*. New Haven: Yale University Press, 1968.

The Life and Art of Andrew Ducrow and the Romantic Age of the English Circus. Hamden, CT.: Archon, 1978.

Schechner, Richard. *Between Theater and Anthropology*. Philadelphia: University of Penn. Press, 1985.

Schwartz, L. 'Occupations and Incomes in Late Eighteeenth-Century London'. *East London Papers* 14 (1972), 87–100.

'Social Class and Social Geography: the Middle Classes in London at the End of the Eighteenth Century'. *Social History* 7 (1982), 167–85.

Senelick, Lawrence. 'Politics as Entertainment: Victorian Music-Hall Songs'. *Victorian Studies* 19 (1975), 149–80.

Sennett, Richard. *The Fall of Public Man*. Cambridge University Press, 1974.

Shepherd, 'The Relationship between Music, Text and Performance in English Popular Theatre 1790–1840' (unpublished doctoral thesis, London University 1991).

Sheridan, Paul. *Penny Theatres of Victorian London*. London: Dennis Dobson, 1981.

Shershow, Scott Cutler. *Puppets and 'Popular Culture'*. Ithaca: Cornell University Press, 1995.

Shiach, Morag. *Discourse on Popular Culture: Class, Gender and History in Cultural Analysis, 1730 to the Present*. Cambridge: Polity, 1989.

Southern, Richard. *Changeable Scenery: Its Origin and Development in the British Theatre*. London: Faber, 1952.

Stallybrass, Peter and Allan White. *The Politics and Poetics of Transgression*. London: Methuen, 1986.

Stephens, John R. *The Censorship of English Drama 1824–1901*. Cambridge University Press, 1980.

The Profession of the Playwright: British Theatre 1800–1900. Cambridge University Press, 1992.

Sypher, Wylie. 'Aesthetic of Revolution: The Marxist Melodrama'. *The Kenyon Review* 10 (1948), 431–44.

Taylor, George. *Players and Performances in the Victorian Theatre*. Manchester University Press, 1989.

Thomas, David. *Restoration and Georgian England, 1660–1788*. Cambridge University Press, 1989.

Thompson, E. P. *The Making of the English Working Class*. Harmondsworth: Penguin, 1963.

'Patrician Society, Plebeian Culture'. Journal of *Social History* 7 (1973–4), 382–405.

Thompson, F. M. L. *The Rise of Respectable Society: A Social History of Victorian Britain, 1830–1900*. London: Fontana, 1988.

Thompson, Peter. 'Thomas Holcroft, George Colman the Younger and the Rivalry of the Patent Theatres.' *Theatre Notebook* 22 (1968), 162–68.

Trussler, Simon, ed. *Burlesque Plays of the Eighteenth Century*. Oxford: Oxford University Press, 1969.

'A Chronology of Early Melodrama.' *Theatre Quarterly* 1 (Autumn 1971), 19–21.

Vicinus, Martha. '"Helpless and Unfriended": Nineteenth-Century Domestic Melodrama'. *New Literary History* 13 (1981), 127–43.

Vickers, Brian. *Returning to Shakespeare*. London: Routledge, 1989.

Wahrman, Dror. *Imagining the Middle Class: The Political Representation of Class in Britain, c. 1780–1840*. Cambridge University Press, 1995.

Waitzkin, Leo. *The Witch of Wych Street: A Study of the Theatrical Reforms of Madame Vestris*. Cambridge, Mass.: Harvard University Press, 1933.

Walvin, James. *Black Ivory: A History of British Slavery*. London: Harper Collins, 1992.

Wang, Shou-ren. *The Theatre of the Mind: A Study of Unacted Drama in Nineteenth-Century England*. London: Macmillan, 1990.

Watkins, Daniel P. *A Materialist Critique of English Romantic Drama*. Gainesville: University Press of Florida, 1993.

Watson, Ernest Bradlee. *Sheridan to Robertson: A Study of the Nineteenth-Century London Stage*. Cambridge, Mass., Harvard University Press, 1926.

Watson, Nicola J. 'Kemble, Scott, and the Mantle of the Bard'. In Jean I. Marsden, ed., *The Appropriation of Shakespeare: Post-Renaissance Reconstructions of the Works and the Myth*. Hemel Hempstead: Harvester, 1991, 73–92.

Webb, Timothy. 'The Romantic Poet and the Stage'. In Richard Allen Cave, ed., *The Romantic Theatre: An International Symposium*. Gerrard's Cross: Colin Smythe, 1986, 9–46.

Wells, Stanley, ed. *Nineteenth-Century Shakespeare Burlesques*. 5 vols. London: Diploma Press, 1977–8.

'Shakespeare in Hazlitt's Theatre Criticism'. *Shakespeare Survey* 35 (1982) 43–55.

West, Shearer. *The Image of the Actor: Verbal and Visual Representation in the Age of Garrick and Kemble*. London: Pinter, 1991.

White, R. S. *Keats as a Reader of Shakespeare*. London: Athlone Press, 1987.

Williams, Clifford. *Madame Vestris: a Theatrical Biography*. London: Sidgwick and Jackson, 1973.

Winter, James. *London's Teeming Streets 1830–1914*. London: Routledge, 1993.

Wolff, Janet and John Seed, eds. *The Culture of Capital: Art, Power and the Nineteenth-Century Middle Class*. Manchester University Press, 1988.

Wood, Leigh. 'Actors' Biography and Mythmaking: The Example of Edmund Kean'. In Postlewait and McConachie, *Interpreting the Theatrical Past*, 230–47.

Zelechow, Bernard. 'The Opera: The Meeting of Popular and Elite Culture in the Nineteenth Century'. *Journal of Popular Culture* 25 (1991), 91–97.

Index

Transgressive & collusion
Romantic ethos
"Others" as non-Radicals
Genres as ideological pursuit
     used
    ie: Shakespeare who gets to make
      what Shakespeare means   Devine
                     idealism

legitimate located in the text (mind)
illegitimate " body (physical)   Base
                            worldly

the Body is "Othered" by the mind

Vestras - identity is changeable/mutable